Montgomery County Texas CSA

A definitive history of Montgomery County's involvement in the War between the States and the men from that county who served in the military of the Confederate States of America

By Frank M. Johnson

Published by Frank M. Johnson

ISBN-978-0615877082

Printed by CreateSpace, An Amazon.com Company

Available from:

frankmjohnson.net, Amazon.com, CreateSpace.com, and other retail outlets

Dedicated to the memory of
Bill Bradley Johnson
(1974 – 2002)

iv

Table of Contents

Chapter 4: Post War & Reconstruction

Bibliography

Appendix A

Appendix B

Acknowledgements

It is only through a systematic study of original materials that relate both to the context and to the events in the lives of Confederate soldiers that an accurate history can emerge. I found this a difficult task, but it is my hope that this book reveals accurately the portions of those soldiers' lives dealt with here.

While preparing this book, I quickly learned that an in-depth account of the individuals and families could only be written with the combined knowledge and research of many others—those with passion and unique perspectives. I was fortunate enough to receive assistance from a substantial number of people with that passion and perspective.

I am first and foremost grateful for the assistance of two special ladies whose talents and tireless research helped to make this book possible. I thank Melinda Cagle for her expertise in editing this publication. In addition to her love for history, she has a unique talent for style and has many publications to her credit. I also thank Karen McCann Hett, a direct descendant of James Marion McCann (McCan) whose biographic sketch is included in this publication. Karen's years of research and detailed biographies of the men who served in the Danville Mounted Riflemen and Company B, 24th Texas Cavalry Regiment are tremendous contributions to the preservation of the histories of these men. Her writings were a major factor in my decision to publish this book.

I would like to thank Karen Lucas-Lawless whose extensive research of early property records of Montgomery County and the family database that she maintains along with Carolyn Terrell has yielded much significant information about early residents of the county. Karen and Carolyn participated in a project led by Melinda Cagle to publish the findings of their work relating to the history of the town of Danville and located several landmarks that still exist at the old town site. Four other members of the Danville project also have contributed information contained in this book. An important source of history concerning transportation and early roads in the area is the research of David Frame, while a substantial amount of family information was drawn from the online database compiled by Elsa Vorwerk and Bill Wood. David Martin was responsible for family information concerning his Confederate ancestors.

My thanks go out to Robert Reichardt, author of *Forever the Cause: The Life and Legacy of Colonel Robert M. Powell*, for the information that he provided about Colonel Powell, Hood's Texas Brigade, and Company D, 5th Texas Infantry.

I thank Kameron K. Searle, JD who has spent many years researching the formative period of Montgomery County and the founding of the town of Montgomery. His writings about these early days and the original settlers of Montgomery County have contributed to a fuller and more accurate understanding of the lives and times of local families that were involved in the War for Southern Independence.

I offer my appreciation to my friend and author, Hewitt Clarke, for his guidance and encouragement in writing this book and to Thomas Adkins for contributing his knowledge of the Brooks family from old Danville.

I am grateful to the late Narcissa "Cissy" Boulware who shared her family history with me and who pointed me to the graves of several Confederate soldiers whose histories were in danger of being lost.

Having spent many years researching the records of the men and women contained in this book, I am certainly grateful for the support of my wife, Denise. The five sons we have raised, Steven Johnson, Brad Johnson, Steven Atkinson, Michael Atkinson, and Jeremy Atkinson, also have supported me and shared in my passion for history.

The burial records of Confederate soldiers buried in Montgomery County and used in this book are due to the tireless efforts of the members of the Sons of Confederate Veterans, United Daughters of the Confederacy, and Texas Society Order of Confederate Rose.

Introduction

Montgomery County, Texas, CSA is a gathering of facts that relate to a select group of men during the time from shortly before the War between the States through the decade that followed it. While there is nothing included in these pages to suggest the personal opinions of these men nor the passions that motivated them, the records and accounts described herein present insight into the people, places, and events that influenced the soldiers' actions and the deeds that defined them as heroes. Regardless of how it is written, history will always confirm that Confederate soldiers and sailors were among the bravest, most dedicated, and most relentless fighters ever known to man. They were men who demonstrated an undying faith in righteousness and honor and a willingness to carry out their tasks regardless of the risks to their own lives or to the challenges they faced. The purpose of this book is to preserve the memory of these remarkable men and the rich heritage that they have left to us and to all future generations.

Identifying and verifying the service of men who served in the Confederate military can be a difficult task. Combinations of many records are required. Confederate service records, census records, pension applications, personal letters, family and church records, burial records, and references from other publications make up the majority of this information. Unfortunately, many of the official military and other government records that would shed light on their service were poorly kept or lost. After the war ended, and again in the early 1900s, the records that had survived were transcribed from the original documents, introducing errors. Misspelled names and misfiled documents are commonplace. These transcriptions are all that remain of many of the original documents. To further isolate records according to a particular region or county is even more difficult.

Completely separating all of the soldiers in Montgomery County from soldiers in adjacent counties cannot always be accomplished. For the purpose of this book, I have defined a Montgomery County soldier as a person who can be placed in Montgomery County prior to the war. While the vast majority of these men were living in Montgomery County at the time of the war, I have included some soldiers who had moved away but still had family or historical ties to the county. Fifteen years before the war, the neighboring counties of Walker, Grimes, and Waller were still part of the original Montgomery County. At the time of the war, communities such as Waverly in Walker County and Danville in Montgomery County had residents who moved back and forth between these areas on a regular basis, further obscuring the locations of some of these soldiers.

No amount of research can produce a perfect list of Confederate soldiers from Montgomery County. It is likely that the names of some of these will never be found. There were certain regiments that were particularly hard to research and possibly contained men from Montgomery County who have not yet been identified as such. Among these regiments are the 1st Texas Heavy Artillery, Waul's Texas Legion, the 17th Texas Militia, and several of the regiments that participated in the New Mexico campaign. Records from the Confederate Navy are almost non-existent.

Many of the graves of these men will never be found. Some are known to have been buried in unmarked graves in other states and in mass graves on the battlefields where they died. Those who made it home from the war returned to communities that had been devastated by four long years of war. The economy had collapsed in the interim, and for many years to follow, these men and their families would be subjugated to the vengeful effects of the process that some historians call "Reconstruction." Some families were too poor to provide permanent markers for the graves of their loved ones, thus these gravesites have been lost to history. Commercial and recreational development continues to obscure the final resting place of many.

This book is designed to provide vital information about these men and their families that will open doors for more detailed research. At the back of the book, there is an alphabetical listing with the necessary information to identify the soldiers and their families with cross-references to additional records in other parts of the book. I hope that this publication serves as a fitting tribute to the men from Montgomery County, Texas who served in the military of the Confederate States of America and that it assists in the preservation of their history.

Chapter 1

Antebellum

Arnold–Simonton House, Montgomery, Texas
photo courtesy of the author

From the early arrivals with Austin's Colony, the fight for independence from Mexico, the building of a new republic, and the molding of a new society in early statehood, the citizens of Montgomery County have played an active role in the history of Texas. The brief period between statehood in 1845 and secession in 1861 marked an era of rapid change for Montgomery County. While this antebellum period was a prosperous one, it was cut short by the great war for Southern independence. From that point forward, the lives and fortunes of the citizens of Montgomery County were forever changed.

Early Montgomery County

The pioneer families of Montgomery County came to the area as part of Stephen F. Austin's second colony in the State of Coahuila y Texas and settled on the prairie between present-day Lake Creek and the San Jacinto River. Many of these early settlers played a role in establishing the Republic of Texas and winning independence from Mexico in 1836. Jonathan Lindley, whose family settled in northern Montgomery County, died defending the Alamo. Many more served in the Texas Army, some who were in Captain William Ware's Company at the Battle of San Jacinto. The struggles to carve out homes in the wilderness while fighting a war to establish a new country inspired among these settlers an uncompromising spirit of independence that would be passed along to future generations.

Montgomery County was officially created on December 14, 1837 by an act of the Congress of the Republic of Texas. The original boundaries extended from the Trinity River in the east to the Brazos River in the west and included all or parts of present-day Grimes, Walker, San Jacinto, Madison, and Waller Counties. An act by the legislature of the new State of Texas and approved on April 6, 1846 created Grimes and Walker Counties out of land from the western and northern portion of Montgomery County. These lands were further divided on January 27, 1853 when Madison County was created from Grimes, Walker, and Leon Counties. By the time of the War between the States, Montgomery County included all of the land that is within its current boundaries in addition to lands to the east that border Liberty and Polk Counties and are now a part of San Jacinto County. Waller County was created from Grimes and Austin Counties in 1873, and the Texas legislature established San Jacinto County with Coldspring as the county seat on August 13, 1870 by taking land from Liberty, Montgomery, Polk, and Walker Counties.

Prior to secession, transportation routes in the area consisted of a complex of trails and roads linking farms and villages to markets and to the local waterways. Railroads were not introduced in Texas until the 1850s and did not extend into Montgomery County until the 1870s. By 1861, there were nine railroad companies in Texas but only about 470 miles of track. Also by 1861, the Houston and Texas Central Railway had reached the town of Millican. This was the northernmost railroad terminus in Texas at that time. The road from the town of Montgomery that stretched westward to Washington intersected the railroad near the town of Navasota and was the closest connection to the railroads for Montgomery County residents. For those shipping cotton, this trail to the railroad avoided high-water issues with Spring Creek and Cypress Creek along the south road from Montgomery to the rail terminal in Cypress City.

From 1845 until 1861, the road system in Montgomery County saw rapid development. While managed by Commissioner's Court, roads were built, paid for, and maintained by the land owners. Although roads and trails connected all of the towns and settlements in the county, weather conditions often dictated the routes to be taken and the modes of transportation. Flooding was common on the San Jacinto River and the many creeks and tributaries that flowed into it. Because of these hazards, the most dependable mode of transportation was horseback.

Stagecoach routes had become well-established by 1860. Funds provided by U.S. mail contracts were the primary reason for the creation and continued success of these routes. The towns of Montgomery and Danville were connected to all the surrounding areas by regularly-scheduled mail stops. Also in 1860, a post office was established at Prairie Home which is present day Pinehurst. It was located on the south route from Montgomery to Cypress City which allowed stage travelers a connection to the railroad stop there.

The economy of Montgomery County prior to the war was based primarily on agriculture. Much like other areas in the South, cotton was the dominant cash crop. By 1860, Montgomery County was producing more than 8,000 bales annually. Although there were several large plantations such as those belonging to Green Wood and John M. Lewis, Sr., the majority of the crop

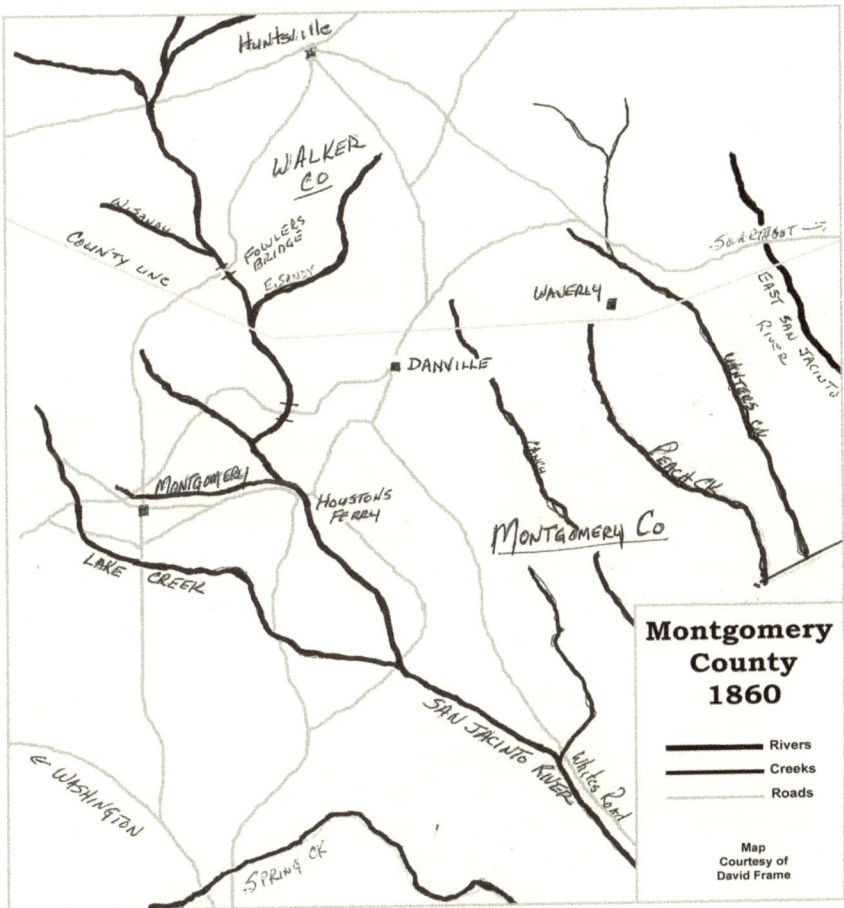

Montgomery
County
1860

	Rivers
	Creeks
	Roads

Map
Courtesy of
David Frame

production came from smaller family farms. While the smaller farms and ranches did not produce large incomes, they were basically self-supporting.

By the time that residents began to seriously consider the idea of disunion from the United States, there were two thriving towns in the county, Montgomery and Danville. Montgomery is one of the oldest towns in Texas, and by the time of statehood in 1845, had doctors, lawyers, churches, schools, a Masonic Lodge, and a telegraph station. That same year, John Marshall Wade established a newspaper in Montgomery. Along with being the county surveyor, he had served in the Republic of Texas Army and would later serve in Captain Lemuel G. Clepper's Company K, 20th Texas Infantry, CSA. Wade published the first issue of his new newspaper, the *Montgomery Patriot* on April 26, 1845. James McCown advertised the sale of town lots in a later edition, stating:

> *The lands surrounding Montgomery, known as the Lake Creek Settlement, being of such a rich and fertile character and having a rich and industrious population, it is destined to be, in a short time, a town of considerable importance.*
>
> *Montgomery is the county site of the most flourishing, populous and intelligent county in the Republic. It is situated on an elevated ridge, which divides the waters of the San Jacinto River and Lake Creek—In point of health, Montgomery is not inferior to any place in the world, lying in the same latitude.*

In the northern part of Montgomery County was the town of Danville. It was located about six miles northwest of present-day Willis along the main route from the Trinity River crossing at Swarthout (Swartwout) which intersected several other major roads in the county.

Although the plat for the town site of Danville was not filed until 1851, settlers had been moving into the area before Texas became a Republic. The *Texas Democrat* newspaper published in Austin, Texas on Saturday, March 21, 1846 mentions the name Danville on a proposed mail route from Opelousas, Louisiana to San Antonio de Bexar, and the April 8, 1846 edition of *Democratic Telegraph and Texas Register* published in Houston shows the election results for a polling place called Danville with 71 people voting for a United States congressional race. This same article shows 118 people voting in the town of Montgomery.

The 1850s would bring a boom to the town of Danville much like that of Montgomery, and by 1856, Danville had reached a population of about 300. An article published in the May 24, 1856 edition of the *State Gazette* describes Danville as "pleasant inland village" situated between Montgomery, Huntsville, and Coldspring in the midst of a dense population of wealthy planters. While that statement may have been somewhat exaggerated, there were several large plantations in the areas of Danville and Waverly supporting this view.

The Road to Secession

Opinions concerning the causes of the War between the States are as divided now as they were at the time of the war. Northern and Southern sentiments are even divided over a definition of "*the cause*." From a Northern perspective, causes refer to the actual events that led to the outbreak of war. From a Southern perspective, "*the cause*" refers to the ideals, beliefs, and principles that were worth protecting at any cost. In the early history of the United States, there had been many issues and disputes that could have escalated into violence, but in 1861, there was one clearly-defined event that was unique to all of the previous encounters. In its strictest sense, the only event that led to the outbreak of war was the secession of Southern states.

Following the road that led to secession is a complicated task. There were many issues that could have led to a final decision to secede among the Southern states, but Texas alone had issues that distinguished it from all of the other states, driving its decision to secede. Texas owned a vast western frontier that posed a continuing threat of Indian attacks, and it bordered a foreign country, Mexico, that did not respect their mutual boundaries. Further, Texas gave up millions of acres of land to the United States to achieve a political compromise in 1850. In exchange for statehood, the United States had promised the Republic of Texas remedies to many of its problems, and yet after statehood, these problems still had not been fully resolved. It is likely that this failure by the United States government to fulfill its promises led many Texans to feel betrayed.

Prior to statehood, Texas had been an independent nation with its own laws and a profound value for sovereignty. Many families in Montgomery County had been a prominent part of that Republic from its beginning, and many of their children had been born as citizens of Texas instead of the United States. It is conceivable that many Montgomery County residents valued Texas sovereignty much more highly than they did statehood.

For most of the Montgomery County citizens, their possessions consisted almost entirely of their lands, their families, and their freedom to chart their own courses, so from the perspective of these citizens, what could so strongly motivate them to risk all of this and go to war? The events of history that unfolded during the War between the States reveal that the men from Montgomery County held fast to what they believed to be a just and honorable cause, and that their families supported them in their beliefs.

On the Issue of Slavery

In the abundance of histories that have been written about the War between the States, many suggest that the American institution of slavery was a major cause of the war. While there is little dispute that slavery was both inhumane and a total abomination to the principals upon which the United States was founded, it was in fact created, protected, and maintained by the Constitution and laws of the United States of America.

By the time that the American colonies declared their independence in 1776, slavery had existed in those colonies for more than 150 years. From its very inception, slavery contributed to a cultural, economic, and sectional division among the colonies. The African slave trade was dominated by merchants whose ships departed from northern ports in Rhode Island, Connecticut, Massachusetts, and New York. The more successful of these merchants would become some of the richest men in the world at that time. The voyage of one ship, while losing a substantial portion of its live cargo, could still net a small fortune. In many northern states, churches, colleges, and entire cities were built with the blood money from the African slave trade.

Northern states, having primarily become an industrial and non-agrarian region, began the process of gradual emancipation of slaves led by Pennsylvania in 1780. Most of the northern states would soon enact similar plans. Despite the fact that Delaware and New Jersey were north of the Mason-Dixon Line, slavery remained legal in those states until after the War between the States when the 13th Amendment was ratified in December 1865. Although the War between the States began in April 1861, slavery was not abolished in Washington D.C. until April 16, 1862.

An act prohibiting importation of slaves to the United States took effect in 1808, and in 1819, U.S. law declared the importation of slaves into the country to be a capital offense thus punishable by death. Despite the harsh penalty for getting caught, American ships departing northern ports continued their involvement in the African slave trade for more than half of the 19th century, and while dozens of these ships were captured by the U.S. Navy, it was not until 1862 that Nathaniel Gordon, captain of the slave ship, *Erie*, became the only American to be executed for slave trafficking. It is believed that the schooner, *Huntress*, which departed New York Harbor in 1864, was likely the last American slave ship to be actively involved in the slave trade.

As slavery diminished in the North and continued to grow in the South, there was seemingly less debate over whether or not slavery would continue than there was about how and where it would continue. As Northern states industrialized and mechanized manufacturing, the need for slave labor in the North diminished. At the same time, the demand for goods in Europe produced by slave labor in the South had significantly increased, competing with Northern wages to produce goods. This continued growth of differences between Northern and Southern economies promoted the fundamental political and ideological divisions between the two regions.

President John Tyler's promotion of the annexation of Texas in 1843 fueled many heated debates in Congress over the issue. At that time, only twelve of the twenty-six states were slave-holding states. This imbalance gave the northern states a considerable advantage in Congress. Texas was a slave-holding state which, if admitted to the Union, would weaken the political power of the northern states. The admission of Florida as a slave state in March 1845 offered even more reason for concern among Northerners. With vast territories in the west destined to be annexed, the free-labor system of the slave-holding states caused great economic concerns among the northern states. When Texas was formally admitted to the Union on December 29, 1845, hostilities began to erupt over where, how, and even if slavery was to be expanded into the new territories. Many Northern politicians contended that it was the obligation of the federal government to prevent any further expansion of slavery while others suggested that slavery should be restricted to the southern regions of the new territories. Political leaders in the South contended that it was the right of each new state to decide the issue of slavery within its own borders. This right of popular sovereignty, included in the Compromise of 1850 and again in the Kansas-Nebraska Act of 1854, triggered a split in the political leadership in the North. The creation of the Republican Party was a result of this split.

To conclude that the Confederate states were fighting to preserve slavery would require that there had been at least some effort or form of legislation generated by the United States government to abolish slavery. No such legislation existed at the time that the first shots were fired in 1861. In fact, the only legislation concerning slavery that had been approved by the United States Congress was an amendment proposed at the beginning of the war by Ohio Republican Representative Thomas Corwin which would prevent Congress from interfering with the domestic institutions of the states, including persons held to labor or service and would forbid subsequent attempts to change the amendment, making this amendment both perpetual and irrevocable. Prior to the war, three northern states had already ratified the Corwin Amendment, including Abraham Lincoln's state of Illinois. Abraham Lincoln supported and promoted the ratification of this amendment.

It is also important to note that after three bloody years of war, a bill addressing slavery was brought before the United States House of Representatives for the first time as a proposed an amendment to the Constitution which would abolish slavery on June 15, 1864. This bill, however, failed to garner the necessary two-thirds majority vote needed to pass and was defeated by a vote of 93 in favor and 65 against, even without the votes of those states now in the Confederacy.

The substantial number of votes by northern congressmen in opposition to abolishing slavery suggests that while the approximately one-third of the southern population that owned slaves were most likely in favor of slavery, an equal or possibly greater number of Northerners were in favor of slavery. This was possibly due to a fear among Northerners that blacks who were set free would move into northern states. Many of the northern states had already adopted immigration laws prior to the war which made it illegal for blacks to immigrate into their states. One of the strictest of these was a law passed by the Illinois in 1853.

Abolition was not a part of the 1860 Republican platform. During Lincoln's 1860 presidential campaign, he stated on more than one occasion that he had no intention of interfering with slavery where it existed, and in his March 4,

1861 inaugural speech he stated, "I have no purpose, directly or indirectly, to interfere with the institution of slavery where it exists. I believe I have no lawful right to do so, and I have no inclination to do so."

For the most part, the only Northerners demanding full and immediate emancipation were well-known abolitionists. Some of these were confessed anarchists who opposed the Constitution of the United States as much as they opposed slavery. As much as these abolitionists might have been hated in South, it is likely that they brought fear and concern in the North as well.

The only act that could end slavery would be an amendment to the Constitution of the United States requiring ratification by three-fourths of the states. With thirty-four states in the Union at the time of the war and with fourteen states opposed to such a ratification, any proposed amendment was a mathematical impossibility.

All of these factors combined give rise to the question of why Southerners would risk their lives, their homes, and the prosperity of their families if slavery as it existed was guaranteed by the U.S. Constitution?

The answer to that question, along with many other suggested causes of the war, has been argued for more than 150 years and likely will continue for centuries to come. While there were many reasons for the North and the South to disagree, it is unlikely that any of these disagreements would have resulted in war without the act of secession. There is no way to predict how long slavery would have lasted had the Southern states agreed to remain in the Union. Secession had been threatened by other states at other times as far back as 1812 in Massachusetts and in 1832 in South Carolina, but when the Southern states carried out their threat in 1860, it most certainly brought war.

The only thing that history can truly attest to concerning those who engaged in this horrific struggle is the incredible bravery, courage, and dedication shown by the men on both sides of this conflict. Regardless of their cause, these men fought with a relentless passion that cannot be denied nor forgotten.

Secession & War

At 11:00 a.m. on February 1, 1861, the delegates to the Texas Secession Convention met to take a final vote on the ordinance of secession. Governor Sam Houston was in attendance. A roll-call vote was cast in alphabetical order. Montgomery County's delegate, Reuben J. Palmer, was among the 166 who cast their votes for secession. There were only eight votes opposed. Among the most vocal of those who opposed secession was James W. Throckmorton who, despite his opposition, would go on to serve in the Confederate Army. Throckmorton also became governor of Texas during Reconstruction but was removed by the Union military authorities for opposing radical Republican policies.

Despite the overwhelming vote in favor of secession, there were several of the delegates who supported Governor Houston's suggestions that Texas should remain an independent nation rather than join the other six states that were beginning to form the Confederate States of America.

Once secession had been approved, the convention created a public-safety committee, sent seven delegates to represent Texas at the Confederate States Convention in Montgomery, Alabama, and used its authority to begin seizing all federal property within the State of Texas. The convention adjourned on February 4, 1861 to await final approval by the voters of Texas.

On February 23, 1861, the citizens of Texas went to the polls and overwhelmingly passed a referendum to secede from the Union. The vote tally for Montgomery County was 318 for and 98 against. Texas officially declared its independence in 1861 just as it did in 1836: on the second day of March. After refusing to take the oath of loyalty to the Confederate States of America, Governor Houston was replaced on March 16 by Lt. Governor Edward Clark. Sam Houston officially resigned as governor on March 30, 1861.

When President Abraham Lincoln was inaugurated on March 4, 1861, a civil war was not a foregone conclusion. In what could have been interpreted by the federal government as acts of war during the Buchanan administration in the 1850s, federal property had been seized in seven states, and cadets from the Citadel in South Carolina had fired on the *USS Star of the West* carrying 200 federal troops and supplies bound for Ft. Sumter in Charleston Harbor. Still, no military action had been taken by the federal government. President Lincoln's immediate call for 75,000 volunteers after Confederate troops fired on Ft. Sumter removed all doubt about a military conflict.

At this point, the structure of the thirty-three militia districts in Texas had already been well-defined. In a matter of weeks, volunteers from Grimes, Montgomery, and Walker Counties were enlisting in the 17th Brigade. Companies were quickly organized and trained for service in the Confederate Army. By the end of the summer of 1861, men from Montgomery County were headed to New Mexico, Kentucky, and Virginia. By the end of 1862, approximately three quarters of the men from Montgomery County between the ages of 18 and 50 were off to war. In the towns of Danville and Montgomery, stores closed, and only a handful of men remained to watch over the communities. Fields that had been filled with crops now lay untended. Wives were left to attend to daily tasks and watch over the children. The county as a whole had made a collective commitment to the war effort. This commitment would alter the lives of virtually everyone in the county. It would result in hundreds of widows and orphans and untold numbers of grieving parents. Some fathers would see their entire bloodlines come to an end. The cost in human lives and in future wealth would devastate Montgomery County. While the town of Montgomery managed to survive, the war marked the beginning of the end for the town of Danville.

Chapter 2

Soldiers
&
Their Families

photo courtesy of Rayford Sandel

The Brooks Family

Samuel Clifford Brooks (1794-1861)

Samuel Clifford Brooks was born on or about January 1, 1794 in Virginia. His family moved from Virginia to Kentucky and then to Tennessee where Samuel served in the Tennessee militia.

He married Elizabeth Hailey on August 26, 1819. Samuel and Elizabeth had two daughters and six sons. After the death of his first wife, Elizabeth, Samuel married Elizabeth Tatum on March 24, 1843. Samuel and his second wife had one daughter and one son before moving to Texas.

Samuel and his family arrived in Texas about 1847. According to the Texas state census records, Samuel was in Montgomery County in 1850, and federal census records show him to have been living in Walker County in 1860. Samuel Clifford Brooks died in Danville, Montgomery County, Texas on October 17, 1861 and was buried in the Danville-Shepard Hill Cemetery.

Six of Samuel's seven sons are known to have served in the Confederate Army. In addition, Samuel's son, Madison D. Brooks claimed that he attempted to join the Confederate Army but was instructed by the Governor of Texas to remain at his job as a prison guard at the state penitentiary in Huntsville. Roland K. Truitt, who married Samuel's youngest daughter, Sina, served in the Danville Mounted Riflemen and served later in Company K of the 20th Texas Infantry Regiment.

John Caperton Brooks (1825-1870)

John Caperton Brooks was born about June 1825 in Tennessee. John served as a private in Company A, 1st Tennessee Mounted Infantry during Mexican-American War. He married Emily Yarbrough Montague on August 8, 1848. John and Emily arrived in Montgomery County, Texas in 1847. John and Emily appear on the rolls of the 1860 U.S. census for Madison County, Texas, along with five children.

John enlisted as a private in Captain W. W. Viser's Company B, 6th Battalion of Texas Cavalry at McNutt's Hill in Louisiana. A muster roll dated January and February 1864 shows that John was present with his company during those months. Another muster roll for April 1865 shows that he was assigned to the Brigade Quartermaster's Department as a teamster on February 8, 1865.

According to the 1870 federal census mortality schedules index, John C. Brooks died from a fever in the month of May in 1870. John was buried in the Cedar Hill/Price Cemetery, Madison County, Texas.

Samuel Houston Brooks (1829-1910)

Samuel Houston Brooks
photo courtesy of
Thomas Adkins

Samuel Houston Brooks was born about January 1829 in Fayette County, Tennessee. He arrived in Texas prior to 1850. Along with several other residents from the Danville area of Montgomery County, Samuel migrated to California during the gold rush. In 1853 at age 24, he was elected treasurer for San Joaquin County, California. Samuel became controller for the State of California in 1860 but resigned in November 1861 to offer his services to the newly-formed Confederate States of America. He married Lucy C. Thornton Judge in Marysville, California on May 21, 1861.

Samuel was appointed captain and placed on the staff of General Benjamin F. Cheatham. He soon was promoted to major and aide-de-camp. In 1864, Samuel and his close friend, David S. Terry, were commissioned to raise a regiment of cavalry in the State of Texas. The new regiment began organizing in Montgomery County, Texas in the late spring of 1864 and was officially mustered into Confederate service on July 6, 1864 as Terry's Regiment Texas Cavalry. This regiment should not be confused with the 8th Texas Cavalry, known as Terry's Texas Rangers which is discussed elsewhere in this book. David S. Terry was appointed colonel of the new regiment, with Samuel H. Brooks, lieutenant colonel, and Joseph M. Evans, major. The regiment was disbanded in 1865 in Texas prior to the final surrender.

Some sources say that Samuel remained in Texas after the war, engaged in cattle ranching, and later drove a herd back to California. Samuel appears in the 1880 federal census in San Francisco, California with his wife and four children. His occupation is shown as stockbroker. He later served one term as treasurer for the city of San Francisco and later served as Assistant United States Treasurer in San Francisco during the Cleveland administration. Samuel Houston Brooks died in Oakland, California on September 16, 1910.

Reding Lafayette Brooks (1832-1908)

Reding Lafayette "Red" Brooks was born March 14, 1832 in Fayette County, Tennessee. He and his family arrived in Montgomery County, Texas about 1847. He married Mary Emily Whitley in Walker County on February 7, 1861.

Reding enlisted as a private in Captain W. W. Viser's Company B, 6th Battalion of Texas Cavalry on March 26, 1862. This unit was attached to the Trans-Mississippi Department and served in Texas and Louisiana. Reding first appears on a muster roll for the month of March 1862 at Camp Burnett in Houston County, Texas. On a muster roll for November and December 1862, he is shown present as a 1st corporal. His final muster roll, dated April 1865, shows that he was at his home and on furlough from the Confederate hospital in Harrisburg. A Confederate pension application filed by Reding on July 12, 1907 was not approved. Reding Lafayette Brooks died August 10, 1908 and was buried at Oakwood Cemetery, Huntsville, Texas.

William Hailey Brooks (1833-1916)

William Hailey Brooks was born June 9, 1833 in Tennessee. He and his family arrived in Montgomery County, Texas about 1847. He married Julia Helen Besser in Walker County on November 5, 1854.

William enlisted as a private in Company G, 20th Texas Infantry on May 5, 1862 at Waverly, Texas. He was promoted to 1st corporal in July 1862 by order of Lt. Colonel Abercrombie. Six muster rolls from July 1864 through January 1865 show 3rd Sergeant W. H. Brooks on detached service to Captain Goff at regimental command in Galveston. William filed a Confederate pension application on September 30, 1907 which was approved on September 28, 1908. William Hailey Brooks died in Freestone County, Texas on April 23, 1916 and was buried in Greenwood Cemetery, Teague, Texas.

Montgomery Somerville Brooks (1835-1908)

Montgomery Somerville Brooks was born November 23, 1835 in Tennessee. He and his family arrived in Montgomery County, Texas about 1847. He married about 1865 to a woman known only as Loretta or Lauretta.

Records from the Texas State Archives show that Somerville Brooks enlisted in Company B, 17th Brigade of Texas State Troops in 1861. In a Confederate pension application filed by M. S. Brooks in Madison County March 20, 1903, M. S. Brooks claims that he also enlisted in Company G, 7th Texas Cavalry in 1861 and served until the close of the war. This pension application was approved on July 16, 1903. One muster roll appears in the records of the 7th Texas Cavalry showing that S. Brooks was enrolled in Company G of the 7th Texas Cavalry by Captain H. W. Fisher in Walker County on October 1, 1861. No further records have been found. Montgomery Somerville Brooks died on February 5, 1908 in Madison County, Texas and was buried in Midway Cemetery.

Andrew Jackson Brooks (1844-1863)

Andrew Jackson Brooks was born on November 8, 1844 in Fayette County, Tennessee. He was the son of Samuel Clifford Brooks and his second wife, Elizabeth J. Tatum Brooks. The Brooks family moved from Tennessee to Mississippi where their youngest child, Sina, was born in October 1847. The family moved to Montgomery County, Texas shortly after her birth.

Andrew was just seventeen when he enlisted in Captain Samuel Wooldridge's Company of the 2nd Texas Lancers on March 29, 1862. This unit was inducted into Confederate service as Company B of the 24th Texas Cavalry. Shortly after arriving at Camp Holmes in Arkansas in the fall of 1862, the 24th Cavalry Regiment was dismounted and was re-designated as the 24th Texas Cavalry (Dismounted). From Camp Holmes, the regiment moved to Ft. Hindman at Arkansas Post. On January 11, 1863, Ft. Hindman was attacked by Union forces along with support from U.S. gunboats. Andrew was mortally wounded during the battle and died the next day. Although the burial site of the Confederate soldiers killed at Arkansas Post is unknown, it is likely that they were buried in a mass grave outside the fort. A marker was placed in memory of Private Andrew Jackson Brooks at the Danville–Shepard Cemetery in Montgomery County, Texas.

The Cartwright Family

Thomas Peter Cartwright, Jr. (1776-1845)

Thomas Peter Cartwright, Jr. is believed to have been born about 1776. He arrived in what is now Montgomery County about 1833. As patriarch of the Cartwrights in Montgomery County, he lived to see two of his sons, Matthew Winston and William P. Cartwright, win independence for Texas at the Battle of San Jacinto. The descendents of Thomas Peter Cartwright, Jr. and the spouses of his descendents contributed no fewer than twenty-two soldiers to the cause of the Confederacy. One of his sons and thirteen of his grandsons served in the Confederate Army. In addition, one of his daughters and seven of his granddaughters were married to Confederate soldiers. Peter, as he was called, did not live to see the extraordinary commitment by his family during the War between the States nor did he have to bear the grief of losing three of his grandsons in combat. He died February 20, 1845 and was buried in what is now the Cartwright–Rabun Chapel Cemetery.

Descendants of Thomas Peter Cartwright, Jr.

Family of Williford B. Cartwright (1802-1860)

Williford B. Cartwright, the oldest son of Thomas Peter Cartwright, Jr. and Elizabeth Ann Shaw, was born March 15, 1802 in Alabama. He married Pinkey Byrd sometime prior to 1836. Together, they had four daughters and four sons. Three of the four sons served in the Confederate Army. The oldest son was killed in a train accident; the second son lost an arm due to wounds received in battle; and the third son died from wounds received in battle. Three of the four Cartwright daughters were married to Confederate soldiers. The oldest daughter, Maria, who was born about 1839, married Private John Barber Nuner of Company B, Waul's Texas Legion. The second daughter, Narcissa, born about 1840, married Private Moses McLain of Company K, 20th Texas Infantry. The third daughter, Letha, born about 1844, married Private Joseph McLain of Company K, 20th Texas Infantry.

Erasmus G. W. Cartwright (1836-1861)

Erasmus "Ras" G. W. Cartwright was born about 1836 in Texas. At age twenty-five, Ras joined Captain P. P. Porter's company of infantry on May 7, 1861. This unit became Company H of the 4th Texas Infantry Regiment and served in the Army of Northern Virginia. In route to Virginia, the regiment made a stop at Holly Springs, Mississippi. While boarding a railroad car to continue his journey, Ras fell beneath a moving train and was killed, thus becoming the first casualty in his company.

Lemuel C. Cartwright (1838-1865)

Lemuel C. Cartwright was born about 1838 in Texas. He enlisted as a private in Company H, 4th Texas Infantry on March 24, 1862 as part of a group of reinforcements recruited by Lieutenant Charles E. Jones. During an engagement on October 7, 1864, southeast of Richmond, Virginia, Private Cartwright received gunshot wounds to the hand and to the thigh. The wounds were severe, and he was transported to the hospital in Richmond where one arm was amputated. He was captured while still in the hospital on April 3, 1865 during the fall of Richmond. Private Lemuel C. Cartwright was paroled on May 3, 1865. He died a short time after returning home and was buried in the Cartwright Family Cemetery near the community of Keenan.

James G. W. Cartwright (1842-1864)

James G. W. Cartwright was born about 1842 in Texas. He enlisted as a private in Captain Procter P. Porter's Company of Infantry on May 7, 1861. Serving in Company H, 4th Texas Infantry, James was promoted to sergeant in September of 1862. He was taken prisoner at the Battle of Sharpsburg (Antietam) on September 17, 1862 and sent to Fort Delaware prisoner-of-war camp. He was later sent to Aikens Landing, Virginia on October 2, 1862 and officially exchanged on November 10, 1862. Second Sergeant James G. W. Cartwright was mortally wounded at the Battle of the Wilderness on May 6, 1864 and was sent to Christian's Factory Hospital in Lynchburg, Virginia where he died June 5, 1862. He is buried in the Old Lynchburg City Cemetery.

Family of Maria C. Cartwright Jones (1803-1860)

Maria C. Cartwright, the oldest daughter of Thomas Peter Cartwright, Jr. and Elizabeth Ann Shaw, was born December 1803 in Washington County, Alabama. She married Charles L. S. Jones in 1824, and together they had three sons and four daughters. Their oldest daughter, Harriett Amelia, married Captain Robert S. Poole who commanded three different companies of Confederate cavalry. The youngest daughter, Mary Isabella, married her first cousin, Benjamin Almary Pierson, who was a sergeant in Company A, 10th Texas Infantry.

Sons of Maria C. Cartwright & Charles L. S. Jones
Charles Edward Jones (1831-1862)

Charles Edward Jones was born about 1831 in Alabama. He enlisted as a sergeant in Captain P. P. Porter's Company of Infantry on May 7, 1861. He was promoted to second lieutenant of Company H, 4th Texas Infantry on October 25, 1861. Lieutenant Jones returned to Montgomery County in February 1862 to recruit reinforcements for the regiment and returned to Virginia in the late spring of 1862 with thirty-seven new recruits. Second Lieutenant Charles Edward Jones was killed in action at the Second Battle of Bull Run (Manassas) on August 30, 1862. His place of burial is unknown.

Matthew Davis Jones (1833-1912)

Matthew Davis Jones was born about 1833. He enlisted in Company A, 24th Texas Cavalry on March 22, 1862. This company was originally commanded by his brother-in-law, Captain Robert S. Poole. He is last shown present with the 24th Texas Cavalry on a roll dated September and October of 1862. Later records show that he was transferred to the Trans-Mississippi Department. It is likely that he was among the men who returned horses to Montgomery County when the 24th Cavalry Regiment was dismounted in the fall of 1862. He appears on the rolls of Company E, 24th/25th Consolidated Regiment as a second lieutenant. Matthew appears on 1870 and 1880 Falls County census rolls in the household of his cousin, Benjamin Pierson. He married Sallie W. Morrison in 1886. Matthew Davis Jones died May 2, 1912. Both he and his wife, Sallie, are buried in Woodland Cemetery, Rosebud, Texas.

Family of Clarissa Ann Cartwright Blount (1810-1883)

Clarissa Ann Cartwright, the second daughter of Thomas Peter Cartwright, Jr. and Elizabeth Ann Shaw, was born about August 10, 1810 in Washington County, Alabama. She married John Thomas Blount in 1826, a union that produced six sons and seven daughters. All six sons were Confederate soldiers. The two oldest, William Peter and John Cartwright Blount, enlisted in the Confederate Army in Mississippi while the four youngest sons, James Koen, Joseph Shaw, Alexander Lutha, and Francis Marion Blount, served in Texas regiments.

At least two of the seven daughters are known to have married Confederate soldiers. Amanda F. Blount married William Farris Montgomery who served in Company K, 20th Texas Infantry. Virginia Adeline "Jennie" Blount married Shephard Franklin Dyer who served in Company A, Terry's Regiment Texas Cavalry.

Three of the four youngest sons of Clarrisa and John T. Blount appear on the U.S. census rolls for Montgomery County in 1860 but enlisted in the Confederate Army in other counties. James Koen Blount enlisted in Company A, 36th Texas Cavalry in San Marcos, Texas on March 18, 1863. Joseph Shaw Blount and Francis Marion Blount enlisted in Company C, 17th Texas Infantry in Wood County about May 18, 1862. Although he does not appear on the Montgomery County census rolls, it is likely that Alexander Lutha Blount was living in Montgomery County when war broke out. He served as a corporal in Company A of Mann's Regiment Texas Cavalry and the 24th/25th Consolidated Regiment Texas Cavalry. Both of these companies were commanded by Captain Robert S. Poole of Montgomery County.

Family of Matthew Winston Cartwright (1815-1884)

Matthew Winston Cartwright, the son of Thomas Peter Cartwright, Jr. and Elizabeth Ann Shaw, was born about January 22, 1815 in Washington County, Alabama. Matthew was a veteran of the Republic of Texas Army and participated in Battle of San Jacinto. He married Susannah Lorraine Sykes in 1838. The couple had four sons and three daughters. Only the first-born son, Pleasant L. Cartwright, was old enough to serve in the Confederate Army. Matthew's youngest daughter, Mary Ann, married John B. Butler who served as a private in Company B, 1st Texas Infantry. Matthew Winston Cartwright died December 4, 1884 and was buried in Cartwright–Rabon Chapel Cemetery in Montgomery County, Texas.

Pleasant L. Cartwright (1840-1899)

Pleasant L. Cartwright, the oldest son of Matthew Winston and Susannah Cartwright, was born October 6, 1840 in Montgomery County, Texas. On May 7, 1861, he enlisted as a private in Captain P. P. Porter's company of infantry that later became Company H, 4th Texas Infantry. Since he is not shown on the rolls of Company H, he apparently did not leave with Captain Porter's company when it departed for Virginia. Instead, Private Cartwright enlisted in Company K, 8th Texas Cavalry on September 8, 1861. A muster roll dated November 7, 1861 to January 1862 shows Private Cartwright as sick at Camp Terry in Kentucky and discharged by way of a surgeon's certificate of disability on January 4, 1862. After returning to Texas, Pleasant appears to have recovered since he enlisted in Company A, 24th Texas Cavalry on April 1, 1862. He traveled with the 24th Cavalry to Arkansas and was captured at the Battle of Arkansas Post on January 11, 1863. He was transported to Camp Butler in Illinois and was later paroled and exchanged at City Point, Virginia. Private Cartwright appears to have gone directly to the hospital in Petersburg, Virginia, suffering from smallpox. He was once again discharged and returned to Texas. He appears on the rolls of Company A, Mann's Regiment, Texas Cavalry and is shown to have been elected as 3rd lieutenant on April 1, 1864, then promoted to 2nd lieutenant in December of 1864. This company was commanded by Captain Robert S. Poole and was later assigned to the 24th/25th Consolidated Cavalry as a detached unit. A muster roll for Company A, 24th/25th Consolidate Cavalry dated March 1865 shows Lieutenant Cartwright absent from Camp Lubbock in pursuit of deserters. He continued to serve with this company until it was disbanded in the spring of 1865.

After the war, Pleasant Cartwright married Joanna Gafford who was the daughter of Abner W. and Rebecca J. Gafford. Joanna had two brothers who also served in the Confederate Army. Her oldest brother, Reuben D. Gafford, was a private in Company H, 4th Texas Infantry and died of disease in the hospital at Richmond, Virginia on May 25, 1862. Another brother, Seaborn W. Gafford, served as a private in Company K, 20th Texas Infantry.

Pleasant L. Cartwright died January 6, 1899 and was buried in the Cartwright–Rabon Chapel Cemetery. His wife, Joanna, died in 1936 and was buried in the Willis Cemetery.

Family of Narcissa Cartwright Pierson (1817-1897)

Narcissa Cartwright, the daughter of Thomas Peter Cartwright, Jr. and Elizabeth Ann Shaw, was born March 16, 1817 in Washington County, Alabama. She married John Goodloe Warren Pierson in 1835.

John and Narcissa's second son, Benjamin Almary Pierson, joined Company A, 10th Texas Infantry in Grimes County on October 12, 1861. He was captured at the Battle of Arkansas Post on January 11, 1863 and sent to Camp Douglas in Illinois as a prisoner of war. After being paroled and exchanged in the spring of 1863, he returned to the 10th Texas Infantry and was promoted to third sergeant. He was present at Chickamauga and the Chattanooga campaign. At the battle of Missionary Ridge, the 10th Tenth Texas Infantry, which had been consolidated with the 6th Texas Infantry and 15th Texas Cavalry (Dismounted), became part of Granbury's Texas Brigade and served during the Atlanta campaign and John Bell Hood's invasions. After the Battle of Nashville, the badly-depleted Granbury's Brigade was reduced to a single regiment known as Granbury's Consolidated Regiment. Benjamin Pierson was promoted second sergeant in Company B of the regiment and was present at the surrender of General Joseph Johnston's Army in North Carolina on April 28, 1865. Benjamin Almary Pierson died January 31, 1905 and was buried at Cedar Springs Cemetery, Falls County, Texas. His mother, Narcissa Cartwright Pierson Roberts, who had remarried after the death of John Pierson, died in 1897 and was also buried in the Cedar Springs Cemetery.

Joseph C. Cartwright (1821-1904)

Joseph C. Cartwright, the youngest son of Thomas Peter Cartwright, Jr. and Elizabeth Ann Shaw, was born May 31, 1821 in Washington County, Alabama. Joseph was drafted into service in the 17th Brigade of Texas State Troops in 1863 and ordered to report to Captain Joseph M. Evans. He was transferred to Company D, 4th Infantry Regiment, Texas State Troops in the fall of 1863, and in the winter of 1864, he enlisted in Company A of Mann's Regiment, Texas Cavalry where his nephew, Pleasant L. Cartwright, was a second lieutenant. When this company became Company A of the 24th/25th Consolidated Cavalry, Joseph was detailed to the Texas District Chief of Transportation as a wheelwright where he served for the remainder of the war. Joseph C. Cartwright died January 24, 1904 and was buried in the Cartwright–Rabun Chapel Cemetery.

Martha Ann Cartwright Laishonce (1825-1897)

Martha Ann Cartwright, the youngest daughter of Thomas Peter Cartwright, Jr. and Elizabeth Ann Shaw, was born about 1825 in Washington County, Alabama. She married Louis Laishonce prior to 1860. Louis D. Laishonce was born about 1817 in Missouri. He enlisted as a private in Captain P. P. Porter's company of infantry on May 7, 1861 but did not appear on the rolls of that company after it left Texas bound for Virginia. He appears on the rolls of Company I, 9th Texas Infantry (Nichols') as a corporal while serving a six-month tour of duty in defense of Galveston Island.

Louis and Martha Ann Laishonce appear on the rolls of the U.S. census for Montgomery County in 1880. No further records are found after that date. Louis was buried in Cartwright–Rabon Chapel Cemetery, but the exact date of his death is unknown. Martha Ann Cartwright Laishonce died June 16, 1896 and is buried in Cartwright Cemetery near Pinehurst in Montgomery County, Texas.

The Cheatham Family

The history of the Cheatham family in Montgomery County, Texas begins with John L. and Martha Cheatham in South Carolina. In the 1850s, at least two daughters and their extended families migrated to Texas. The youngest child, Alfred Cheatham, remained in South Carolina. With the start of the war in 1861, Alfred joined the Confederate Army, serving in the 7th Battalion, South Carolina Infantry (Nelson's). He was killed in action at Drury's Bluff, Virginia, May 16, 1864.

Among those who made their way to Texas were Helena Cheatham Golding and her husband, Reuben G. Golding, and their children. The children of Louvinda Cheatham Foshee (Fooshe) and her former husband, John Madison Golding, along with Louvinda, also made the journey. Two children of John L. and Martha Cheatham's son Robert also made their way to Texas. These children were William Alexander Cheatham and his sister, Amanda Cheatham who married William W. Roten about 1856. William Roten's mother and four of his siblings also migrated to Texas.

Helena Cheatham Golding (1816-1889)

Helena Cheatham was born about 1816 in South Carolina. She was the daughter of John L. and Martha Cheatham. She married Reuben Griffin Golding in South Carolina on May 27, 1837. Helena and Reuben and their family migrated to Texas prior to 1860. Reuben Golding served in Company B, 17th Brigade of Texas State Troops. Helena and Reuben were believed to have had five sons. The youngest three sons served in the Confederate Army. Helena died about 1889 in Matagorda County, Texas.

Children of Helena Cheatham Golding
Anthony Foster Golding (1841-1886)

Anthony Foster Golding was born March 27, 1841 in South Carolina. He was the son of Helena and Reuben G. Golding. Anthony enlisted in Captain Robert M. Powell's Company D, 5th Texas Infantry at Danville, Texas on August 20, 1861. He was wounded in the side at the Battle of Manassas on August 30, 1862 and sent to the hospital. He returned to duty and in October and served with the 5th Texas Infantry until the end of the war. He was present when General Robert E. Lee surrendered the Confederate Army of Northern Virginia. Private Anthony Golding was paroled at Appomattox Courthouse, Virginia on April 9, 1865.

After the war, Anthony returned to Montgomery County and worked as a farmer. He married Sallie A. Sample in Montgomery County on February 17, 1877. Anthony Foster Golding died September 7, 1886 and was buried in the Willis City Cemetery, Montgomery County, Texas.

Thomas D. Golding (1843-1863)

Thomas D. Golding was born December 6, 1843 in South Carolina. He was the son of Helena and Reuben G. Golding. Thomas enlisted as a private in Company B, 24th Texas Cavalry (Dismounted) at Danville, Texas on March 29, 1862. Thomas was captured at the Battle of Arkansas Post on January 11, 1863 and was transported to City General Hospital in St. Louis, Missouri. He died there on February 13, 1863 from typhoid fever and chronic diarrhea. He was buried in what is now Jefferson Barracks National Cemetery.

Nimrod Chiles Golding (1845-1912)

Nimrod Chiles Golding was born March 9, 1845 in South Carolina. He was the son of Helena and Reuben G. Golding. The exact date that N. C. Golding joined the Confederate Army is uncertain. He appears on one muster roll of Captain Robert S. Powell's Company A, 24th/25th Consolidated Cavalry. This roll is dated April 1865 and indicates that Private Golding was a bugler for the company. Nimrod was never known to have married. He appears on the rolls of the 1880 Montgomery County census in the household of his brother Anthony Golding. Nimrod Chiles Golding died February 16, 1912 and was buried in the Willis City Cemetery, Montgomery County, Texas.

Louvinda Cheatham Golding Foshee (1824-1912)

Louvinda Cheatham was born about August 24, 1824 in South Carolina. She was the daughter of John L. and Martha Cheatham. At age seventeen, Louvinda married John Madison Golding on November 7, 1841. The couple was known to have had at least two sons and one daughter. The two sons, Henry and John, served in the Confederate Army. Their daughter, Elizabeth Helena Golding, married Thomas Jefferson Liles who served in the Confederate Army in several units from Montgomery County. John Madison Golding, Sr. died in October 1848.

Louvinda then married George Washington Foshee about 1850. The exact number of children born from that union is unknown. Louvinda and George migrated with their family to Texas prior to 1860. After arriving in Montgomery County, George enlisted in the 17th Brigade of Texas State Troops. Their daughter, Martha Irene Foshee, married Timothy Jackson Cude who served in the 24th and 26th Texas Cavalries. Louvinda died October 12, 1912 and was buried in Cude Cemetery, Montgomery County, Texas.

Children of Louvinda Cheatham Golding Foshee
Henry Richard Golding (1844-1883)

Henry Richard Golding was born October 31, 1844 in South Carolina. He was the son of John Madison and Louvinda Cheatham Golding. After John's death in 1848, Louvinda and her second husband migrated to Texas with their family prior to 1860. Henry enlisted as a private in Company B, 24th Texas Cavalry (Dismounted) at Danville, Texas on March 29, 1862. He was captured at the Battle of Arkansas Post on January 11, 1863 and transported to the City General Hospital in St. Louis, Missouri. After being discharged from the hospital, Richard was incarcerated at Gratiot Street Prison in St. Louis. He was paroled in 1863 and was sent to City Point, Virginia where he was exchanged. Henry was admitted to the hospital in City Point where he was diagnosed with a general wasting condition shown as "a debility" and given a sixty-day furlough. After his furlough, Henry is once again shown as absent and in the hospital. It appears that Henry never fully recovered and likely was discharged after the fall of Atlanta in 1864, but all muster rolls for the regiment end in April of 1864, leaving no further record.

After the war, Henry returned to Montgomery County, and on August 16, 1868 he married Sidney Elizabeth Sapp Alston. Family records indicate that Henry died on November 20, 1883. His place of burial is unknown.

John Madison Golding, Jr. (1846-1920)

John Madison Golding, Jr. was born August 6, 1846 in South Carolina. He was the son of John Madison Golding, Sr. and Louvinda Cheatham Golding. After John, Sr.'s death in 1848, Louvinda and her second husband migrated to Texas with their family prior to 1860.

John Madison Golding, Jr. does not appear in the official Confederate service records. In a Confederate widow's pension application filed by Nancy Delia Sunday Golding, she claimed that her late husband had served as a cook in Captain Poole's Company of the 24th/25th Consolidated Texas Cavalry and was discharged with his company at Columbus, Texas in 1865. Despite affidavits from several witnesses, the application was denied. It was common for records to be missing in the late days of the war, and by the time many of the pension applications were filed, there were few veterans still living to give testimony. It is likely that John M. Golding, Jr. did serve in the Confederate Army, but evidence to substantiate that claim has long been lost.

Robert Cheatham (1805-1845)

Robert Cheatham was born about 1805 in South Carolina. He was the son of John L. and Martha Cheatham. He married Frances Sadler about 1825. Family histories tell that Robert and Frances had four children with only two living to adulthood. The two surviving children, Amanda and William Alexander, migrated to Texas in the 1850s.

Children of Robert Cheatham
Amanda Cheatham Roten Bryant (1836-unknown)

Amanda Cheatham was born about 1836 in South Carolina. She was the daughter of Robert and Frances Sadler Cheatham. Amanda married William Roten in South Carolina about 1856. The couple migrated to Texas prior to 1860. William Roten served in Company B, 24th Texas Cavalry along with his brother, Larkin J. Roten. William is believed to have died in 1862. David Edward Roten, another brother of William, served in Company I, 9th Texas Infantry and Company K, 20th Texas Infantry.

Amanda remarried in Montgomery County on January 6, 1867 to Jacob Bryant. During the war, Jacob had served in Company I, 9th Texas Infantry and Company K, 20th Texas Infantry. No records have been found for the date of Amanda's death nor for the place of her burial.

William Alexander Cheatham (1837-1900)

William Alexander Cheatham was born December 27, 1837 in South Carolina. He was the son of Robert and Frances Sadler Cheatham. William migrated to Texas prior to 1860. It is likely that he traveled to Texas with the Roten family.

Confederate service records show that William A. Cheatham enlisted as a private in Captain Thomas Brandon Shannon's Company C of the 1st Texas Lancers. This regiment, which was organized and commanded by Colonel George W. Carter, was later designated as the 21st Texas Cavalry. Private Cheatham is shown on a company muster roll dated February 26, 1862 at Camp Hèbert near Hempstead, Texas. He is shown present with a rank of 3rd corporal on a roll for the period of August 31, 1862 through February 28, 1863. The last muster roll in William's file shows him present for the months of September and October of 1863. Since there are no records that state otherwise, it is likely that Corporal Cheatham remained with his regiment until it returned to Texas and was disbanded in the spring of 1865.

After the war, William returned to Montgomery County where he married Sarah Elizabeth Walker on December 18, 1867. Sarah's father and two of her brothers served in the Confederate Army. Her father, William Walker, served in Company B, 24th Texas Cavalry and died of disease at Arkansas Post on November 11, 1862. Sarah's oldest brother, Samuel Walker, also served in Company B, 24th Texas Cavalry and had previously served in Company I, 9th Texas Infantry (Nichols'). Her brother, John Madison Walker, served in Company A, 24th/25th Consolidated Texas Cavalry. William Alexander Cheatham died January 4, 1900 and was buried in Cude Cemetery, Montgomery County, Texas. Sarah Elizabeth Walker Cheatham died September 27, 1905 and also was buried in Cude Cemetery.

The Thomas Chilton Family

Thomas Chilton (1798-1854)

The story of the Chilton family is deeply rooted in the history of the Baptist church, the Republic of Texas, and the War between the States. A son of Reverend Thomas John Chilton and Margaret Peggy Bledsoe, Thomas Chilton was born near Lancaster, Kentucky, July 30, 1798. His mother was the daughter of Reverend Joseph Bledsoe. His aunt, Jane Bledsoe Baylor, was the wife of Captain John Walker Baylor who came to the Republic of Texas in 1839 and was almost immediately elected a judge of the Supreme Court of the Republic. John and Jane Baylor's son, Robert Emmett Bledsoe Baylor, co-founded Baylor University in 1845 with the Reverend William Tryon and Reverend James Huckins. Their grandson, George W. Baylor, was a Texas Ranger and a colonel in the Confederate Army, and their grandson, John Robert Baylor, was a lieutenant colonel in the Confederate Army.

Thomas B. Chilton attended schools in Paris, Kentucky. One week before his seventeenth birthday, he married Francis Tribble Stoner and began his study for ordination as a Baptist minister. He simultaneously began studying law with his uncle, Jesse Bledsoe. Family histories indicate that there may have been as many as six children born to Thomas and Francis Chilton. Census records confirm two daughters, Sarah Elizabeth (b.1819) who married Franklin Welsh Bowdon and Margaret (b.1824) who married Hugh G. Barclay. Records also confirm three sons, Thomas J. (b.1825); George W. (b.1828); and Horace B. (b.1836). In addition, there may have been a fourth son, William P. (b.1829).

After being admitted to the bar and beginning a law practice in Owingsville, Bath County, Kentucky, Thomas became a member of the Kentucky House of Representatives in 1819. Chilton was elected as a U.S. Representative from Kentucky to fill a vacancy in Congress and first took his seat in the U.S. House of Representatives on January 11, 1828. While in Washington, DC, he took residence at the boarding house of Mary Ball. He was lodged in the same room as a representative from Tennessee named David Crockett. The two men rapidly became friends and spent the better part of six years working together in Congress. It is rumored that a book claiming to be an autobiography published in 1834 and titled *Narrative of the Life of David Crockett of the State of Tennessee* was actually written by Thomas Chilton. In a letter to his publisher in 1834, Crockett admits that Thomas Chilton was entitled to a portion of the copyright and profits from the book.

After leaving Congress, Chilton returned to Kentucky, and in 1839, he moved his family to Talladega, Alabama near his younger brother, William Parish Chilton. Thomas practiced law in Alabama but also accepted the pulpit of the Hope Baptist Church in Talladega. During one of his revival meetings on the fourth Sunday of 1839, Chilton baptized his maternal cousin, Robert Emmett Bledsoe Baylor, who, after thirteen years of avowed atheism, converted to Christianity through the influence of Chilton. Baylor was so inspired by the sermons of Reverend Chilton that he soon became a Baptist preacher and moved to Texas where he assisted in the creation of the Union Baptist Association in 1840 and founded Baylor University at Independence Texas in 1845.

After the death of his wife Frances on October 6, 1842, Thomas Chilton married Louisa Eleanor Conklin, January 3, 1843. Together they had seven sons. They were William Henry (b.1843); Frank Bowden (b.1845); Matthias Dayton (b.1846); Hugh Barclay (b.1848); Lysias Brown (b.1849); Jenkins Conklin (b.1851); and Samuel Thomas (b.1853).

Thomas and Louisa moved their family to Texas in 1851 when Thomas was invited to pastor the First Baptist Church of Houston in August of that year. Resigning as pastor of the church in Houston on October 28, 1853, he became pastor of the Baptist church in Montgomery, Texas. While delivering a sermon on August 15, 1854, he suddenly clutched his chest, collapsed, and died in front of his congregation. Fellow Pastor Z. N. Morrell had this to say about the tragedy: "On the fifteenth day of August, 1854, while serving as pastor of the church at Montgomery, he died in the midst of his flock, who loved him much. His sojourn among us in Texas was short, but his name and deeds of love live on, and will, in the memory of many Texas Baptists."

Old Methodist Cemetery, Montgomery, Texas
photo courtesy of the author

The Reverend Thomas Chilton is buried in the Old Methodist Cemetery in downtown Montgomery, Texas. The inscription on his grave marker reads:

In Memory of
Rev. Tho. Chilton
who was born in Ky.
July 30, 1798 and
DIED
Among us Aug. 15, 1854

When Reverend Thomas Chilton died, he left a widow, ten sons, and two daughters. One of his sons served in the Confederate Army from Alabama, and five sons served from Texas. Four of these sons were living in Montgomery County in 1860.

George Washington Chilton (1828-1884)

George Washington Chilton, the second son of Thomas and Francis Tribble Stoner Chilton, was born near Elizabethtown, Kentucky on June 4, 1828. He migrated to Alabama with his parents and siblings in 1839. After briefly attending Howard College in Marion Alabama, he enlisted as a private in Company B of Colonel John Coffee Hays' First Regiment, Texas Mounted Rifles during the Mexican War. Following discharge, he returned to Alabama where he was admitted to the bar in 1848 and set up practice in Talladega. In 1851, Chilton set up a law practice in Tyler, Texas, and in 1852, he married Ella Goodman. Chilton was elected as a delegate from Smith County to

George Washington Chilton
photo courtesy of Southern Methodist University,
DeGolyer Library,
Lawrence T. Jones III Collection

the Secession Convention and served from January 28 until February 4, 1861. During the convention, he was given the task of informing Governor Sam Houston that if Houston did not take the oath to the Confederacy, he would be replaced as governor of Texas. In May 1861, George Chilton enlisted as a private in the 12th Brigade of Texas State Troops, but having had previous military experience, he was quickly promoted to major and assigned to the 3rd Texas Cavalry. Chilton received a minor head wound while leading the regiment at the Battle of Chustenahlah, Indian Territory, on December 26, 1861. The one-year enlistment period for the 3rd Texas Cavalry expired on May 8, 1862, and new officer elections were held at which time Chilton was dropped from the rolls. He was later appointed chief ordinance officer on the staff of General Hamilton Bee where he served for the remainder of the war. After the war, George Chilton was elected to the United States House of Representatives but was removed by the radical majority in Congress. He died on August 10, 1884 and was buried in Oakwood Cemetery, Tyler, Smith County, Texas.

Horace B. Chilton (1836-1862)

Horace B. Chilton, the youngest son of Thomas and Francis Tribble Stoner Chilton, was born in Bath County, Kentucky about 1836. At age twenty-five, he enlisted as a private in Company G of the 5th Alabama Infantry at Cahaba, Alabama on April 10, 1861. This regiment was originally commanded by Colonel Robert E. Rhodes and saw its first action during the sweeping Confederate victory at the First Battle of Manassas (Bull Run) on July 21, 1861. Just eleven months later, Private Chilton was killed in action as the 5th Alabama Infantry led an assault on the right flank of the Union Army at the Battle of Gaines' Mill. His place of burial is unknown.

William Henry Chilton (1843-1897)

William Henry Chilton was born on October 6, 1843 in Alabama. He was the oldest son of Thomas and Louisa Eleanor Conklin Chilton. He appears on the rolls of 1860 Montgomery County census in the household of his mother, L. E. Chilton.

On the twenty-first day of September 1861, William enlisted in Captain Benjamin F. Neal's Company I, 8th Texas Infantry in Corpus Christi, Texas. His first muster roll describes him as being eighteen years of age, five-foot-nine-and-one-half inches tall, blue eyes, and light-colored hair. It is unclear why William traveled all the way from Montgomery County to Corpus Christi to enlist in the Confederate Army. It is possible that he was related to Lieutenant George E. Conklin of Company I or to Harriett E. Conklin Moore, the wife of prominent Corpus Christi businessman, John M. Moore. Company I, was a light artillery company commanded by former Corpus Christi Mayor Benjamin Franklin Neal. This unit was involved in the Battle of Corpus Christi which was fought between August 12 and August 18, 1862. A list dated March 22, 1863, shows William to be among the able-bodied men at Fort Brown who were desirous of entering the naval service. Conflicting service records show a William Chilton enlisting at Tarrant County in Captain Samuel Evans' Company of Griffin's Regiment, Texas Infantry. This man appears to be the son of William Richard Chilton of Tennessee and not the son of Thomas Chilton. William appears on the 1880 Harris County, Texas census rolls with a wife shown only as Martha who was born in Texas. William's occupation is listed as "printing house." It is believed that William died in Marlin, Texas on November 2, 1897 and is buried in Falls County.

Frank Bowden Chilton (1845-1926)

Franklin Bowden Chilton, the son of Thomas Chilton and his second wife, Louisa Eleanor Conklin Chilton, was born February 27, 1845 in Marion County, Alabama. He was only nine years of age when his father died. He appears on the 1860 U.S. census rolls in Montgomery County with his mother and six brothers. His name appears on the roll as "F. Chitton." He was sent to school for a short time, then started to work at a very young age as a laborer at a neighboring sawmill, at six dollars a month. In less than a year, he was driving an ox team, hauling lumber to area towns, and frequently made the fifty-mile trip from Montgomery to Houston.

When Houston and Texas Central Railway extended its service to the town of Navasota in 1859, young Chilton secured a sub-contract to deliver mail from Montgomery to that point for a wage of fifteen dollars per month. Although the thirteen-year-old Chilton was often faced with crossing swollen creeks and streams, he never missed a stop nor wet a mail sack. Twice each week, he made the sixty-mile round trip without fail. By age sixteen, Frank was studying law under the guidance of a local attorney named Charles Jones. During the day, he clerked in the store of P. J. Willis at Montgomery, and at night and on Sundays, read his law books.

When the call to war sounded in 1861, Frank Chilton was persuaded by another attorney from Montgomery named Procter P. Porter to join his newly-formed company of troops. Lieutenant James T. Hunter from the town of Cincinnati in Walker County enrolled Frank Chilton in the company known as the Porter Guards at Montgomery, Texas on May 7, 1861. The company soon marched to Red Top in Grimes County where it was mustered into Confederate service. After leaving Red Top, the Porter Guards marched to Harrisburg where the company boarded a train to Beaumont. From Beaumont, the company was taken by boat up the Sabine River to Niblett's Bluff, and from there, the men marched through the treacherous swamplands of Louisiana to waiting rail cars in New Orleans for the long ride to Virginia. After arriving in Virginia, the Porter Guards were designated as Company H of the 4th Texas Infantry under the command of Colonel John Bell Hood.

Like many of the soldiers in Company H, Frank Chilton had become ill from exposure to the elements during the long trip from Texas to Virginia. As winter approached, many of the men in the regiment were in hospitals or on sick leave. Confederate service records show that Frank Chilton was on sick leave as of February 18, 1862. It is believed that he was suffering from yellow fever. He appears to have returned to his company by the end of February and participated in the fighting during the Peninsula campaign. Frank is shown to be on sick leave again on June 18, 1862. It was during this second period of absence that the bloody Battle of Gaines' Mill was fought. While recuperating, Frank learned that several of the men in has company had been killed and that his beloved Captain Procter Porter was mortally wounded and died several days after the battle. To add to the heartbreak, he learned that his brother, Horace B. Chilton, serving in the 5th Alabama Infantry, also had been killed at Gaines' Mill.

Either because he was under age or because he had chronic bouts with fever, Frank Chilton was honorably discharged from Company H, 4th Texas Infantry Regiment on September 15, 1862. Back home in Montgomery, Frank spent only a short time recuperating before re-enlisting in the Confederate Army.

While serving as a sergeant in Company B of Baylor's Texas Cavalry, the regiment of his cousin, Colonel George W. Baylor, he was promoted to 2nd lieutenant for having proved himself a gallant and meritorious soldier. At the time of his promotion, he was wounded and disabled, and being unfit for service in the field, was made post commander and provost marshal at Navasota. On January 27, 1865, by request of General Jerome B. Robertson, Lieutenant Chilton was promoted to captain and transferred to the reserve corps in Austin where he would remain until the end of the war.

Following the war, Frank Chilton worked tirelessly to preserve the memory of the Confederate soldier. Serving as president of the Hood's Texas Brigade Monument Committee, Frank Chilton led the memorial ceremony when the famed monument was dedicated in 1910 on the grounds of the Texas State Capitol. With the help of former comrades, H. T. Sapp and James T. Hunter, Frank drafted a detailed account of the men who served in Company H of the 4th Texas Infantry. Franklin Bowden Chilton died in Harris County on May 19, 1926 and is buried in Willis City Cemetery, Willis, Texas.

Matthias Dayton Chilton (1846-1918)

Matthias Dayton Chilton was born at Greensboro, Alabama on November 6, 1846. He was the third son of Thomas and Louisa Eleanor Conklin Chilton. He appears on the rolls of the 1860 Montgomery County census in the household of his mother, L. E. Chilton. In the spring of 1863,

Matt Chilton traveled from Montgomery to the nearby settlement of Courtney which was just south of Navasota in Grimes County. Here he enlisted in Company B, Madison's Regiment, Texas Cavalry on March 23, 1863 for a one-year period of service. Confederate service records show that he was discharged by a surgeon's certificate of disability at Camp Lee, Louisiana on August 31, 1863. This certificate describes Private Chilton as being age sixteen, five-foot-six inches tall, with light complexion, blue eyes, and light hair. The document shows that his former occupation was "school boy." A muster roll dated March 1865 shows M. D. Chilton to be a member of Company C, Terry's Regiment of Texas Cavalry. After the war, Matt returned to Montgomery County and later settled in Falls County, Texas. He married Clara Thompson of Fort Bend County, Texas on May 14, 1874. Matt and Clara appear on the 1910 census rolls in Falls County. Some time prior to 1918, Matt was admitted to the Confederate Veterans Home in Austin, Texas. He died at the home on March 19, 1918 and was buried in the Texas State Cemetery in Austin.

Hugh Barclay Chilton (1848-1872)

Hugh Barclay Chilton was born at Greensboro, Alabama on May 22, 1848. He was the fourth son of Thomas and Louisa Eleanor Conklin Chilton and was the youngest of their sons to serve in the Confederate Army. He appears on the rolls of the 1860 Montgomery County census in the household of his mother, L. E. Chilton. Hugh Chilton enlisted in Captain Robert S. Poole's Company A of Mann's Regiment, Texas Cavalry. This company, composed primarily of men from Montgomery County, spent much of its time rounding up conscripts and deserters. In 1865, the company was assigned to the 24th/25th Consolidated Texas Cavalry and served as Company A, Captain Poole's detached cavalry. Private Hugh Chilton was mistakenly listed on the rolls as N. B. Chilton and is shown to have been left sick in Austin County, Texas on April 29, 1865. Hugh Barclay Chilton is believed to have passed away on January 12, 1872 in Corsicana, Texas. His place of burial is unknown at this time.

The Clepper Family

There were five members of the Clepper family in Montgomery County who served in the Confederate Army. All were sons or grandsons of James and Christine Winfred Collier Clepper. The two sons were Lemuel Gilliam Clepper and Joseph Collier Clepper. The three grandsons, Lorenzo Dow Clepper, Charles Duncan Clepper, and James Clepper, were sons of John Clepper. John was the oldest son of James and Christine Clepper.

Lemuel Gilliam Clepper (1813-1893)

Lemuel Gilliam Clepper was the second son of James and Christine Clepper. He was born in Tennessee on October 28, 1813. According to Clepper family histories, Lemuel left his home in Tennessee at an early age and moved to Alabama where he married Rebecca Broadnax in 1836. He is said to have moved to Texas about 1837. Rebecca Broadnax Clepper is believed to have died about 1841. Lemuel married Mary Ann Faulkner in Polk County, Texas on September 28, 1848.

Prior to the war, Lemuel had served as a sheriff, justice of the peace, and district clerk in Montgomery County. In the spring of 1861, he began organizing a company of men, known as the Montgomery County Rifle Boys. Some of the men from the Rifle Boys joined the 9th Texas Infantry (Nichols') for a period of six months before returning to Montgomery County. In the spring of 1862, Lemuel Clepper recruited and organized a new company of men which became Company K of the 20th Texas Infantry. He was elected captain of the company and commanded the unit until the end of the war.

After the war, Lemuel once again served as a justice of the peace and as a county commissioner. Lemuel Gilliam Clepper died June 19, 1893 and was buried in the Magnolia Cemetery, Montgomery County, Texas.

Joseph Collier Clepper (1831-1910)

Joseph Collier Clepper was born June 30, 1831 in Tennessee. He was the son of James and Christine Clepper. He appears on the rolls of the 1850 Montgomery County census in the household of his brother, Lemuel G. Clepper.

Joseph enlisted as a private in Company K, 8th Texas Cavalry, better known as Terry's Texas Rangers. His exact date of enlistment is unclear. He appears on a muster roll for the months of September and November of 1861 which states that he was enrolled by Captain John G. Walker at Bowling Green, Kentucky on October 26, 1861. It also states that he was placed on leave until November 4, 1861. He is last shown present on a roll dated November 7, 1861 to January 7, 1862. The last service record in his file states that he was discharged with a surgeon's certificate of disability but the certificate is not dated. It is known that many of the men in the 8th Texas Cavalry became severely ill in travels through Tennessee and Kentucky. It is likely that Joseph is one of those who could not quickly recover from his illness and was discharged.

After the war, Joseph returned to Montgomery County for a brief period. Census records show him in Washington County in 1870. Joseph married Penelope Hatfield Burney on October 2, 1878. They appear on the census rolls of Burleson County in 1880. Joseph Collier Clepper died in Caldwell, Burleson County, Texas on May 14, 1910.

Lorenzo Dow Clepper (1839-1904)

Lorenzo Dow Clepper was born January 30, 1839 in Tennessee. He was the son of John and Amanda M. Birdwell Clepper. He married Sarah Ann Travis in Montgomery County on April 26, 1861. She was the daughter of John and Mary Rayborn Travis and a distant cousin of William Barrett Travis who died at the Alamo in 1836. Her brother, Henry Travis, served with Lorenzo in Company H of the 4th Texas Infantry and was killed at the Battle of the Wilderness in 1864.

Lorenzo enlisted as a private in Company H, 4th Texas Infantry in Montgomery County on March 18, 1862. He was discharged due to disability in 1863. After returning to Montgomery County, Lorenzo enlisted in Company K, 20th Texas Infantry which was commanded by his uncle, Captain Lemuel Clepper. He last appears on a muster roll of the 20th Infantry in March 1865. This roll states that he had been sick in the hospital at Houston since November 29, 1865. He was once again discharged from Confederate service by a surgeon's certificate of disability March 5, 1865 with a cause given as "Phthisis Pulmonalis," an archaic medical term which generally meant consumption or tuberculosis. Family histories tell that Lorenzo Dow Clepper died July 1, 1904 and was buried in Shiloh Cemetery in Waller County, Texas.

Charles Duncan Clepper (1840-1923)

Charles Duncan Clepper was born November 6, 1840 in Tennessee. He was the son of John and Amanda M. Birdwell Clepper. Family histories state that Charles arrived in Montgomery County with his parents in 1857. He appears on the rolls of the 1860 Montgomery County census in the household of his father, John Clepper.

Charles Clepper enlisted as a private in Company I of the 9th Texas Infantry (Nichols') on November 7, 1861. The men of this regiment were enlisted for a period of six months for the purpose of defending Galveston Island. After being mustered out of the 9th Infantry at Galveston in April 1862, Charles enlisted as a private in Captain Lemuel G. Clepper's Company K of the 20th Texas Infantry and was given a short furlough. A muster roll for the months of November and December 1862 states that Charles was absent on sick leave and was at home in Montgomery County from November 10, 1862 to January 1, 1863. It is unclear if Charles made it back to the regiment prior to the Battle of Galveston on New Year's Day, but he is shown present on the rolls for the months of January and February 1863. Charles is last shown present with the regiment as a sergeant on a roll for the month of December 1864.

Charles Duncan Clepper married Mary Jane McAlpine in Montgomery County on October 17, 1866. The couple moved from Montgomery County to Washington and Grimes Counties, then back to Montgomery County. They finally settled in an area near Fields Store in Waller County. Charles Clepper died in 1923 and was buried in Fields Store Cemetery.

James Clepper (1844-unknown)

James Clepper was born about 1844 in Tennessee. He was the son of John and Amanda M. Birdwell Clepper. He appears on the rolls of the 1860 Montgomery County census in the household of his father, John Clepper.
Along with his brother Charles Duncan Clepper, James enlisted as a private in Company I of the 9th Texas Infantry (Nichols') in Montgomery County on November 7, 1861. After being mustered out of the 9th Infantry at Galveston in April 1862, James enlisted as a private in Captain Lemuel G. Clepper's

Company K of the 20th Texas Infantry at age eighteen. On October 7, 1863, James was detailed as a guard on the gunboat *USS Sachem* at Sabine Pass, Texas. In October 1864, he was detailed to procure winter clothes for his company. James Clepper is last shown on the rolls of the 20th Texas in November 1864. No further records, neither military nor personal, have been found for James Clepper.

The Cude Family

It was not unusual for every male family member of fighting age to join the Confederate Army. Some families would be fortunate enough to see most of their sons come home while some families would be destroyed by the war. The Cude family of Montgomery County was among those families, with the largest number of soldiers. Two brothers, William Arthur Cude, Jr. and Timothy Wright Cude, would furnish no fewer than thirteen sons for the Confederate Army.

The William Arthur Cude, Jr. Family

William Arthur Cude, Jr. was born in Tennessee about 1801 and died in Montgomery County, Texas on May 1, 1847. He was first married to Eleanor Long on August 13, 1821 in Alabama. William and Eleanor lived in Alabama until about 1826 or 1827 where they had four children: James Washington Cude (b.ca.1822); Sylvania Cude (b.1823); Tobias A. Cude (b.1825); and Dorcus Cude (b.1827). The family moved to Texas, settling first in Frio County, and from there, they moved to Gonzales County where they had another son, Solomon Marion Cude who was born in 1831. It is uncertain where William and Eleanor were living when their next two children were born, John M. Cude in 1833 and Nathaniel Wiley in 1836, but Eleanor passed away October 31, 1837 in Gonzales County, Texas. On June 30, 1839, William married Lydia Ellen "Lillie" Winters in Montgomery County, Texas where they had four sons: Alfred Jackson Cude (b.1840); Richard Dowling Cude (b.1842); Willis Franklin Cude (b.1844); and Timothy J. Cude (b.1846). In all, William Arthur Cude had nine sons who joined the Confederate Army. While the sons of William Cude, Jr. enlisted in the Confederate Army from counties other than Montgomery, each of these nine soldiers, with the exception of James Washington Cude, either had been born in or lived in Montgomery County for a substantial amount of time prior to the War between the States.

James Washington Cude (1822-1908)

James Washington Cude, the oldest son of William Arthur Cude, Jr. and Eleanor Long, was born in 1822 in Jefferson County, Alabama. He and his wife, Rachel Ann Walker Cude, are shown in the 1860 U.S. census rolls for Gonzales County as "James and Rachel Corde," living with their five children and another child named James Walker who was probably a nephew. Living nearby was the family of brother-in-law, Billington Taylor Winters and a sister, Dorcus Cude Winters. Two brothers, Tobias A. and Nathaniel Wiley Cude, also appear to have been living in the Winters' household. Another brother, Solomon Marion Cude, also is shown living nearby with wife, Mary Ann Jones Cude, and their four children. In July

1861, James Washington Cude and his brother-in-law Billington Taylor Winters entered Confederate service by joining Captain Malvern Harrell's company of the Hopkinsville Mounted Cavalry, 25th Brigade, Texas State Troops for a period of one year. While Billington Winters went on to serve in the 17th Texas Infantry, there are no further Confederate service records for James Washington Cude. With James being age 40, he would have been beyond the conscription age-limit of 35, and no further service was required. Family histories state that James died May 12, 1908 near the town of Devine in Medina County, Texas. James Washington Cude's place of burial is uncertain.

Tobias A. Cude (1825-1863)

Tobias A. Cude was born in Alabama about 1825. He was the second son of William Arthur Cude, Jr. and Eleanor Long. Tobias enlisted as a private in Co. K, 2nd Texas Cavalry at Fort Brown in Brownsville, Texas on September 23, 1861. He is shown as being on detached service as coast guard on January 1, 1862. A company muster roll for February 28 through June 30, 1863 indicates that he was sick in the hospital in Louisiana. A surgeon's certificate of disability for disease was issued for Tobias Cude on July 6, 1862 stating that he had lost the use of his left foot from paralysis caused by a cut. A company muster roll for the months of July and August 1863 states that T. A. Cude died in the hospital at Columbus, Texas on July 13, 1863. It is known that there was a Confederate cemetery in Columbus, Texas although the exact location of the cemetery has not been found. It is likely that Tobias A. Cude is buried there in an unmarked grave. A diary kept by James Pitman Saunders shows that Saunders visited the cemetery in April 1863 and wrote:

There are about fifty graves here so new that there is no grass growing on them and men at the hospital dying at the rate of 2 or 3 a week. They are buried in a very plain coffin, a shallow grave without a vault in a very loose sandy piece of ground, dressed in their own everyday wearing clothes. No fencing whatever about the graves.

Solomon Marion Cude (1831-1877)

Solomon Marion Cude
photo used by permission of
owner, Earlayne Chance

Solomon Marion Cude was born on or about October 3, 1831. He was the third son of William Arthur Cude, Jr. and Eleanor Long. He enlisted in the Pedernales Cavalry, 31st Brigade, Texas State Troops on August 24, 1861. After his service in the militia, Solomon enlisted as a private in Company C of Colonel George M. Flournoy's 16th Texas Infantry on March 19, 1862. While participating in the Red River campaign, Solomon was captured at Pleasant Hill, Louisiana on April 9, 1864 and was shown on a roll of prisoners of war delivered by U.S. General Banks to Confederate General Taylor on April 20, 1864 at Blair's Landing in Louisiana. There are no records of his parole or exchange. Solomon Marion Cude died at Hopkinsville, Gonzales County, Texas on March 23, 1877 and was buried in Delhi Cemetery, Caldwell County, Texas.

John M. Cude (1833-1895)

John M. Cude was born in Texas on November 19, 1833. He was the fourth son of William Arthur Cude, Jr. and Eleanor Long. John was enrolled as a private in Company C, 16th Regiment, Texas Infantry (Flournoy's) by Captain M. H. Bowers in Blanco, Frio County, Texas, on March 19, 1862. He was shown as sick in Blanco, Texas in September of 1862 and was discharged for disability October 1, 1862. No other records have been found for him. John M. Cude died in Frio County, Texas, March 7, 1895. He is buried in Longview Cemetery, Big Foot, Frio County, Texas.

Nathaniel Wiley Cude (1836-1916)

Nathaniel Wiley Cude was born in Texas on February 16, 1836. He was the youngest son of William Arthur Cude, Jr. and Eleanor Long. Nathan enlisted as a private in Company K, 2nd Regiment, Texas Cavalry (2nd Mounted Rifles) in Columbus, Texas, January 1862. It appears that Nathan spent the better part of a year either in the hospital or sick on leave and is last shown having returned to duty from the hospital in Houston on January 26, 1863. According to Nathaniel Cude's pension application #29030 filed in Frio County, he later re-enlisted under Colonel Rip Ford's Command. A Texas muster roll index card in the Texas State Archives indicates that N. W. Cude enlisted as a sergeant in Captain D. M. Wilson's Company of Colonel Benavides Regiment, Texas Cavalry. Colonel Benavides was in fact under Colonel John S. Ford's command at that time. While no service records for Nathaniel Cude or Captain D. M. Wilson of Austin have been found, it was not uncommon for regimental records to be missing late in the war. Nathaniel Wiley Cude died December 11, 1916 in Devine, Medina County, Texas. He is buried in Longview Cemetery, Big Foot, Frio County, Texas.

Alfred Jackson Cude (1840-1867)

Alfred Jackson Cude was born about 1840 in Montgomery County, Texas. He was the oldest son of William and Lydia Winters Cude. He appears on the rolls of the 1850 Montgomery County census in the household of his mother and step-father. Alfred enlisted as a sergeant in the Mounted Rangers of Colonel John S. Ford's Rio Grand Regiment of Texas State Troops on February 21, 1861 in Oakville, Texas. This regiment later became a part of the 2nd Texas Cavalry. Alfred enlisted as a corporal in Company K, 2nd Regiment, Texas Cavalry (2nd Mounted Rifles) in Brownsville, Texas, September 23, 1861. On January 1, 1862, Cude was shown to be on detached service as coast guard. On a company muster roll for February 15 through June 30, 1863, he is listed as "in hospital" of wounds received June 21, 1863 which would have been during the Battle of Lafourche Crossing in Louisiana. Apparently, James did not recover completely from his wounds and was discharged for disability on December 31, 1863. Alfred Jackson Cude is believed to have died about 1867.

Richard Dowling Cude (1842-1895)

Richard Dowling Cude was born in Montgomery County, Texas on March 26, 1842. He was the second son of William and Lydia Winters Cude. He appears on the rolls of the 1850 Montgomery County census in the household of his mother and step-father. Richard enlisted as a private in Captain Charles De Montel's Ranger Company, Colonel J. M. Norris' Frontier Regiment, Texas State Troops, on February 17, 1862 in Uvalde, Texas. He re-enlisted in Colonel James E. McCord's Frontier Regiment, Texas Cavalry, on December 29, 1862. After his service in the Frontier Regiments, Richard enlisted in Company K, 2nd Regiment, Texas Cavalry (2nd Mounted Rifles) in Moulton, Texas, October 1, 1863. After enlisting as a private, Richard Cude had reached the rank of 1st sergeant by the time that he was paroled with the rest of his regiment on July 25, 1865 in Columbus, Texas. He died in Dripping Springs, Hays County, Texas on June 9, 1895 and is buried in Wrightsboro Cemetery, Wrightsboro, Gonzales County, Texas.

Willis Franklin Cude (1844-1932)

Willis Franklin Cude was born in Montgomery County, Texas, on April 4, 1844. He was the third son of William and Lydia Winters Cude. He appears on the rolls of the 1850 Montgomery County census in the household of his mother and step-father. Willis enlisted as a private in Company K, 2nd Regiment, Texas Cavalry (2nd Mounted Rifles) in Brownsville, Texas, September 23, 1861. A company muster roll of January 1862 shows Willis on detached service as coast guard. He participated in the recapture of Galveston on January 1, 1863. Confederate service records indicate that Willis Cude was taken prisoner at the Battle of Lafourche Crossing in Louisiana on June 21, 1863 and transported to Algiers POW camp in New Orleans on June 22, 1863. He appears on the rolls of Company K in Galveston, January 1864. Willis Cude remained in Galveston until he was paroled with the rest of his regiment on July 25, 1865 in Columbus, Texas. Willis Franklin Cude died November 7, 1932 in Frio County, Texas and is buried in Pearsall Cemetery, Frio County, Texas.

Timothy J. Cude (1846-1929)

Timothy J. Cude was born in Montgomery County, Texas on March 29, 1846. He was the youngest son of William and Lydia Winters Cude. He appears on the rolls of the 1850 Montgomery County census in the household of his mother and step-father. His records are sometimes confused with those of his first cousin, Timothy Jackson Cude, who was the son of Timothy Wright Cude.

There are no records found for Timothy's service in the Confederate Army, but a Confederate pension application #14657, approved on August 31, 1909, shows that he enlisted in February 1864 and served close to one year in Company K, 2nd Texas Cavalry. Affidavits by A. B. Butler and C. Jones of Company K, attest to his service. Timothy J. Cude died in San Antonio, Bexar County, Texas on September (17, 1929 and is buried in Oakville Cemetery, Three Rivers, Live Oak County, Texas.

The Cude-Winters Connection

While all but one of William Cude's sons were either born in or spent time in Montgomery County, most of them moved to other parts of the state after his death in 1847. This explains their service in Confederate regiments that were not common to Montgomery County. Their migration was influenced by the Winters families. William's last wife, Lydia Ellen "Lillie" Winters Cude, was the daughter of James Washington Winters, Sr. James and his family came to Texas in 1835 and settled along a bayou now known as Winters Bayou near present-day New Waverly in Walker County. James, Sr. and three of his sons served in the Republic of Texas Army, and all three sons fought in the Battle of San Jacinto while James drove a wagon to supply the troops. The oldest son, William Carven Winters, was severely wounded during the battle. On February 1, 1838, William Winters was granted land in Montgomery County. On June 28, 1838, he was issued 640 acres of land for having participated in the Battle of San Jacinto. On January 24, 1861, he received additional land for having been wounded at San Jacinto. And for having served in Houston's army from March 12, 1836, to May 3, 1836, he was issued another 320 acres of land. By 1850, William and his family had moved to Guadalupe County. In 1854, William purchased land in Hays County, and by 1856, he, his wife, Levina, and some of his children and their spouses operated a gristmill and sawmill. William's brother, James Washington Winters, Jr., also lived at the Winters' mill for a short time while he helped his brother with the mill and the building of his home. The community that grew up around the mill became known as Winters' Mill. After William's death in 1864, his widow, Levina, and their son, William Elisha Winters, moved to Frio County, Texas. They sold their shares of the mill to John M. Cude and his wife Nancy Naomi Winters Cude who was William and Levina's daughter. The Cudes operated the mill until 1874 when they sold it to Pleasant Wimberley for whom the town of Wimberley was later named. It seemed that wherever the Winters boys went, the Cude boys followed. Sons of William Cude could be found in Gonzales, Hays, Frio, Lavaca, and even Caldwell Counties.

The Timothy Wright Cude Family

Timothy Wright Cude, the youngest son of William Arthur Cude, Sr. and Dorcus Jones Cude, was born in Grainger County, Tennessee, about 1804. He married Serena Johnson in July of 1829 in Jefferson County, Alabama. The marriage between Timothy and Serena is believed to have produced five daughters and seven sons. Timothy received a land grant from the Mexican government on September 15, 1835 for 4,428.40 acres on the east side of the San Jacinto River's west fork in what is now Montgomery County. While it does not appear that Timothy took part in the Battle of San Jacinto during the Texas Revolution, his name does appear on a list of Republic of Texas Army soldiers in a company of Washington County volunteers from the east side of the Brazos River. Timothy Wright Cude died just a few months after the start of the War between the States but had four sons who served in the Confederate Army.

William Johnson Cude (1834-1908)

William Johnson Cude
photo courtesy of Margaret Carraway

William Johnson Cude is said to have been born on September 25, 1834 in what is now Montgomery County, Texas. U.S. census records from 1850 through 1900 state that he was born in Texas sometime between 1835 and 1837. Since his father, Timothy, did not receive his land grant until September 15, 1835, it is likely that William was born sometime after that date. Confederate service records show that William enlisted in Captain Procter Prentice Porter's company of infantry on April 10, 1862. Known as the Porter Guards, this company was inducted into Confederate service as Company H, 4th Texas Infantry. By the time of William's enlistment, Company H was already in Virginia. Private Cude apparently became ill during the exhausting trip to Virginia and is first shown on the rolls as sick in Charlottesville on May 20, 1862. It is unclear when he caught up with the rest of his company, but in July 1862, Captain Porter, along with several other men from Montgomery County, were killed at the Battle of Gaines' Mill. William Cude may or may not have been present for that battle. He is first shown as present with his company on a roll dated November-December 1862. William is shown to be present with his company from that point until March 27, 1864 when he is shown to be furloughed for 40 days. Being present during that period would have placed him at the battles of Fredericksburg, Gettysburg, and Chickamauga. Records indicate that William did not return to his company after his furlough in March 1864. William's wife, Gatsy Ann, filed a widow's pension application which was approved on October 15, 1910. Included in this application was a sworn affidavit by a Company H veteran named W. B. Barry which states that he knew William Johnson Cude, that he was a member of Company H, 4th Texas Infantry, that William was disabled on or about the 15th or 16th of September 1863, and that his leg had been amputated. These dates were less than a week after the Battle of Chickamauga, and it is possible that his wounds were actually received during that engagement. William Johnson Cude died on November 10, 1908 and is buried in Plantersville Cemetery, Grimes County, Texas.

James Hyrum Cude (1839-1907)

James Hyrum Cude was born March 15, 1839 in Montgomery County, Texas. At age 22, James enlisted in Captain Horatio White Fisher's Company G, 7th Texas Cavalry in Walker County, Texas on August 24, 1861. This company was mustered into Confederate service on October 26, 1861 at Camp Pickett near San Antonio, Texas. Confederate service records indicate that James was present for duty with his company through December 30, 1862 which would have included participation in the New Mexico campaign. It is likely that James participated in the re-taking of Galveston Island on January 1, 1863 because records after that date show that he was with his company in Louisiana. He appears on a roll of prisoners of war captured by the U.S. 19th Army Corps near Camp Pratt, Louisiana on November 20, 1863. Written remarks on this roll state that he was captured by a reconnaissance party. James later appears on a register of prisoners of war being held at the customs house in New Orleans. A roll of prisoners of war dated December 21, 1863 states that James Cude was taken from New Orleans to New Iberia, Louisiana for exchange. No further service records are found. Confederate pension application #06958 filed by J. H. Cude in Robertson County, Texas and approved on March 29, 1900 states that James served with the 7th Texas Cavalry from September 1861 to the close of the war. James Hyrum Cude died of tuberculosis in Robertson County, Texas on June 2, 1907 and is buried in Boring Cemetery in that same county.

Timothy Jackson Cude (1843-1877)

Timothy Jackson Cude was born in Montgomery County, Texas on the 30th of June 1843. Timothy enlisted in Captain Samuel D. Wooldridge's company of Texas Lancers at age 18. Records show that Timothy joined for duty on March 29, 1862 in Danville, Texas and was enrolled by J. E. George. This company later became Company B, 24th Texas Cavalry. A company muster roll for April 28 to August 31, 1862 states that Timothy was discharged on July 28, 1862. It is likely that Private Cude was one of the many soldiers who became ill while the company was camped near El Dorado, Arkansas and probably sent home due to illness. Since his father had died just a few days before he left Arkansas, it is likely that he and the rest of the family were staying in the home of his brother, William Johnson Cude, who was off to war in Virginia. This was in an area of South Montgomery County where Franklin G. Dupree was recruiting men for the 26th Texas Cavalry. Timothy enlisted in Company H, 26th Texas Cavalry near Hockley, Texas on September 1, 1863 and is shown as present with this company on a roll for January and February 1864. No other service records have been found. Tim Cude appears on the 1870 Montgomery County census rolls living in the same household with his mother, Serena, brothers, Jackson and Willis, and sister, Minerva Caroline, on Tillis Prairie. They are shown to be living near his oldest brother, William Johnson Cude. Tim Cude married Martha Irene "Mattie" Foshee (Forshee) on August 30, 1871. Together they had a daughter, Elizabeth, and two sons, Henry and Zebedee. Family histories say that Timothy Cude died October 27, 1877 and is buried in an unmarked grave in Cude Cemetery which is now at the edge of Lake Conroe. Mattie Cude appears on the 1880 Montgomery County census rolls, living with her three children in the household of her parents.

George Travis Cude (1845-1933)

George Travis Cude was born in Montgomery County on November 9, 1845. While there are no Confederate service records to confirm George Cude's involvement in the Confederate Army, a Confederate pension application that he filed in Upshur County on December 27, 1907 contains documents that support a claim that he had been a Confederate soldier. Texas Confederate pension application #13562, which was approved on March 21, 1908, claims that George Travis Cude served in Company G, 7th Texas Cavalry from March 4, 1864 until the end of the war. This application contained sworn affidavits from Rush B. Wood and John Knight, former members of the 7th Texas Cavalry Regiment who attested to having served with George Travis Cude in Company G while in Louisiana. This, along with other testimony by his brother, James Hyrum Cude of Company G, was conclusive enough for the State of Texas to approve the application. George Travis Cude spent his final years in Liberty County, Texas. A Liberty County death certificate shows that George died from a hemorrhage of the bowels at age 87. George Travis Cude died January 7, 1933 and was buried in the Cleveland City Cemetery in Liberty County.

The Dupree Family

Family histories state that Lewis and Levene Adeline Daves Dupree migrated to the Republic of Texas from Georgia about 1842. They first settled near present-day Chapel Hill and later in Montgomery County. The Lewis Dupree plantation was southwest of present-day Dobbin on what is now the Montgomery and Grimes Counties' line. According to census records, Lewis and Levene Adeline had two daughters and six sons. Two of the sons, James T. (1840) and Robert P. (1848) appear to have died before adulthood. The remaining four sons served in the Confederate Army along with a nephew of Lewis Dupree, John Lewis Dupree, who was raised on the Lewis Dupree plantation. Lewis and Levene Adeline's youngest daughter, Rebecca Caroline Ann "Carrie" Dupree, married her cousin, John L. Dupree, about 1865. Lewis Dupree died on August 23, 1855 and was buried on the family property.

Franklin Goldstein Dupree (1826-1914)

Frank Goldstein Dupree
photo courtesy of Mary Ann Pratt

Franklin Goldstein Dupree, the son of Lewis and Levene Adeline Daves Dupree, was born April 14, 1826 in Georgia. He migrated to Texas with his family about 1842. He married Canzada Tynes Springer in Montgomery County, Texas on December 15, 1847. Canzada was the daughter of John May and Elizabeth Landrum Springer who were among the earliest settlers in the county. From about 1850 to 1855, Frank Dupree and his father-in-law, John May Springer, operated a sawmill in Leon County. It is likely that Frank returned home to be near his mother after the death of his father in 1855.

Frank Dupree enlisted as a corporal in Company E of Davis's Mounted Battalion on October 15, 1861. This unit was later designated as the 26th Texas Cavalry. He was enrolled by Captain George W. Owens who was the commander of Company E at that time. In December 1861, Frank was commissioned to raise a new company of mounted riflemen, and on January 3, 1862, he was appointed captain of the newly-organized unit designated as Company H. Frank's brother-in-law, Zachariah Landrum Springer, served as 2nd lieutenant, and Frank's first cousin, John Lewis Dupree, served as junior 2nd lieutenant.

The 26th Texas Cavalry participated in the Battle of Galveston on January 11, 1863. A family legend contends that after the Battle of Galveston, Captain Frank Dupree took the boiler from the *USS Harriet Lane* and shipped it by ox-drawn wagon to his mill in Montgomery County. Since it is known that the ship was put into Confederate service as a blockade runner following its capture, the story seems very unlikely. It is possible that such a boiler may have been taken from the *USS Westfield* which ran aground during the battle. Some accounts indicate that Captain Dupree and his men salvaged what they could from the wreckage.

During the remainder of 1863 and the winter of 1864, the 26th Texas Cavalry served in defense of the upper Texas coast. In the spring of 1864, the regiment marched to Louisiana and participated in the Red River campaign where it remained for several months. After returning to Texas, the regiment remained intact until receiving news of the Confederate surrender when the men were discharged and returned to their homes.

After the war, Frank Dupree returned to the sawmill business in Montgomery County. His mill was located near the Joshua Griffith property which was south of present-day Dobbin and was east of the Lewis Dupree plantation. Frank's first wife, Canzada Tynes Springer, died in 1882 and is said to be buried in the Dupree Cemetery on the old Lewis Dupree plantation. On November 3, 1885, Frank married Samantha Heflin. Franklin Goldstein Dupree died April 22, 1914 and was buried in Magnolia Cemetery.

Joel Reed Dupree (1827-1912)

Joel Reed Dupree, the son of Lewis and Levene Adeline Daves Dupree, was born November 27, 1827 in Georgia. His name also appears as "Joseph" on some records. He married Roana Collier in Montgomery County on April 11, 1848. J. R. appears in the 1860 census with a female born about 1836 in Tennessee who is likely a second wife, said to be Amanda Perkins or Perkinson. Montgomery County marriage records show that he was married to Susan J. Ellis on June 12, 1870.

J. R. Dupree enlisted as a private in Company G, 20th Texas Infantry on April 26, 1862. His last muster roll in that regiment is dated April 30, 1863 and states that he had transferred to Debray's Regiment of Texas Cavalry. No records for J. R. Dupree are found in Debray's Regiment, however. J. R. Dupree died August 5, 1912 and was buried in Glenwood Cemetery in Houston, Texas.

Jesse Gee Dupree (1834-1922)

Jesse Gee Dupree, the son of Lewis and Levene Adeline Daves Dupree, was born December 10, 1834 in Georgia. He was married to Lydia Ann Springer on November 25, 1858. Lydia was the sister of Canzada Tine Springer who was the wife of Franklin Goldstein Dupree.

Jesse enlisted as a sergeant in Company H, 26th Texas Cavalry in May 1862. He was enrolled by his brother Captain Franklin G. Dupree. There are no Confederate services records shown for Jesse after 1862, and although he did not die until 1922, he did not file a Confederate pension application. Texas death records show that J. G. Dupree died in Harris County on April 11, 1922.

John Lewis Dupree (1841-1925)

John Lewis Dupree was born about 1841 in Georgia. He was a nephew of Lewis and Levene Adeline Daves Dupree and was raised by his aunt and uncle on the Lewis Dupree plantation. Family histories relate that Lewis Dupree went back to Georgia after the sudden death of John's parents and brought John back to the Dupree plantation.

In August of 1861, John Lewis Dupree and his first cousin were recruited for the 5th Texas Cavalry by Captain Denman W. Shannon from Grimes County. On their way to join their regiment in San Antonio they were accompanied by another cousin, Charles Robert Scott, who was not yet eighteen years of age. Once they arrived at camp near San Antonio, Charles enlisted in Company A, 7th Texas Cavalry. All three of these young men were enrolled in the Confederate Army by Lieutenant Joseph Sayers. Joseph D. Sayers was recommended for promotion for capturing five Union cannons at the Battle of Val Verde in New Mexico. In 1899, Joseph D. Sayers became the 22nd governor of Texas.

John Lewis Dupree was discharged by a surgeon's certificate of disability because of chronic diarrhea before his regiment departed for New Mexico. He returned to Montgomery County and re-enlisted in the 26th Texas Cavalry. He was appointed junior second lieutenant in Company H, commanded by his first cousin, Captain Franklin G. Dupree. He was promoted to second lieutenant after the death of Lieutenant Zachariah Springer. He was detached for duty as a scout under Colonel Luckett in February 1864 and last appeared on the rolls of Company H in March 1865.

Soon after the war, John Lewis Dupree married his first cousin, Caroline "Carrie" Dupree. Carrie died in 1896. John Lewis Dupree died January 3, 1925 and was buried in Washington Cemetery in Houston, Texas.

Samuel Francis Dupree (1841-1862)

Samuel Francis Dupree, the son of Lewis and Levene Adeline Daves Dupree, was born about 1841. At the age of 20, Samuel enlisted as a private in Company C, 5th Texas Cavalry in August of 1861. Sam participated in the New Mexico campaign of 1862. He was wounded at the Battle of Glorieta Pass and died some time later in the hospital. It is possible that he died in Santa Fe and was one of a handful of Confederate soldiers buried in unmarked graves in what is now the Santa Fe National Cemetery.

The Estill Family

Milton B. Estill was born about 1807 in Kentucky. He married Louise Boulton about 1833. The Reverend Milton Estill established the first Presbyterian Church in Texas, the Shiloh Cumberland Presbyterian Church, in Red River County in 1833. He moved his family to Texas between and 1838 and 1841. Reverend Estill was elected justice of the peace for beat five in Montgomery County in 1841. He was elected as the first chief justice of Walker County when that county was established in 1846. The family moved to Danville prior to 1860. He performed marriages in the county and was a member of the San Jacinto Masonic Lodge in Danville. Milton and Louise Estill appear on the rolls of the 1860 Montgomery County census with their five sons. The story of the Estill family's contribution to the cause of the Confederacy is a tragic one. Four brothers went off to war and never returned.

Sons of Milton B. Estill
Charles B. Estill (1836-1863)

Charles B. Estill was born about 1836 in Tennessee. He was the oldest son of Milton and Louise Boulton Estill. He married Nancy Jane Fowler McCracken in Montgomery County on September 19, 1860. Charles served as a private in Company B, 24th Texas Cavalry (Dismounted). He was captured at the Battle of Arkansas Post on January 11, 1863 and transported to prison at Camp Butler in Sangamon County, Illinois. He died at the Camp Butler hospital on April 13, 1863 and was buried in what is now the Confederate section, number 320, in Camp Butler National Cemetery.

Benjamin P. Estill (1839-1862)

Benjamin P. Estill was born about 1839 in Tennessee. He was the second son of Milton and Louise Boulton Estill. Benjamin served as a private in Company D, 5th Texas Infantry. He was mortally wounded at the Second Battle of Manassas on August 30, 1862 and died in the hospital at Warrenton, Virginia on October 5, 1862. The cause of death was listed as a "gunshot wound to the breast." He was buried in Warrenton Confederate Cemetery, Fauquier County, Virginia.

James Black Estill (1841-1862)

James Black Estill was born about 1841 in Texas. He was the third son of Milton and Louise Boulton Estill. Benjamin served as a private in Company D, 5th Texas Infantry. He was admitted to the Chimborazo Hospital, number three, in Richmond, Virginia on May 9, 1862, suffering from typhoid fever. He died May 21, 1862 and was buried in Oakwood Confederate Cemetery, Richmond, Virginia.

Milton Estill (1844-1863)

Milton B. Estill was born about 1844 in Texas. He was the fourth son of Milton and Louise Boulton Estill. Milton served as a private in Company B, 24th Texas Cavalry (Dismounted). He was killed in action at the Battle of Arkansas Post on January 11, 1863. His exact place of burial is unknown.

The Griffith Family

Noah Griffith and his wife, Esther Randall Wightman Griffith, arrived in Texas in the early part of 1829 along with Esther's brother, Elias R. Wightman, who was a surveyor in Stephen F. Austin's first colony. They arrived at the port of Matagorda which had been platted earlier by Elias Wightman. Noah Griffith received a league of land in Stephen F. Austin's second colony which was about four miles south of present-day Dobbin in Montgomery County, Texas. Noah and his wife Esther moved to the property with their three sons about 1831. The two oldest sons of Noah and Esther, Leroy A. and Joshua D. Griffith, served in the Confederate Army. Their youngest son, John Maynard Griffith, married Angelina Elizabeth Dickinson who was better known as "the babe of the Alamo." Angelina was the daughter of Almeron and Susannah Wilkerson Dickinson. She was just two years old when she and her mother survived the Siege of the Alamo where her father was killed in 1836. John and Angelina married in 1851 and lived at the Griffith homestead in Montgomery County where they had three children. According to family histories, Angelina missed the glamour of the city culture in which she had been raised. Shortly after the birth of her third child, Angelina abandoned her family and never returned. It is said the John Maynard Griffith went off to find Angelina, and little is known about him after his departure. Some believed that he died about 1868 and was buried in the family cemetery. His three young children were raised by his brother, Alonzo.

Sons of Noah Griffith
Leroy Alonzo Griffith (1821-1883)

Leroy Alonzo Griffith was born December 17, 1821 In Dutchess County, New York. He was the son of Noah and Esther Wightman Griffith. He arrived in Montgomery County with his parents and two brothers in 1831. He married Nancy Rebecca Hogan in 1847.

Leroy enlisted as a private in Captain Robert S. Poole's Company A of the 2nd Texas Lancers in Montgomery County on March 10, 1862. After training at Camp Carter near Hempstead, he traveled with his company to Arkansas where the entire regiment was dismounted and designated as the 24th Texas Cavalry (Dismounted). After the regiment was dismounted, Leroy was among the men detailed to return the horses to Montgomery County. It is unclear why Leroy was not with the 24th Texas Cavalry when it was captured at the Battle of Arkansas Post on January 11, 1863. It is possible that he did not make it back from Montgomery County before his regiment was captured. He is shown as a 4th sergeant on a roll of Company D, 17th Texas Consolidated Cavalry for the months of January and February 1864. This regiment was made up of men from the five Texas cavalry regiments that were not captured at Arkansas Post. Confederate service records for Leroy A. Griffith end with that muster roll.

After the war, Leroy returned to the Griffith property in Montgomery County. He moved his wife and children, along with his youngest brother's children, to Bell County prior to 1870. Leroy Alonzo Griffith died on February 29, 1883 and was buried in Salado Cemetery, Bell County, Texas.

Joshua Delos Griffith (1825-1887)

Joshua Delos Griffith was born about 1825 In Dutchess County, New York. He was the son of Noah and Esther Wightman Griffith. He arrived in Montgomery County with his parents and two brothers in 1831. He married Amelia Ellen Conley in Montgomery County on March 20, 1852.

Unlike his brother Alonzo, Joshua Griffith did not join the 24th Texas Cavalry. After Captain Robert Poole returned to Texas, however, Joshua joined Poole's 24th/25th Consolidated Texas Cavalry. The exact date of Joshua's enlistment is uncertain. His name appears on a company return for the month of April 1865 stating that he had been left sick in Austin County on April 29, 1865. The 1860 Montgomery County census lists Joshua's occupation as a "miller" which, according to conscription laws, possibly could have exempted him from military service. He apparently chose to join the Confederate Army anyway. It is likely that he chose to enlist in the 24th/25th Consolidated Texas Cavalry in order to remain close to the Griffith farm since he was the only adult male to watch over his and his two brothers' families. Joshua Delos Griffith died June 14, 1887 and was buried in the family cemetery on the Griffith property.

The Irvine Family

Benjamin Fielding Irvine was born about 1797 in Kentucky. He married Mary "Polly" Belles (originally Bellesfelt/Bellesfeldt) on March 1, 1817 in Mercer County, Kentucky. The Irvine family arrived in Montgomery County between the years of 1837 and 1839. They settled in the northern part of the county, northwest of present-day Willis. Benjamin had three sons who served in the Confederate Army. Sadly, two of these sons did not return home from the war.

Benjamin Franklin Irvine (ca 1821-1902)

The first son, Benjamin Franklin Irvine, was born about 1821. He was married to Catherine L. Tabor who was the daughter of Reverend Isaac Tabor. Benjamin served as a private in the Danville Mounted Riflemen, 17th Brigade, Texas State Troops and survived the war. He died on January 6, 1902 and was buried in Eureka Cemetery, Navarro County, Texas.

Peter Belles Irvine (ca 1823-1863)

The second son, Peter Belles Irvine, was born about 1823 in Kentucky. Peter married Minerva Angelia Tabor in Montgomery County on November 23, 1847. Minerva also was a daughter of Reverend Isaac Tabor. Peter served in the Danville Mounted Riflemen, 17th Brigade, Texas State Troops and later enlisted in Company B of the 24th Texas Cavalry (Dismounted). Peter was killed in action at the Battle of Arkansas Post on January 11, 1863. It is likely that Peter was buried in an unmarked grave on the battlefield. Family histories relate that Peter's wife, Minerva, sent a servant with a wagon to bring Peter's body back to Montgomery County, but he was unable to locate Peter's remains.

Henry Reid Irvine (ca 1841-1863)

The youngest son, Henry Reid Irvine, was born in Montgomery County, Texas about 1841. He served in Captain Robert M. Powell's Company D, of the 5th Texas Infantry, also known as the Waverly Confederates. Muster rolls show that Private H. R. Irvine was sent to the hospital on June 23, 1862. It is unclear if Henry was sick or wounded, but he died on July 1, 1863 and was buried in Hollywood Cemetery, Richmond, Virginia.

The Lewis Family

John McClanahan Lewis, Sr. was born in Virginia about 1802. He married Susan Madison Bowyer in Fincastle, Virginia in 1831. Shortly after their marriage, the couple moved to Franklin County, Alabama where they had three sons and one daughter. The family moved to Texas about 1842. Lewis represented Montgomery County in the Republic of Texas House of Representatives in the eighth and ninth congresses. He was the Speaker of the House during the ninth congress. John was well known for his beautiful plantation home which he named Elmwood. His daughter, Lanthe Alabama Lewis, married Miller A. Woodson who served as a private in Company D, 24th Texas Cavalry. All three of John's sons served in the Confederate Army, but only one returned home from the war. The story of the Lewis family is one of many tragic tales of lives that were destroyed by the War between the States.

Sons of John McClanahan Lewis, Sr. (1802-1862)
William Eldon Lewis (1833-1864)

William Eldon Lewis, the oldest son of John McClanahan and Susan Bowyer Lewis, was born in Virginia about 1833. He married Frances A. "Fannie" Arnold on December 24, 1857.

Eldon Lewis enlisted as a private in Captain Samuel Wooldridge's Company of the 2nd Texas Lancers at Danville, Texas on March 29, 1862. This unit was later designated as Company B, 24th Texas Cavalry (Dismounted). Eldon was captured at the Battle of Arkansas Post on January 11, 1863 and was transported to prison at Camp Butler, Illinois. He was paroled in the spring of 1863 and exchanged at City Point, Virginia. Eldon is shown to be present with his company from April 30, 1863 through the months of January and February of 1864. His service during this period would have placed him at the Battle of Chickamauga, the Chattanooga campaign, and the Battle of Ringgold Gap. According to a letter written by his brother, John M. Lewis, Eldon was slightly wounded at Ringgold Gap. A list of casualties published in the *Galveston Tri-Weekly News* on Wednesday, November 9, 1864 states that Private Eldon Lewis was wounded during the Atlanta campaign. The last record in Eldon's file is a receipt for clothing issued to Private "Edwin" Lewis, Company B, 24th Texas Cavalry at Hill Hospital, Cuthbert, Georgia, in December 1864. According to family histories, Benjamin F. (Doc) Cheshire was contracted to go to Georgia and return Eldon's body to Montgomery County in 1865. It is not known if the body was ever returned, but it is known that there were graves under the cedar trees at the front of the Lewis plantation which is now under the Lake Lewis power station reservoir near Willis, Texas.

Clinton A. Lewis (1836-1862)

Clinton A. Lewis, the second son of John McClanahan and Susan Bowyer Lewis, was born in Alabama about 1836. He traveled to Texas with his parents and three siblings about 1842.

Clint Lewis enlisted as a private in Company H, 4th Texas Infantry on May 7, 1861. He received a gunshot wound to the shoulder at the Battle of Gaines' Mill on June 27, 1862. A muster roll for the months of July and August 1862 states that he was absent and still in the hospital. A report from the Chimborazo Confederate Hospital No. 2 in Richmond, Virginia states that Clint Lewis was admitted June 29, 1862, transferred to exchange hotel July 23, 1862, and died at Fincastle, Virginia on July 28, 1862. The report of his death appears to have been given by Clint's uncle, H. W. Bowyer, who was clerk of the Botetourt County Court at the time. Since Fincastle was his mother's hometown, it is likely that Clint was staying with his mother's family at the time of his death and may have been buried in a family plot in that county.

John McClanahan Lewis, Jr. (1837-1908)

John McClanahan Lewis, Jr., the youngest son of John McClanahan and Susan Bowyer Lewis, was born November 29, 1837 in Alabama. He traveled to Texas with his parents and three siblings about 1842.

John M. Lewis enlisted in Company I, 9th Texas Infantry (Nichols') on October 10, 1861 for a period of six months. After being mustered out of the 9th Infantry at Galveston, John enlisted as a private in Captain Samuel Wooldridge's Company B of the 2nd Texas Lancers and was enrolled by Colonel F. C. Wilkes at Shreveport, Louisiana on June 20, 1862 in the regiment which was designated as the 24th Texas Cavalry (Dismounted). He was promoted to second lieutenant on December 1, 1862. He was captured at the Battle of Arkansas Post on January 11, 1863. Since John was an officer, he was transported up the Mississippi River and then transferred by rail to the prison at Camp Chase in Ohio. John was later transferred to Fort Delaware where he was paroled on April 25, 1863 and sent to City Point, Virginia where he was exchanged. After the men of the 24th Cavalry had been exchanged, Captain Wooldridge was in a weakened condition from his stay in prison and was discharged. First Lieutenant Jabez S. Thomason was placed in command of Company B but was soon transferred to the Trans-Mississippi Department by order of General Bragg. John Lewis then took command of the company with the rank of third lieutenant. John remained in command of Company B until he was captured near Atlanta on July 21, 1864. He was once again transported to prison and eventually returned to Camp Chase in Ohio where he remained until the end of the war.

After the war, John returned to Montgomery County where he married Martha "Mattie" Cook Woodson on November 15, 1865. John McClanahan Lewis, Jr. died April 8, 1908 and was buried in the Willis City Cemetery, Montgomery County, Texas.

The Lindley Family

Samuel Washington Lindley was born about 1788 in South Carolina. Samuel and his second wife, Elizabeth Whitley, migrated to Texas from Illinois about 1833. The couple had six sons, three who served in the Confederate Army. The oldest son, Jonathan, died at the Battle of the Alamo in March 1836. While there are no records indicating that the second son, William Nathan Lindley, served in the Confederate Army, William's oldest son, John Wood Lindley, served in Company G, 7th Texas Cavalry. A third son, Samuel Washington Lindley, Jr. died in 1848.

John Lindley (1829-1911)

John Lindley, the fourth son of Samuel and Elizabeth Lindley, was born June 8, 1829 in Sangamon County, Illinois. John married Eliza Ann Martin in Walker County, Texas on September 4, 1851. John served in the Danville Mounted Riflemen, 17th Brigade, Texas State Troops and later enlisted in Company B, 24th Texas Cavalry (Dismounted) and survived the war. He died on February 20, 1911 and was buried in the Madisonville City Cemetery, Madison County, Texas.

James Lindley (1831-1895)

James Lindley, the fifth son of Samuel and Elizabeth Lindley, was born March 13, 1831 in Bond County, Illinois. He married Mary Lee R. Irvine in Montgomery County on November 22, 1853. James served in the Danville Mounted Riflemen, 17th Brigade, Texas State Troops and later enlisted in Company B, 24th Texas Cavalry (Dismounted) and survived the war. He died on October 18, 1895 and was buried in the Shepard Hill Cemetery at Danville, Texas.

Elijah Lindley (1835-1880)

Elijah Lindley, the sixth son of Samuel and Elizabeth Lindley, was born in Texas on March 20, 1835. He married Eliza Tolbert Kelton in Walker County, Texas on August 20, 1855. Elijah served in the Danville Mounted Riflemen, 17th Brigade, Texas State Troops and later enlisted in Company B, 24th Texas Cavalry (Dismounted) and survived the war. After the death of his wife, Eliza, about 1870, he moved to Madison County. Shortly afterward, he married Margaret E. McGill. Elijah died July 28, 1880 and was buried in Ferguson Cemetery, Limestone County, Texas.

The Little Family

An integral part of the history of Montgomery County is the history of the old town of Danville which was home to the Hiram Little family. Hiram Little was born in Bond County, Illinois. Family histories give his date of birth as April 9, 1809. Hiram married Mary "Polly" Lindley in Illinois on July 11, 1831. According to his sworn testimony before the Montgomery County Land Commission, Hiram claimed to have arrived in Texas on January 20, 1835. It is believed that he first settled in the Sabine District. Prior to 1836, he moved to an area of Washington County which is now Montgomery County. Hiram purchased land near the Danville townsite in 1848. When the city of Danville was platted in 1848, the inner wall of Hiram Little's water well was used as the beginning point for the survey.

Hiram served in both the Republic of Texas Army and the Confederate Army. In April 1861, Hiram enlisted as a private in Captain Sam Wooldridge's cavalry company known as the Danville Mounted Riflemen, 17th Brigade, Texas State Troops. Being well over age, Hiram did not continue with the unit when Captain Wooldridge's company became Company B of the 2nd Texas Lancers.

Hiram's three oldest sons served in the Confederate Army. Three of Hiram's daughters were married to Confederate soldiers. Aphadelia "Delilah" Little married William M. Tolbert who was a private in the 23rd Brigade of Texas State Troops. Catherine Little married Thomas J. Prindle who was a junior second lieutenant in Madison's Regiment, Texas Cavalry. Mary Emily Little married Oscar F. Holmes who was a private in Madison's Regiment, Texas Cavalry.

Sons of Hiram Little
Jonathan Little (1836 – 1865)

Jonathan Little was born in Montgomery County, Texas on May 26, 1836. He was the oldest son of Hiram and Mary "Polly" Lindley Little. He married Mary Elizabeth Smith In Montgomery County on April 22, 1858. Jonathan joined Captain Samuel Woodridge's Company of 2nd Texas Lancers on March 29, 1862. After training at Camp Carter near Hempstead, Jonathan traveled with the company to Arkansas where it was designated as Company B, 24th Texas Cavalry (Dismounted). Jonathan is shown as absent on detail on a muster roll dated August 31, 1862. It is likely that he was one of the men who was detailed to return the horses home to Montgomery County after the regiment was dismounted. A muster roll for September and October 1862 shows that Jonathan was sick and on furlough. It is unclear if Jonathan was furloughed while in Arkansas or if he became sick before returning from detail and was furloughed in Texas. Family histories state that Jonathan died near Fort Smith, Arkansas, but no records have been found to confirm that story.

William M. Little (1840 – 1913)

William M. "Doc" Little was born in Texas on November 18, 1840. He was the second son of Hiram and Mary "Polly" Lindley Little. He appears on the rolls of the 1860 Montgomery County census in the home of his parents along with three siblings.

William enlisted as a private in Company G, 7th Texas Cavalry on October 26, 1861. This company was commanded by Captain H. W. Fisher from Walker County. During the New Mexico campaign, Company G was held in reserve near Mesilla, New Mexico and did not make the journey to Santa Fe and Glorietta Pass. A muster roll for the period of October 26, 1861 to February 28, 1862 shows William to be on detailed service to General Sibley. A roll for the period ending April 30, 1862 tells that William's horse broke down and was abandoned but that he had been re-mounted. The 7th Texas Cavalry returned to Texas in time to participate in the Battle of Galveston on January 1, 1863. During the rest of 1863 and all of 1864, the 7th Texas Cavalry was involved in numerous conflicts in Louisiana including the Red River campaign. In a Confederate pension application filed by William in July of 1909, he states that he enlisted in the spring of 1862 and served until he was discharged in May 1865.

Prior to the end of the war, William married Sarah Catherine Paulsel in Walker County on April 12, 1865. William died in February of 1913 and was buried in the Willis City Cemetery, Montgomery County, Texas.

Samuel Little (1842-1874)

Samuel Little was born in Texas on November 4, 1842. He was the third son of Hiram and Mary "Polly" Lindley Little. He was their last child to be born in the Republic of Texas.

Samuel enlisted as a third corporal in Captain Robert S. Poole's Company of the 2nd Texas Lancers on January 1, 1862. After training at Camp Carter near Hempstead, Samuel traveled with his company to Arkansas where it was designated as Company A, 24th Texas Cavalry (Dismounted). He was captured at the Battle of Arkansas Post on January 11, 1863 and transferred to prison at Camp Butler, in Illinois. Samuel was paroled in the spring of 1863 and sent to City Point, Virginia for exchange. Samuel last appears on the rolls of the 24th Texas Cavalry in April of 1864. It is likely that Samuel was discharged during or at the end of the Atlanta campaign in the summer of 1864 but there are no records to indicate exactly when or why he was discharged.

Samuel married Mary Mahalia Ellisor in Montgomery County, Texas on December 15, 1864. The couple had four children, the last one being born in April 1874. It is believed Samuel died around the time of his last child's birth. His place of burial is unknown.

The Morris Family
Alfred William Morris, Sr. (1821–1866)

Alfred William Morris, Sr.
photo courtesy of Jan Stovall

Alfred William Morris was born on June 11, 1821 in Mississippi. Although very little is known about him before his arrival in Texas, it is believed that he was the son of John and Sarah Hooker Morris. According to family histories, Alfred migrated to the Republic of Texas about 1840. In the spring of 1842, Alfred enlisted in the Republic of Texas Army, responding to an invasion by Mexican General Rafael Vasquez. On February 22, 1845, Alfred married Matilda Parmer in Jasper County, Texas. Matilda was the daughter of Martin Parmer who was a prominent legislator, judge, and signer of the Texas Declaration of Independence. During the Mexican-American war, Alfred enlisted as a private in Captain James Chesser's Company G of the 1st Texas Foot Riflemen in Jasper County, Texas. He was mustered out of service near Camargo, Mexico on August 24, 1846.

Alfred and Matilda, along with their young son, Alfred W. Morris, Jr., moved to Walker County, Texas about 1847. Alfred joined in the 1849 California gold rush. During his absence, Matilda and her two small children lived with her brother, Anthony C. (Parmer) Palmer, in Walker County. It is unknown if Alfred ever found gold. After Alfred returned to Texas, he moved his family to Montgomery County where he was elected sheriff in 1856.

Alfred and his fifteen-year-old son enlisted in Company K, 8th Texas Cavalry on September 7, 1861. Alfred was elected first lieutenant. During the regiment's first major engagement at Woodsonville, Kentucky on December 17, 1861, Colonel Benjamin F. Terry was killed, and Alfred was seriously wounded. An account by Chaplain Robert F. Bunting states that Lieutenant Morris was shot through the arm and lungs. Private Alfred W. Morris, Jr. was detailed to escort his father back to Montgomery County. Back in Montgomery County, Lieutenant Morris served for a brief period as a recruiting agent but was forced to resign in August 1862 because of his health. Alfred W. Morris, Sr., a veteran of the Republic of Texas Army, Mexican-American War and the War between the States died in Montgomery County, Texas on September 29, 1866 at the age of forty-five.

Alfred William Morris, Jr. (1846-1925)

Alfred William Morris, Jr. was born in Texas on January 10, 1846. He was the son of Alfred William and Matilda Parmer Morris. He moved with his parents to Montgomery County, Texas in the 1850s.

Alfred enlisted as a private in Company K of the 8th Texas Cavalry on September 7, 1861. His father served as a first lieutenant in the company. Although Alfred was only fifteen years of age, he is shown on the rolls as age eighteen. A muster roll for the period of November 7, 1861 through January 7, 1862 indicates that Private A. W. Morris was sick in the hospital at Nashville, Tennessee. After his father was wounded at the Battle of Woodsonville in Kentucky on December 17, 1861, he was detailed to escort his father back to Montgomery County. At some point, Private Morris was dropped from the rolls of the 8th Texas Cavalry. He appears on a muster roll for March of 1865 in Captain Robert S. Poole's Company A, 24th/25th Consolidated Texas Cavalry.

After the war, Alfred married Mary Permilia Bobbitt on January 28, 1867. He was elected sheriff of Montgomery County in 1871. He later served three terms in the Texas House of Representatives and one term in the Texas State Senate. After Mary's death in 1890, Alfred was married three more times. He died on June 25, 1925 and was buried in the Palestine City Cemetery, Anderson County, Texas.

The Peel Family

Thomas R. Peel (1807-1888)

Thomas R. Peel was born about 1807 in Kentucky. He was the son of Richard and Elizabeth Wilson Peel. In 1831, he married Ann E. Wood in Arkansas. Richard and Ann moved to Montgomery County, Texas prior to 1850. They appear on the rolls of the 1860 Montgomery County census with two sons, John R. and Thomas J. Peel.

Thomas Peel appears on one muster roll of Company K, 16th Texas Infantry for the month of June 1862. He is shown to be absent with leave. His oldest son, John R. Peel, was captain in command of Company K at the time, and his youngest son, Thomas J. Peel, was a second lieutenant. It is likely that Thomas had the desire to go off to war with his two sons but at age fifty-five was simply too old to serve in an infantry regiment. There are no further Confederate service records found for Thomas R. Peel.

John R. Peel (1832-unknown)

John R. Peel was born about 1832 in Arkansas. He was the oldest son of Thomas R. and Ann Wood Peel. He married Sarah E. Creath prior to 1860 and moved to Madison County, Texas.

On October 25, 1861, John R. Peel enlisted as a sergeant in Captain James Gillaspie's Company E of the 9th Texas Infantry (Nichols'). This regiment was formed for a period of six months in order to defend Galveston Island from invasion. His brother, Thomas Jefferson Peel, served in Company I of the regiment. After mustering out of the 9th Texas Infantry, John enlisted in Company K of the 16th Texas Infantry while still in Galveston and was elected captain. John resigned from the 16th Texas Infantry on January 29, 1863. In the summer of 1864, John enlisted in Company G of Bradford's Regiment (later Mann's Regiment) of Texas Cavalry and was elected captain on June 16, 1864. John remained as captain of Company G until the end of the war.

After the war, John and his family appear on the rolls of the 1870 and 1880 Montgomery County censuses. The 1880 census shows John with his wife, Sarah, and five children. His occupation is shown as lawyer. No further records have been found for John or for his wife, Sarah.

Thomas Jefferson Peel (1837-1901)

Thomas Jefferson Peel was born in Texas on February 2, 1837. He was the youngest son of Thomas R. and Ann Wood Peel. He appears on the rolls of the 1860 Montgomery County census with his parents and brother, John R. Peel.
Thomas J. Peel enlisted as a sergeant in Captain Robert F. Oliver's Company I of the 9th Texas Infantry (Nichols') on October 10, 1861. This regiment was formed for a period of six months in order to defend Galveston Island from invasion. His brother, John R. Peel, served in Company E of the regiment. Thomas was promoted to second lieutenant after the resignation of Lieutenant J. G. Cobb. After mustering out of the 9th Texas Infantry, Thomas enlisted in Company K of the 16th Texas Infantry while still in Galveston on April 25, 1862 and was elected junior second lieutenant. Although the date is not shown, Thomas was eventually promoted to captain and commanded Company K until the end of the war.

Prior to the end of the war, Thomas married Anamelia "Annie" Arnold in Montgomery County on February 2, 1864. Thomas died on October 31, 1901 and was buried in the Old Methodist Church Cemetery in Montgomery, Texas.

Procter Prentice Porter (1826-1862)

Procter Prentice Porter was born about 1826 in Tennessee. There is little known about him before his arrival in Montgomery County. He served as a second lieutenant in Company G of the 5th Tennessee Infantry during the Mexican-American War. He is shown to have been mustered in at Knoxville, Tennessee on November 17, 1847 and mustered out of service at Memphis, Tennessee on July 20, 1848. He does not appear on the federal census rolls for the year 1850. He appears on the rolls of the 1860 Montgomery County census in the household of Ann Arnold who was the widow of Dr. E. J. Arnold. His occupation is shown as lawyer.

Procter Porter was among the earliest men in Montgomery County to recruit and organize a company of men to support the Confederate war effort and was chosen by his men to serve as captain. It is known that Procter Porter was well liked by most of the men who served under him. His newly-formed company left Montgomery County in August of 1861 bound for Virginia where Porter's company was designated as Company H, 4th Texas Infantry. Leading his company at the bloody Battle of Gaines' Mill on June 27, 1862, Procter Porter was mortally wounded. Captain Porter, along with Captain John Hutcheson from Grimes County, were transported from the battlefield to the Richmond home of Corbin Warwick where Captain Hutcheson died. Captain Porter was transferred to a hospital in Richmond where he died on July 20, 1862 and was buried at Hollywood Cemetery in Richmond.

Robert Micajah Powell (1826-1916)

Robert Micajah Powell
photo courtesy of Robert Reichardt

Robert Micajah Powell was born September 23, 1826 in Alabama. He was the oldest son of George Francis and Nancy Williamson Powell. Robert arrived in Texas in 1849 and began a law practice with his uncle, Robert M. Williamson. On November 27, 1851, Robert married Elizabeth Green Wood at her father's home in Montgomery County, Texas. Elizabeth was the daughter of wealthy planter Green Wood and Evelina Alexander Barnes Wood. After his marriage to Elizabeth, Robert moved his law practice to Montgomery County. Robert and Elizabeth had one child, William Wood Powell who was born on December 17, 1852. Elizabeth Powell died on June 14, 1856.

Robert M. Powell was a dedicated secessionist and worked diligently to persuade the residents of Montgomery County to support disunion. Soon after the governor of Texas called for the enlistment of troops for the Confederate Army, Robert Powell began recruiting and organizing his own company and was elected captain. Captain Powell's company was known as the Waverly Confederates. Upon arrival in Virginia, Captain Powell's company was designated as Company D of the 5th Texas Infantry.

Powell quickly rose in the ranks of the 5th Texas Infantry. He was promoted to major on August 22, 1862 and to colonel in command of the 5th Texas Infantry Regiment on November 1, 1862. While leading the 5th Texas Infantry at the Battle of Gettysburg on July 2, 1863, Colonel Powell was wounded and taken prisoner. After leaving the field hospital at Gettysburg, Colonel Powell was confined for a short period of time in the hospital of the military prison at Ft. McHenry and then transferred to Johnson's Island Prison in Ohio. During the five-week stay in the hospital at Fort McHenry, Robert fell in love with Elizabeth R. Grace. Powell was later transferred to Fort Monroe in Virginia where he was released and exchanged. After his exchange, he returned to the 5th Texas Infantry. In March of 1865, Colonel Powell became the last commander of Hood's Texas Brigade.

After the surrender at Appomattox, Powell traveled to Baltimore to be reunited with and marry Elizabeth Grace. The couple soon journeyed back to Montgomery County, Texas. Post-war life in Texas was not kind to Powell and his new wife. In late 1867, the couple moved back to Baltimore, along with their young son, Wood Powell. In 1882, Robert Powell moved his family to St. Louis, Missouri where he lived until his death on January 15, 1916. He was buried in Calvary Cemetery in St. Louis.

The Sandel (Sandell) Family

Sandel family histories indicate that George Henry Sandel was born in South Carolina about 1755. He is believed to have married Mary Catherine Nobels about 1790. Family histories also state that George and Mary Catherine had six sons and one daughter and moved their family to Pike County, Mississippi prior to 1820. The surname sometimes appears as Sandell. Census records show that two of these sons, Henry Sandel and Peter Warren Sandel, moved their families to Texas between 1850 and 1860. Another son, Darius Sandel, settled in Louisiana and did not migrate to Texas, but Darius' son, James Monroe Sandel, arrived in Texas sometime prior to 1860 and served in Company I, 9th Texas Infantry (Nichols') and also in Company K, 20th Texas Infantry. James died December 3, 1881 and was buried in the Willis City Cemetery, Montgomery County, Texas.

Henry Sandel (1796-1866)

Henry Sandel is believed to have been born in South Carolina on November 23, 1796. Little is known about Henry's fist wife. Family history mentions her as "Emily M." who was born in Georgia about 1801. Henry and Emily are believed to have been married about 1821 in Mississippi. Census records indicate that there were at least two daughters and seven sons born from this marriage. It is possible that the two daughters, Martha and Atha, were twins. Census records also show that both girls were born in Mississippi in 1822. Prior to 1850, Martha married John Edmond George who joined the Danville Mounted Riflemen in 1861. Atha married John Wren Naul who served in Company E, 1st Infantry, Texas State Troops. Six of the seven sons served in the Confederate Army.

Henry and Emily moved to Walker County, Texas prior to 1855. Henry Sandel died about October 1863 and was buried in the Foster Cemetery near the Loma community in Walker County.

Martin Luther Sandel (1826-1893)

Martin Luther Sandel was the oldest son of Henry and Emily Sandel. He was born December 20, 1826 in Mississippi. He married Sarah Jackson Bay about 1856. Sarah was the daughter of Robert Thomas Bay who established a community in Montgomery County which is now known as Bay's Chapel. Martin enlisted in Captain Robert S. Poole's Company A of the 24th/25th Consolidated Texas Cavalry in January 1865. He is last shown on the rolls of Company A in April 1865 with a notation that he had been left sick in Austin County on April 29, 1865. After the war, Martin returned to Walker County and took up farming. Martin died April 24, 1893 and was buried in the Foster Cemetery near the Loma community in Walker County.

James Wesley Sandel (1829-1890)

James Wesley Sandel, the second son of Henry and Emily Sandel, was born May 14, 1829 in Pike County, Mississippi. He married Harriet S. King in Mississippi about 1851. James enlisted as a corporal in Company H, 20th Texas Infantry at Huntsville, Texas on April 26, 1862. While stationed in Galveston, he was detailed to pick up clothing at the state penitentiary in Huntsville. He was transferred to the engineer's corps at Galveston in June 1864. James returned to Walker County after the war and took up farming. He died May 2, 1890 and was buried at Ebenezer Cemetery in Walker County, Texas.

Harvey J. Sandel (1831-1896)

Harvey J. Sandel, the third son of Henry and Emily Sandel, was born about 1831 in Mississippi. Harvey married Mary Dunlap in Montgomery County on November 1, 1855. They appear in the 1860 Walker County census with two daughters, ages two and one. Henry enlisted as a private in Company H, 20th Texas Infantry in Huntsville, Texas on June 29, 1862. He was transferred to the engineer's corps at Galveston in June 1864. No records have been found showing what happened to Harvey's first wife. He is known to have married Sarah Armenda Pittman in Grimes County on June 2, 1887. Harvey died in Grimes County in 1896. His place of burial is unknown.

Dewitt Clinton Sandel (1834-1903)

Dewitt Clinton Sandel was the fourth son of Henry and Emily Sandel. He was born January 12, 1834 in Pike County, Mississippi. He married Zerena Palmer about 1857. Zerena was the daughter of Thomas Henry and Rachel Teel Palmer, and she was the granddaughter of John Martin Palmer (Parmer), a signer of the Texas Declaration of Independence. Dewitt enlisted in Company E of the Cavalry Battalion in Waul's Texas Legion at Houston, Texas on May 13, 1862 and was appointed fifth sergeant on May 20. He last appears on the rolls of Waul's Texas Legion in February 1863. Dewitt filed a Confederate pension application in Harris County, Texas on November 12, 1902 in which he claims the he spent the last year of the war in Captain Poole's Company of the 24th Texas Cavalry. Dewitt Clinton Sandel died in Harris County on October 6, 1903 and was buried in Hollywood Cemetery in Houston.

Erastus Emory Sandel (1836-1901)

Erastus Emory Sandel was the fifth son of Henry and Emily Sandel. He was born June 27, 1836 in Pike County, Mississippi. He appears on the rolls of the 1860 Montgomery County, Texas census in the household of his sister, Martha, and her husband, John Edmond George. On May 4, 1861, E. E. Sandel joined the Danville Mounted Riflemen, one of the earliest companies formed in the 17th Brigade of Texas. When a call was made for troops to defend the island of Galveston, E. E. enlisted in Company I, 9th Texas Infantry (Nichols') for an enlistment term of six months. After being mustered out of the 9th Texas Infantry, E. E. enlisted as a private in Company H, 20th Texas Infantry at Huntsville, Texas on May 10, 1862. He was promoted to third corporal on August 20, 1862. He was transferred to the engineer's corps at Galveston in June 1864 along with his brothers, James Wesley and Harvey J. Sandel, and his cousin, James Monroe Sandel. It is unclear whether E. E. was soon discharged or was allowed to go home on furlough, but he married Rachel Sanner Lindley in Grimes County on September 14, 1864. E. E. appears in the 1870 Walker County census as a farmer with property valued at fifteen-hundred dollars. Erastus Emory Sandel died in March 1901 and is believed to be buried in Brazos County, Texas.

Henry Columbus Pinkney Sandel (1841-1909)

Henry C. P. Sandel was the youngest son of Henry and Emily Sandel. He was born about 1841 in Pike County, Mississippi. There are very few verifiable records for Henry C. P. Sandel. He appears on the rolls of the 1860 Walker County census in the household of his father and stepmother, but no spouse is shown.

Confederate service records show that at the age of nineteen, Henry enlisted in Captain John R. Kennard's Company A, 10th Texas Infantry at Anderson, Texas on October 12, 1861. This company was also known as the Grimes County Boys. Henry took part in the Battle of Arkansas Post on January 11, 1863 along with his cousins, John Oliver and Peter Sandel, who were in the 24th Texas Cavalry (Dismounted). He was captured and transported to Camp Douglas, Illinois where he arrived on February 8, 1863. He was paroled from Camp Douglas on April 1, 1863 and exchanged at City Point, Virginia on April 7, 1863. Like many of the men who were sent to prisoner-of-war camps after the Battle of Arkansas Post, on being exchanged, Henry spent a great deal of time in the hospital. He is shown present for the months of November and December 1863 when his regiment was consolidated with the 6th Texas Infantry and the 15th Texas Cavalry and then was assigned to Granbury's Texas Brigade. He is shown present on a muster roll dated March and April 1864 which was the last roll reported by his regiment. It is likely that Henry was with his regiment throughout the Atlanta campaign and at the Battle of Franklin and the Battle of Nashville during Confederate General John Bell Hood's ill-fated invasion of Tennessee. Henry was admitted to the Way Confederate Hospital in Meridian, Mississippi in January 1865, indicating that he was still with his regiment when it retreated into Mississippi after the Battle of Franklin.

After the war, Henry appears on the 1867 voter registration roll for Montgomery County. He is shown in the 1880 Milam County census with wife, Isabella A. Sandel. She is shown to be age twenty and to have been born in Florida in 1860. Henry filed a Confederate pension application in Milam County on June 30, 1904 claiming that his only property was one hog worth five dollars. Henry Columbus Pinkney Sandel died on May 19, 1909 and was buried in the Friendship United Methodist Church Cemetery at Davilla in Milam County, Texas.

Peter Warren Sandel (1806-1866)

Peter Warren Sandel is believed to have been born in South Carolina on September 6, 1806. After moving to Pike County, Mississippi, Peter met and married Winifred Tabor. Winifred was the daughter of Methodist minister Isaac Tabor and Susanah Bullock Tabor. Isaac moved his wife and eight children to Texas about 1837 while Winifred stayed in Mississippi. Isaac and his family arrived in the Montgomery County area about 1841 where he served as a Methodist minister. It is possible that Isaac's arrival in Montgomery County may have influenced Peter Sandel to move to Texas. During their time in Pike County, Mississippi, Peter and Winifred had eight children. They were: William Fletcher (b.1827), James Franklin (b.1829), John Oliver (b.1831), Levisa Elizabeth (b.1832), Isaac Benson (b.1834), Eliza Ann (b.1835), David Wiggins (b.1839), and Peter Tabor (b.1842). Family history tells that Winifred died from complications with the birth of her youngest child, Peter Tabor. After the death of his first wife, Peter Warren Sandel married Louisa Winbourne while still in Mississippi. The couple had two children, Mary Matilda (b.1847) and Thomas Griffith (b.1849). Sometime after November 1850, Peter and Louisa left Pike County, Mississippi. Peter's oldest son, William Fletcher, who is shown on the 1850 Pike County census rolls as a teacher at age 22, did not follow the rest of the family to Texas initially but appears in Walker County prior to the war. No military records have been found for William who may have been exempt from service because he was a teacher.

The Peter W. Sandel family arrived in Walker County, Texas about October 1851 settling on Sandy Creek just a few miles north of Danville. This community came to be known as East Sandy and still carries that name today along with East Sandy Cemetery where Peter, his wife, Louisa, and his son, Peter Tabor Sandel, are buried. Peter Warren Sandel was known to have had two sons who served in the Confederate Army, and in addition, his daughter, Eliza Ann Sandel, married James Thomas Vick, who served as a private in Company H, 20th Texas Infantry.

John Oliver Sandel (1831-1864)

John Oliver Sandel, the son of Peter Warren and Winifred Tabor Sandel, was born January 1, 1831 in Pike County, Mississippi. John arrived in Texas in the early 1850s. He married Roxana S. Harrison on June 19, 1856 in Walker County. According to the 1860 census, the couple had two children, Mary W. Sandel (b.1857) and Isaac H. Sandel (b.1860). John also appears on the 1857 roll of San Jacinto Masonic Lodge 106 in Danville.

Confederate service records show that J. O. Oliver was enlisted as a private into Captain S. D. Wooldridge's Company B, 24th Texas Cavalry Regiment on March 29, 1862 by John E. George. He is first shown present at Camp Carter near Hempstead, Texas on April 28, 1862. This record shows him to be age 31, having travelled 50 miles to his rendezvous, with a horse valued at $200, and equipment valued at $20. After training at Camp Carter, John traveled with the 24th Cavalry through East Texas and Louisiana into Arkansas where they were dismounted and their horses sent home. The 24th Cavalry Regiment was assigned to Garland's Brigade and was sent to Camp Holmes at Sulphur Springs, Arkansas. At Camp Holmes, John was trained as an infantryman before being sent to defend Fort Hindman at Arkansas Post.

At the Battle of Arkansas Post on January 11, 1863, John was among the men captured who were sent by boat to Camp Butler in Illinois. Treatment of the prisoners and exposure to the harsh winter both during the trip and after their incarceration resulted in the deaths of several of the members of Company B. John was able to survive the ordeal and was later paroled and exchanged, allowing him to rejoin his regiment that had been assigned to the Army of Tennessee. A muster roll for May and June 1863 showed that he had been sick and in the hospital.

Five consecutive muster rolls show that J. O. Sandel was present from July 1863 through April 1864 and also show that he still had not been paid for use of his horse, his gun, nor for his trip to Camp Carter when he first enlisted. Service during that period of time would have placed him at the Battle of Chickamauga, September 19-20, 1863 and the Chattanooga campaign, October through November 1863.

The records for John and most of those for the 24th Texas Cavalry come to an end at the beginning of the Atlanta campaign in May 1864. Apparently the intense fighting in Atlanta and Hood's subsequent invasion of Tennessee did not allow enough time for proper record keeping.

Family records for John Oliver Sandel say that John was killed at the Battle of Franklin on November 30, 1864. Nothing in his Confederate service records disputes those statements. It is reasonable to believe that the family records are accurate because his brother Peter Tabor Sandel was with him at Franklin. The burial place of John Oliver Sandel is unknown. If he died in the Battle of Franklin, he likely is buried in McGavock Cemetery at the Carnton plantation. One researcher concludes that Oliver is buried in Texas Section 6, Grave

No. 79, which currently shows the name of Sanders. The names of many soldiers who are buried in this cemetery are still unknown and many more are incorrectly marked.

Peter Tabor Sandel (1842-1932)

Peter Tabor Sandel, the son of Peter Warren and Winifred Tabor Sandel was born September 15, 1842 in Pike County, Mississippi. Peter appears on the rolls of the 1860 Walker County census in the household of his parents.

At the age of nineteen, Peter enlisted in Captain Robert F. Oliver's Company I, Ninth Texas Infantry (Nichols') on October 10, 1861. This regiment was organized for a period of six months for the purpose of defending Galveston Island from Union invasion. While still in Galveston, Peter was mustered out of service from the 9th Texas Infantry and enlisted in Company B, 24th Texas Cavalry. This company was commanded by Captain Samuel Wooldridge and was primarily comprised of men from Montgomery County. Peter first appears on the rolls of Company B at Camp Carter near Hempstead, Texas. This roll shows his horse to be valued at $200 and equipment valued at $20. After training at Camp Carter near Hempstead, Texas, Peter rode with this company to Arkansas where it became Company B, 24th Texas Cavalry (Dismounted). He was captured at the Battle of Arkansas Post on January 11, 1863. While most of the men captured at Arkansas Post were sent to Camp Butler in Illinois, Peter was sent to the City General Hospital in St. Louis, Missouri to be treated for a gunshot wound on January 22, 1863. He later was transferred to Gratiot Street Prison in St. Louis where he was paroled in April 1863. After being paroled, Peter was exchanged at City Point, Virginia. Records show that he was hospitalized prior to returning to his regiment. Private P. T. Sandel is shown present on the rolls of Company B for the month of September 1863 through February 1864 and participated in the Battle of Chickamauga, Battle of Missionary Ridge, and numerous engagements in Georgia, including the Atlanta campaign. He was with his regiment as a part of General John Bell Hood's invasion of Tennessee and was at the Battle of Franklin on November 30, 1864 where his brother, John Oliver, was killed in action. Private Peter T. Sandel was one of only nine men in Company B, 24th Texas Cavalry (Dismounted) to survive the war. This regiment was reorganized as Company I, Granbury's Consolidate Regiment, Texas Cavalry and was among the troops surrendered by General Joseph Johnston in North Carolina in April 1865.

After the war, Peter returned to Walker County were he married Priscilla A. Samuels on December 17, 1868. After Priscilla's death in 1888, he married Mollie E. Gibson. On May 8, 1908, Peter filed a Confederate pension application at the age of sixty-five. In his application, he states that he was a resident of Willis, Texas and that he had moved there from Walker County on December 11, 1907. He further states that he was generally "broke down, nearly blind and totally blind in one eye." He also states that he was suffering from exposure during the war, rheumatism, and old age. Peter lists his only property as a pony and a buggy which were valued at sixty dollars. Peter Tabor Sandel died April 2, 1932, just five months shy of his ninetieth birthday. He was buried in East Sandy Cemetery near New Waverly, in Walker County, Texas.

The Shannon Family

Among the most written-about families in the history of Montgomery County is the Shannon family. While it is known that the family was among the earliest settlers in the area, at least some of the written history is based on family lore and conjecture. The Confederate history of this family is derived from Owen Shannon and his nephew Aaron Shannon, and the family's contributions in the War between the States is well documented.

The Owen Shannon Family

Owen Shannon, the son of Eleanor and Thomas Shannon, Sr., was born about 1762 in Georgia. It is believed that Owen was married to Margaret Montgomery in Wilkes County, Georgia in October of 1792. Around 1821, the couple and five of their six children immigrated to the Mexican province of Texas. Owen and his two sons, John and Jacob, each received a league of land in Stephen F. Austin's colony in an area which is now Montgomery County. Four of Owen's grandsons and two of his great grandsons fought for Southern independence during the War between the States.

Family of John Shannon (1794-1838)

John Shannon, the oldest son of Owen and Margaret Montgomery Shannon, was born about 1794 in Georgia. He is believed to have married Louisa Compton in Franklin County, Georgia in 1816. Family histories state that John and Louisa had two sons and four daughters. The last four of these children were born after the Shannon family's migration to Texas. After the death of Louisa, John married Charlotte Wilson, a union that produced three more sons and two daughters. As members of Stephen F. Austin's colony, John and his wife settled in Montgomery County where he, along with his father Owen and his brother Jacob, received a league of land. John Shannon died in Texas about 1838. His place of burial is unknown. John's widow, Charlotte, married David Clarke in 1839 and appears in the 1850 Walker County census with her son, Josias Shannon, and daughter, Rebecca Shannon.

Five of John Shannon's sons and two of his grandsons served in the Confederate Army. Only his oldest son, Owen Shannon, and grandson, William T. Shannon, served as Confederate soldiers from Montgomery County. John's son, William C. Shannon, moved to Grimes County prior to 1850 and served in 17th Brigade of Texas State Troops. John's three youngest sons moved to Walker County prior to 1850. Simon Shannon, born about 1825, served in the 4th Infantry Regiment of Texas State Troops. James W. Shannon, born in 1826, and Jonas Shannon, born in 1829, served in the 24th/25th Consolidated Texas Cavalry. James W. Shannon's oldest son, John W. Shannon, served in the 35th Texas Cavalry from Walker County. John's grandson William Absolum Denman served in the 17th Brigade and 4th Infantry Regiment of Texas State Troops. In addition to having five sons and three grandsons in the Confederate Army, John's daughter, Rebecca Shannon, married Montgomery County soldier Walter Leigh who served in Company K of the 20th Texas Infantry.

Sons of John Shannon
Owen Shannon (1821-1880)

Owen Shannon, son of John Shannon, was born about 1821. Records show that Owen Shannon married Maranda Raney in Montgomery County on October 2, 1842. The couple appears on the 1850 census rolls of Walker County along with Margaret Shannon, age eleven; Isaac Shannon, age seven; William Shannon, age three; and Martha Shannon, age four months. Neither Margaret Shannon nor Isaac Shannon appear to be the children of Owen and Maranda Shannon. Isaac, however, did serve in the Confederate Army. Census records indicate that by 1860, Owen and Maranda had returned to Montgomery County where they remained until sometime after 1870 and prior to Owen's death in Johnson County, Texas on February 5, 1880. Records in the Texas State Archives show that Owen Shannon joined Captain J. M. Montgomery's Company C, 17th Brigade of Texas State Troops on August 28, 1863 at age 42. Records from the National Archives show that Owen served in Company B of David S. Terry's Texas Cavalry. A pension application filed by Owen's son, William Thomas Shannon, on September 20, 1928, states that William also served in Terry's Regiment, Texas Cavalry. Owen Shannon died in 1880. Both Owen and his son, William, are buried in Cleburne Memorial Cemetery, Johnson County, Texas.

William Compton Shannon (1822-1874)

William Compton Shannon was born about 1822. Although it is likely that William lived with his father, John, when he first arrived in Montgomery County, there are no records to indicate that he was a citizen of the county. He married Martha J. McNair in Grimes County on June 27, 1850 and appears on the Grimes County census rolls for 1860 and 1870. Records indicate that William C. Shannon enlisted in Captain James W. Barnes' Company A of the 17th Brigade of Texas States Troops on December 27, 1862 as a first corporal but substituted W. H. Maupin in his place. He is later shown to have re-enlisted in the 17th Brigade in Captain J. M. Montgomery's Company C as a fourth corporal at age 42 for a period of six months. William C. Shannon died in Grimes County on January 26, 1874 and is buried in Bethel Cemetery near Bedias, Texas.

Simon Shannon (1825-unknown)

Simon Shannon was born about 1825 and moved to Walker County prior to 1850. Simon and his wife, Eppa Denman Shannon, appear on the Walker

County census rolls from 1850 through 1870 and in Madison County in 1880. Records show that Simon Shannon enlisted for a term of six months in Captain R. D. Hightower's Company B, 17th Brigade of Texas State Troops in Walker County on August 28, 1863 at the age of 38. A muster roll dated January 30, 1864 shows that Simon Shannon was enrolled in Company E, 4th Infantry Regiment of Texas State Troops. A certificate witnessed by Captain Joseph M. Evans states indicates that Simon was discharged on February 8, 1864. No further service records have been found. Simon died sometime after 1880, and his place of burial is unknown.

James W. Shannon (1826-1886)

James W. Shannon was born in Texas on September 5, 1826. He married Minerva Wilson in 1847 in Walker County. A muster roll dated April of 1865 shows that James was enrolled in Company E, 24th/ 25th Consolidated Texas Cavalry on April 29, 1865. Remarks on this roll state that he joined by enlistment. No further records have been found. James died on December 12, 1886 and is buried in Chalk Mountain Cemetery, Erath County, Texas.

Jonas Shannon (1829-1907)

Jonas Shannon was born in Texas on October 23, 1829. Some records show his name as Jonah or Josias as indicated by the 1850 Walker County census roll which shows him in the household of his stepfather, David Clarke, along with his mother, Charlotte, and his sister, Rebecca. Jonas married Ruth Mills in Walker County January 30, 1851. Jonas and Ruth appear on the Walker County census rolls from 1850 through 1870. The couple appears on the 1880 Milam County census rolls. A Confederate service record file for Company H, 20th Texas Infantry Regiment labeled "Jonas Shannon" lists a group of men detailed to transport cotton to Mexico. The name shown on this record is "James Shannon, age 38" which is the approximate age of his brother James, so it is likely that the records of these two brothers are confused. A muster roll dated April of 1865 shows Jonah Shannon in Company H, 24th/25th Consolidated Regiment having been transferred to Company G, 25th Texas Cavalry. Jonas died on May 12, 1907 and is buried in Friendship United Methodist Church Cemetery, Milam County, Texas.

Family of Jacob Montgomery Shannon (1804-1878)

Jacob Montgomery Shannon, the youngest child of Owen and Margaret Montgomery Shannon, was born March 6, 1804. Jacob married Catherine "Kitty" Yoakum about 1823. Jacob and Kitty had three sons and five daughters. As members of Stephen F. Austin's colony, Jacob settled in Montgomery County where he, along with his father, Owen, and his brother, John, received a league of land. Jacob Shannon died May 22, 1878 and is buried in the Shannon-Evergreen Cemetery near the town of Dobbin in Montgomery County, Texas.

All three of Jacob's sons served in the Confederate Army. In addition, two of his daughters married Confederate soldiers. Margaret Shannon married William

Aylett Dean who served in Company A, 17th Brigade of Texas State Troops, and Josephine Shannon married M. A. Connell who served in Company G, 20th Texas Infantry and Company H, 26th Texas Cavalry.

Sons of Jacob Montgomery Shannon
Mathis Ward Shannon (1824-1909)

Mathis Ward Shannon was born July 24, 1824. He married Mary Steele before 1850. Matt Shannon joined Captain Franklin G. Dupree's Company H, of the 26th Texas Cavalry on January 1, 1863. Records do not indicate that he participated in the Battle of Galveston on that date. Other records show that he was detailed as a courier for General Bagby on October 15, 1864. No further records of his Confederate service have been found. Mathis Ward Shannon died on July 13, 1909 and was buried in Shannon-Evergreen cemetery near Dobbin.

Jacob Montgomery Shannon, Jr. (1828-1877)

Jacob Montgomery Shannon, Jr. was born September 29, 1828. No records have been found showing that he was married. He is shown on the rolls of the 1870 Montgomery County census as single, age forty-one, and living in the household of his father. Jacob joined Company K, of the 18th Texas Cavalry (Terry's Texas Rangers) on September 7, 1861. He appears on a muster roll for November 1861 through January 1862 and is shown as absent in the hospital at Nashville. The final record in his file is an order dated February 24, 1862 to furnish transportation for J. M. Shannon from New Iberia to Niblett's Bluff, Louisiana. No further records of his Confederate service have been found. Jacob Montgomery Shannon, Jr. died December 4, 1877 and was buried in Shannon-Evergreen cemetery near Dobbin.

Benjamin Franklin Shannon (1843-1922)

Benjamin Franklin "Frank" Shannon was born in Montgomery County on February 21, 1843. Frank Shannon was first married to Mary E. Scott. After Mary's death in 1878, he married Anna Davidson Harbin on February 23, 1882. Confederate service records show that Frank Shannon enlisted in Company G, 20th Texas Infantry on April 28, 1862 at age nineteen and appears to have been present at the Battle of Galveston on January 1, 1863. The last record in his file shows him present with his company for the months of March and April 1863. Anna Shannon states in her Confederate widow's pension application filed in Walker County on April 23, 1925, that her husband, B. F. Shannon, served in the 20th Texas infantry for more than three years. Benjamin Franklin "Frank" Shannon died March 5, 1922 and was buried in Shannon-Evergreen cemetery near Dobbin.

Family of Aaron Shannon (1796-1865)

Aaron Shannon, the son of Sarah and John Shannon, was born in South Carolina on or about June 8, 1796. He married Elizabeth Kilpatrick in the Pendleton District of South Carolina in August 1818. Family histories suggest that Aaron

Shannon was commissioned as colonel in the army by Andrew Jackson and also state that he served on the Board of Regents at the University of Alabama. While these statements are unconfirmed, it is known that Aaron Shannon was one of the original trustees of Baylor University and offered a portion of his land as a site for the new college. Aaron was the nephew of Owen Shannon who immigrated to Montgomery County with his sons John and Jacob as part of Stephen F. Austin's Colony. Although Aaron and his family were not part of Austin's Colony, it is believed that they arrived in the Montgomery County area sometime before 1845. Aaron and wife, Elizabeth Shannon, appear on the rolls of the 1850 Grimes County census along with their four sons and the two youngest of his three daughters. The oldest daughter, Clarrisa was married to Theodore Smyth at that time. Aaron Shannon died July 27, 1865 and was buried in Shannon-Evergreen Cemetery near Dobbin.

Before his death, Aaron would see three of his sons serve in the Confederate Army. Aaron's oldest son, John, appears to have died prior to the war. Aaron's grandson, Reginald Smyth, served in Company L, of the 8th Texas Cavalry (Terry's Texas Rangers). On November 29, 1867, Aaron's youngest daughter, Mary Elizabeth, married Andrew Roane Dillon who served as a private in the 3rd Texas Infantry.

Sons of Aaron Shannon
William Alexander Shannon (1828-1862)

William Alexander Shannon was born in Pickens County, Alabama in 1828. William arrived in Montgomery County with his father Aaron and the rest of the family prior to 1845. Texas marriage records show that William A. Shannon married S. A. Farquhar on December 22, 1851. This appears to be the same person as Celesta Ann Farquhar born about 1835 in Mississippi. A twenty-year-old female shown as C. Forkner appears on the rolls of the 1860 Montgomery County census in the household of W. A. Shannon along with a seven-year-old female shown as H. Shannon. This is likely Celesta Ann and daughter Hulda. The residence is shown to be near the home of William's younger brother, Thomas Brandon Shannon. William enlisted in a company of cavalrymen organized by Captain Denman W. Shannon in Grimes County in the summer of 1861. He was elected first lieutenant and was second in command. This group of men was mustered into Confederate service as Company C, 5th Texas Cavalry in San Antonio, Texas on August 31, 1861. The 5th Texas Cavalry traveled westward with General H. H. Sibley's Brigade as part of the New Mexico campaign. William is shown present with his company for the month of December 1861 which would have been in the area of El Paso. At some time during the Confederate invasion of New Mexico in the winter of 1862, he tendered his resignation. The fact that General Sibley's Confederate force had lost approximately one thousand men to pneumonia, small pox, and dysentery by February 1862 suggests that William might have been in failing health. His resignation was approved on March 13, 1862. Since there are no further records of William's Confederate service, it is likely that he died in New Mexico. In November of 1863, Celesta Ann petitioned the State of Texas for thirteen weeks of pay due 1st Lt. William A. Shannon, deceased. She stated in her petition that she was the lawfully-married wife of William A. Shannon, the legal heir to his estate, and the natural guardian of their child. She signed the document as "C. A. Shannon" and was awarded $243.33 on November 21, 1863.

Thomas Brandon Shannon (1831-1921)

Thomas Brandon Shannon was born in Pickens County, Alabama on New Year's Day of 1831. He arrived with the Shannon family in Montgomery County prior to 1845. Thomas married Mary Jane Hayes on January 8, 1852. The couple appears on the rolls of the 1860 Montgomery County census with five children. Thomas enlisted in Colonel G. W. Carter's 21st Texas Cavalry on December 15, 1861. After training at Camp Carter near Hempstead, Thomas and his company of cavalry traveled to Arkansas with Colonel Carter's three regiments of cavalry. Like many of the other regiments at winter camp in Arkansas, the 21st Texas Cavalry was plagued with illness due to poor living conditions and the continued spread of disease. After being examined by a doctor and found to be physically unfit for duty, Thomas rendered his resignation as captain on December 2, 1862 and returned to Texas. Texas militia records show that Thomas joined Company C, 17th Brigade Cavalry, Texas State Troops on August 23, 1863 for a period of six months. No further military records have been found. Thomas Brandon Shannon died in on June 21, 1921 and was buried in Old Independence Cemetery in Washington County, Texas.

Aaron Shannon, Jr. (1838-1864)

Aaron Shannon, Jr. was born in Pickens County, Alabama about 1838. He is shown in the household of his father, Aaron Shannon, Sr. on the rolls of the 1860 Grimes County census. His brothers, William and Thomas Brandon, were living in Montgomery County at that time. He enlisted in Company C, 21st Texas Cavalry on December 15, 1861. He was elected first lieutenant and was second in command to his brother, Captain Thomas Shannon. Both the life and the military career of Aaron Shannon would end very soon. He apparently became seriously ill during the trip to Arkansas as indicated by a muster roll dated September 2, 1862 which states, "left behind on march sick." It is unclear when or how Aaron returned home, but he died February 12, 1864 and was buried in Shannon-Evergreen Cemetery, Montgomery County, Texas.

Reuben Davis Simonton (1842-1900)

Reuben Davis Simonton was born about 1842. Family histories tell that he was born in Robertson County, Texas. He was the son of William Sylvester and Eliza Melinda Halbert Simonton. He first appears on the Montgomery County census rolls in 1850.

Reuben enlisted as a private in Company K, 8th Texas Cavalry on September 7, 1861. This regiment was more commonly known as Terry's Texas Rangers. While a very large number of men in the regiment were sick in the hospital in Tennessee during the fall of 1861 and winter of 1862, muster rolls indicate that Reuben was present throughout the war. He was promoted to fifth sergeant on April 1, 1863. According to an account by Chaplain Robert F. Bunting, Reuben was severely wounded in the head while on picket duty at Hoover's Gap, Tennessee in June of 1863. Sergeant Simonton was paroled on May 26, 1865 and released at Vicksburg, Mississippi on June 1, 1865.

After his release, Reuben returned to Montgomery County where he married Louisa "Ludy" Arnold on December 7, 1865. Ludy was the daughter of Dr. E. J. Arnold. A home given to Reuben and Ludy by Dr. Arnold was used as the Montgomery city hall for many years. Reuben Davis Simonton died on June 10, 1900 and was buried in the New Montgomery Cemetery.

The Willis Family

Two brothers, Peter James Willis and Richard Short Willis made their way to Montgomery County shortly after Texas became a Republic in 1845. The lives of these two men and their families substantially impacted the histories of both Montgomery and Galveston Counties. The wealth derived from their mercantile business known as P. J. Willis & Bro. allowed them the means to become known as gracious philanthropists. Among their contributions were the land for what is now the New Montgomery Cemetery and the land for the original townsite of Willis which still carries the family name. While both Peter and Richard remained active in the cotton trade during the War between the States, both men were Confederate soldiers. Peter had two sons who also served in the Confederate Army.

Peter James Willis, Sr. (1815-1873)

Peter James Willis was born March 26, 1815 in Delaware. About 1822, his family moved to Maryland where Peter grew up. An unverified account says that Peter came to Texas in January 1836, then went back to Maryland for a few months and returned to Texas in 1837 with three of his brothers. In 1844, he married Caroline Womack, daughter of John N. and Tabitha Ford Womack. Together, the couple had six children: William Henry (b. 1845); Peter James (b. 1847); Mary Ella (b. 1849); Tabitha Ann (b. 1852); Magnolia (b. 1854); and Caroline (b. 1857). Peter enlisted in Company G, 20th Texas Infantry on May 14, 1862 and is shown present in Hempstead. With the exception of a brief stay in the Confederate Hospital at Houston on December 13, 1862, Peter is shown present with his company until a muster roll for the months of March and April 1863 indicate that he was discharged by civil authority. A muster roll index card from the Texas State Archives shows Peter enlisted in Company A, 17th Brigade TST (militia) on August 28, 1863 and later transferred back to the Confederate States Army but no further records of his service have been found. This break in service may have been related to the death of his wife, Caroline, on September 19, 1863 and just eleven months later, the death of his daughter, Tabitha Ann. After the war, Peter and Richard Willis moved their mercantile business to Galveston but continued to pursue business interests in Montgomery County. The

P. J. Willis & Bro. company continued to grow and prosper even after Peter's death in 1873. His two sons, William and Peter, Jr. remained active in the family business along with J. G. Goldthwaite, the husband of daughter, Ella. Peter's daughter, Magnolia, married wealthy entrepreneur George Sealy. The home that George built for his wife, Magnolia, in 1889 stood as the grandest mansion in Galveston until the completion of what is now known as the Moody Mansion, built by Narcissa Worsham Willis after the death of her husband, Richard Short Willis.

William Henry Willis (1845-1888)

William Henry Willis, the oldest son of Peter James and Caroline Womack Willis, was born in Montgomery County on December 7, 1845. Confederate service records do not give the exact date of William's enlistment in the Confederate Army. A letter from William, dated April 1, 1864, states that he was a sergeant in Captain Williamson's Corps of Cadets attached to Colonel Cook's regiment of heavy artillery. In this letter, he requests a transfer to Company G, of the 20th Texas Infantry Regiment. There are no records of that request being granted. He first appears on a muster roll dated July 1864 in W. M. Williamson's Corps of Cadets, Mann's Texas Cavalry. A roll dated January of 1865 shows that William and his company were on detached service with the signal corps stationed at Bolivar Point. His last record of service is a roll dated March 1865 indicating that he was a private in Company B, Mann's Regiment, Texas Cavalry, so it is likely that he was with Mann's Regiment on Galveston Island, when it was surrendered on June 2, 1865. After his father's death in 1873, William became a managing partner in the P. J. Willis & Bro. mercantile company. On December 19, 1877, he married Emma Beverly Price. While at his home in Galveston, William was murdered in an apparent home invasion on May 16, 1888. He is buried in the family plot at Trinity Episcopal Cemetery, Galveston, Texas.

Peter James Willis, Jr. (1847-1912)

Peter James Willis, Jr., the second child of Peter James and Caroline Womack Willis, was born in Montgomery County on November 9, 1847. The first record of Peter's service in the Confederate Army is a muster roll dated July 1864 showing him to be a private in W. M. Williamson's Corps of Cadets, Mann's Texas Cavalry on detached service to the signal corps on Bolivar Point. He was only sixteen years of age at that time. His last record of service is a roll dated March 1865 indicating that he was a private in Company B, Mann's Regiment, Texas Cavalry so it is likely that he was with Mann's Regiment on Galveston Island, when it was surrendered, June 2, 1865. Peter became a managing partner in the P. J. Willis & Bro. mercantile company after his father's death in 1873. On September 30, 1868, Peter married Martha Sterling Price, the daughter of former Missouri governor and Confederate General Sterling Price. Peter died October 31, 1912 and was buried in the family plot at Trinity Episcopal Cemetery, Galveston, Texas.

Richard Short Willis (1821-1892)

Richard Short Willis, son of Short Adam and Mary Polly Willis, was born October 17, 1821. He is believed to have arrived in Texas with his brother Peter James Willis in 1837. In 1847, Richard married Narcissa Worsham, daughter of Jeremiah and Catherine Landrum Worsham. Narcissa was the brother of Israel Worsham who served as a lieutenant colonel in the 17th Brigade of Texas State Troops (militia). Richard S. Willis enlisted in Company K, 20th Texas Infantry on April 1, 1864. From this date until the end of the war, Richard is on detached service with the quartermaster's department. An application from the Texas Cotton Office signed by Lieutenant Colonel W. J. Hutchins dated May 26, 1864, requests that Private R. S. Willis, Company K, Colonel Elmore's Regiment (20th), Texas Volunteer Infantry be detailed for ninety days for duty as wagon master in charge of a train of wagons transporting cotton from Montgomery County to the Rio Grande. The application describes R. S. Willis as 43 years old, six feet tall, dark hair and eyes, and dark complexion. The last record on file for Private R. S. Willis, Company K, 20th Texas Infantry is a parole of honor, number 577 signed at Houston, Texas, June 27, 1865. Following the war, Richard and his brother Peter moved their families and the P. J. Willis & Bro. company to Galveston. Richard remained active as a partner in the business until his death on July 27, 1892. After Richard's death, his widow Narcissa Worsham Willis contracted for the construction of a 28,000-square-foot mansion on Broadway Avenue in Galveston. The home was completed about 1895 and Narcissa died just four years later on September 6, 1899 at her son's summer home in New Jersey. Her heirs sold the home soon after the great hurricane of 1900 to William L. Moody, Jr., and the former residence is now a popular tourist attraction known as the Moody Mansion. Both Richard and Narcissa are buried in the Old City Cemetery in Galveston.

Samuel Dunbar Wooldridge, MD
photo courtesy of Carlton Cranor

Samuel Dunbar Wooldridge (1823-1890)

Samuel Dunbar Wooldridge was born in Hinds County, Mississippi on September 21, 1823. He was the son of Samuel C. and Elizabeth Ann McDaniel Wooldridge. Samuel served as a corporal and sergeant in Company G, 1st Regiment Mississippi Infantry during the Mexican-American War. He attended medical lectures in Kentucky, and in 1847 he went to New Orleans where he took a course at the New Orleans Medical College. He became a physician before moving to Texas about 1850 to be near his mother and step-father. Samuel married Catherine Elizabeth McCan in the Baptist Church at Danville, Texas on April 29, 1852. He was a member of San Jacinto Masonic Lodge #106 at Danville and remained a member until his death.

Soon after secession, Sam Wooldridge began recruiting and organizing a company of cavalrymen named the Danville Mounted Riflemen. The Riflemen were organized under Texas Militia laws as part of the 17th Brigade of Texas State Troops at Danville, Texas on May 4, 1861. The company was incorporated on September 13, 1861 and elected Samuel Wooldridge as its captain.

In the spring of 1862, Captain Wooldridge and more than forty of the Danville Mounted Riflemen enlisted in the regular Confederate Army as part of the 2nd Texas Lancers which was the second of three cavalry regiments organized by Colonel George W. Carter. In total, about one hundred men from Danville and surrounding areas joined the company for training at Camp Carter near Hempstead, Texas. After training, the company traveled to Arkansas where it was dismounted and designated as Company B, 24th Texas Cavalry (Dismounted). The men of the 24th Texas Cavalry were captured following the Battle of Arkansas and were transported to prison camps. The commissioned officers were transported to St. Louis, Missouri and then to Camp Chase in Ohio. In April, Sam was transferred to Fort Delaware and later sent to Virginia for exchange. Like many of the men who were subjected to exposure and harsh conditions in prison camps, he was sent directly to the hospital following his exchange. It is likely that Sam was unable to fully recover from his prison ordeal and was probably discharged due to disability. He was ordered to the Trans-Mississippi Department on July 18, 1863, after which he went home to Montgomery County for the duration of the war. Samuel Dunbar Wooldridge died in Montgomery County on May 18, 1890 and was buried in the Willis City Cemetery.

Chapter 3
Soldiers
&
Their Regiments

photo courtesy of David Frame

Over the many decades since the great War between the States, countless histories have been written about the numerous battles along with the bravery and determination of the men who fought these battles. While the individual efforts of many of these men are well documented, it is important to recognize the overall participation by communities and their nearly unanimous support of war effort. The county of Montgomery was a stunning example of that participation and support.

While Montgomery County overwhelmingly passed a referendum to secede from the Union by a vote of 318 for and only 98 against, the participation in the war effort was even greater. It is estimated that at the time of secession there were fewer than eight hundred white males between the ages of fourteen and fifty in the county. Out of that number, more than ninety percent served in the Confederate military. Within weeks of the firing on Fort Sumter, Dr. Samuel Wooldridge of Danville had organized a company of cavalrymen known as the Danville Mounted Rifles, and by the summer of 1861, three new companies of infantry had been formed in the county. By the fall of 1861, more than two hundred soldiers from Montgomery County had been deployed. One hundred of these men were at Galveston, defending the Texas coast, and more than one hundred were in other states as far away as Virginia.

Of the more than seven hundred men from Montgomery County who went to war, about one out of five did not return home. Many of those who did return home were disabled for the rest of their lives and some did not live to see Texas return to statehood in 1870. The ages of these men ranged from the mid-teens to more than fifty years of age. The youngest-known soldier from Montgomery County was Reuben Campbell Copeland who enlisted as a private in Company C of Ragsdale's Texas Cavalry at age thirteen. The oldest known soldier from Montgomery County was Peter Pincham who enlisted in Captain Samuel Wooldridge's Danville Mounted Riflemen on May 4, 1861 at the age of sixty-four. The youngest soldier from Montgomery County to die in service was William L. Pitts who served as a private in the 8th Texas Cavalry and died in Tennessee at the age of seventeen. He is buried in the Mt. Olivet Cemetery at Nashville. The oldest soldier from Montgomery County to die while in service was Israel Hewitt who served as a private in Company B, Twenty-Fourth Texas Cavalry and died in the City General Hospital at St. Louis, Missouri on February 2, 1863 at the age of fifty. He is buried in the Jefferson Barracks National Cemetery at St. Louis. The last Montgomery County veteran, Private Robert Charles Scott of Company A, 7th Texas Cavalry, died on July 5, 1940 at the age of ninety-six.

Identifying Confederate Soldiers

The process of proving the Confederate soldier's service can be a difficult task. Most of the Confederate service records are in the National Archives, but the muster rolls in the Archives were transcribed from the original records resulting in many errors. The accuracy of these transcriptions depended largely on the quality of handwriting of the original records. Often there were alternate spellings of a soldier's name. Since there were no identifiers such as soldiers' identification numbers, soldiers' records often were misfiled or confused with other soldiers. A national database called the Civil War Soldiers & Sailors System is maintained by the National Park Service, but indexing the thousands of records in the National Archives created yet another opportunity for human error, so although the database is a helpful tool, it is still necessary to view the actual transcribed record for a more reliable conclusion. Records for Texas State Troops or militia can be found only in the files of the Texas State Library and Archives Commission in Austin, Texas.

For the purpose of this book, a more difficult task is distinguishing the Montgomery County soldiers from those soldiers in other counties. The first qualifier for records contained in this book is that the soldier was a resident of Montgomery County at the time of the war. Other soldiers included in these records are those who had lived in the county prior to the war and still had family in the county at the time of the war or those who came back to Montgomery County to enlist. Various records used to establish this citizenship include census rolls, voter registrations, and tax rolls. Family histories, letters, and newspaper articles sometimes aid in research but are not considered to be necessarily reliable sources for proving residency. While other publications might be listed as sources for gathering information, all of the records contained in this book have been verified by and are a result of the individual research of the author although sometimes aided by those experienced researchers who have been previously acknowledged.

One of the necessary requirements for identifying Confederate soldiers from Montgomery County is a knowledge of how the Texas and Confederate military was organized. Soldiers were generally solicited for service and inducted into a company of men by one or more local recruiters. A company was comprised of one hundred or more men on average who, in most cases, elected their own officers. It was common for the recruiters to become the officers in the company. The elected officers of a company were a captain who commanded the company and three or more lieutenants. Ten companies, identified by letters "A" through "K" (excluding "J" because it looked too much like "I" when written), were the average make-up of a regiment. Each regiment was numbered and was often identified with the name of its original commander (example: 20th Texas Infantry "Elmore's"). The regimental officers were comprised of a colonel who commanded the company, along with a lieutenant colonel, and a major. A brigade was generally comprised of three or more regiments, and unlike the Union Army, was given a name (example: Hood's Texas Brigade). For identification purposes, regiments and brigades often kept the same names throughout the war regardless of who became their commanders.

Aside from the Texas State Troops (militia), the vast majority of the soldiers from Montgomery County were members of sixteen companies in fourteen regiments. These companies were Company H, 4th Texas Infantry; Company

D, 5th Texas Infantry; Company G, 7th Texas Cavalry; Company K, 8th Texas Cavalry; Company I, 9th Texas Infantry; Company K, 16th Texas Infantry; Companies G & K, 20th Texas Infantry; Company C, 21st Texas Cavalry; Company A & B, 24th Texas Cavalry; Company A, 24th/25th Consolidated Texas Cavalry; Company H, 26th Texas Cavalry; Company A, Mann's Regiment Texas Cavalry; Company K, Terry's Regiment Texas Cavalry; and Company C, Waul's Texas Legion.

Navy and Marines

The official records of the Confederate States Navy were destroyed at the end of the war. Most were destroyed by the burning of the city of Richmond, Virginia where the records were housed, and many other records likely were destroyed by officers fearing retaliation by the federal government. Some records still exist in the Texas State Library & Archives identifying Texans who served in the Confederate Navy, but they offer little information about the service of these men.

The only resident from Montgomery County who is known to have served in the Confederate Navy was Britton B. Wilkes. Both Britton and his brother, T. O. Wilkes, originally joined Captain P. P. Porter's Company H of the 4th Texas Infantry and traveled to Virginia. After his brother was killed at the Battle of Gaines' Mill on June 27, 1862, Britton Wilkes continued to serve with the 4th Texas Infantry through February of 1864. A pay voucher signed by 2nd Lt. J. S. Spivey at Bull's Gap, Tennessee and dated March 2, 1864 shows that B. B. Wilkes, a resident of Montgomery County, Texas, was entitled to be discharged by reason of appointment as midshipman in the Confederate States Navy. This is the last service record found on file for B. B. Wilkes.

Although very few historians have written about it, the Confederate States of America did have a Marine Corps stationed at naval bases, shorefront fortifications, and on many Confederate warships. One Confederate battery was headquartered at Fort Darling on Drewry's Bluff above the James River in Virginia. Most of the officers in this unit were former veterans of the United States Marine Corps who resigned their commissions to support the Southern war effort. Among the most notable of these was Lieutenant Israel Greene who commanded the first-ever rapid deployment of the United States Marine Corps in the siege of the federal arsenal at Harper's Ferry held by radical abolitionist John Brown. It is also interesting to note that the first Medal of Honor awarded to a United States Marine was issued to Sergeant John F. Mackie for his actions during the battle involving the ironclad *USS Galena*. This ship lost most of its crew while receiving heavy fire from Confederate Marines at Fort Darling atop Drewry's Bluff. In the famous clash of the ironclads at Hampton Roads, Company C of the Confederate States Marine Corps served aboard the *CSS Virginia* (*Merrimac*). The official Confederate States Marines served east of the Mississippi River.

In Texas, as well as in other states in the Western theater, cavalry units were often used aboard Confederate warships. Boarding and capturing the enemy's ship was a frequently-used tactic during the War between the States. This required additional troops to be placed on warships. Such was the case during the re-taking of Galveston on January 1, 1863 when Texas cavalrymen were placed aboard the *CSS Bayou City* and *CSS Neptune*. During the battle, the *Bayou City* used a boarding device similar to the ancient Roman corvus, by attaching itself to the *USS Harriet Lane,* allowing the Confederate cavalrymen to board and capture the Union gunboat. As a result of using cavalry aboard vessels, these units received the nickname "Horse Marines." Montgomery County men in Captain Franklin G. Dupree's Company H, 26th Texas Cavalry are believed to have been among the men aboard the Confederate cottonclads at the Battle of Galveston.

Black Confederate Soldiers

Opinions concerning the role of blacks in the Confederate Army vary as much as opinions concerning the cause of the War between the States. Some of the more popular contemporary views insist that black Confederate soldiers simply did not exist, despite substantial evidence to the contrary. Historians who accept the existence of black Confederate soldiers widely disagree on the actual number blacks in Confederate service, with estimates ranging from a few thousand to more than fifty-thousand men.

Despite the differing views, the involvement of blacks in the Confederate Army and Navy is not newly-found history but is often difficult to track. Although a multitude of records can be found in the National Archives, in many cases, the service records of blacks were not kept. Among the problems with researching the service records that were kept is the way that they were indexed. Black Confederate soldiers had given names but not usually surnames. Further, a wide range of terminologies were used to describe individuals, including "Negro," "black," "colored," "colored man," "body servant," "body guard," "black Confederate," and "black Confederate soldier."

Confederate pension applications are sometimes more helpful in identifying black Confederate soldiers. These files often contained the sworn affidavits of witnesses who gave a detailed account of the soldiers' services. These pensions were paid individually by each Southern state and were awarded to both white and black soldiers. In addition to drawing veteran's benefits, blacks were involved in numerous Confederate veteran activities and reunions after the war.

Still another way of verifying the existence of black Confederate soldiers and veterans is through newspaper and eyewitness accounts. An address given in September 1861 by the renowned abolitionist Frederick Douglass states:

> *There are in the present moment many colored men in the Confederate army doing duty not only as cooks, servants and laborers but as real soldiers, having muskets on their shoulders and bullets in their pockets.*

Confederate officers in Texas regiments were not consistent in recording the service of blacks. The services of these men were rarely recorded at all except in cases of soldiers being captured and becoming prisoners of war. Such is the sad but true story of six black Confederate soldiers from Montgomery County, Texas. These men, known only in existing records as Alexander, George Estill, Green, Nelson, Worthy Sell, and L. Williams, traveled from Texas to Arkansas with a company of cavalrymen commanded by Captain Samuel Wooldridge. After being dismounted and inducted into Confederate service as Company B, 24th Texas Cavalry (Dismounted), this company participated in Battle of Arkansas Post on January 11, 1863. Neither muster rolls nor records of this battle give an indication as to the involvement of these six men during conflict. In most cases, blacks served as cooks, laborers, or teamsters and were commonly referred to as body servants. As shown in the histories of other Confederate regiments, the term "body servant" can have diverse meanings, and the extent to which a black man would serve in any role varied widely from one individual and regiment to the next. During the intense battle at Arkansas Post, these six men may have sheltered in place or could have been involved in support roles such as tending to the wounded or reloading weapons, but the possibility that these men took up arms during the battle cannot be eliminated.

What we do know is that after the surrender, the six black men were treated in the same manner as their white counterparts. During the middle of winter, all captured men were loaded onto transport ships without blankets or warm clothing and suffered the long journey up the Mississippi River to prison camps. All six appear on a roll of prisoners of war received at Camp Butler, Illinois on January 31, 1863 with remarks stating, "negro, liberated." No further records of these men have been found. If they were released, they would have had to face the brutal cold of the Illinois winter without proper clothing, with no money, and no safe place to go. A law passed by the State of Illinois in 1853 made it illegal for blacks to immigrate to that state. Under this law, no black from another state could remain in Illinois for more than ten days. If unable to pay the fine for remaining beyond ten days, local sheriffs were authorized to sell the offender to the highest bidder. It is possible that at least some of these men were able to make their way to a place of safe refuge but the prospects for a happy ending to their journey were not good. There is no way to know to what extent these men were committed to the cause of the Confederacy, but their service cannot be ignored.

It would be difficult to determine the exact number of blacks from Montgomery County that were involved in some form of service to the Confederate Army, but it is safe to assume that it was a significant number. Accounts from the day book of plantation owner Green Wood state that at least nine of his own blacks, in addition to another half-dozen or more from the Danville area, worked as laborers constructing the defenses at Galveston under the supervision of his son, Green Mark Wood. Upon completing their duties there, all returned to their homes in Montgomery County freely and unattended.

Accounts such as this suggest that many blacks who were involved with the Confederate Army carried out their duties with a certain degree of willingness and often had little or no supervision. While many historians contend that any involvement of blacks in Confederate service would have been strictly against their wills, the fact that these men had access to weapons and horses would raise the question of why they did not attempt to escape. The numerous accounts of black men carrying weapons and being involved in actual combat raises another question: If the Confederate Army subjected a black man to forced labor and sometimes placed him in a life-threatening situation, at what point during his involuntary servitude would he be handed a gun? While we do not know the reasons nor forces that compelled these men in their service to the Confederacy, the history of their participation cannot be denied.

Texas State Troops (Militia)

Paramilitary volunteers existed in Texas as far back as the days of Stephen F. Austin when in May 1823, he appointed Moses Morrison as commander of a scouting company comprised of ten men recruited to control the Karankawa Indians around the Colorado and Tres Palacios Rivers. On December 20, 1836, the 1st congress passed "an Act to organize and fix the Military establishment of the Republic of Texas." This was the first of several congressional acts which established various military groups. Throughout the 19th century, they were given many names. Among those names were Mounted Volunteers, Texas State Troops, Frontier Rangers, State Rangers, and Texas Rangers. At the time of secession, Texas already had thousands of trained troops ready to enter the Confederate Army. These early Confederate soldiers were most commonly identified as Texas State Troops.

Shortly after becoming the twenty-eighth state, Texas enacted its first militia law on April 21, 1846. This law provided for the formation of militia units throughout various counties within the state. It became the duty of the Texas Adjutant General to maintain all records of appointments, promotions, resignations, deaths, and commissions, in addition to the receipt of monthly and annual returns, and muster rolls from the various military units. The adjutant general was also required to keep the records of recruitment and enrollment of both the Texas Rangers and all militiamen.

The Seventh Texas Legislature passed the Militia Act of 1858 which provided for incorporating uniformed military companies already organized or to be organized in the future. It also provided for the election of officers by the members, a schedule for filing a list of the names of members, and mandatory parades once a month.

The adjutant general position was re-established by the militia law passed on February 14, 1860, whereby the adjutant general assumed the duties of quartermaster general and ordnance officer of the state. This act mandated that every able-bodied free male inhabitant of this state between the ages of eighteen and forty-five years would be liable to perform military duty with certain exceptions. Exemptions included supreme, district, and probate court judges, postmasters, post riders, millers, ferrymen on public roads, teachers, and professors. The state militia was to be divided into thirty-three districts having one brigade in each district. The 17th Brigade, Texas State Troops consisted of men from Grimes, Montgomery, and Walker Counties.

During the early part of the war, virtually all Confederate soldiers from Montgomery County were in the 17th Brigade TST. Four of the earliest companies to be formed had very distinct identities. Former 17th Brigade General Procter P. Porter organized a company of men known as the Porter Guards which would later be inducted into the Confederate Army as Company H of the 4th Texas Infantry.

Robert M. Powell organized a militia company of men known as the Waverly Confederates, which was later inducted into the Confederate service as Company D of the 5th Texas Infantry. The men were primarily from the Danville area of Montgomery County and the community of Waverly in Walker County.

Dr. Samuel Wooldridge organized a company of cavalrymen from the Danville area which was known as the Danville Mounted Riflemen and later became Company B of the 24th Texas Cavalry (Dismounted).

In the southern part of the county, Lemuel G. Clepper formed a company of men known as the Montgomery County Rifle Boys. The majority of the men from the Rifle Boys joined Company K of the 20th Texas Infantry. Lemuel G. Clepper served as captain in Company K.

Montgomery County Rifle Boys

One of the units formed in the 17th Brigade from Montgomery County was known as the Montgomery County Rifle Boys. Recruiting was done primarily in the town of Montgomery, southward to the Harris County line and eastward to the Liberty County line. The officers who were elected to lead the Rifle Boys were Captain Lemuel G. Clepper, 1st Lieutenant L. W. Smith, 2nd Lieutenant William T. Jones, and 3rd Lieutenant Horatio D. Etheridge.

Last Name	First, Middle Name	Born	Died
Bailey	James A.	05/07/1829	06/3/1911
Baker	William Henry	about 1841	unknown
Bell	James Jefferson	about 1829	04/7/1915
Bender	John F.	10/22/1829	10/19/1904
Benhousen *	Henry	---------	---------
Bland *	H.	---------	---------
Boon(e)	J. A.	about 1846	unknown
Boon(e)	E. A.	06/22/1822	08/26/1902
Bosel *	August	---------	---------
Brautigam	George C.	08/06/1837	01/17/1916

Burk *	Daniel	- - - - - - - - -	- - - - - - - - -
Carter	Hampton Wesley	12/15/1835	06/18/1896
Cartwright	Joseph C.	05/31/1831	01/24/1904
Cathey	B. H.	about 1839	04/1863
Cathey	J. C.	about 1817	unknown
Clepper	Lemuel Gilliam	10/28/1813	06/19/1893
Close	J. E.	about 1825	unknown
Corgey	Louis	08/09/1833	01/02/1901
Corgey	Henry	07/01/1836	09/29/1885
Davis	William Humphrey	about 1826	about 1899
Davis	Franklin C. Davis	01/1843	05/16/1910
Day *	E. S.	- - - - - - - - -	- - - - - - - - -
Decker	Christler	02/23/1832	about 1873
Dickinson	W. W.	about 1838	- - - - - - - - -
Etheridge	Horatio D.	about 1835	unknown
Ford	James A.	about 1839	12/28/1899
Gatlin	John Davidson	03/22/1841	02/08/1916
Gatlin	William Riley	05/13/1833	06/29/1918
Goodson	Arthur	about 1798	02/18/1863
Goodson	Edward	about 1834	unknown
Goodson	James	10/27/1820	01/25/1891
Goodson	William Walter	about 1824	03/30/1899
Graves	Jesse Cox	09/21/1841	01/06/1923
Graves	James W.	about 1840	unknown
Griffin	S. D.	about 1842	08/07/1862
Hamby	Isaac	about 1820	unknown
Harris *	J. D.	- - - - - - - - -	- - - - - - - - -
Holden *	H.	- - - - - - - - -	- - - - - - - - -
Ingle *	S. B.	- - - - - - - - -	- - - - - - - - -
Jenkins	James C.	about 1830	after 1920
Jobert*	Emile	about 1834	about 1892
Johnson	John Wesley	03/22/1843	05/18/1925
Johnson	Jesse	about 1816	04/18/1914
Jones*	B.	- - - - - - - -	- - - - - - - - -
Jones	William T.	about 1839	unknown
Kise *	John	- - - - - - - - -	- - - - - - - - -
Lacey	Milan Carile	about 1844	about 1875
Lacey	Cicero Daniel	about 1842	01/12/1927
Mack	George W.	11/08/1842	02/19/1907
Mack	Jesse	11/15/1840	06/26/1910
Martin	John William	05/14/1836	10/4/1904
McCaskell	James M.	about 1843	unknown
Morris	Samuel	about1825	unknown
Mostyn	Henry	about 1841	unknown
Pillow	Ransom Doc	05/01/1842	10/14/1914
Pillow	Andrew M.	10/03/1838	08/18/1913
Roberts	E.	about 1835	unknown
Roberts	Green	about 1840	unknown

Rodgerson	William	11/30/1816	10/13/1900
Sanders	J. F.	about 1823	unknown
Shilling	Christopher	12/03/1833	05/30/1874
Smith	L. W.	before 1828	unknown
Surles	Robert	about 1838	02/10/1864
Tandy *	James E.	- - - - - - - - -	- - - - - - - - -
Vance	Seaborn S.	about 1836	unknown
Vance	Davis W.	about 1830	after 1880
Vance	Joshua J.	about 1841	unknown
Warren *	William H.	- - - - - - - - -	- - - - - - - - -
Whitaker	Thomas J.	about 1841	- - - - - - - - -
Wickson	James	about 1836	unknown
Wickson	Peter	about 1841	unknown
Williams	J. F.	unknown	unknown

* Denotes men who have not been identified as Confederate soldiers from Montgomery County. This roster was compiled from a report included in the records of the Texas State Troops in the adjutant general's correspondence files in the Texas State Archives, dated July 22, 1861, from Captain Lemuel G. Clepper to the commander of the 17th Brigade TST, General Procter P. Porter. Some of the names shown here have been corrected and may not appear as they did on the original document. Birth and death dates also have been added to further identify these men.

Danville Mounted Riflemen*

It had been fewer than three weeks since Confederate troops had triggered a national crisis by firing on Fort Sumter in Charleston Harbor when Dr. Samuel Dunbar Wooldridge began forming a company of cavalrymen from Danville and the surrounding area. While not all of these men were residents of Montgomery County at the time of their enlistments, virtually all of them had been previous residents of the county or still had immediate family living in Montgomery County. This company of mounted volunteers, known as the Danville Mounted Riflemen, was incorporated on September 13, 1861, then sworn before the justice of the peace, John E. George, and recorded with the clerk of the county court of Montgomery, Appleton Gay, on September 23, 1861. Samuel D. Wooldridge was elected captain; Moses Grayham, first lieutenant; Augustus Richards, second lieutenant; and W. H. Woodson, third lieutenant. In April 1862, Captain Wooldridge and forty-four of the Danville Mounted Riflemen, along with some fifty other men from the Danville area, joined the 2nd regiment of Colonel George W. Carter's Texas Lancers. After training at Camp Carter near Liendo Plantation in Hempstead, Captain Wooldridge and his men marched off to Arkansas where this company later became Company B, 24th Texas Cavalry (Dismounted).

When Confederate General Paul Octave Hébert called for troops to defend the city of Galveston in the summer of 1861, nine of the Riflemen answered the call. They were John A. Guynn, James W. Hulon, John M. McClanahan, Jr., William F. Malone, James McCarley, James H. Norsworthy, David E. Roten, E. E. Sandel, and James B. Thomason. They joined Company I, Colonel E. B. Nichols' 9th Texas Infantry for a period of six months but upon mustering out, rejoined Captain Wooldridge's company of lancers. A more detailed account of these men and their Confederate service is included in the history of the 24th Texas Cavalry (Dismounted).

Last Name	First, Middle Name	Born	Died
Adams	William G.	1822	1878
Anderson	Edward A.	02/01/1820	12/11/1896
Baugass	J. R.	unknown	03/26/1863
Brake	William B.	1843	03/04/1863
Cates	Benjamin F.	1839	10/19/1861
Chambers	Daniel L.	1841	09/20/1863
Chambers	John F.	1828	01/17/1863
Chambers	John H.	1838	09/20/1863
Chambers	Thomas	1842	02/26/1863
Childers	Reuben	1840	07/10/1862
Fowler	Charles	1843	09/20/1863
Fox	Samuel	1825	unknown
George	John E.	07/22/1821	09/24/1875
Gibson	Anthony	11/17/1818	02/24/1895
Graham	Moses	03/04/1825	01/13/1904
Green	Wiley	02/02/1842	02/4/1905
Guynn	John A.	05/22/1843	06/08/1894
Hall	James H.	07/17/1824	1901
Hardy	John	1808	09/01/1884
Harrison	William	1821	after 1870
Hoskins	John C.	1837	1867
Hostetter	John H.	03/01/1799	04/06/1871
Hulon	James W.	1840	04/16/1907
Hulon	John	10/30/1845	9/9/1915
Hulon	William	1803	unknown
Irvine	Benjamin F.	08/19/1821	01/6/1902
Irvine	Peter Belles	1823	01/11/1863
Kellett	John G.	1826	07/29/1865
Kellett	James M.	1811	before 1870
Kelsey	Samuel L.	Feb. 1816	02/10/1878
King	Thomas E.	03/21/1840	02/8/1919
Lewis	Eldon	10/29/1833	Dec. 1864
Lewis	John M.	11/29/1837	04/8/1908
Lindley	Elijah	03/20/1835	07/28/1880
Lindley	James	03/20/1835	07/28/1880
Lindley	John	03/13/1831	10/18/1895
Little	Hiram	04/09/1809	09/13/1891
Little	Jonathan	05/26/1836	unknown
Long	E. A.	unknown	unknown
McCarley	James	1840	02/08/1836
McCrory	Marion A.	04/1834	12/30/1895
McGilvary	Alexander	about 1844	11/30/1864
McIntyre	James R.	1832	after 1911

McIntyre	Jesse	03/03/1835	06/13/1903
Malone	Thomas M.	11/18/1835	about 1867
Malone	William F.	1835	10/8/1907
Mayfield	Samuel B.	about 1825	03/13/1905
Nichols	George J.	about 1831	03/18/1863
Norsworthy	James H.	1840	11/11/1862
O'Banion	John R.	about 1831	after 04/1864
O'Banion	William H.	04/22/1827	05/09/1913
Perry	William	1835	unknown
Pincham	Peter	1797	10/15/1867
Quick	George J.	about 1831	03/29/1863
Reding	George W.	02/12/1825	10/18/1888
Reding	John B.	03/05/1817	10/27/1877
Richards	Augustus	10/02/1816	11/18/1913
Rogers	William D.	about 1827	unknown
Roten	David E.	05/01/1834	09/10/1917
Sandell	Erastus E.	06/27/1836	03/1901
Seale	William J.	about 1844	unknown
Spear	Thomas J.	09/27/1837	08/02/1862
Tarpley	Barbee	01/29/1842	04/8/1909
Terry	Samuel	about 1831	after 04/1865
Thomason	Francis M.	01/26/1843	12/16/1876
Thomason	Jabez S.	11/27/1827	06/13/1908
Thomason	James B.	abt 1832	01/11/1863
Truitt	Roland K.	08/23/1841	05/18/1930
Viser	William W.	06/19/1830	09/25/1901
Waters	William	02/07/1825	05/6/1907
Webb	George W.	about 1820	unknown
Weisinger	Samuel	06/27/1818	01/16/1897
Whitten	John D. G.	10/27/1836	10/20/1894
Westmoreland	John T.	about 1838	10/29/1911
Westmoreland	Joseph M.	1827	1904
Woodson	John C.	1844	unknown
Woodson	William H.	04/13/1834	01/13/1894
Wooldridge	Edmond D. T.	05/31/1854	10/20/1926
Wooldridge	Samuel D.	09/21/1823	05/18/1890
Worthy	Albert V.	about 1820	after 1880

* KAREN McCANN HETT is the historian for The Danville Mounted Rifeman, a militia company of 80 men raised in Montgomery County by Captain Samuel D. Wooldridge. Profiles for each of these men, as well as a capsule history, can be viewed on her website. She provided the information about these men found in this book on pages 22; 54-55; 57-58; 60-61; 68-69; 83; 173-175) as well as other information. For other works about the Riflemen by Ms. Hett, see *The Herald* (Conroe, Tx: MCG&HS), Vols. 27-31 and her website at *http://freepages.genealogy.rootsweb.ancestry.com/~barrettbranches/Researchers/Karen%20Hett/B24cavindex.html*.

17th Brigade (17th Militia District)

For most Confederate soldiers, joining the local militia was a staging period which led to their induction into the regular army, but for some soldiers, service in the militia would be their chief contribution to the Southern cause. These men reported to camp, drilled, and trained just as the men in the regular army but because of age or other encumbrances, were unable to travel to far-away battlefields. In addition to continued military training, these men served as the home guard to protect the local citizens in the event of hostile Indian incursions, riots, civil unrest, or general lawlessness. The 17th Brigade, as well as the other brigades of Texas militia, was a constantly-changing unit. Frequent elections were held to replace officers who transferred to the regular army. While it is likely that some soldiers tried to use their service in the militia to avoid regular service, there are few records that would indicate that they were successful in avoiding conscription (the draft). Listed here are the names of ninety-five Confederate soldiers from Montgomery County who have not been found on the rolls of any units other than the 17th Brigade of Texas State Troops (militia).

Last Name	First, Middle Name	Born	Died
Abney	H. H.	about 1827	about 1870
Anders	Jacob	02/14/1827	06/27/1909
Anderson	E. A.	02/01/1820	12/11/1896
Bailey	James A.	05/07/1829	06/03/1911
Baker	William Henry	about 1844	unknown
Bay	Andrew F.	04/01/1817	04/25/1878
Bay	William Harrison	11/10/1815	08/10/1897
Brooks,	Somerville M.	about 1844	02/05/1908
Caldwell,	William	03/10/1844	08/15/1897
Cathey	J. C.	about 1817	after 1870
Childers	Douglas	10/19/1819	08/09/1911
Collier	A. B.	about 1825	about 1908
Collins	R. D.	about 1841	about 1865
Cone	Monroe Martin	06/22/1846	09/12/1921
Curry	James L.	about 1824	unknown
Dabney	Joel G.	about 1825	unknown
Davis	Nathaniel Hart	11/06/1815	10/08/1893
Davis	William Humphrey	about 1826	about 1899
Day	E. S.	unknown	unknown
Dean	William Aylett	03/22/1827	01/19/1899
Decker	Isaac Cryle	02/18/1829	after 1874
Denman	Chapleigh Hampton	05/16/1819	05/07/1894
Dunlap	James Marion	about 1825	after 1900
Forshee	George Washington	about 1820	10/15/1881
Fowler	John W.	about 1816	05/28/1899
Fox	Samuel	about 1825	unknown
Gatlin	William Riley	05/13/1833	06/29/1908
George	John Edmund	07/22/1821	09/24/1875
Gibson	Anthony Palmer	11/17/1818	02/24/1895

Gholston	Frank Henry	about 1822	about 1869
Golding	Reuben Griffin	about 1815	unknown
Goodson	Arthur	about 1799	02/18/1863
Hardy	John	about 1808	09/01/1884
Harrington	William Calvin	about 1822	05/23/1918
Harrison	William	about 1821	after 1870
Holland	W. P.	about 1821	unknown
Hughes	Henry S.	about 1818	unknown
Hulon	John Spiller	10/30/1845	09/09/1915
Hulon	William Henry	about 1803	unknown
Irvine	Benjamin Franklin	08/19/1821	01/06/1902
Jefferies	William Cantrel	about 1826	05/17/1888
Jones	William T.	about 1839	unknown
Kellett	John Garland	about 1826	07/29/1865
Kellett	James Madison	about 1811	before 1870
Kelsey	Samuel L.	about 1816	02/10/1878
Kirby	Jeff	about 1821	unknown
Lacey	Cicero Daniel	06/22/1839	01/12/1927
Lacey	Milan Carile Lacey	about 1844	before 1873
Lindsey	G. W.	about 1828	unknown
Linton	William	about 1831	05/21/1898
Lipscomb	A. S.	07/26/1826	04/01/1873
Little	Hiram	04/09/1809	09/13/1891
Long	E. A.	unknown	unknown
Love	A. J.	unknown	unknown
Mayfield	Samuel Brooks	about 1825	1899
McClure	A. J.	about 1843	unknown
McGilvary	John Martin	12/20/1812	05/18/1878
McRae	James M.	about 1822	unknown
McNeese	Ivy	about 1811	unknown
Moorfield	Henry	about 1824	unknown
Morris	Samuel	about 1825	unknown
Mostyn	Henry	about 1841	before 1866
Muckle	Jeptha	03/17/1828	07/20/1899
Norsworthy	Wyley B.	about 1816	about 1883
O'Banion	William Hamilton	04/22/1827	05/09/1913
Palmer	Reuben Jonathan	01/18/1829	03/20/1868
Pankey	F. B.	about 1798	unknown
Phillips	Abram B.	about 1820	about 1877
Phillips	George Nix	10/09/1825	03/11/1877
Pincham	Peter	about 1797	10/15/1867
Pinkston	Nathaniel	about 1834	02/28/1905
Rankin	Thomas Berry	03/30/1815	09/30/1885
Reding	James A.	about 1825	about 1864
Richards	Augustus	10/02/1816	11/18/1913
Robb	J. A.	about 1817	unknown
Roberts	Green	about 1811	1870
Rogers	James M.	09/06/1824	01/28/1871

Scott	John N.	08/15/1825	01/01/1913
Singletary	J. M.	about 1838	unknown
Simonton	Robert S.	about 1816	about 1863
Steed	Willis H.	about 1818	after 1880
Stewart	James Samuel	09/11/1823	02/07/1908
Walters	William W.	02/07/1825	05/06/1907
Weatherford	Jones E.	05/15/1828	06/01/1883
Webb	George Washington	08/02/1820	05/02/1898
Westmoreland	Joseph Mark	about 1827	about 1904
Wickson	James	about 1836	unknown
Wickson	Peter	about 1841	unknown
Williams	Williamston	05/15/1817	10/18/1897
Wood	Green Mark	09/07/1814	03/05/1898
Wood	William H.	05/17/1814	02/20/1884
Woodson	John C.	about 1844	after 1880
Worsham	Israel	about 1820	about 1882
Wyche	G. W.	about 1823	03/04/1871

4th Infantry Regiment, Texas State Troops
(1863-1864) (for six months)

A conflict which is often overlooked in both Texas history and accounts of the War between the States is an invasion of the Texas coastline by Union troops in the late fall of 1863. In November 1863, a U.S. Army force of approximately 7,500 men under the command of Major General Nathaniel Banks landed near the mouth of the Rio Grand River at Brazos Santiago. Accompanied by Union gunboats, the force made its way northward along the Texas coast seizing ports at Corpus Christi and Aransas Pass. By the end of December, Union troops had taken Fort Esperanza at the end of Matagorda Island and Fort Velasco at the mouth of the Brazos River.

Fearing the Union forces might attempt to retake Galveston or make its way up the Brazos River behind the Texas coastal defenses, Confederate General John Bankhead Magruder moved his headquarters to the McNeel plantation near present-day Lake Jackson. In addition, he ordered men from the 17th Brigade and other militia districts into immediate Confederate service forming the 4th Infantry Regiment of Texas State Troops.

Although the regiment carried the title Texas State Troops, these soldiers were now regular Confederate Army soldiers and no longer militia. They were enlisted for a period of six months and were detailed to fortify and maintain a stronghold on the Texas coast near the mouth of Caney Creek. The fortification known as Camp Caney was a crude sand and earth structure with several cannons guarding the opening of Caney Creek into Matagorda Bay. These structures were connected to rifle pits which guarded the rear of the camp.

While no infantry battles occurred, the fortress was intermittently shelled by Union gunboats. The men of the 4th Infantry Regiment were joined by numerous cavalry and artillery regiments from the Trans-Mississippi Department and with such a formidable force focused on the this area, General Banks decided to withdraw from the Texas coastline and support the failing Union effort in Louisiana. On March 31, 1864, the U.S. troops returned to their ships and did not return to Texas until the final battle of the war was fought and won by Confederate troops at the Battle of Palmetto Ranch near Brownsville.

There are few Confederate service records for the men in this regiment and the few files that exist are likely incomplete, but some of the muster rolls for the men from Montgomery County state that they were "camped in the field near Caney." After these men served their six-month tour of duty, some re-enlisted in Colonel D. S. Terry's Regiment of Texas Cavalry. There are no records to show that the 17th Brigade still existed after the creation of Terry's Cavalry, but it is likely that there was some remnant of a home guard.

Montgomery County Men the 4th Infantry TST

Company D

Last Name	First, Middle Name	Born	Died
Abbott	George	about 1820	unknown
Bailey	William Henry	04/12/1821	01/11/1895
Bay	James H.	11/26/1821	01/27/1884
Brantner	George H.	about 1827	about 1871
Caldwell	S. H.	about 1846	unknown
Campbell	Clark Calhoun	about 1824	7/27/1907
Campbell	John Wesley	05/12/1829	12/8/1915
Cartwright	Joseph C.	05/31/1831	01/24/1904
Close	J. E.	about 1825	unknown
Culbertson	James M.	about 1826	about 1889
Darden	W. T.	1823	unknown
Davis	Gary	1826	1899
Deadrick	John	1818	unknown
Dean	John	01/08/1822	1879
English	J. E.	about 1816	about 1886
Evans	Joseph M.	about 1820	unknown
Gafford	James O.	1824	12/1879
Glass	William	about 1829	11/15/1894
Goodrich	J. M.	about 1819	unknown
Goodson	William Walter	1824	03/30/1899
Griffin	J. E.	about 1823	12/19/1888
Griffin	W. R.	1844	unknown
Hays	Lewis	about 1840	unknown
Hicks	James Monroe	about 1818	unknown

Johnson	G. W.	about 1833	unknown
Judson	John	about 1817	unknown
Kelsey	Samuel L.	02/1816	02/10/1878
Liles	Thomas Jefferson	07/14/1840	06/26/1881
Love	R. O.	about 1818	unknown
Lowery	Allen	about 1818	about 1900
Lucky	John F.	about 1820	unknown
Lynch	D. B.	02/14/1823	06/20/1878
Martin	Claiborne A.	1844	unknown
Matthews	Harmon	about 1845	unknown
Meeks	Archibald	about 1818	after 1870
Mochman	Wilhelm Robert E.	04/28/1828	01/01/1880
Morehead	Sanford V.	about 1816	unknown
Morris	Benjamin F.	about 1822	before 1880
Norman	J.	about 1816	unknown
Oliver	Robert F.	about 1817	after 1890
Pitts	James Harrison	10/02/1818	04/20/1884
Reding	John Baker	03/05/1817	10/27/1877
Reding	George W.	02/12/1825	10/18/1888
Rodgerson	William	1816	1900
Sanders	J. F.	1823	unknown
Sheets	A.	about 1834	unknown
Stowe	John W.	about 1817	about 1871
Thomas	William	about 1823	about 1870
Uzzell	Elisha Bryant	12/26/1843	05/25/1928
Weisinger	Samuel	06/27/1818	01/16/1897
Westbrook	J. A.	about 1834	after 1880
Williamson	John H.	11/03/1823	5/16/1905
Winslow	William	06/10/1824	06/18/1896
Womack	Francis Hancock	05/26/1815	about 1875

Company E

Denmon	William Absolum	03/25/1846	09/1/1919

Company H

Horton	Thomas	1822	unknown
Sapp	Forsyth H.	02/14/1834	04/7/1908

The Texas Brigades

Hiram B. Granbury
photo courtesy of Southern Methodist
University, DeGolyer Library,
Lawrence T. Jones III Collection

John Bell Hood
photo courtesy of
U. S. Library of Congress

When the title of "Texas Brigade" is mentioned in the history of the War between the States, it is most often referring to "Hood's Texas Brigade" in the Confederate Army of Northern Virginia. Although it is seldom noted, there were two prominent Texas infantry brigades. While Hood's Brigade is widely known for its role in major battles such as Gettysburg and Antietam, only Granbury's Texas Brigade participated in campaigns in both the eastern and western theaters of the war, and both Texas brigades participated in the Battle of Chickamauga. Approximately eighty-three men from Montgomery County served in Hood's Texas Brigade. Thirty of those are known to have died during the war. There were twenty-three men from Montgomery County who are known to have served in Granbury's Texas Brigade. All of these men in Granbury's Brigade were members of the 24th Texas Cavalry (Dismounted). While the number of Montgomery County men in Granbury's Texas Brigade is lower than the number of men who served in Hood's Texas Brigade, it should be noted that Granbury's Brigade was not formed until November 1863. This does not take into account the one-hundred-and-ten men from Montgomery County who originally enlisted in the 24th Texas Cavalry or the two Montgomery County men who enlisted in Company A, 10th Texas Infantry.

Hood's Texas Brigade

The first Texas Brigade was organized on October 21, 1861 in Richmond, Virginia and was commanded by Colonel Louis T. Wigfall. It originally consisted of the 1st, 4th, and the 5th Texas Infantry Regiments and the 18th Georgia Infantry Regiment. On June 1, 1862, eight infantry companies from Wade Hampton's South Carolina Legion were added. In November 1862, the 3rd Arkansas Infantry joined the brigade, replacing the Georgia and South Carolina units. Wigfall resigned as commander of the brigade in February 1862 to take a seat in the Confederate Congress. On March 7, Colonel John Bell Hood, commander of the 4th Texas Infantry Regiment, was promoted to Brigadier General and placed in command of the brigade. This unit would become known as Hood's Texas Brigade for the remainder of the war. This brigade participated in the battles of Eltham's Landing, Seven Pines (Fair Oaks), Gaines' Mill, Second Manassas, Antietam (Sharpsburg), Fredericksburg, Gettysburg, Chickamauga, Wilderness, Cold Harbor, Petersburg, and Appomattox.

Two attorneys from Montgomery County, Procter P. Porter and Robert M. Powell, were among the first in their area to organize groups of men to serve in the Confederate Army. Robert M. Powell organized a company of men known as the Waverly Confederates which became Company D, 5th Texas Infantry, and Procter P. Porter organized a company of men known as the Porter Guards which became Company H, 4th Texas Infantry. They were joined by a company of men primarily from Grimes County known as Captain John W. Hutcheson's Grimes County Grays. Both Porter and Hutcheson were mortally wounded during the Battle of Gaines' Mill on June 27, 1862. Both captains were transported to the Richmond home of Corbin Warwick where Captain Hutcheson died two days later. His body was taken to his childhood home in Mecklenburg County, Virginia and buried on the grounds of his father's plantation. Captain Porter was transferred to a Confederate hospital in Richmond where he died on July 10, 1862. His body was interred at Hollywood Cemetery in Richmond. Lieutenant J. T. Hunter from Walker County was promoted to captain of Company H, and he served as company commander for the remainder of the war.

Col. Robert M. Powell
photo courtesy of
Robert Reichardt

Robert Micajah Powell of Danville, Texas rose from the rank of captain to major on August 22, 1862 and to colonel in command of the 5th Texas Infantry Regiment on November 1, 1862. While leading the 5th Texas Infantry at the Battle of Gettysburg on July 2, 1863, Colonel Powell was wounded and taken prisoner. After leaving the field hospital at Gettysburg, Colonel Powell was confined for a short period of time at the military prison at Fort McHenry and then transferred to Johnson's Island Prison in Ohio. After two hard winters in Ohio, Colonel Powell was transferred from Johnson's Island to Fort McHenry and later to Fortress Monroe, Virginia where he was released and exchanged on February 6, 1865. In March of 1865, Colonel Powell became the last commander of Hood's Texas Brigade. The brigade had dwindled from over 5,000 men to about 700, and on April 9, 1865, Colonel Powell surrendered with his brigade and the rest of the Army of Northern Virginia at Appomattox Court House. Of the original eighty-four Montgomery County men in Hood's Texas Brigade, only fifteen were present at the final surrender.

Granbury's Texas Brigade

Although Granbury's Texas Brigade existed for only eighteen months, the men in this brigade participated in some of the bloodiest battles in the war while suffering some of the highest casualties of any unit in the Confederacy. When Confederate Brigadier General James Deshler was killed at the Battle of Chickamauga on September 20, 1863, command of his brigade was temporarily transferred to Colonel Roger Q. Mills. By mid-October, Brigadier General James A. Smith was given permanent command of the brigade. At this time, the brigade consisted of the 6th and 10th Texas Infantry and 15th Texas Cavalry (Consolidated), the 17th, 18th, 24th, and 25th Texas Dismounted Cavalry (Consolidated), and the 9th and 24th Arkansas Infantry (Consolidated). In early November, the Arkansas regiments were reassigned and were replaced by the 7th Texas Infantry commanded by Colonel Hiram Granbury forming an all-Texas brigade. At the Battle of Missionary Ridge on November 25, 1863, General James A. Smith was severely wounded, and Colonel Hiram Granbury took command of the brigade.

As a part of Major General Patrick Cleburne's Division, Granbury's Texas Brigade began its road to fame by holding the Confederate Army's right flank against an all-out attack by Union General William Tecumseh Sherman. Despite intense fighting and heroic efforts, Cleburne's Division, the center of the Confederate line, collapsed, forcing the army to retreat into Georgia.

The reputation of Granbury's Texas Brigade continued to grow while covering the Confederate retreat into Georgia. At a mountain pass known as Ringgold Gap, the 4,100 men of Cleburne's Division halted the advance of General Joseph Hooker's 12,000 Union troops for more than five hours, allowing the Confederate wagons and artillery to pass through the gap unharmed.

On November 28, 1863, after giving his report of the Chattanooga campaign, Confederate General Braxton Bragg asked to be relieved as commander of the Army of Tennessee. President Jefferson Davis ordered General Joseph E. Johnston to replace him on December 18, 1863.

On May 4, 1864, General William T. Sherman, replacing General U. S. Grant as commander of the Military Division of Mississippi, began his campaign to take Atlanta. Now having three U.S. armies under his command, Sherman began a series of flanking that continuously pushed Johnston's army back toward Atlanta. Jefferson Davis' concerns that General Johnston would not stand and fight prompted him to replace Johnston on July 17, 1864 with the more aggressive John Bell Hood. Although the fighting intensified, the results of the Confederate efforts saw little change, and on September 1, 1864, the city of Atlanta was evacuated.

In an attempt to draw General Sherman's troops out of Georgia, General Hood began his ill-fated invasion of Tennessee. Among the most costly of Hood's engagements in Tennessee was the Battle of Franklin on November 30,

1864. In a massive assault by eighteen brigades and almost 20,000 men, the Confederate Army of Tennessee lost fourteen generals. Seven generals were wounded, one was captured, and six were killed or mortally wounded. Among the dead were Major General Patrick Cleburne and Brigadier General Hiram Granbury. Although General Hood changed strategies and used defensive tactics at the ensuing battle of Nashville, his army was forced to retreat from the battlefield by overwhelming Union forces.

After Hood's Tennessee campaign, Granbury's Texas Brigade was reduced to approximately 440 men and was reorganized as Granbury's Consolidated Brigade, Texas Cavalry (1st Consolidated Regiment). Only eight men from Montgomery County were present when this regiment surrendered at Durham Station, North Carolina on April 26, 1865.

The Regiments

1st Texas Regiment, Heavy Artillery
(Cook's Regiment Heavy Artillery)

At the time Texas seceded from the Union, the largest city in the state was Galveston. In addition, it was the state's largest seaport. With the arrival of Union ships off the coast of Galveston in July 1861, the 3rd Battalion of Texas Artillery was formed to defend the city. In early 1862, many of the infantry and cavalry regiments that had been stationed in Galveston had been transferred out of state. As a result, the artillery battalion was expanded to a full regiment, becoming the 1st Texas Regiment, Heavy Artillery and commanded by Colonel Joseph Jarvis Cook. This regiment was the primary line of defense during the first battle of Galveston, fought on October 4, 1862 and supported the re-taking of the island during the second battle of Galveston on New Year's Day 1863.

The 1st Texas Heavy Artillery is most often remembered for the exploits of Company F, better known as the Davis Guards. This company, named for Confederate President Jefferson Davis, was composed of forty-five enlisted men, one engineer, one surgeon, and commanded by Captain Frederick H. Odlum. The men were all Irish, all under the age of thirty, and had been hand-picked from dock workers in Houston and Galveston. This unit had originally been created as more of a social club and held meetings at a bar in Houston known as the Bank of Bacchus. This bar was owned by Captain Odlum's son-in-law, 1st Lt. Richard "Dick" Dowling, who would later become captain and commander of the company.

In the spring of 1863, General John Magruder ordered the Davis Guards to man a defensive position at the mouth of the Sabine River near Sabine Pass. On September 8, 1863, the Davis Guards, under the command of Richard "Dick" Dowling, routed a Union invasion force, capturing two Union gunboats and taking 350 prisoners without having a single casualty.

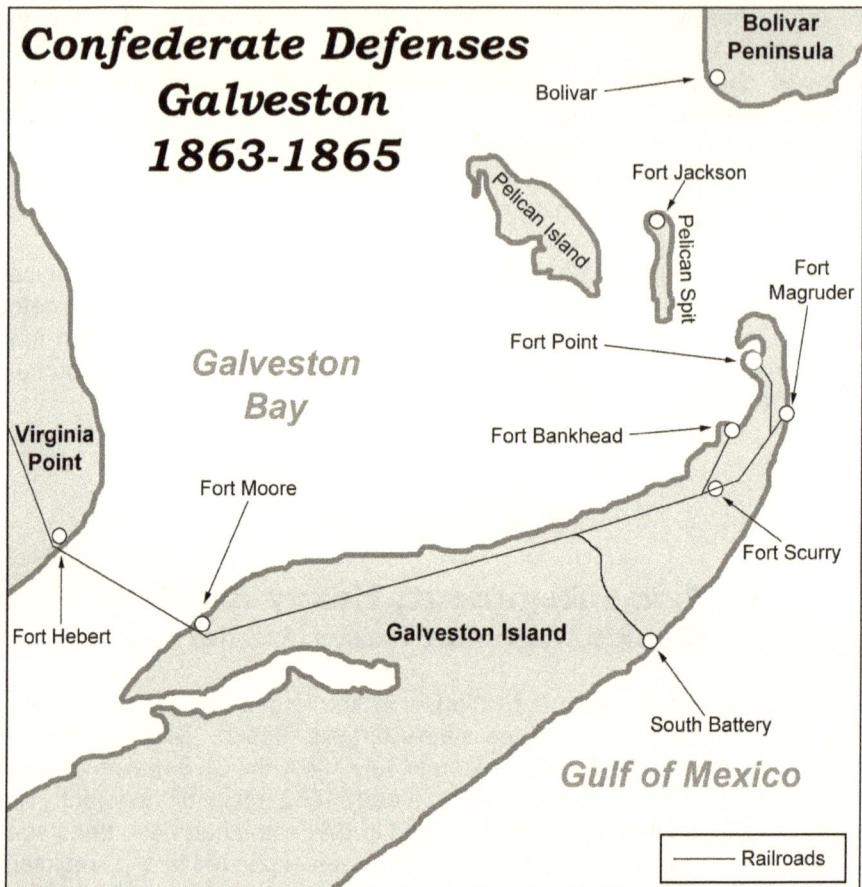

Confederate Defenses
Galveston
1863-1865

Bolivar Peninsula
Bolivar
Fort Jackson
Pelican Island
Fort Magruder
Pelican Spit
Fort Point
Galveston Bay
Fort Bankhead
Virginia Point
Fort Moore
Fort Scurry
Fort Hebert
Galveston Island
South Battery
Gulf of Mexico
Railroads

After the re-taking of Galveston in 1863, the 1st Texas Heavy Artillery prevented any further invasion of the island. The regiment's defenses were so formidable that the greatest threat to its men became boredom and yellow fever. Soldiers transferred in and out of the regiment on a regular basis. For this reason, many of the men were not recorded on the muster rolls, and since nearly all enlistments took place at Galveston, there are few references to the soldier's county of residence. All of these elements combined makes it nearly impossible to determine how many men from Montgomery County actually served in the 1st Texas Heavy Artillery. However, if their names do not appear on the official rolls as having served in the 1st Texas Heavy Artillery, they often appear on the rolls of other regiments.

Four of the members of Company D, 1st Texas Heavy Artillery were from an area in southeastern Montgomery County known as the Boggy Precinct or Boggy Prairie. All four of these men, Benjamin F. Martin, Francis Marion Metts, Joseph Robert Metts, and Richard Outlaw, transferred to Company C, 9th Texas Infantry (Nichols) just one month after enlisting in the artillery. Daniel A. McCaskill of Company D, transferred to the 20th Texas Infantry in the spring of 1863.

The muster rolls for Company G, 1st Texas Heavy Artillery show that four brothers, Calvin, Daniel, Henry, and Sabert Oglesby, enlisted on March 25, 1862. All four of these men spent the majority of their periods of service with the 1st Heavy Artillery—either in the hospital or sick at home—and the oldest brother Daniel, died in camp at Galveston in February 1865. Since none of these men appear on subsequent census rolls in Texas, it is possible that all died before 1870. Their father, Sabert Oglesby, Sr., who married Lucrecy Ford in Montgomery County, Texas on August 26, 1852, died in Coryell County, Texas in 1877 at the age of one-hundred-and-one years old.

Montgomery County Men in the 1st Texas Regiment, Heavy Artillery

Company B

Bell, James Henry – Enlisted as private at age 40 on October 19, 1861. Discharged July 1, 1862 being over age and term of enlistment having expired.

Company D

Martin, Benjamin F. – Enlisted as private at age 17 on October 3, 1861. Mustered into service by Major Cook as member of Pelican Battery. Transferred to Waul's Texas Legion.

McCaskill, Daniel A. – Enlisted as private at age 23 on September 17, 1861. Mustered into service by Lt. Sparks at Houston, Texas. Member of Pelican Battery, Galveston, Texas, December 27, 1861. On detached service November & December 1862. Last shown present in April 1863.

Metts, Francis Marion – Enlisted as private at age 17 on October 3, 1861. Mustered into service by Major Cook as member of Pelican Battery. Last shown present in November 1861. Transferred to Waul's Texas Legion.

Metts, Robert – Enlisted as private at age 20 on October 3, 1861. Mustered into service by Major Cook as member of Pelican Battery. Last shown present in November 1861. Transferred to Waul's Texas Legion.

Outlaw, Richard - Enlisted as private at age 20 on October 3, 1861. Mustered into service by Major Cook as member of Pelican Battery. Last shown present in November 1861. Transferred to Waul's Texas Legion.

Company G

Oglesby, Calvin – Enlisted March 25, 1862. Sick at home June 26, 1862. Sick in hospital at Houston, September 1864. Sick at home in Montgomery, February 1865.

Oglesby, Daniel – Enlisted March 25, 1862. Died in camp at Galveston in February 1865.

Oglesby, Henry – Enlisted March 25, 1862. Sick in Harris County, March & April 1863.

Oglesby, Sabert – Enlisted March 25, 1862. Sick in Montgomery County, January 1864.

2nd Regiment, Texas Cavalry (2nd Mounted Rifles)

The 2nd Regiment, Texas Cavalry, also known as the 2nd Mounted Rifles, was first formed in May of 1861 with six companies as the 2nd Texas Mounted Rifles under the command of Lieutenant Colonel John Robert Baylor and participated in the New Mexico campaign. This regiment was reorganized in April of 1862 as the 2nd Texas Cavalry and was involved with the recapture of Galveston on January 1, 1863. It went on to participate in many battles in Louisiana. While it appears that at the time this cavalry was formed, there were no Montgomery County residents who served in this regiment, six members of Company K were former residents of Montgomery County and prominently linked to county history. All six of these men were the sons of William Arthur Cude, Jr. who moved to Montgomery County in 1839 and died there on May 1, 1847.

Company K

Cude, Alfred Jackson – Corporal. Enlisted age 21 on September 23, 1861 at Fort Brown, Brownsville, Texas. Wounded in action on June 21, 1863 in Louisiana.

Cude, Nathaniel Wiley – Private. Enlisted age 25 in January, 1862 at Columbus, Texas. Last appears on roll of Confederate General Hospital in Houston showing to have been admitted on January 19, 1863 and returned to duty on January 26, 1862.

Cude, Richard Dowling – Sergeant. Enlisted age 19 on October 1, 1863 at Moulton, Texas. Last shown present on roll of January & February 1864. Signed Parole of Honor at Columbus, Texas on July 25, 1865.

Cude, Timothy J. – Does not appear on rolls but Confederate pension application #14657 which was approved on August 31, 1909 shows that he enlisted in February 1864 and served close to one year in Company K, 2nd Texas Cavalry. Affidavits by A. B. Butler and C. Jones of Company K, attest to his service.

Cude, Tobias A. – Private. Enlisted age 36 on September 23, 1861 at Fort Brown, Brownsville, Texas. Roll of February 28 to June 30, 1863 shows sick in hospital in Louisiana. Died in hospital at Columbus, Texas, July 13, 1863

Cude, Willis Franklin – Private. Enlisted age 17 on September 23, 1861 at Fort Brown, Brownsville, Texas. POW at Algiers Prison in New Orleans, Louisiana after being captured June 21, 1863 at Lafourche Crossing. Shown detached as courier February, 1865. Signed Parole of Honor at Columbus, Texas on July 25, 1865.

4th Texas Infantry

In April of 1861, the Confederate States War Department sent requests to Texas Governor Edward Clark asking Texas to raise a total of 8,000 troops for Confederate service. Among the earliest regiments to be organized as a result of this request was the 4th Texas Infantry Regiment. Its members were recruited in the counties of Bexar, Ellis, Falls, Freestone, Goliad, Grimes,

Guadalupe, Henderson, Hill, McLennan, Montgomery, Navarro, Robertson, Travis, and Walker. After being brigaded with 1st and 5th Texas Infantries, it became know as the Texas Brigade, and after Colonel John Bell Hood of the 4th Texas Infantry was promoted to the rank of brigadier general in command of this brigade, it would forever become known as Hood's Texas Brigade. The 4th Texas Infantry Regiment served with the Confederate Army of Northern Virginia from the Peninsula campaign in the spring of 1862 until the final surrender at Appomattox Court House in April of 1865. It also fought with the Confederate Army of Tennessee at the Battle of Chickamauga.

Perhaps the best-known Confederate unit from Montgomery County was Company H, 4th Texas Infantry. More than one-third of the total number of men who served in this company were from Montgomery County. Company H, also known as the Porter Guards, has often been touted as the largest group of Confederate soldiers from the county. While that statement is far from being accurate, Company H, was one of only two companies to serve in the Army of Northern Virginia and played a major role in some of the most significant battles of the War between the States. Alongside Company D, the Waverly Confederates of the 5th Texas Infantry, this company served in the famed Hood's Texas Brigade. One-hundred-three men in Company H left Texas to join the Army of Northern Virginia in 1861, being reinforced by thirty-seven new recruits in 1862 and another five recruits in 1863, totaling 145 men. When General Robert E. Lee surrendered the Army of Northern Virginia at Appomattox in 1865, only eleven men remained in Company H, including two soldiers from Montgomery County, Corporal James H. Hall and Private Henry Keyser. Of the fifty-one men from Montgomery County to serve in this company, twenty-one either were killed in action or died in hospitals, and another nineteen were discharged due to disability.

At least one Montgomery County man, Lawrence A. Daffin, traveled to Anderson in Grimes County and enlisted in Captain John Hutcheson's Company G, of the 4th Texas Infantry. This company also was known as the Grimes County Grays. Daffin was part of a second wave of recruits that traveled to Virginia in the spring of 1862. Although he was shown on the rolls of the 1860 Montgomery County census, he may have moved to Grimes County prior to enlistment.

Soon after Texas had officially seceded, several units began gathering men to be inducted into the Confederate States Army. One of the earliest of these units to be organized was the Porter Guards, named for Procter Prentice Porter, an attorney from the town of Montgomery and a former general of the 17th Brigade of Texas State Troops. Porter, with the aid of James T. Hunter of Walker County, raised a company of more than one hundred men in Montgomery, Grimes, and Walker Counties and organized them at Red Top (Prairie Plains) in Grimes County on May 7, 1861. Here, Procter Porter was elected captain, James T. Hunter of Walker County was elected first lieutenant, Thomas M. Owens of Grimes County was elected second lieutenant, and Benton Randolph of Walker County was elected third lieutenant.

In August of 1861, the Porter Guards marched to Harrisburg where they boarded a train heading east toward the Sabine River. There the men boarded a steamer bound for Neblett's Bluff. Leaving Neblett's Bluff, they were subjected to heavy rains and treacherous swamps on their march to Brashear City where they boarded a train to New Orleans. Arriving at New Orleans in early September, the Porter Guards stopped briefly to prepare for the long rail trip to Virginia. The first casualty among the newly-formed company occurred at Holly Springs, Mississippi when Private E. G. Cartwright was killed in a tragic train accident. An unconfirmed story relates that Private Cartwright was trying to impress the local ladies as he attempted to jump onto a moving rail car. He supposedly tripped and fell beneath the departing train, severing both legs.

The company reached Richmond, Virginia in mid-September and set up camp near the James River. The 4th Texas Infantry Regiment mustered into Confederate service on September 30, 1861. Once the men had been formally mustered in, they began demanding that their current commander, Colonel R. T. P. Allen, be replaced. Colonel Allen resigned, and the men of the 4th Texas quickly elected Colonel John Bell Hood as his replacement.

A combination of traveling for weeks and poor living conditions within the camp began taking its toll on the regiment. Many of the men became ill within a few days. In October, Privates D. D. Farrow, Albert Faulkner, T. R. Mathews, Alex Taylor, and Frank H. Wade were all seriously ill in nearby hospitals. John P. Rogers died October 17, 1861, and D. D. Farrow died December 12, 1861. Privates Albert Faulkner and T. R. Mathews both were discharged in December 1861 and were sent home. The harsh winter and the soldiers' exposure to the elements continued to take its toll throughout the winter and early spring of 1862. Corporal A. C. Morris died from typhoid fever in Dumfries, Virginia on February 2, 1862. Private Albert Holt was admitted to the hospital March 30, 1862 with frost bite and discharged on a surgeon's certificate of disability, July 28, 1862. Private Theodore W. Wilcox was left sick in Fredricksburg on April 8, 1862 and died there on April 12, and Private Bennett H. Cathey died April 30, 1862. Forty-eight-year-old Private C. B. Sanders entered the hospital on May 20, 1862 and was discharged by a surgeon's certificate of disability on July 28, 1862. Private W. G. Leach died of typhoid fever in the hospital at Danville, Virginia on June 20, 1862.

In March of 1862, the Union Army commanded by Major General George B. McClellan began a large-scale offensive known as the Peninsula campaign. McClellan had a few small successes against the conservative Confederate General Joseph Johnston, but most of these battles were inconclusive. Corporal Hartwell T. Sapp of Company H was wounded in one such battle known as Yorktown or Eltham's Landing. When General Joseph Johnston was wounded at the Battle of Seven Pines, General Robert E. Lee took command of the Army of Northern Virginia. Now McClellan was confronted by a much more aggressive opponent.

Second Lieutenant Charles Edward Jones, who had been detailed to Montgomery County in February of 1862 to enlist more men for Company H, returned to Virginia during the Peninsula campaign with thirty-seven new recruits. Two of these new recruits were admitted to the hospital soon after their arrival in Virginia. Private R. D. Gifford died of disease at Richmond, May 25, 1862, and Private Thomas J. Myers died August 25, 1862.

General Lee reorganized his army in June 1862 and commanded the Army of Northern Virginia in a series of offensives known as the Seven Days Battles. Robert E. Lee's first major victory as commander would come on June 27, 1862 at the Battle of Gaines' Mill but at a very high price with nearly 8,000 casualties. It was the 4th Texas Infantry and the rest of Hood's Texas Brigade that turned the tide of that battle but also sustained some of the heaviest casualties. Among the greatest losses of the 4th Texas Infantry in the battle were Captain Procter P. Porter of Company H and Captain John William Hutcheson of Company G. Both men were mortally wounded and died a few days later. Other casualties from Company H included three men killed in action: Corporal C. M. Conrow, Private Reverious Quigley, and Private T. O. Wilkes. Among the wounded from Company H were Privates William Fisher, James Kirby, Clint Lewis, John Smith, Matthew Steussy, and Henry Travis. Private Clint Lewis, the son of John McClanahan Lewis, Sr., was permanently disabled during the battle and was sent to stay with family members in nearby Fincastle, Virginia where he died on July 28, 1862.

Following the Seven Days Battles, the 4th Texas Infantry participated in another decisive victory at the second Battle of Manassas (Bull Run), August 28 through August 30, 1862. It was here that 2nd Lieutenant Charles E. Jones, after working so diligently to reinforce Company H, was killed in action. Privates Samuel King, Lewis Levanture, James Sharp, and B. B. Wilkes were wounded. Private Levanture was taken prisoner, and Private King died from his wounds on October 4, 1862.

The 4th Texas Infantry left the Manassas Battlefield on September 1, 1862 moving north and crossing the Potomac River into Maryland where it set up camp on the Monocacy River near Frederick City before marching to Hagerstown, Maryland. While in Maryland, a copy of General Lee's order detailing his troop movements fell into the hands of the Union Army. Learning that General Lee had split his troops, Union General George McClellan hoped to attack the Army of Northern Virginia before it could reunite its forces. The 4th Texas Infantry was instrumental in temporarily halting the Union Army at South Mountain, Maryland, allowing Robert E. Lee to withdraw to Sharpsburg where he rejoined his divided army leading up to the Battle of Sharpsburg (Antietam) on September 17, 1862. Hood's Texas Brigade, which now consisted of the 18th Georgia Regiment, Hampton's Legion, and the 1st, 4th, and 5th Texas Infantries, was once again a prominent force in the fighting. Of the two hundred men left in the 4th Texas Infantry, more than half became casualties at the Battle of Sharpsburg. Privates Albert Faulkner and Richard Fox of Company H were killed in action. Sergeant James Cartwright, and Privates Burrel Anders and Thomas Mitchell were captured during the battle. While the Union Army claimed victory, the Battle of Sharpsburg was tactically inconclusive. Despite being outnumbered two-to-one, the Confederate Army still held the battlefield when the fighting was over and slowly moved back across the Potomac River into Virginia.

In December of 1862, the Confederate and Union Armies collided in Virginia at the battle of Fredricksburg. While the Confederate Army suffered more than 4,700 killed and wounded, this was less than half the number of Union casualties in yet another decisive Confederate victory. The men of Company H, escaped the battle virtually unscathed. This was the last major conflict before the Army of Northern Virginia took to winter quarters.

In June of 1863, General Robert E. Lee prepared for his second invasion into northern territory, and on the first day of July 1863, two great armies came face-to-face near the town of Gettysburg, Pennsylvania. The bloody three-day battle—from July 1st to July 3rd—would be the pivotal battle for the Army of Northern Virginia. A Confederate victory would have left Washington D.C. virtually cut off from most of the rest of the nation. Instead, it was a Union Army victory that turned the tide of the war and sent Lee's army back to Virginia for the last time.

On July 2, the 4th Texas Infantry was part of an offensive designed to break through the Union line near a hill known as Little Round Top. The rugged terrain of Little Round Top proved to be as formidable an enemy as the Union Army itself which, combined with 20,000 reinforcements from the Union V Corps, repulsed the Confederate attack. The intense fighting left Corporal Zach Landrum and Private Jacob Steussy of Company H permanently disabled. Corporal Landrum was shot through the thigh, and Private Steussy had to have his leg amputated. Private Robert Rankin, who was also wounded during the battle, was taken prisoner. The final day of battle on July 3 would include the failure of Pickett's charge, leading to the defeat and eventual retreat of the Army of Northern Virginia.

Because of the struggles with General Braxton Bragg's Confederate Army of Tennessee against his Union opponents, General Lee was forced to dispatch Longstreet's Corps to his aid. This corps included the 4th Texas Infantry and the rest of Hood's Texas Brigade. Their first major battle as part of the Army of Tennessee would be at Chickamauga Creek in Georgia. The Battle of Chickamauga on September 19th and 20th of 1863 would be the only major battle where the 4th Texas Infantry fought in the same army with fellow Montgomery County soldiers in the 10th Texas Infantry and 24th Texas Cavalry (Dismounted). It would prove to be the last major victory for the Confederate Army of Tennessee and would also come at a high price. Chickamauga would leave over 2,300 Confederate soldiers dead and almost 15,000 wounded. Among the dead was Private James A. Kirby of Company H, 4th Texas Infantry. Privates Burrel Anders and William S. Fisher were wounded in the battle.

In late September of 1863, General Longstreet led his corps of men on a campaign in eastern Tennessee near Knoxville. The only real effect of the Knoxville campaign was that it deprived General Bragg of badly-needed troops and prevented Longstreet from returning to Virginia before the armies went into winter quarters. One Montgomery County man, Private Lawrence A. Daffin of Company G, was captured near Kingston, Tennessee. He was first transferred to Louisville, Kentucky and then to Rock Island, Illinois where he spent the rest of the war.

In April 1864, the 4th Texas Infantry was back in Virginia and participated in the Battle of the Wilderness, fought May 5-7, 1864. Here Sergeant James G. W. Cartwright and Private Henry Travis were killed in action. Sergeant G. W. Dale was wounded during the battle.

In the summer of 1864, General U. S. Grant, commander of the Union Army, began his siege of Petersburg, Virginia, a struggle that would last until March 1865. On June 22, 1864, Private James H. Sharp was killed in action while in the trenches outside Petersburg. He was the last soldier from Montgomery County in Company H to be killed in the war.

On October 7, 1864 the Texas Brigade was ordered to spearhead an attack against Union breastworks on Darbytown Road southeast of Richmond. Many of the men found themselves pinned down short of the breastworks by artillery fire and Union sharpshooters along with Union cavalry armed with Spencer repeating rifles. Here Private Lemuel Cartwright and Sergeant Hartwell Sapp of Company H were wounded. Sergeant Sapp was taken prisoner and sent to the POW camp at Point Lookout, Maryland. Wounds received by Private Cartwright would result in has arm being amputated. He was later captured in 1865 while in the hospital at Richmond. Confederate General John Gregg commanding the Texas Brigade was shot through the neck and killed instantly during the battle.

In November 1864, the 4th Texas Infantry settled into winter quarters inside the Confederate defenses at Richmond. The spring of 1865 would include the fall of Richmond and of Petersburg as the Confederate Army was pushed to its final stand near Appomattox Court House. When General Lee surrendered the Army of Northern Virginia, only eleven men from Company H were present. The only remaining Company H member from Montgomery County was Private James H. Hall although former Company H member Private J. R. P. Jett was shown present as a member of the regimental staff.

Montgomery County Men
in the 4th Texas Infantry

Company G

Daffan, Lawrence Aylette – Private. Enlisted Grimes County, March 15, 1862. Sick at Charlottesville, May, 1862. Captured near Kingston, Tennessee November 19, 1863. Forwarded to Louisville, KY. POW at Rock Island, Illinois. January 20, 1864. Paroled at Rock Island Barracks June 19, 1865.

Company H

Officers:

Porter, Procter Prentice – Captain. Served as captain of Company H, from time of organization in May 1861 until he was wounded in the thigh at the Battle of Gaines' Mill, Virginia June 27, 1862. Died in Institute Hospital, Richmond, Virginia July 20, 1862 and buried in Hollywood Cemetery.

Jones, Charles Edward – 2nd Lieutenant. Enlisted Montgomery County, May 7, 1861 by James T. Hunter. Promoted from sergeant to 2nd lieutenant October 25, 1861. Detailed to Montgomery County recruiting for regiment February 1862. Killed at 2nd Battle of Manassas August 30, 1862.

Enlisted Men:

Anders, Burrel (Burrill) – Private. Enlisted April 7, 1862 by C. E. Jones. Captured in hospital at Sharpsburg. Paroled September 30, 1862. Wounded at Chickamauga, September 19, 1863. Roll for July & August 1864 shows absent in hospital permanently disabled, gunshot wound, fractured left leg. Discharged December 22, 1864.

Cartwright, E. G. – Private. Enlisted at Prairie Plains by James T. Hunter May 7, 1861. Killed in train accident at Holly Springs, Mississippi September 11, 1861.

Cartwright, James G. W. – Sergeant. Enlisted Montgomery County, May 7, 1861 by James T. Hunter. Captured at Sharpsburg, Maryland. Exchanged November 9, 1862. Died of wounds, Battle of the Wilderness May 6, 1864.

Cartwright, Lemuel C. – Private. Enlisted Montgomery, March 24, 1862 by C. E. Jones. Gunshot wounds to hand and thigh October 7, 1864 Darbytown Rd. Arm amputated. Captured at hospital in Richmond April 3, 1865. Paroled May 3, 1865.

Cathey, Bennett H. – Private. Enlisted Montgomery April 5, 1862 by C. E. Jones. Died in hospital April 30, 1863.

Chilton, Franklin Bowden – Private. Enlisted Montgomery County, May 7, 1861 by James T. Hunter. Discharged September 15, 1862 for being under age.

Clepper, Lorenzo Dow – Private. Enlisted Montgomery March 18, 1862. Sick in hospital with rubella June 2, 1862. Returned to duty July 23, 1862. Put in substitute 1863. No further records found.

Collier, Arthur H. – Private. Enlisted Montgomery, March 14, 1862 by C. E. Jones. Last appeared as present on company roll May & June 1863. Transferred to regimental staff as musician.

Conrow, C. M. – Corporal. Enlisted May 7, 1861 Montgomery County by James T. Hunter. Killed in Battle of Gaines' Mill June 27, 1862.

Cude, William Johnson – Private. Enlisted Montgomery April 5, 1862 by C. E. Jones. Furloughed March 27, 1864. No further records found.

Dale, G. W. – Sergeant. Enlisted Montgomery March 17, 1862 by C. E. Jones. Gunshot wound May 6, 1864. Admitted to hospital September 12, 1864. Returned to duty September 16, 1864. No further records found.

Farrow, D. D. – Private. Enlisted May 7, 1861 by James T. Hunter. Died Dumfries, Virginia in December 12, 1861.

Farrow, S. W. – Sergeant. Enlisted Montgomery, March 20, 1862 by C. E. Jones. Admitted to Howard's Grove Hospital, Richmond, Virginia July 19, 1864. Furloughed August 18, 1864 for 60 days. No further records found.

Faulkner, Albert – Private. Enlisted Montgomery County May 7, 1861 by James T. Hunter. Discharged December 26, 1861. Re-enlisted Montgomery March 29, 1862 by C. E. Jones. Killed at Antietam September 17, 1862.

Fisher, William S. – Private. Enlisted Montgomery County May 7, 1861 by James T. Hunter. Wounded Gaines' Mill June 27, 1862. Wounded Battle of Chickamauga September 19, 1863. Discharged due to disability in 1864.

Fox, Richard – Private. Enlisted in Montgomery March 24, 1862 by C. E. Jones. Killed at Battle of Antietam September 17, 1862.

Gafford, R. D. – Private. Enlisted in Montgomery March 15, 1862 by C. E. Jones. Died of disease at Richmond May 25, 1862.

Hall, James H. – Corporal. Enlisted Montgomery County May 7, 1861 by James T. Hunter. Appointed 4th corporal May 6, 1864. Present at surrender of the Army of Northern Virginia, Appomattox Courthouse, Virginia. Paroled April 12, 1865.

Holt, Albert C. – Private. Enlisted Montgomery County May 7, 1861 by James T. Hunter. Admitted to the hospital March 30, 1862 with frost bite. Discharged on surgeon's certificate of disability July 28, 1862.

Jeffers, M. S. – Private. Enlisted in Montgomery March 24, 1862 by C. E. Jones. Sick in hospital August 28, 1862. Furloughed November 1862. Clerk in Q. M. Department, Hempstead, Texas 1864. Signed Parole of Honor at Galveston June 22, 1865.

Jett, J. R. P. – Private. Enlisted Montgomery County May 7, 1861 by James T. Hunter. Detailed as litter bearer June 27, 1862. Transferred to regimental staff. Appears on roll of Prisoners of War paroled at Appomattox Court House April 9, 1865.

Kirby, James A. – Private. Enlisted in Montgomery March 24, 1862 by C. E. Jones. Admitted to Chimborazo Hospital June 29, 1862 with wound to arm received in Battle of Gaines' Mill. Killed in action at Battle of Chickamauga September 19, 1863.

Keyser, Henry – Private. Enlisted Montgomery County March 18, 1862 by C. E. Jones. Sick in hospital at Richmond June 26, 1862. On extra duty detailed as butcher in Texas Brigade Quartermaster Department November 1862. Present at surrender of the Army of Northern Virginia, Appomattox Courthouse, Virginia April 9, 1865. Parole not dated.

Landrum, Willis J. – Private. Enlisted Montgomery County May 7, 1861 by James T. Hunter. Left service on surgeon's certificate of disability June 19, 1863. Returned to duty August 1, 1863. Said to have deserted at White's Tavern, Virginia August 16, 1864 (possibly POW instead). Signed Parole of Honor April 26, 1865 Ashland, Virginia.

Landrum, Zachariah – Corporal. Enlisted Montgomery County May 7, 1861 by James T. Hunter. Wounded at Battle of Gettysburg July 2, 1863. Permanently disabled.

Leach, W. G. – Private. Enlisted at age 25 on April 20, 1862 by C. E. Jones. Died of typhoid fever in hospital at Danville, Virginia June 20, 1862.

Lewis, Clint A. – Private. Enlisted Montgomery County May 7, 1861 by James T. Hunter. Wounded in shoulder at Gaines' Mill June 27, 1862. Died from wound July 28, 1862.

Lewis, William – Private. Enlisted Montgomery County May 7, 1861 by James T. Hunter. Discharged, surgeon's certificate of disability (heart trouble) June 28, 1862.

Mathews, T. R. – Private. Enlisted Montgomery County May 7, 1861 by James T. Hunter. Sick in hospital October 6, 1861. Discharged at Richmond, Virginia December 3, 1861.

Mitchell, Thomas R. – Private. Enlisted in Montgomery March 20, 1862 by C. E. Jones. Taken prisoner at Sharpsburg, Maryland and sent to Fort Delaware. Took oath of allegiance 1862. Did not return to his regiment.

Morris, A. C. – Corporal. Enlisted Montgomery County May 7, 1861 by James T. Hunter. Died from typhoid fever in Dumfries, Virginia February 2,1862.

Myers, Thomas J. – Private. Enlisted by C. E. Jones March 20, 1862. Died of chronic diarrhea and pneumonia August 25, 1862.

Quigley, Reverious – Private. Enlisted Montgomery County March 17, 1862 by Charles E. Jones. Killed at Battle of Gaines' Mill, Virginia June 27, 1862.

Rankin, Robert – Private. Enlisted Montgomery County March 17, 1862 by Charles E. Jones. Wounded at Battle of Gettysburg July 2, 1863. Captured while in hospital at Richmond, Virginia April 3, 1863.

Sanderlin, J. M. – Private. Enlisted Montgomery County May 7, 1861 by James T. Hunter. Discharged November 23, 1861.

Sanders, Claiborne B. - Private. Enlisted Montgomery County March 24, 1862 by Charles E. Jones. Sick in hospital in Richmond, Virginia May 20, 1862. Discharged by surgeon's certificate of disability July 28, 1862, age 48.

Sapp, Hartwell T. – Sergeant. Enlisted as 2nd Corporal, Montgomery County May 7, 1861 by Procter P. Porter. Wounded May 7, 1862 at Battle of West Point, Virginia. Discharged for disability September 4, 1862. Rejoined company July 2, 1863. Promoted to sergeant May 6, 1864. Captured on Darbytown Rd. near Richmond October 7, 1864. POW Point Lookout, Maryland. Exchanged January 17, 1865.

Sharp, James H. – Private. Enlisted Montgomery County May 7, 1861 by James T. Hunter. Wounded at 2nd Battle of Manassas August 30, 1862. Killed in trenches below Petersburg, Virginia June 22, 1864.

Smith, John I. – Private. Enlisted by Charles E. Jones March 7, 1862. Wounded at Battle of Gaines' Mill, Virginia June 27, 1862. Appointed 3rd corporal May 6, 1864. Wounded near Williamsburg Rd. in Virginia on October 27, 1864.

Steussy (Steussey), Jacob – Private. Enlisted Montgomery County March, 1862 by Charles E. Jones. Wounded at Battle of Gettysburg July 2, 1863. Leg amputated. Permanently disabled.

Steussy (Steussey), Matthew – Private. Enlisted Montgomery County March, 1862 by Charles E. Jones. Wounded at Battle of Gaines' Mill, Virginia June 27, 1862. Arm amputated. Permanently disabled.

Talley, J. C. – Private. Enlisted in Montgomery March 15, 1862 by C. E. Jones. Sick in hospital in fall of 1862. Died at Danville, Virginia in 1864.

Talley, Reuben – Private. Enlisted in Montgomery March 15, 1862 by C. E. Jones. Shown present with Company H, from May 1862 through January 1865. Admitted to Howard's Grove Hospital January 21, 1865. Signed parole of honor in Houston, Texas. July 27, 1865.

Taylor, Alex - Private. Enlisted Montgomery County May 7, 1861 by James T. Hunter. Sick in hospital at Richmond, Virginia October 15 to November 6, 1861. Wounded in arm Battle of the Wilderness May 6, 1864. Wounded in arm and jaw Petersburg, Virginia June 19, 1864. Furloughed September 1864.

Taylor, C. L. – Private. Enlisted in Montgomery March 20, 1862 by C. E. Jones. Accidentally shot in the foot November 1, 1862. Furloughed to Texas permanently disabled. Transferred to Company A, Mann's Regiment Texas Cavalry.

Travis, Henry – Private. Enlisted Montgomery County May 7, 1861 by James T. Hunter. Wounded in arm at Battle of Gaines' Mill June 27, 1862. Killed in action at Battle of the Wilderness May 6, 1864.

Wade, Frank H. – Corporal. Enlisted Montgomery County May 7, 1861 by James T. Hunter. Sick in hospital at Richmond, Virginia October 15, to November 6, 1861. Appointed 4th Corporal February 3, 1862. AWOL from hospital in Richmond, November 1862. Reported to have transferred to the artillery in 1863.

Willcox, Theodore W. – Private. Enlisted Montgomery County May 7, 1861 by James T. Hunter. Left sick at Fredricksburg April 8, 1862. Died at Fredricksburg April 12, 1862.

Wilkes, Britton B. – Private. Enlisted in Montgomery March 18, 1862 by C. E. Jones. Wounded at 2nd Battle of Manassas August 29, 1862. Transferred to Confederate Navy in 1864.

Wilkes, T. O. – Private. Enlisted Montgomery County May 7, 1861 by James T. Hunter. Killed in action at Battle of Gaines' Mill June 27, 1862.

Note: **Private P. L. Cartwright** was shown on the rolls of the Porter Guards May 7, 1861 but did not make the journey to Virginia. He enlisted in Company K, 8th Texas Cavalry (Terry's Texas Rangers) September 7, 1861.

5th Texas Cavalry
(5th Mounted Volunteers)

The 5th Texas Cavalry, also known as the 5th Mounted Volunteers, was organized in the summer of 1861. The original officers were Colonel Thomas Green, Lt. Colonel Henry C. McNeill, and Major Samuel A. Lockridge. This regiment served in the New Mexico campaign, the Battle of Galveston, and numerous conflicts in Louisiana and Arkansas.

There were only four men from Montgomery County who are known to have served in the 5th Texas Cavalry. Three of these men, John Dupree, Samuel Dupree, and William Shannon, were from families that were among the earliest settlers in Montgomery County. Two of these men died during the New Mexico campaign of 1862.

John Lewis Dupree was a cousin of Samuel Frances Dupree. John enlisted in the 5th Texas Cavalry at San Antonio on August 19, 1861. He was discharged on a surgeon's certificate of disability on September 26, 1861. One January 3, 1862, he re-enlisted in Company H, 26th Texas Cavalry as a junior 2nd lieutenant.

Samuel Frances Dupree was the son of Lewis and Levene Adaline Daves Dupree. He enlisted as a private in Company C, 5th Texas Cavalry on August 19, 1861. Sam was wounded at the Battle of Glorieta Pass on March 28, 1862 and is believed to have died in the hospital at Santa Fe, New Mexico. His place of burial is unknown.

James Matthew Gary was the son of James M. and Wilmuth Watson Dibrell Gary. The exact date that James moved to Montgomery County is uncertain. He married Susan E. Nobles in Montgomery County on June 15, 1864. James enlisted in Company C of the 5th Texas Cavalry in Grimes County on August 19, 1861. He was discharged by furnishing a substitute on January 2, 1863.

William Alexander Shannon was the son of Aaron Shannon (1796-1865). His brothers, Thomas Brandon Shannon and Aaron Shannon, Jr., were officers in the 21st Texas Cavalry. William enlisted as a 1st lieutenant in Company C, 5th Texas Cavalry on August 31, 1861. He apparently became seriously ill during the New Mexico campaign and resigned effective March 13, 1862. It is uncertain exactly where or when William died, but it does not appear that he made it back to Texas.

5th Texas Infantry

After Confederate forces fired on Ft. Sumter in April of 1861, leaders in the militia districts of Texas rapidly organized companies of men to serve in the Confederate Army. Records in the archives of the Texas State Library show that Robert M. Powell, an attorney in Danville and son-in-law of wealthy planter Green Wood, had organized a company of fifty-three men from the 17th Brigade of Texas State Troops by the end of April of that year. These recruits were primarily from the areas of Danville in Montgomery County and Waverly in Walker County. Powell, along with William Traylor Hill from Walker County, continued to recruit men for the company through most of the summer.

This company assumed the name of Waverly Confederates and trained near Anderson in Grimes County. Robert Powell was elected captain. Other elected officers were William T. Hill, 1st lieutenant, A. C. Woodall, 2nd lieutenant, and Campbell Wood, 3rd lieutenant. After training through the summer, the company traveled to Harrisburg where the Waverly Confederates were officially inducted into Confederate service as Company D, 5th Texas Infantry. There were thirty-two men from Montgomery County among its ranks.

In September 1861, the 5th Texas Infantry arrived in Virginia and on October 22, 1861 was placed in a brigade with the 1st Texas, 4th Texas, and 18th Georgia Infantries under the command of Brigadier General Louis T. Wigfall. By the end of the year, most of the men had spent time in hospitals due to disease or exposure to the elements. The brigade was realigned in February 1862 when Colonel John Bell Hood of the 4th Texas Infantry was promoted to Brigadier General and placed in command. From that date, and through the rest of the war, the brigade was known as Hood's Texas Brigade.

Four Montgomery County soldiers, Privates James B. Estill, James J. Tomlinson, Joseph D. Rose, and Thomas R. Wallace died in camp or in Richmond hospitals prior to the brigade's first major engagement. In June of 1862, Jerome B. Robertson was promoted to colonel and placed in command of the 5th Texas Infantry. On August 28, 1862, the 5th Texas Infantry took part in the Second Battle of Manassas. It was during this battle that the regiment received the nickname "The Bloody 5th." On the afternoon of August 30, 1862, the 5th Texas Infantry led an attack against the 5th and 10th New York Infantries, driving them from the field while inflicting more than 300 casualties in a matter of minutes. The fierce attack virtually destroyed the 5th New York Infantry regiment by killing or wounding almost two-thirds of the regiment. Privates Joseph Burden, Ben Estill, and James Harris of Montgomery County were mortally wounded during the battle. Sergeant Robert Brantley, Private Anthony Golding, Corporal William Smith, and Private Alex Traylor were also wounded but survived.

During the Battle of South Mountain on September 14. 1862, Colonel Jerome Robertson collapsed from exhaustion and was carried from the battlefield. He was replaced by Captain Ike Turner as commander of the 5th Texas. Three days later, at the Battle of Antietam, Privates T. J. Edwards and F. M. Ridg(e)way of Montgomery County were killed in action.

Major Robert M. Powell was promoted to colonel in command of the 5th Texas Infantry Regiment on November 1, 1862. While leading the regiment in an assault on Little Round Top at the Battle of Gettysburg on July 2, 1863, Colonel Powell was seriously wounded and taken prisoner. Private William T. McGilvary was also taken prisoner. Second Lieutenant Campbell Wood was wounded in the foot, and Sergeant Robert Brantley was wounded and taken prisoner during the assault. During the Confederate retreat from Gettysburg, Private Robert Hewitt was captured by Union forces under the command of Brigadier General Benjamin F. Kelly on July 18, 1863. He arrived at Camp Chase as a prisoner of war on July 24, 1863 but is shown to have escaped.

In August of 1863, the 5th Texas Infantry, as a part of Lieutenant General James Longstreet's Corps, was temporarily transferred to the Confederate Army of Tennessee. On September 19, 1863, the 5th Texas Infantry took part in the Battle of Chickamauga in Georgia. During the overwhelming Confederate victory, Private John Tomlinson of Montgomery County was killed in action, and Private Alex Traylor was wounded.

Following the victory at Chickamauga, Longstreet's Corps began an independent campaign against Union forces commanded by General Ambrose Burnside. During this campaign, Sergeant William Campbell of Montgomery County was taken prisoner. In 1864, the 5th Texas Infantry returned to the Army of Virginia. Under the command of Brigadier General John Gregg, the Texas Brigade took part in the Wilderness campaign. John Gregg was killed October 7, 1864 and was replaced by Colonel F. S. Bass who was wounded on the same day, leaving the Texas Brigade under the command of Lt. Colonel C. M. Winkler. Privates John Burden and William Traylor were wounded, and Private Robert Stanton was taken prisoner.

Colonel Robert M. Powell, the organizer and original commander of the Waverly Confederates, was released and exchanged on February 6, 1865. In March of 1865, Colonel Powell became the last commander of Hood's Texas Brigade. Colonel Powell, Private Anthony Golding, and Private William Traylor were the only men from Montgomery who were present at the surrender of the Army of Northern Virginia at Appomattox Court House on April 9, 1865.

Montgomery County Men
in the 5th Texas Infantry
Company D

Officers:

Powell, Robert M. – Captain. Organized the company in the summer of 1861 and elected captain. Promoted to major August 22, 1862. Promoted to colonel on November 1, 1862. Wounded at Battle of Gettysburg, July 2, 1863. Prisoner of war, Johnson's Island Prison in Ohio. Released and exchanged February 6, 1865. Appointed commander of Texas Brigade March 1865. Surrendered his brigade April 9, 1865.

Wood, Campbell – 3rd Lieutenant. Enlisted August 2, 1861. Sick in Camp December 2, 1861. Promoted to 2nd lieutenant August 23, 1862. Wounded at Gettysburg July 2, 1863. Retired December 9, 1864 due to disabling wounds received at Gettysburg.

Enlisted Men:

Brantley, Robert Augustus – 2nd Corporal. Enlisted August 2, 1861. Promoted to 1st corporal February 1, 1862. Wounded Manassas August 30, 1862. Promoted to 4th sergeant April 1863. Wounded and Captured Gettysburg, July 2, 1863. POW Ft. Delaware. Released June 1865.

Burden, John Gillard – Private. Enlisted August 2, 1861. Wagon master May 2, 1862. Wounded Wilderness May 6, 1864. Retired June 24, 1864 for disability from wounds.

Burden, Joseph C. – Private. Enlisted August 2, 1861. Wounded Manassas August 30, 1862. Died August 31, 1862.

Burke, Ephraim – Private. Enlisted August 2, 1861. Detailed as ambulance driver April 1, 1863. Captured at Gettysburg July 2, 1863. Confined at Ft. McHenry, Maryland and transferred to Ft. Delaware July, 6, 1863. Took Oath of Allegiance Ft. Delaware. Released June 9, 1865.

Campbell, Douglas M. – Private. Enlisted August 2, 1861. Discharged for inability at Richmond, Virginia June 28, 1862.

Campbell, John Wesley – 3rd Sergeant. Enlisted August 2, 1861. Discharged on surgeon's certificate of disability June 26, 1862 at Dumfries, Virginia.

Campbell, William B. – 1st Corporal. Enlisted August 2, 1861. Promoted to 4th sergeant December 1, 1861. Promoted to 3rd sergeant February 1, 1862 replacing J. W. Campbell. Promoted to 2nd sergeant August 23, 1862. Furloughed for 30 days September 29, 1862. Captured in Tennessee, December 1863. POW at Rock Island, Illinois. January 1, 1864. Paroled May 23, 1865.

Dikeman, William K. – Private. Enlisted August 2, 1861. Discharged, surgeon's certificate of disability due to hernia, January 24, 1862.

Edwards, T. J. – Private. Enlisted August 2, 1861. Killed at Battle of Antietam September 17, 1862.

Estill, Ben P. – Private. Enlisted August 2, 1861. In hospital at Petersburg, Virginia September 1861. Returned to duty October 1861. Wounded in breast Manassas August 30, 1862. Died from wounds September 28, 1862.

Estill, James Black – Private. Enlisted August 2, 1861. Admitted to hospital, Richmond, Virginia with typhoid fever May 9, 1862. Died May 21, 1862.

Golding, Anthony F. – Private. Enlisted August 20, 1861. Wounded in side Manassas August 30, 1862. Returned to duty October 1862. Paroled at Appomattox Courthouse, Virginia April 9, 1865.

Guynn, William James (J. W.) – Private. Enlisted August 20, 1861. Sick at St. Charles Hospital, Richmond, Virginia October 15, 1861. Sick at private home October 23, 1861. Discharged, surgeon's certificate, December 1, 1861.

Harris, James K. P. – Private. Enlisted in Virginia November 10, 1861. Captured Yorktown, Virginia May 4, 1862. Exchanged August 11, 1862. Wounded in thigh, Manassas, August 30, 1862. Died from wounds September 18, 1862.

Hewitt, Robert – Private. Enlisted March 28, 1862. Captured near Bunker Hill, Virginia July 18, 1863. POW received at Champ Chase, OH July 24, 1863. Shown to have escaped.

Irvine, Henry Reid – Private. Enlisted August 2, 1861. Sent to hospital June 23, 1862. Died in Richmond, Virginia July 1, 1862.

Malone, Henderson F. – Private. Enlisted August 2, 1861. Discharged, surgeon's certificate of disability, Richmond, Virginia December 5, 1861.

McGilvary, William Thomas – Private. Enlisted August 2, 1861. Captured at Gettysburg, PA July 2, 1863. POW Ft. Delaware, Maryland. Took oath of allegiance June 9, 1865 and was released.

Ridg(e)way, F. M. – Private. Enlisted August 2, 1861. Wounded and left on battlefield, died at Antietam, September 17, 1862.

Rose, Joseph D. – Private. Enlisted April 8, 1862. Died in camp near Richmond, Virginia June 3, 1862.

Scott, John Franklin – Private. Enlisted August 2, 1861. Sent to hospital in Richmond, Virginia May 25, 1862. Discharged by order of Secretary of War on certificate of disability July 1, 1862.

Smith, William Oliver – Private. Enlisted August 2, 1861. Wounded Manassas August 30, 1862. Returned to duty November 1862. Promoted to 4th corporal March 1863. Promoted to 3rd corporal September 20, 1863. Promoted to 2nd corporal October 31, 1863. Detailed as courier for General Fields February 10, 1864. Paroled Montgomery, AL May 23, 1865.

Stanton, Robert – Private. Enlisted August 2, 1861. Extra duty, carpenter services, December 10, 1861. Captured Wilderness May 6, 1864. POW at Point Lookout, Maryland. Exchanged February 18, 1865. Paroled Appomattox Court House, Virginia April 9, 1865.

Tomlinson, James J. – Private. Enlisted March 28, 1862. Died in hospital, Richmond, Virginia May 26, 1862.

Tomlinson, John – Private. Enlisted March 28, 1862. Killed in action Chickamauga September 19, 1863.

Traylor, Alex H. – Private. Enlisted August 2, 1861. Wounded Manassas August 30, 1862. Returned to duty November 1862. Wounded Chickamauga September 20, 1863. Furloughed to Alabama for 60 days October 10, 1863. Retired July 16, 1864 due to wounds received at Chickamauga.

Traylor, William A. – Private. Enlisted March 28, 1862. Wounded Wilderness May 6, 1864. Returned to duty June 1864. Paroled Appomattox Courthouse, Virginia April 9, 1865.

Wallace, Thomas R. – Private. Enlisted March 28, 1862. Died in Richmond, Virginia June 12, 1862.

Wood, Robert L. – Private. Enlisted August 2, 1861. Sick in hospital November 30, 1861. Discharged by surgeon's certificate of disability January 30, 1862.

Woodson, Creed T. – Private. Enlisted August 2, 1861. Appointed 4th corporal February 1, 1862. Sick in hospital June 10, 1862. Appointed 3rd corporal August 23, 1862. 90-day furlough April 12, 1863. Transferred to cavalry in Trans-Mississippi Department by order of General Kirby Smith July 10, 1863.

7th Texas Cavalry
(7th Mounted Volunteers)

The 7th Texas Cavalry, also known as the 7th Mounted Volunteers, was organized in the summer of 1861. The original officers were Colonel William Steele, Lt. Colonel John S. Sutton and Major Arthur P. Bagby. This regiment was involved in the New Mexico campaign, the Battle of Galveston, and numerous engagements in Louisiana including the Red River campaign of 1864.

Company G of the 7th Texas Cavalry was organized and commanded by Captain Horatio White Fisher from Walker County, Texas. The men in this company were primarily from the Waverly and Danville areas. These were the first groups of cavalrymen to leave the Montgomery County area. There were twenty-seven men from Montgomery County who were known to have served in this company. The majority were enlisted near Waverly, Texas by Captain H. W. Fisher on August 24, 1861 and traveled to Camp Pickett in San Antonio where they were inducted into Confederate service on October 26, 1861. Another young man from Montgomery County, Charles Robert Scott, served in Company A, 7th Texas Cavalry. Charles rode from his home near Montgomery to San Antonio and was mustered into the 7th Cavalry on October 4, 1861 at age 17. Private Scott was enlisted in the Confederate Army by Lieutenant Joseph D. Sayers who later became the twenty-second Governor of Texas in 1899.

In the late fall of 1861, the 7th Texas Cavalry traveled west through Indian territory along previously-established stagecoach routes. During the journey, Private Lee Burke was hospitalized at Fort Lancaster but soon recovered and rejoined his company. The 7th Cavalry arrived at El Paso in December, and it was here that Private Benjamin F. Cates, a former member of the Danville Mounted Riflemen, became ill and died.

In January 1862, the 7th Texas Cavalry, as a part of General H. H. Sibley's Brigade, made its push into New Mexico. The terrain was treacherous, and many of the horses died along the way. In early February, Private Peter T. Sessums was struck with a severe case of measles and sent to the hospital at Fort Bliss where he was later discharged from Confederate service. Company G was one of five companies that served as a rear guard for Sibley's Brigade, spending much of its time in the area of Mesilla, New Mexico and saw very little action during the New Mexico campaign. Company A was part of the five-company-advance unit of the 7th Cavalry and was heavily engaged at both the Battle of Val Verde and the Battle of Glorieta Pass.

After a decisive Confederate victory at Val Verde, New Mexico, Sibley's Brigade continued northward to occupy Albuquerque and Santa Fe. On March 26, 1862, the 7th Texas Cavalry participated in the Battle of Glorieta Pass in the Sangre de Cristo Mountains southeast of Santa Fe. Although this conflict has been nicknamed the "Gettysburg of the West", it was actually a Confederate victory. By March 28, 1862, Confederate forces had driven the Union Army through the pass and down the trail toward Fort Union. During the intense battle, Union Major John Chivington with four companies of troops slipped behind the Confederate lines looting and destroying approximately eighty wagons, spiking several cannons, and killing or driving off more than five hundred horses and mules. With all of their reserve horses and supplies gone, Sibley's Brigade was forced to retreat toward Santa Fe. Unable to re-supply his troops, Sibley abandoned the New Mexico campaign and eventually returned to Texas.

Back in Texas and under the command of Colonel Arthur Pendleton Bagby, the 7th Texas Cavalry participated in the re-taking of Galveston on January 1, 1863. Many of the men served as "Horse Marines" aboard the *CSS Bayou City* and *CSS Neptune*. Private G. Willis Ellisor of Company G was killed during the battle.

After establishing control of Galveston, the 7th Texas Cavalry was transferred to the Army of Western Louisiana and during the rest of 1863, participated in many conflicts including Fort Bisland (Berwick Bay), Brashear (Morgan) City, Donaldsonville, Cox's Plantation, Stirling's Plantation, and Bayou Bourbeau. During these engagements, Private Levi Zim Burke was captured at the Battle of Bayou Teche on April 27, 1863, and Private Felix R. Collard was wounded at Donaldsonville on June 28, 1863. Privates James Hiram Cude and John Wood Lindley of Company G, and Private Charles Robert Scott of Company A were captured near Camp Pratt, Louisiana on November 20, 1863.

In 1864, the 7th Texas Cavalry participated in the Red River campaign and participated in battles at Mansfield, Pleasant Hill, and Monett's Ferry, in addition to several smaller skirmishes. In September of 1864, the 7th Texas Cavalry was assigned to the 3rd Texas Cavalry Brigade (Hardeman's), 1st Texas Cavalry Division (Wharton's), 2nd Corps, Trans-Mississippi Department, and in April 1865, they were assigned to Bagby's Cavalry Brigade, District of West Louisiana. These units were included in the surrender of the Trans-Mississippi Department by General E. Kirby Smith on May 26, 1865.

Montgomery County Men
in the 7th Texas Cavalry
Company A

Scott, Charles Robert – Private. Enlisted October 4, 1861. Lost horse March 7, 1862, remounted next day. Shown present throughout the New Mexico campaign. Captured near Camp Pratt, LA November 20, 1863. POW at Customs House, New Orleans November 23, 1863. Exchanged at New Iberia, LA December 21, 1863.

Company G

Officers:

Sessums, Blount D. – 2nd Lieutenant. Enlisted August 24, 1861. Appointed orderly sergeant October 26, 1861. Elected 3rd lieutenant December 21, 1862. Elected 2nd lieutenant December 22, 1862. Resigned May 4, 1864.

Enlisted Men:

Barrett, David Albert – Private. Enlisted February 1865. No further records found.

Barrett, Stephen Reding – Private. Enlisted July 15, 1862. Shown present on roll dated July 1 to December 30, 1862. No further records found.

Barrett, William Robert – Corporal. Enlisted August 24, 1861. Shown as 2nd corporal on roll dated July 1 to December 30, 1862. No further records found.

Barrett, William Robert – Corporal. Enlisted August 24, 1861. Shown as 2nd corporal on roll dated July 1 to December 30, 1862. No further records found.

Betts, Menter – Private. Enlisted August 24, 1861. Shown present on roll dated October 26, 1861 to April 30, 1862. Transferred to Company A, 24th/25th Consolidated Texas Cavalry.

Burden, George Larkum – Private. Enlisted August 24, 1861. Shown present on roll dated October 26, 1861 to April 30, 1862. Transferred to Company A, Mann's Regiment Texas Cavalry.

Burke, Lee – Private. Enlisted August 24, 1861. Shown absent—sick at Ft. Lancaster on roll dated October 26, 1861 to April 30, 1862. Shown present on roll dated July 1 to December 30, 1862.

Burke, Levi Zim – Private. Enlisted August 24, 1861. Shown present on roll dated July 1 to December 30, 1862. Captured at Bayou Teche, LA April 27, 1863. Paroled at Prophet's Island below Port Hudson May 5, 1863.

Burke, Nathan – Private. Enlisted August 24, 1861. Lost horse January 12, 1862 remounted May 1, 1862. No further records found.

Cates, Benjamin Franklin – Private. Enlisted August 24, 1861. Died near El Paso, December 19, 1861.

Chesher, James F. – Private. Enlisted August 24, 1861. Hospital attendant at Fort Bliss January 1862. Discharged due to disability May 28, 1862.

Clark, E. A. – Private. Enlisted August 24, 1861. Absent on special duty at Fort Bliss February 27, 1862. Admitted to CS Field Hospital, Virginia Point, Texas. November 14, 1863. Admitted to CSA General Hospital, Shreveport, LA September 19, 1864. Returned to duty September 22, 1864.

Collard, Felix R. – Private. Enlisted August 24, 1861. Shown present during New Mexico campaign. Wounded at Donaldsonville, LA June 28, 1863. Paroled June 24, 1865.

Cude, George Travis – Private. Enlisted March 4, 1864. No further records found.

Cude, James Hiram – Private. Enlisted August 24, 1861. Shown present during New Mexico campaign. Captured near Camp Pratt, LA November 20, 1863. POW at Customs House in New Orleans November 23, 1863. Exchanged at New Iberia, LA December 21, 1863.

Ellisor, G. Willis – Private. Enlisted July 15, 1862. Killed at Battle of Galveston January 1, 1863.

Ellisor, Nathan Thomas – Private. Enlisted August 24, 1861. Shown muster rolls from October 26, 1861 through December 30, 1862. No further records found.

Knight, John Arthur – Private. Enlisted August 24, 1861 in Walker County. Captured at the Battle of Donaldsonville, Louisiana, June 28, 1863. No records of parole or discharge.

Lindley, John Wood – Private. Enlisted August 24, 1861. Shown present during New Mexico campaign. Captured near Camp Pratt, LA November 20, 1863. POW at Customs House in New Orleans, November 23, 1863. Exchanged at New Iberia, LA December 21, 1863.

Little, William M. – Private. Enlisted August 24, 1861. Muster roll dated October 26, 1861 to February 28, 1862 shows on extended service to General Sibley. Muster roll dated October 26, 1861 to April 30, 1862 notes horse broken down and abandoned while on extended duty with Company C, 7th Texas Cavalry. Remounted April 5, 1862. Discharged in May 1865.

Perry, C. William – Private. Enlisted August 24, 1861. Shown present from October 26, 1861 to December 30, 1862. No further records found.

Rose, Elisha Alexander – Private. Enlisted July 15, 1862. Shown present July to December 30, 1862. No further records found.

Rose, Sterling A. – Private. Enlisted July 15, 1862. Shown present July to December 30, 1862. No further records found.

Seale, William J. – Private. Enlisted August 24, 1861. Shown present during New Mexico campaign. Discharged at Morgan's Ferry, LA by surgeon's certificate of disability on September 19, 1863.

Sessums, George W. – Private. Enlisted August 24, 1861. Shown present from October 26, 1861 to December 30, 1862. No further records found.

Sessums, Peter Thomas – Private. Enlisted August 24, 1861. In hospital at Fort Bliss with measles February 10, 1862. Discharged by surgeon's certificate of disability May 3, 1862.

Wood, Rush Brevard – Private. Enlisted March 1864. Discharged in May 1865. No further records found.

8th Texas Cavalry
(Terry's Texas Rangers)

Soon after the adjournment of the Texas Secession Convention, Thomas S. Lubbock traveled to Montgomery, Alabama seeking a commission to raise troops for the Confederate Army, but his request was denied. After returning to Texas, Thomas teamed up with fellow soldier, Benjamin Franklin (Frank) Terry, to organize a small group of men to travel to Virginia and join the Confederate Army. One of these men was Thomas Jewett Goree who had opened a law office in Montgomery, Texas in 1858. Arriving in Virginia, these men were attached to the staff of General James Longstreet and participated in the first major battle of the war at Manassas (Bull Run). General Longstreet was so impressed by the service of these men that he appointed Thomas Goree to his staff as his aide-de-camp and recommended that Frank Terry and Thomas Lubbock be allowed to return to Texas to raise a regiment of troops.

By August of 1861, Terry and Lubbock were back in Texas, recruiting and organizing their new regiment. There were twenty-three men from Montgomery County who were known to have served in the 8th Texas Cavalry, all of whom were in Company K. This company was commanded by Captain John G. Walker of Harris County with the majority of the recruiting in Montgomery County being done by Sheriff Alfred W. Morris who became a 1st lieutenant in the company.

By early September, the new regiment was more than one thousand men strong and on its way to Virginia. Somewhere during the trip from Houston to New Orleans, some of the men began calling themselves Texas Rangers. For whatever reason, the name stuck, and the regiment would be known as Terry's Texas Rangers for the remainder of the war.

While in New Orleans, Frank Terry received a telegram from a friend of the Terry family, General Albert Sidney Johnston, asking the 8th Texas Cavalry to join his command in the west. It is believed that General Johnston promised Terry that his men would serve as an independent regiment and would be mounted on the finest horses in Kentucky. Yielding to the temptation of such promises, Terry and his men accepted General Johnston's offer and boarded train cars headed to Nashville. While in Nashville, the regiment was struck by an outbreak of measles, and many of the men had to be hospitalized. Private William L. Pitts of Montgomery County died on December 1, 1861 and was buried in the Old Nashville Cemetery.

While many of its men were still sick in hospitals at Nashville, the 8th Texas Cavalry was engaged at the Battle of Woodsonville, Kentucky on December 17, 1861. This engagement would have had little impact on the history of the 8th Cavalry had it not been for the death of their commander Colonel Frank Terry. Captain John G. Walker and 1st Lieutenant Alfred W. Morris, Sr. were among the wounded. Thomas Lubbock, still in the hospital at Nashville, was elected colonel to replace Terry but never took command due to his death on January 23, 1862. Captain John Wharton was then promoted to colonel in command of the regiment. Captain John G. Walker of Company K was promoted to lieutenant colonel over the unpopular Major Thomas Harrison but later resigned, and Harrison was promoted to lieutenant colonel in his place. Third Lieutenant Samuel P. Christian was promoted to captain in command of Company K.

Still suffering from wounds received at Woodsonville, 1st Lieutenant Alfred W. Morris, Sr. returned to Montgomery County in February 1862, detailed as a recruiter for the regiment. He was accompanied by his sixteen-year-old son, Private Alfred W. Morris, Jr.

In the early spring of 1862, the 8th Texas Cavalry had moved to Corinth, Mississippi where it was joined by survivors of the winter illness in Nashville along with new recruits from Texas. Seven new recruits from Montgomery County, Privates Thomas Chatham, Samuel Epperson, John Foster, John Glover, Theodore Goalder, John Katchler, and Jabez Mitchell, were added to the ranks of Company K.

In the two days of fighting at the Battle of Shiloh on April 7-8, the 8th Texas Cavalry was involved in several charges against Union forces. At least one of these charges was executed while dismounted. General Albert Sidney Johnston was mortally wounded during the battle. Colonel John Wharton was also wounded and temporarily relinquished command to Lt. Colonel Thomas Harrison. Harrison took permanent command of the regiment when Wharton was promoted to brigadier general on November 18, 1862.

From the end of 1862 through most of 1863, the 8th Texas Cavalry, as a part of Wharton's Brigade, fought numerous battles in Tennessee, including at Murfreesboro, Stones River, and Fort Pillow. Private Samuel Epperson of Montgomery County was captured near Stones River, Tennessee on December 31, 1862 and later died as a prisoner of war at the infamous Camp Douglas in Illinois. Two more Montgomery County men, Privates Noah W. Chatham and Daniel Mitchell, were captured near McMinnville, Tennessee on October 4, 1863 and transported to the prisoner-of-war facility at Camp Morton, Indiana. Private Mitchell died there on October 30, 1863 and was buried at Greenlawn Cemetery but later was reinterred in a mass grave at Crown Hill Cemetery. Private Chatham was transferred from Camp Morton to City Point, Virginia and exchanged on March 4, 1865.

At the bloody Battle of Chickamauga on September 19-20, Terry's Texas Rangers were part of Wheeler's Division that turned the Union right flank in a sweeping Confederate victory. After Chickamauga, John Wharton was promoted to major general, and Terry's Cavalry, in a brigade commanded by Thomas H. Harrison, supported General James Longstreet during his campaign into eastern Tennessee. By April 1864, the 8th Texas Cavalry was back in Georgia with the main body of the Confederate Army of Tennessee during the Atlanta campaign. For several months, the Rangers hacked away at the advancing Union forces commanded by General William Sherman. After General John Bell Hood took the main body of the Confederate Army on an invasion into central Tennessee, the 8th Cavalry continued engaging Sherman's Union forces all the way through Georgia and then northward into North Carolina.

As Terry's Texas Rangers made its final charge at Bentonville, North Carolina on March 19, 1865, the men from Montgomery County in Company K were under the command of Captain John F. "Doc" Matthews from Chappell Hill, Texas. During his four years with the 8th Texas Cavalry, Matthews had been wounded seven times and once captured but managed to escape. He was described as a smooth-face boy who had been promoted by the bullets of the enemy. After the Battle of Bentonville, Captain Matthews became the last commander of the 8th Texas Cavalry.

In four years of service, the 8th Texas Cavalry was involved in more than two-hundred-seventy-five engagements in seven states. Although many were wounded and countless numbers of horses were lost, the men in Terry's Texas Rangers from Montgomery County suffered only four fatalities. The bodies of three of these men, Privates Samuel Epperson, Daniel Mitchell, and William L. Pitts were reinterred after the war in mass graves. The final resting place of Private David C. Muckle, killed near Savannah, Georgia in 1864, is unknown at this time.

Montgomery County Men
In the 8th Texas Cavalry
Company K

Officers:

Hottlel (Hottle), Jarred M. (A. W.) – Major. Enlisted in Montgomery County as 1st sergeant. Transferred to quartermaster's department as forage master. Promoted to major in quartermaster's department.

Morris, Alfred William, Sr. – 1st Lieutenant. Enlisted September 7, 1861. Wounded at Battle of Woodsonville, KY December 17, 1861. Hospitalized in Nashville, Tennessee Returned to Texas as recruiter for the regiment February 1862. Resigned August 18, 1862.

Enlisted Men:

Burrows, Thomas J. – Private. Enlisted September 7, 1861. Discharged October 31, 1862 surgeon's certificate of disability.

Cartwright, Pleasant L. – Private. Enlisted September 7, 1861. Discharged January 4, 1862 surgeon's certificate of disability.

Chatham, Thomas Jefferson – Private. Enlisted March 15, 1862. Shown present from March 15, 1862 to February 29, 1864.

Chatham, Noah W. – Private. Enlisted September 7, 1861. Captured near McMinnville, Tennessee October 4, 1863. POW Camp Morton, IN October 10, 1863. Transferred to City Point, Virginia for exchange March 4, 1865.

Clepper, Joseph Collier – Private. Enlisted October 26, 1861. Last shown present January 7, 1862. Discharged surgeon's certificate of disability.

Davis, A. J. – 4th Sergeant. Enlisted as private September 7, 1861. Appointed 4th Sergeant October 26, 1861. Last shown present January 7, 1862.

Elam, Frances Marion – Corporal. Enlisted as private September 7, 1861. Promoted to 3rd corporal in 1863. Last shown present February 29, 1864. Rumored to have had thirteen horses killed or wounded under him.

Epperson, Samuel – Private. Enlisted April 10, 1862. Captured near Stones River, Tennessee December 31, 1862. Died as POW at Camp Douglass, Illinois.

Foster, John A. – Private. Enlisted March 15, 1862. Last shown present February 29, 1864.

Glover, John Allen – Private. Enlisted March 15, 1862. Last shown present February 29, 1864. On roll of prisoners of war paroled at Columbus, Mississippi. May 17, 1865.

Goalder, Theodore O. – Private. Enlisted March 31, 1862. Appears on roll dated October 31, 1863 to February 29, 1864 as POW.

Katchler, John A. – Private. Enlisted March 15, 1862. Last shown present February 29, 1864.

Mitchell, Jabez N. – Private. Enlisted May 4, 1862. Last shown present February 29, 1864.

Mitchell, Daniel – Private. Enlisted September 7, 1861. Captured near McMinnville, Tennessee October 4, 1863. Died as POW at Camp Morton, IN October 30, 1863.

Morris, Alfred William, Jr. – Private. Enlisted September 7, 1861. Sick in hospital at Nashville January 1862. Detailed to transport his father, 1st Lieut. A. W. Morris back to Montgomery County, Texas. February 1862. No further records found.

Muckle, David C. – Private. Enlisted September 7, 1861. Killed in action near Savannah, GA November 28, 1864.

Pinchback, James Howard – Private. Enlisted September 7, 1861. Last shown present February 29, 1864.

Pitts, William L. – Private. Enlisted September 7, 1861. Died in Nashville December 2, 1861.

Shannon, Jacob Montgomery, Jr. – Private. Enlisted September 7, 1861. Furloughed February 24, 1862. No further records found.

Simonton, Reuben Davis – Sergeant. Enlisted as a private September 7, 1861. Received a head wound during battle in Tennessee. Appointed 5th sergeant April 1, 1863. On roll of prisoners of war paroled in Mississippi May 26, 1865.

Vaught, Columbus Wright - Private. Enlisted September 7, 1861. Absent sick near Bowling Green, KY, November, 1861. Shown present on muster roll for October 31, 1863 to February 29, 1864.

9th Texas Infantry (Nichols')
(5th Texas Volunteer Infantry)

When Union gunboats appeared off the coast of Galveston in the summer of 1861, Brigadier Gen. Paul O. Hébert, commanding the Confederate District of Texas, called for volunteers to defend the island. Galveston merchant and banker Ebenezer B. Nichols began recruiting and organizing a regiment of men which was originally known as the 5th Texas Volunteer Infantry. In October of 1861, the new regiment was mustered into Confederate service as the 9th Texas Infantry (Nichols') with each man volunteering to serve for a period of six months. E. B. Nichols was appointed colonel with Josiah C. Massie serving as lieutenant colonel and Fred Tate serving as major.

In late 1861 and early 1862, the Union forces off the coast of Galveston continued to grow, and General Hébert believed that Galveston Island was no longer defensible. As preparations were being made to evacuate the island, the 9th Texas Infantry disbanded in March 1862 at the end of its six-month term of service. While still on the island, most of the men from the 9th Texas Infantry re-enlisted in other regiments such as the 1st Texas Heavy Artillery, Waul's Texas Legion, the 16th and 20th Texas Infantries, and the 24th and 26th Texas Cavalries.

Eighty men from the Montgomery County area were known to have served in Company I of the 9th Texas Infantry. The officers of this company were Captain Robert F. Oliver, 1st Lieutenant Thomas Wesley Smith, 2nd Lieutenants Thomas J. Peel and J. G. Cobb, and 3rd Lieutenant M. H. Elliott. Nine men were known to have served in Company C and at least two in Company E of the 9th Texas Infantry.

Montgomery County Men
In the 9th Texas Infantry (Nichols')

Company C

Collins, Isom S., Cpl
Collins, John J., Pvt
Collins, Johnson, Pvt
Collins, Meshak, Pvt
Martin, Benjamin F., Pvt

Metts, Francis Marion, Pvt
Metts, George Washington, Sgt
Metts, Joseph Robert, Pvt
Outlaw, Richard, Pvt

Company E

McCan, James Marion, Pvt

Peel, John R., Sgt

Company I

Adams, E. W., Pvt
Adams, Thomas R., Pvt
Arnold, Owen W., Sgt
Atchison, James W., Pvt
Bass, B. E., Pvt
Bass, T. W., Pvt
Berkley, William Henry, Pvt
Bridgers, Leonedus Moore, Pvt
Brown, R. J., Pvt
Bryant, Jacob, Pvt
Carson, R. L., Pvt
Clepper, Charles Duncan, Pvt
Clepper, James, Pvt
Cobb, J. G., 2nd Lt
Cone, Thomas J., Pvt
Dean, Henry Ingraham, Pvt
Dean, Robert T., Pvt
Dildia, George W., Pvt
Doughtie, Jacob, Pvt
Downing, Timothy, Pvt
Elliott, Mason H., 3rd Lt
Ellis, John, Pvt
Etheridge, Horatio D., Pvt
Evans, Henry, Pvt
Farmer, David, Pvt
Ferguson, John L., Pvt
Gafford, Seaborn W., Pvt
Graves, Jesse Cox, Pvt
Guynn, John A., Pvt
Hall, Hiram H., Pvt
Harrington, Robert, Pvt

Malone, William Farrington, Sgt
Martin, J. B., Pvt
Mathews, Newman, Pvt
Matthews, Harmon, Pvt
Matthews, Jacob, Pvt
McAlpin, William K., Pvt
McCarley, James, Pvt
McClain, Joseph, Pvt
McClain, Moses, Pvt
McGrew, William J., Pvt
McKinney, Gilbert, Pvt
McKinney, Albert Wrinkles, Pvt
McKinzie, Joseph, Sgt
McLeod, Chris, Pvt
McLeod, George, Pvt
Meredith, Jacob A., Pvt
Mitchell, John M., Pvt
Neal, Lewis, Pvt
Noble, P. H., Pvt
Norsworthy, James H., Pvt
Oliver, Robert F., Capt
Parker, D. H., Pvt
Peel, Thomas Jefferson, 2nd Lt
Powell, J. G., Pvt
Ratliff (Ratcliff), James R., Pvt
Rigby, Eli, Pvt
Roten, David Edward, Pvt
Sandel, Erastus Emery, Pvt
Sandel, James Monroe, Cpl
Sandel, Peter Tabor, Pvt
Sanders, James Madison, Pvt

Henry, John K., Pvt

Hulon, James William, Pvt

Laishonce, Louis, Cpl

Lauderdale, Thomas Josiah, Pvt

Lewis, John McClanahan, Jr., Pvt

Lipscomb, Nathan, Pvt

Lowry, Simpson, Pvt

Mack, Edward, Pvt

Mack, Jesse, Pvt

Sanders, John, Pvt

Smith, Thomas Wesley, 1st Lt

Surghnor, L. W., Sgt

Thomas, D. J. L., Pvt

Thomason, James Burke, Cpl

Walker Samuel T. (T. S.), Pvt

Warren , William H., 1st Sgt

Waters, N. M., Pvt

16th Texas Infantry (Flournoy's)
(7th Infantry or Flournoy's Infantry)

The 16th Texas, also known as the 7th Infantry or Flournoy's Infantry was organized and trained at Camp Groce near Hempstead, Texas in the spring of 1862. It was commanded by former Texas Attorney General and fiery secessionist, Colonel George M. Flournoy. In addition to Colonel Flournoy, the original officers were Lt. Colonel James E. Shepard of Washington County and a former Texas Ranger, Major William H. Redwood.

After completing training at Camp Groce, the 16th Texas Infantry boarded railroad cars bound for Virginia Point, an area which is now a part of Texas City. In July 1862, the regiment was ordered back to Camp Groce in preparation for a march to Arkansas. In October 1862, the regiment made its winter quarters at Camp Nelson near Little Rock, Arkansas. While in winter quarters, the 16th Texas Infantry was assigned to the 3rd Brigade of General Henry E. McCulloch's Division. Colonel Flournoy was promoted to brigade commander. In December 1862, Major General John G. Walker assumed command of the division, returning General McCulloch to command of the 3rd Brigade and once again placing Colonel Flournoy in command of the 16th Texas Infantry. On April 23, 1863, the division was ordered to Monroe, Louisiana and reported to Lieutenant General E. Kirby Smith. General Smith ordered Walker's Division to march to the Mississippi River to offer support for the besieged city of Vicksburg, Mississippi and during a minor skirmish at Perkins' Landing, some twenty-five miles southwest of the city, interrupted Union General Ulysses S. Grant's supply line.

From Perkins' Landing, Walker's Division moved up the west bank of the Mississippi to an area near Richmond, Louisiana known as Milliken's Bend. On the morning of June 7, 1863, Walker's Texas Division attacked Union forces under the command of Union Colonel Hermann Lieb, inflicting heavy casualties and driving the Union forces to the bank of the Mississippi River. Heavy fire from Union gunboats eventually caused the Confederate forces to withdraw, ending all hope of aid to the city of Vicksburg.

In October 1863, Brigadier General William Read Scurry took command of the 3rd Brigade of Walker's Division. As a part of Scurry's Brigade, the 16th Texas Infantry participated in the Red River campaign and the Camden expedition during the spring of 1864. In late February 1865, the regiment, now commanded by Major X. B. Saunders, was transferred to the 4th Brigade under the command of Brigadier General W. H. King and soon returned to Texas. The 16th Texas Infantry had already disbanded prior to General Edmund Kirby Smith's surrender of the Trans-Mississippi Department on May 26, 1865.

Twelve of the fifteen Montgomery County men who are known to have served in the 16th Texas Infantry enlisted in Company K. This company was recruited and organized by John R. Peel and his brother Thomas Jefferson Peel. Captain John R. Peel, the son of Thomas R. Peel of Montgomery County, was the original commander and was living in Madison County at the outbreak of war. While John recruited in Madison, Grimes, and Walker Counties, his brother, Senior Second Lieutenant Thomas Jefferson Peel, recruited men from Montgomery County. After the resignation of John R. Peel in February 1863, Thomas J. Peel was promoted to captain and served as commander of Company K for the remainder of the war. Thomas Ray Peel, the father of John and T. J. Peel, appears to have trained at Camp Groce, then returned home on leave before the company left for Louisiana.

Private Lloyd Walter Surghnor recruited two men for Company A of the 16th Texas Infantry. Although the men in this company were primarily from Washington and Bell Counties, it appears that Private Surghnor may have joined and recruited for this company because of a possible relationship to Annie Surghnor Saunders whose husband, X. B. Saunders, was the original captain of Company A.

Montgomery County Men
in the 16th Texas Infantry

Company A

Surghnor, Lloyd Walter, Pvt
Welch, John, Pvt

Welch, Thomas, Pvt

Company K

Collins, Isom S., Cpl
Collins, John J., Pvt
Collins, Johnson, Pvt
Coward (Cowart), Myrick Milburn, Pvt
Jenkins, J.F., Pvt
Needham, Kyle Grundy, Pvt

Outlaw, Alexander, Pvt
Outlaw, Frances Marion, Pvt
Peel, John R., Capt
Peel, Thomas Jefferson, Capt
Peel, Thomas Ray, Pvt
Stanley, Stephen S., Pvt

20ᵗʰ Texas Infantry

The 20ᵗʰ Texas Infantry began organizing in the spring of 1862. Most of the men in this regiment were recruited in Austin, Grimes, Montgomery, Polk, Robertson, Walker, and Washington Counties. When the six-month term of service for the 9ᵗʰ Texas Infantry (Nichols') expired in March 1862, many of the men from that regiment re-enlisted in the 20ᵗʰ Texas Infantry while they were still stationed in Galveston. On May 14, 1862, wealthy planter Henry Marshall Elmore of Waverly was elected colonel of the 20ᵗʰ Infantry, and on that same date, Leonard Anderson Abercrombie was elected lieutenant colonel while Robert Bell was elected major. Two Montgomery men served on the regimental staff. These men were Assistant Surgeon John L. Irion and Chaplain Calvin Herlock Brooks.

From its very inception, the 20ᵗʰ Texas Infantry was designated to serve as a home guard and was charged with patrolling the Texas Gulf Coast and the border along the Sabine River. Many of the men were over the conscription age of thirty-five and were too old to travel long distances with the regiments that had already left Texas. There were also many very young men who were sole providers for their young families and who joined the 20ᵗʰ Texas Infantry in ordered to stay close to home in the event of a family emergency. It was common for the men in this regiment to receive lengthy furloughs to return home and care for their farms and families.

Several companies of the 20ᵗʰ Texas Infantry were involved in the Battle of Galveston on January 1, 1863, and while most the regiment did not see service outside of Texas, records show that at least four companies of the 20ᵗʰ Texas Infantry guarded supply routes between Niblett's Bluff and Vermillion (present-day Lafayette), Louisiana. It is known that among these four companies was Company H, commanded by Captain Jesse C. Dickie of Walker County; Company I, commanded by Captain James B. Stephenson of Grimes County; and Company K, commanded by Captain Lemuel G. Clepper of Montgomery County.

At least one-hundred-fifty-six men from Montgomery County served in the 20ᵗʰ Texas Infantry. No fewer than one hundred of these men were in Captain Lemuel G. Clepper's Company K which was likely the most active company in the regiment. The large number of Montgomery County men in this regiment can be attributed to Lemuel Clepper having organized the Montgomery County Rifle Boys early in the war. Fourteen of the former Rifle Boys served in Company K. Most of the men in Company K were from the southern half of Montgomery County and had been recruited by Captain Clepper personally. After training at Camp Groce near Hempstead, Company K was stationed in Houston from November 1862 through April 1863. In October 1863, Captain Clepper and forty-two men in his company were detailed to the Sabine River near Orange to guard the gunboat USS Sachem that had been captured at the Battle of Sabine Pass. In the summer of 1863, Company K was in Louisiana guarding supply routes. A detachment of the company under the command of 1ˢᵗ Lieutenant William Rigby acted as couriers. Records show that the company was stationed in Galveston from January to May of 1864 but was back in Louisiana by June. On June 22, 1864, 1ˢᵗ Lieutenant William Rigby was dispatched to Houston by Captain Stephenson of Company I. In August 1864,

Lt. Rigby was ordered to Fort Randall on Galveston Island where he later contracted yellow fever and died on September 13, 1864. William J. McGrew from the town of Montgomery was promoted to 1st lieutenant as his replacement. By November of 1864, the rest of Company K was at Fort Randall. Captain Clepper and some of his men spent a brief period of time guarding prisoners at Camp Groce near Hempstead but were back in Galveston before the regiment was surrendered in June 1865.

No fewer than forty-seven men from Montgomery County served in Company G of the 20th Texas Infantry. This company was commanded by Captain Dixon Hall Lewis from Waverly in Walker County. Captain Lewis was a nephew of 20th Infantry Commander, Colonel Henry Elmore. After training at Camp Groce, this company participated in the Battle of Galveston on New Year's Day 1863. Once the Confederate reoccupation of Galveston was complete, Company G spent most of the war guarding the island. In January 1863, Company G was stationed at Fort Moore in Eagle Grove on the bay side of the island. Fort Moore was an earthen fortification overlooking the railroad bridge which connected Galveston Island to the mainland at Virginia Point. In January 1864, the men of Company G were transferred to the south battery which faced the Gulf of Mexico and then were transferred to Fort Magruder in the fall. With the guns of the 1st Texas Heavy Artillery occupying every vantage point on and around Galveston Island, there was virtually no threat of another invasion, so the two biggest enemies facing Company G were boredom and disease. Outbreaks of yellow fever were common. Private Cyrus D. McRae died October 2, 1864 and was the only member of Company G from Montgomery County who is known to have died from the disease.

Four men from Montgomery County served in Company H of the 20th Texas Infantry. Three of these men—Privates Thomas Monroe Malone, William Farrington Malone, and Erastus Emory Sandel—were former members of the Danville Mounted Riflemen. These men were enlisted at Huntsville, Texas in April of 1862 by the company commander, Captain Jessie C. Dickie of Walker County. After participating in the Battle of Galveston, January 1, 1863, Company H was stationed at Fort Moore guarding the railroad bridge leading into the city. Through most of 1863 and 1864, Company H traveled back and forth between Louisiana and Galveston and is shown to have been stationed at Galveston in March 1865.

Five men from Montgomery County served in Company I of the 20th Texas Infantry. All of these men were residents of a community known as Bay's Chapel. Company I was commanded by Captain James B. Stephenson from Grimes County. After the Battle of Galveston, this company was stationed at Fort Moore. From November 1863 through the spring of 1864, Company I was stationed at Pelican Spit in Galveston Bay and was detailed to guard the CSS *Bayou City*. In the summer of 1864, Company I and three other companies of the 20th Texas Infantry were sent to Louisiana to protect the supply routes between Niblett's Bluff and Vermilion, Louisiana and then returned to Galveston in the fall to serve out the remainder of the war.

Montgomery County Men
in the 20th Texas Infantry
Company G

Abbott. Johnson, Pvt
Adams, Thomas R., Pvt
Anders, James, Pvt
Anders, James, Pvt
Arnold, E. L., Pvt
Arnold, Owen W., Pvt
Barker, G. F., Sgt
Boyd, A. R., Pvt
Brooks, William Haley, Sgt
Brown, R. J., Pvt
Burke, Charles, Pvt
Carson, Elihis Lemuel, Pvt
Chambers, Edward C., Pvt
Chatham, Andrew Singleton, Pvt
Cobb, J. G., Sgt
Compton, Barton William, Cpl
Connell, J. W., Pvt
Connell, M. A., Pvt
Dean, Reuben B., Pvt
Decker, Crisler, Pvt
Dupree, J. R., Pvt
Edwards, James Lemic, Pvt
Ellis, John, Pvt
Farmer, David, Pvt
Ferguson, John L., Pvt

Gerloff, Carl, Pvt
Herring, Asa Franklin, Pvt
Johnson, Jesse, Pvt
Kerr, William, Pvt
Lee, Andrew E., Pvt
Lipscomb, Nathan, Pvt
McCormack, J. P., Pvt
McRae, Cyrus D., Pvt
Parker, A. M., Pvt
Pool, Henry Joseph, Pvt
Pool, John William, Pvt
Rankin, W. M., Pvt
Rogers, Charles Lewis, Pvt
Sapp, John M., Sgt
Shannon, Benjamin Franklin, Pvt
Smith, Robert T., Pvt
Sones, Benson, Pvt
Wallace, Hugh Theodore, Pvt
Wallace, William Goodwin, Pvt
West, J. M., Pvt
Westbrook, J. A., Pvt
Willis, Peter James, Pvt
Womack, John Francis, Pvt
Womack, William G., Pvt

Company H

Malone, Thomas Monroe, Pvt
Malone, William Farrington, Pvt

Sandel, Erastus Emory, Pvt
Slaughter, Henry Travis, Pvt

Company I

Bay, James Henry, Jr., Pvt
Bay, Thomas Bowen, Pvt
Carrington, Edward William, Pvt

Carrington, Thomas Preston, Pvt
Dooley, Jesse, Pvt
Thomas, Simeon, Pvt

Company K

Adams, E. W., Pvt
Atchison, James W., Pvt
Baggerly, Isaac J., Pvt
Bailey, Pister M., Pvt
Bass, Tom W., Pvt

Bender, John F., Pvt
Boyd, T. D., Pvt
Boyd, Alex, Pvt
Brautigam, Friedrick, Pvt
Brautigam, George C., Pvt

Bradley, R. R., 2nd Lt
Brantley, Edward, Pvt
Bryant, Jacob, Pvt
Burton, George, Pvt
Carroll, David Allison, Pvt
Carson, R. L., Pvt
Catharino, David, Pvt
Clark, J. Edward, Pvt
Clark, John, Pvt
Clepper, Charles Duncan, Sgt
Clepper, James, Pvt
Clepper, Lemuel Gilliam, Capt
Clepper, Lorenzo Dow, Pvt
Cone, Thomas J., Pvt
Corgey, Henry, Pvt
Corgey, Lewis, Pvt
Curry, Tobias Franklin, Pvt
Davis, Franklin C., Pvt
Davis, John C., Pvt
Dikeman, William K., Sgt
Doughtie, Jacob, Pvt
Elliott, Mason H., 2nd Lt
Elliott, William D., Pvt
Ethridge, Horatio D., 2nd Lt
Evans, Henry, Pvt
Gafford, Seaborn W., Pvt
Gerloff, C. H. L., Pvt
Gilliam, James Wiley, Sgt
Glenn, Joseph C., Pvt
Goble, Thaddeus Lynn, Pvt
Goodson, Ed, Pvt
Graves, James W., Pvt
Graves, Jesse Cox, Pvt
Green, Levi, Pvt
Griffin, W. R., Pvt
Hall, Hiram H., Pvt
Hamby, Isaac, Pvt
Harrington, Robert Calvin, Pvt
Henry, John K., Pvt
Johnson, William Wilburn, Pvt
Kerr, William, Pvt
Lee, Alexander, Pvt
Leigh, Walter, Pvt
Lewin, C. W., Pvt
Mack, Jesse, Pvt
Martin, C., Pvt
Martin, James P., Pvt

Martin, John William, Pvt
Matthews, G. A., Pvt
Matthews, Jacob, Pvt
Matthews, Lamar Littleberry, Pvt
Matthews, Neuman Isaac, Pvt
Matthews, T. R., Pvt
McAlpine, William K., Pvt
McCaskell, Daniel A., Pvt
McCaskell, H. C., Pvt
McGrew, William J., 1st Lt
McLain, Joseph, Pvt
McLain, Moses, Pvt
McRae, R. W., Pvt
Meredith, Jacob A., Cpl
Norsworthy, Thomas Wiley, Pvt
Nuner, William P., Pvt
Oats, Stephen, Pvt
Outlaw, Alexander, Pvt
Outlaw, Frances Marion, Pvt
Parker, Joseph C., Pvt
Pillow, Andrew M., Pvt
Pinchback, George, Pvt
Ratliff, James R., Pvt
Rigby, A. H., Cpl
Ribgy, Eli, Pvt
Ribgy, William, 1st Lt
Roten, David Edward, Pvt
Sandel, J. M., Cpl
Sanders, James Madison, Pvt
Sanders, John, Pvt
Sanders, William F., Pvt
Shannon W., Pvt
Smith, Lewis Andrew, Pvt
Surles, Robert, Pvt
Travis, Joseph, Pvt
Tubb, James M., Pvt
Vick, Jesse, Pvt
Vick, Vincent C., Pvt
Wade, John M., Cpl
Walters, August, Pvt
Wickson, Cyrus, Pvt
Williams, Frances James, Pvt
Willis, Richard Short

21st Texas Cavalry

The 21st Texas Cavalry was the first of three regiments of Texas Cavalry that was organized by Methodist minister George Washington Carter. The other two regiments were the 24th Texas Cavalry and the 25th Texas Cavalry. These regiments were originally known as the 1st, 2nd, and 3rd Lancers or Carter's Lancers. Prior to their separation in Arkansas, these regiments were jokingly referred to as the Methodist Brigade because all three of their commanders were Methodist ministers.

The 1st Texas Lancers began enlisting men at Camp Hebert in December of 1861. The regiment was organized and trained in the spring of 1862 at Camp Carter near Hempstead Texas. The original officers of the regiment were Colonel George Washington Carter, Lieutenant D. C. Giddings, and Major Benjamin D. Chenoweth. The majority of the men in this regiment were from Austin, Bell, Brazos, Burnet, Goliad, Grimes, Lavaca, McLennan, Milam, Montgomery, Orange, Parker, Travis, Walker, and Washington Counties.

After training at Camp Carter, the three regiments of lancers assembled at Crockett, Texas in May of 1862 and began a long trip toward Arkansas. They arrived and camped near El Dorado, Arkansas in early July where they were designated the 21st, 24th, and 25th Texas Cavalries. With the need for infantry so great and fodder for the horses of three regiments of cavalry becoming so difficult to provide, the three regiments were ordered to dismount. In order to save the horses of his own 21st Texas Cavalry, Colonel George W. Carter aligned his regiment with Parson's Brigade and continued to operate as regular cavalry while the 24th and 25th Texas Cavalries were dismounted and assigned to Garland's Brigade.

There are very few official records that detail the activities of the 21st Texas Cavalry. It is known that as a part of Parson's Brigade, the regiment participated in Brigadier General John S. Marmaduke's invasion of Missouri in the spring of 1863 and was back in Arkansas prior to September of that year. During most of this time, the 21st Cavalry was commanded by Lieutenant Colonel D. C. Giddings. After a battle at Pine Bluff, Arkansas in October 1863, the regiment continued operations in Arkansas, serving primarily as a scouting unit. From March through May 1864, the 21st Texas Cavalry participated in the Red River campaign and under the command of Major Benjamin D. Chenoweth, was instrumental in the Confederate victory at the Battle of Mansfield. A see-saw battle on May 18, 1864 at Yellow Bayou in Louisiana is the last-known military engagement involving the 21st Texas Cavalry, after which the regiment returned to Arkansas and was assigned to Walter P. Lane's Brigade. The regiment returned to Texas in the spring of 1865 where it was disbanded.

Fifteen men from Montgomery County, Texas served in Company C of the 21st Texas Cavalry. This company was recruited and organized by Thomas Brandon Shannon who was elected captain of the company on February 26, 1862. His younger brother, Aaron Shannon, was elected 1st lieutenant. After arriving at camp in Arkansas, many of the men became seriously ill. Corporal W. B. Reynolds died in camp in September 1862. Captain T. B. Shannon resigned March 21, 1863 and returned to Texas. Records show that Lieutenant Aaron Shannon was left behind at camp near Cotton Plant, Arkansas in September of 1862 and was dropped from the rolls of the regiment on March 3, 1863. Aaron Shannon died in Montgomery County, Texas on February 12, 1864. A report for August 31, 1862 through February 28, 1863 states that Company C was in the field in Arkansas and that one man was without a gun, three men were without cartridge boxes, and only five men had six shooters. A report for September and October 1863, issued by Captain R. Sample Howard, states that frequent changes of encampments had been beneficially healthful to the troops and that most movements had been rapid and at night. The report goes on to state that Company C was involved in an attack of Union troops at Pine Bluff, Arkansas on October 25, 1863 and that the troops had conducted themselves with boldness of character.

Another soldier from Montgomery County, Private Hampton Wesley Carter, enlisted in Company H at Courtney in Grimes County on March 24, 1862. He was last shown present on a muster roll for Company H for the months of September and October of 1863.

Montgomery County Men
in the 21st Texas Cavalry
Company C

Bell, James Jefferson, Sgt
Carvell, William M., Pvt
Cheatham, William A., Cpl
Curtis, F. S., Pvt
Davis, James R., Pvt
Ford, T. M., Cpl
Gott, Thomas, Pvt
McCaskill, J. M., Pvt

Morse, M. H., Pvt
Ramsdell, Charles H., Pvt
Reynolds, W. B., Cpl
Ryals, William Alexander, 2nd Lt
Shannon, Aaron, 1st Lt
Shannon, Thomas Brandon, Capt
Shilling, Christopher, Pvt

Company H
Carter, Hampton Wesley, Pvt

24th Regiment, Texas Cavalry (Dismounted)
(2nd Texas Lancers)

The 24th Regiment, Texas Cavalry, also known as the 2nd Texas Lancers, was the second of three cavalry regiments raised by Methodist minister George Washington Carter. The first muster was on April 24, 1862 at Camp Carter which was near Camp Groce and not far from Hempstead, Texas. Originally, there were ten companies, A through K, in what was sometimes called the 2nd Regiment Carter's Brigade Texas Mounted Volunteers. The first commander of the regiment was another Methodist minister, Colonel Franklin C. Wilkes.

Other officers included Lt. Colonel Robert R. Neyland, Major Patrick H. Swearingen, and Major William A Taylor. First Lieutenant Benjamin D. Griffin of Montgomery County, served as adjutant. Captain Sam Wooldridge's Company B boasted 100 volunteers, almost all of whom were men from Montgomery County, Texas. Another fourteen men from Montgomery County enlisted in Captain Robert S. Poole's Company A.

After training at Camp Carter, the troops assembled at Crockett, Texas, in early May 1862 and began marching toward Arkansas. In June, many of the men became sick with the measles. Private Charles H. Thomas died June 12, 1862. While camped in Smith County on June 20th, twenty-four-year-old Private Larkin Roten died, presumably a victim of measles. The next day, Private Alex C. Copeland also died of disease. The exact burial places of these men are unknown. Private Walter W. Nichols was discharged on June 21, 1862.

By July 10th, most of the companies of the 2nd Lancers had crossed over into Arkansas and proceeded to El Dorado where they made camp. The August muster roll noted that Private Reuben Childers had died in the hospital at Shreveport. Louisiana, on July 10. It is uncertain if Captain Robert S. Poole and 1st. Lieutenant J. W. Maddox made the trip into Arkansas or remained in Shreveport, but at some point 2nd Lieutenant C. C. Hope assumed command of Company A.

Before being designated as the 21st, 24th, and 25th Texas Cavalry Regiments, the regiments were ordered to be dismounted by General Thomas C. Hindman. The order was likely given because the need for infantry was so great, and fodder for horses was so scarce. Regardless of the reasons, being dismounted met with strong protest from the men of the Lancers. The orders stated that one man from each company was to be elected to lead a detail of one man per ten horses to take the horses home and then return to their companies. Private L. A. Griffith was elected for Company A. It is believed that he was accompanied by Private L. M. Bridgers, Private M. D. Jones, and Private M. M. Uzell. These men did not return to Arkansas. While it is unclear who was elected to lead the detail from Company B, First Lieutenant Moses Graham, Sergeant J. H. Chambers, Private Jonathan Little, Private M. J. Milburn, Private John Smith, Private Samuel Terry, Private R. B. White, and Private J. E. Wilson made the trip to Montgomery County.

After being dismounted, Colonel G. W. Carter's 2nd Regiment of Lancers, under the command of Colonel F. C. Wilkes, was given the designation of 24th Texas Cavalry (Dismounted), and the 3rd Regiment of Lancers, under the command of Colonel C. C. Gillespie, was designated as the 25th Texas Cavalry (Dismounted). These two regiments were assigned to the brigade of Colonel Robert Garland and sent to Camp Holmes near Pine Bluff Arkansas for training as infantrymen. Colonel Carter's 1st Regiment of Lancers, designated as the 21st Texas Cavalry, was remounted and headed north toward Missouri as a part of Colonel W. H. Parson's brigade.

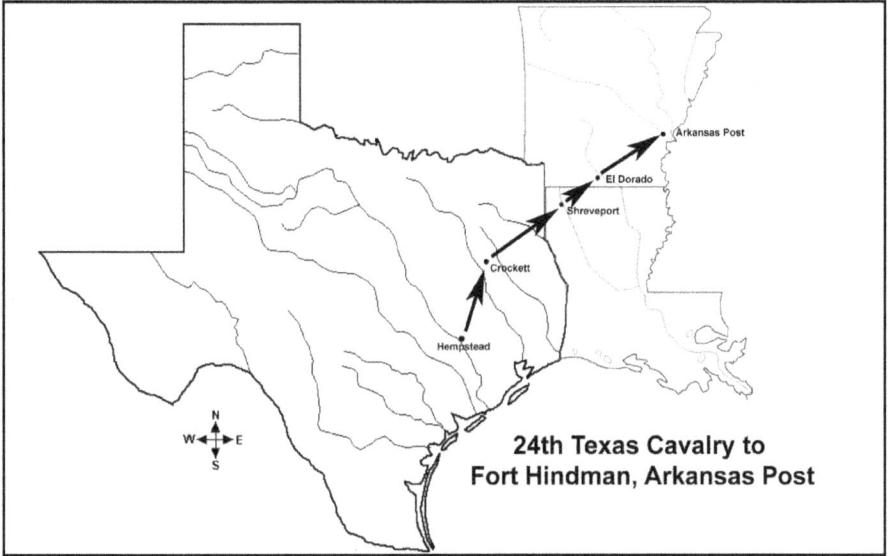

24th Texas Cavalry to
Fort Hindman, Arkansas Post

While at Camp Holmes, illness continued to plague the 24th Texas Cavalry. More than a dozen of the men from Company B, were reported absent on sick leave. Confederate service records indicate that Private Thomas J. Spear died of disease on August 2, 1862. Montgomery County probate records indicate that Private Spear might have made it home before he died, but in any case, there is a marker honoring him in the Camp White Sulphur Springs Confederate Cemetery near Pine Bluff, Arkansas. Private Wiley Green, the brother-in-law of T. J. Spear, died of disease on August 31, 1862 and is believed to be buried in an unmarked grave in this same cemetery. Confederate service records show that William W. Roten was on detached service in Texas on December 15, 1862. It is believed that he died during his detached service and never returned home to Montgomery County.

In the late fall of 1862, the men of the 24th Texas Cavalry broke camp and made their way toward Fort Hindman at Arkansas Post. It was a cold and miserable trip contributing to even more illness and death. Civilian inhabitants in the village of Arkansas Post provided a building to serve as a hospital which quickly filled up with the sick and dying. Private James H. Norsworthy and Private William Walker died of illness on November 11, 1862 and Private Thomas J. Wilson died of illness on November 19, 1862. Another member of Company B, Private John Smith, died December 13, 1862. It is not known if he was at Arkansas Post at the time.

Although hundreds of Confederate soldiers died at Arkansas Post prior to the siege of Fort Hindman, no cemetery nor burial site has been found. It is possible that change in the river channel over time has washed the burial sites away just as it did with Fort Hindman itself. It is known that after the battle, Confederate soldiers were not allowed time to bury their dead so the burial location of the men killed in action is also unknown.

By January 10, 1863, Union troops and Union gunboats began converging on Fort Hindman. The Confederate force of fewer than 6,000 men faced nearly 33,000 Union troops accompanied by a flotilla of Union gunboats. Heavy fire from Union gunboats had silenced the guns of Fort Hindman by mid-afternoon of January 11. Around 4:30 p.m., as Union forces under Major General John A. McClernand prepared to launch a final assault on the fort, white flags appeared along the Confederate lines. It is unknown who raised the first flag, but it was raised within the ranks of the 24th Texas Cavalry. No officer reported giving orders to raise a surrender flag, but Colonel F. C. Wilkes was later court-martialed and acquitted. The raising of the white flag caused a chain reaction, and soon the entire Confederate command was forced to surrender.

While historical accounts seldom expound on the significance of the Battle of Arkansas Post, the fall of Fort Hindman was a major contribution to the Union Army's effort to control the Mississippi River and to divide the Confederacy. It was also one of the most devastating events in the history of the town of Danville. One hundred of the Danville area's finest men left Montgomery County in support of the war effort. Eleven of these men died on the way to Arkansas Post, and four men, Private Milton Estell, Private Peter B. Irvine, Private James B. Thomasson, and Private R. B. White were killed in action, and the rest of Company B, eight men from Company A, and Private Greenberry Springer of Company D, 24th Texas Cavalry (Dismounted) became prisoners of a merciless enemy. While an element of shame might have existed among some the families of Montgomery County due to the fact that the first surrender flag had appeared from the ranks of the 24th Texas Cavalry (Dismounted), it was likely overridden by the grief from the deaths and the uncertain fate of those who survived the battle. Unfortunately, the grief would continue to escalate.

After the battle at Arkansas Post, Confederate soldiers were ordered to stack their weapons and to gather at the river for boarding transport ships. They were not allowed to return to their quarters to gather coats or blankets, and the cold January weather added to their discomfort and disheartenment. While awaiting transport, Private Andrew Jackson Brooks died from wounds received during the battle.

On January 13, 1863, the transport ships lifted anchor and headed toward the Mississippi River. The hopes of some soldiers that they might be taken to Vicksburg and paroled ended when the transports reached the Mississippi and turned northward toward Union prison camps. The weather was treacherously cold, and heavy snow was falling as they made their way up river to Memphis. Private John F. Chambers died in the hospital at Memphis on January 17, 1863 from wounds that he received in battle.

The prisoners reached St. Louis, Missouri about January 23, 1863. Many of the men had become severely ill during the voyage and were transferred to hospitals. In the period from January 23 to February 26, six members of Company B died in St. Louis hospitals. They were Private Jonathan T. McGary, Private Israel Hewitt, Private James McCarley, Private Thomas D. Golding, Private David Henry Parker and Private Thomas Chambers, Jr. All of these men are buried in Jefferson Barracks Cemetery. The last member of Company B to die in St. Louis was Private James E. Wilson who died on March 20, 1863. A burial location for James Wilson has not been determined. It is possible that his body was taken back to Texas.

After leaving St. Louis, the remaining prisoners were transported to Illinois. Enlisted men were sent to Camp Butler in Sangamon County, and officers were forwarded to Camp Chase in Ohio. The winter weather at Camp Butler was no less than brutal. The lack of proper clothing, exposure to the elements, and unsanitary living conditions led to widespread illness and death. In all, ten men from Montgomery County serving in the 24th Texas Cavalry (Dismounted) died at Camp Butler. Two men from Company A were Private C. A. Bridge(r)s who died on April 15, 1863 and Private Alfred Dafford who died on April 17, 1863. Eight men from Company B were Corporal James R. Baugass who died March 26, 1863, Private William B. Brake who died March 4, 1863, Private I. J. Burgess who died April 25, 1863, Private M. L. Elam who died March 19, 1863, Private Charles B. Estill who died April 13, 1863, Private M. J. Milburn who died March 14, 1863, Private George J. Nichols who died March 18, 1863, and Private George J. Quick who died March 29, 1863. All of these men were buried in Camp Butler Cemetery.

A single muster roll from Camp Butler Prison gives the only account of six black Confederate soldiers from Company B. Their names were listed as Alexander, George Estill, Green, Nelson, Worthy Sell, and L. Williams. This single roll simply reads "Liberated" which would indicate that they were possibly released from prison. No other records have been found that tell the fate of these men nor their involvement at the Battle of Arkansas Post. The outlook for their survival was bleak. None of the men were allowed to leave Arkansas Post with their winter coats or blankets, so being left to fend for themselves in the harsh Illinois winter would have been perilous. In addition, Illinois immigration laws made it illegal for blacks to immigrate to that state, so if these men did survive the winter elements, they likely would have had to evade local law enforcement to avoid being locked up or possibly even killed.

After several months of harsh prison life, most of the remaining men were paroled and later exchanged at City Point, Virginia. Those who were healthy enough were reassembled in the Army of Tennessee in the late spring of 1863. The men who were no longer fit for duty were transferred to the Trans-Mississippi Department and sent back to Texas. Due to dwindling numbers, the 24th was consolidated with the 25th Texas Cavalry (Dismounted) to form the 24th/25th Dismounted Texas Cavalry and assigned to Brigadier General James Deshler's Brigade.

By September 1863, General Braxton Bragg's Army of Tennessee had retreated into northern Georgia. Soon, two armies found themselves facing off from either side of a creek known as Chickamauga. Although the ensuing battle would result in a major victory for the Confederate Army of Tennessee, it was the first of many bloody battles that would eventually devastate the 24th/25th Dismounted Cavalry.

Because the Confederate forces under General Bragg were faring poorly, General Robert E. Lee dispatched two divisions of General Longstreet's Corps to assist Bragg's Army of Tennessee. On September 18, 1863, Major General John B. Hood of Longstreet's Corp arrived at Chickamauga Creek and took command of General Bushrod Johnson's Division. The men of 24th Texas Cavalry were consolidated with the 17th, 18th, and 25th Texas Cavalries to form a regiment commanded by Colonel F. C. Wilkes. This regiment was a part of Deshler's Brigade in General Patrick Cleburne's Division. The ensuing two-day battle resulted in a combined total of nearly 4,000 killed, 25,000 wounded, and 6,300 captured or missing. The costly battle would be the last major victory for the Confederate Army of Tennessee. The victory also came at a high price for Deshler's Brigade and the 24th Texas Cavalry (Dismounted). On the second day of battle, General James Deshler was killed instantly by a Union artillery shell which exploded in front of him, tearing his heart from his body. Private Charles A. Fowler of Company B along with Private Daniel L. Chambers and Sergeant John H. Chambers were killed in action. Another Montgomery County boy, Private Greenberry Springer of Company D, lost his left army in the fighting. Colonel Roger Q. Mills took temporary command of Deshler's Brigade as the army moved northward to occupy Chattanooga.

After a decisive victory at Chickamauga, Confederate General Braxton Bragg's Army of Tennessee besieged the city of Chattanooga, Tennessee, establishing themselves on the high grounds of Lookout Mountain and Missionary Ridge overlooking the city and Union supply lines therefore threatening to starve the forces into surrender. Due to dwindling numbers, the 24th Texas Cavalry (Dismounted) was consolidated with the 17th, 18th, and 25th Texas Cavalry (Dismounted) to form a new regiment under the command of Major William A. Taylor. They now joined with the 7th Texas Infantry regiment, commanded by Colonel Hiram B. Granbury along with a regiment formed by the consolidation of the 6th and 10th Texas Infantries and the 15th Texas Cavalry (Dismounted), commanded by Colonel Roger Q. Mills organizing General James A. Smith's Brigade.

On November 24, 1863, Smith's Brigade established a position at the far right of the Confederate battle line along Missionary Ridge at Tunnel Hill. Repulsing numerous attacks by Union forces commanded by Major General William T. Sherman, Smith's Brigade held its position at Tunnel Hill until reinforcements from Confederate General Patrick Cleburne's Division arrived and routed Union positions. During the intense fighting, General James A. Smith and Colonel Roger Q. Mills were both severely wounded. As a result, Colonel Hiram B. Granbury was appointed commander of the Smith's Brigade which would now become known as Granbury's Texas Brigade.

Despite the success of the Texas Brigade at Tunnel Hill, Major General U. S. Grant ordered his Union forces to attack the center of the Confederate line, which collapsed, thereby forcing Bragg's Confederate Army to retreat into Georgia. An attack by Union forces against the retreating Confederate Army was thwarted by the Texas Brigade and Cleburne's Division near Dalton, Georgia at the Battle of Ringgold Gap, inflicting heavy Union casualties.

On November 28, 1863, General Braxton Bragg sent a report of the Chattanooga campaign to President Jefferson Davis in which he asked to be relieved of his command. After several debates between President Davis and his cabinet members, General Joseph E. Johnston was selected to replace Bragg. This took place as the two armies made camp for the winter of 1864.

In May 1864, U.S. Major General William T. Sherman began his infamous Atlanta campaign with several aggressive flanking maneuvers to which Confederate General Joseph Johnston responded by continuously withdrawing deeper into Georgia. These consistent withdrawals caused President Davis to replace General Johnston with the more aggressive General John Bell Hood on July 17, 1864. There are very few individual records of the men in the 24th Texas Cavalry after April 1864, but battlefield reports show that the 24th Cavalry as a part of Granbury's Texas Brigade were involved in almost every major conflict between May 1864 and the fall of Atlanta in September of that year. Confederate service records for Lt. John M. Lewis indicate that he was in command of Company B, 24th Texas Cavalry from April 1863 until his capture near Atlanta on July 21, 1864. Records also show Lt. William H. Woodson had returned to Company B sometime during the Atlanta campaign and may have been company commander at the time that he was wounded in August 1864. Private Rufus R. Dean of Company A died of pneumonia on June 1, 1864, Ocmulgee Hospital, Macon, Georgia.

During the months of September and October 1864, Hood attacked Sherman's positions wherever and whenever possible, attempting to halt the Union Army's relentless march through Georgia. After conferring with President Davis, General Hood devised a plan to invade Tennessee, hoping that it would draw Sherman out of Georgia. In mid-October, Hood's army moved into Alabama on its way to Tennessee.

In an attempt to prevent General John Bell Hood's Confederate Army from invading Nashville, 27,000 Union troops under the command of Major General John Schofield began preparing strong defensive positions in the town of Franklin, Tennessee around entrenchments originally constructed for a previous engagement in 1863. On November 30, 1864, Hood's Confederate Army formed a two-mile front in preparation for the attack on Union troops in Franklin with Granbury's Texas Brigade in the center along the Columbia Pike. At 4:00 p.m. on November 30, more than 20,000 battle-hardened Confederate soldiers advanced toward Union defenses at Franklin. Granbury's Texas Brigade was the first to strike and ultimately to route Major General Wagner's two brigades, forcing them back behind the earthworks in Franklin. At just after 4:30 p.m., amidst a blizzard of rifle and cannon fire, General Hiram B. Granbury was shot through the head, killing him instantly. Within minutes, Granbury's commander, General Patrick Cleburne was killed. The fighting became so intense that one soldier commented that "it was if the devil had full possession of the earth." By 9:00 p.m., the fighting faded, leaving six of the Confederate Army's finest generals dead or dying. Private Alexander McGilvary and Private John Oliver Sandell of Company B, 24th Texas Cavalry were also killed in action. At midnight, the Union Army abandoned the battlefield and continued its march toward Nashville.

The Battle of Franklin has been called the bloodiest six hours of combat in the War between the States. The massive frontal assault was larger than Pickett's Charge at Gettysburg. In addition to losing six generals, Hood's army suffered approximately 6,300 casualties with more than 1,750 killed, 3,800 wounded, and 700 missing or captured. The 24th Texas Cavalry (Dismounted) had paid its price as well. Of the almost 100 men in Company B who left Montgomery County in 1862, not more than fourteen remained with this unit.

On December 2, 1864, General Hood's Confederate Army took up positions just south of Nashville. After having his army devastated at the Battle of Franklin, Hood decided to take a defensive position rather than to repeat a potentially-fruitless frontal attack. He entrenched his army and waited, hoping that the Union Army under the command of General George H. Thomas would attack his heaving defenses, allowing him to launch a counter attack and take Nashville. Having lost General Hiram B. Granbury and Lt. Colonel Robert Young at Franklin, Granbury's Texas Brigade was now commanded by Captain E. T. Broughton of the 7th Texas Infantry. On December 15, 1864, Union forces attacked the Texas Brigade which was manning a stout four-gun lunette on the west side of a deep cut on the Nashville & Chattanooga Railroad and were struck by very heavy close-range fire and were forced to retreat. On December 16, Thomas launched a massive assault which disintegrated the Confederate left flank, forcing Hood's army to abandon its defensive position and to retreat toward Franklin.

The Battle of Nashville marked the end of Hood's invasion of Tennessee. The Confederate Army of Tennessee retreated to Tupelo, Mississippi where General Hood resigned his command on January 13, 1865. Legend states that the retreating Texas Brigade adopted a song which they sang to the tune of the "Yellow Rose of Texas":

> *Oh, now I'm headed southward,*
> *For my heart is full of woe.*
> *I'm going back to Georgia*
> *To find my Uncle Joe.*
> *You may talk about your Beauregard*
> *And sing of General Lee,*
> *But the gallant Hood of Texas,*
> *Played hell in Tennessee!*

On January 23, 1865 in Tupelo, Mississippi, Lt. General John Bell Hood gave a farewell address to his troops and turned over the command to Lt. General Richard Taylor. The few remaining members of the 24th Texas Cavalry along with the rest of Granbury's Texas Brigade left Tupelo by train on January 25,

McGavock Confederate Cemetery, Franklin, Tennessee
photo courtesy of Karen McCann Hett

headed for Mobile, Alabama. The brigade continued traveling slowly through Georgia and South Carolina reaching its final destination in North Carolina by early March. On March 20, 1865, Granbury's Texas Brigade, now under the command of Major William A. Ryan, arrived at Bentonville, North Carolina where Confederate General Joseph Johnston's army was engaged with the Union Army of General William T. Sherman. By the time that the Texans joined in the battle, the Confederate Army was outnumbered five to one. Only nine members from Company B, 24th Texas Cavalry remained.

On April 9, 1865, General Johnston restructured his army, and the eight Texas regiments that had formed Granbury's Texas Brigade were now consolidated into one and designated Granbury's Consolidated Brigade, Texas Cavalry (1st Consolidated Regiment). The nine former members of Company B, 24th Texas Cavalry: O. P. Chambers, William Forrest, J. G. Gooch, James Hulon, Adam King, James McCan, Albert McKinney, Peter Sandel, and John Whitten were included in Company I of that regiment. The history of this new regiment would prove to be a short one. On April 26, 1865, General Johnston agreed to the terms of surrender offered by Union General William T. Sherman. All of the men would turn in their weapons and be paroled at Greensboro, North Carolina. Privately-owned horses and mules could be retained by their owners, and officers could retain their side arms. In addition, transportation would be furnished for the soldiers to their home states by the federal government wherever possible. This small group of men from Montgomery County could now make its way home.

Montgomery County Men in the
24th Texas Cavalry (Dismounted)

Regimental Officers:

Griffin, Benjamin D. – 1st Lieutenant/Adjutant. Enlisted age 28. Appointed 1st Lieutenant/Adjutant, April 24, 1862 at Camp Carter, Hempstead, Texas. Captured at Arkansas Post January 11, 1863. Forwarded from St. Louis Missouri to Camp Chase, Ohio, January 27,1863. Paroled at Ft. Delaware April 25, 1863. Exchanged at City Point, Virginia, April 29, 1863. Relieved of duty June 10, 1863. Ordered to Trans-Mississippi Department by General Bragg July 31, 1863. No further Confederate service records have been found.

Company A

Officers:

Poole, Robert S. – Captain. Enlisted age 35, December 15, 1861, Montgomery, Texas by Colonel G. W. Carter. First shown present April 4, 1862 Camp Carter, Hempstead, Texas. Shown present September-October 1862. Transferred to Trans-Mississippi Department.

Enlisted Men:

Bridge(r)s, C. A. – Private. Enlisted age 23, March 21, 1862, Montgomery, Texas by Robert S. Poole. First shown on roll April 4-August 31, 1862 on detached service. Captured at Arkansas Post January 11, 1863. Died in prison, Camp Butler, Illinois, April 15, 1863.

Bridge(r)s, Leonidas Moore – Private. Enlisted by Robert S. Poole. First shown on rolls May-June 1863. Transferred to Trans-Mississippi Department.

Cartwright, Pleasant L. – Private. Enlisted age 21, April 1, 1862, Montgomery, Texas by Robert S. Poole. First shown present April 4-August 31, 1862. Captured at Arkansas Post January 11, 1863. POW Camp Butler January 31, 1863. Paroled and exchanged in April 1863. Shown in hospital at Petersburg with smallpox April 17, 1863. Transferred to Trans-Mississippi Department prior to July 1863.

Dafford, Alfred – Private. Enlisted age 24, February 20, 1862, Montgomery, Texas by Robert S. Poole. First shown present April 4, 1862 Camp Carter, Hempstead, Texas. Captured at Arkansas Post January 11, 1863. Died in prison, Camp Butler, Illinois, February 17, 1862.

Dean, Henry Ingraham – Private. Enlisted age 19, May 12, 1862, Montgomery, Texas by Robert S. Poole. First shown April 4-August 31, 1862. Captured at Arkansas Post January 11, 1863. POW, Camp Butler, Illinois. Last shown present March-April 1864 in Georgia.

Dean, Robert T. – Private. Enlisted January 7, 1862, Galveston, Texas by Adjutant Steele. First shown present May-June 1863. Captured at Arkansas Post January 11, 1863. POW, Camp Butler, Illinois. Last shown present March-April 1864 in Georgia.

Dean, Rufus R. – Private. Enlisted January 6, 1863, Montgomery, Texas by Judge Bell. Died of pneumonia June 1, 1864, Ocmulgee Hospital, Macon, Georgia.

Dorwin, W. H. C. – Private. Enlisted age 28, May 13, 1862, Montgomery, Texas by Robert S. Poole. First shown present on roll dated April 4-August 31, 1862. Captured at Arkansas Post January 11, 1863. POW, Camp Butler, Illinois January 31, 1863. Discharged June 20, 1863.

Griffith, Leroy A. – Sergeant. Enlisted age 40, March 10, 1862, Montgomery, Texas by R. S. Poole. First shown present April 4, 1862 at Camp Carter, Hempstead, Texas. Detailed to return horses from Arkansas to Montgomery County. Transferred to Trans-Mississippi Department.

Hall, C. C. – Private. Enlisted age 21, March 1, 1862. First shown present April 4, 1862 at Camp Carter, Hempstead, Texas. Captured at Arkansas Post January 11, 1863. POW, Camp Butler, Illinois. In hospital at Petersburg, Virginia with smallpox April 21, 1863. Died while in Trans-Mississippi Dept. 1864.

Jones, M. D. – Private. Enlisted age 27, March 22, 1862, Montgomery, Texas by R. S. Poole. First shown present on roll dated April 4-August 31, 1862. Last shown present with his company on roll dated September and October 1862. Transferred to Trans-Mississippi Department. Promoted to 2nd Lt., Co. E, 24th/25th Consolidated Regiment 1865.

Little, Samuel – Corporal. Enlisted age 19 on January 1, 1862 by Robert S. Poole. First shown present April 4, 1862 Camp Carter, Hempstead, Texas. Captured at Arkansas Post January 11, 1863. POW, Camp Butler, Illinois January 31, 1863. Last shown on roll dated March-April 1864.

Shaw, John – Private. Enlisted age 18, February 20, 1862 by Robert S. Poole. First shown present April 4, 1862 Camp Carter, Hempstead, Texas. Shown present for September-October 1862. Last shown as sick on furlough.

Uzell, M. M. – Private. Enlisted age 27, March 22, 1862, Montgomery, Texas by R. S. Poole. First shown present April 4, 1862 Camp Carter, Hempstead, Texas. Shown present on roll of September-October 1862. Transferred to Trans-Mississippi Department.

Company B*

Officers:

Wooldridge, Samuel D. – Captain. Enlisted age 38, March 29, 1862 Danville, Texas by John E. George. First shown present April 28, 1862 Camp Carter, Hempstead, Texas. Captured Arkansas Post January 11, 1863. Forwarded from St. Louis, Missouri to Camp Chase, Ohio January 27, 1863. Paroled at Ft. Delaware April 25, 1863. Exchanged City Point, Virginia. Ordered to Trans-Mississippi Department July 18, 1863 by General Bragg.

Graham, Moses – 1st Lieutenant. Enlisted age 37, March 29, 1862 Danville, Texas by John E. George. First shown present April 28, 1862 Camp Carter, Hempstead, Texas. Detailed to return horses to Texas from Arkansas August 1862. Returned to Arkansas and shown present on roll September-October 1862. Resigned November 1862.

Thomason, Jabez S. – 1st Lieutenant. Enlisted age 34, March 29, 1862 Danville, Texas by John E. George. First shown present April 28, 1862 Camp Carter, Hempstead, Texas. Captured Arkansas Post January 11, 1863. Forwarded from St. Louis, Missouri to Camp Chase, Ohio January 27, 1863. Paroled Ft. Delaware April 25, 1863. Exchanged City Point, Virginia April 29, 1863. Last shown present on roll April 30, 1863 signing as commander of the company. Ordered to Trans-Mississippi Department by General Bragg.

Woodson, William H. – 2st Lieutenant. Enlisted age 28, March 29, 1862 Danville, Texas by John E. George. First shown present April 28, 1862 Camp Carter, Hempstead, Texas. Captured Arkansas Post January 11, 1863. Forwarded from St. Louis, Missouri to Camp Chase, Ohio January 27, 1863. Paroled Ft. Delaware April 25, 1863. Exchanged City Point, Virginia. Ordered to Trans-Mississippi Department by General Bragg. Returned to regiment 1864. Appears on register of patients Ocmulgee Hospital, Macon, Georgia August 11, 1863, stating left battle August 10 with fractured leg. Record also shows his leg was amputated. Returned to duty October 12, 1864. No later records shown.

Lewis, John McClanahan, Jr. – 2nd Lieutenant. Enlisted age 22 Galveston, Texas April 17, 1862 by Lieutenant Steel, mustered into service by Colonel F. C. Wilkes at Shreveport, Louisiana. First shown present on roll April 28-August 31, 1862. Last shown present on roll March-April 1864. Captured Arkansas Post January 11, 1863. Forwarded from St. Louis, Missouri to Camp Chase, Ohio January 27, 1863. Paroled Ft. Delaware April 25, 1863. Exchanged City Point, Virginia. Shown present July 1863-February 1864 as commander of company. Last shown present on roll March-April 1864.

Enlisted Men:

Adams, William G. – Sergeant. Enlisted age 39, March 29, 1862, Danville, Texas. First shown present April 28, 1862 Camp Carter, Hempstead, Texas. Discharged September 6, 1862.

Alexander, Negro – No age shown. Appears on roll of prisoners of war received at Camp Butler, Illinois January 31, 1863. Shown as liberated. No further records appear in file.

Baugass, J. R. – Corporal. Enlisted age 27, March 29, 1862, Danville, Texas. First shown present April 28, 1862 Camp Carter, Hempstead, Texas. Captured Arkansas Post January 11, 1863. POW Camp Butler, Illinois. Died of disease Camp Butler, Illinois March 26, 1863. Buried Camp Butler National Cemetery.

Bell, Henry Ellsworth – Private. Enlisted age 18, March 29, 1862 Danville, Texas. First shown present April 28, 1862 Camp Carter, Hempstead, Texas. Captured Arkansas Post January 11, 1863. Gratiot Street Prison in St. Louis, Missouri. Took Oath of Allegiance to U.S. March, released from hospital and allowed to leave.

Bolton, John T. – Private. Enlisted age 32, March 28, 1862 Danville, Texas. Confederate Service also recorded as John T. Boulton. First shown present April 28, 1862 Camp Carter, Hempstead, Texas. Captured Arkansas Post January 11, 1863. POW Camp Butler, Illinois. Took Oath of Allegiance to U.S. March 3, 1863.

Name last appears on roll dated August 1, 1863 stating "deserted, took oath of allegiance at Camp Butler, Ill." No further trace of him has been found.

Brake, William B. – Private. Enlisted age 18, March 29, 1862 Danville, Texas. First shown present April 28, 1862 Camp Carter, Hempstead, Texas. Captured Arkansas Post January 11, 1863. POW Camp Butler, Illinois. Died at Camp Butler, Illinois, March 4, 1863. Cause of death unknown. Buried Camp Butler National Cemetery.

Brooks, Andrew J. – Private. Enlisted age 18, March 29, 1862 Danville, Texas. First shown present April 28, 1862 Camp Carter, Hempstead, Texas. Mortally wounded Battle of Arkansas Post January 11, 1863. Died January 12, 1863. Burial site unknown.

Burgess, I. J. – Private. Enlisted age 18, April 8, 1862, Montgomery, Texas. First shown present April 28, 1862 Camp Carter, Hempstead, Texas. Captured Arkansas Post January 11, 1863. POW Camp Butler, Illinois. Died at Camp Butler, Illinois March 13, 1863. Cause of death unknown. Buried Camp Butler National Cemetery.

Chambers, Daniel L. – Private. Enlisted age 21, March 29, 1862 Danville, Texas. First shown present April 28, 1862 Camp Carter, Hempstead, Texas. Captured Arkansas Post January 11, 1863. POW Camp Butler, Illinois January 31, 1863. Paroled and exchanged City Point, Virginia April 1863. Killed in action Battle of Chickamauga September 20, 1863.

Chambers, John F. – Private. Enlisted age 36, March 29, 1862 Danville, Texas. First shown present April 28, 1862 Camp Carter, Hempstead, Texas. Captured Arkansas Post January 11, 1863. Died at Memphis, Tennessee from wounds received in Battle of Arkansas Post.

Chambers, John H. – Sergeant. Enlisted age 23, March 29, 1862 Danville, Texas. First shown present April 28, 1862 Camp Carter, Hempstead, Texas. Captured Arkansas Post January 11, 1863. POW Camp Butler, Illinois January 31, 1863. Paroled and exchanged City Point, Virginia April 1863. Killed in action Battle of Chickamauga September 20, 1863.

Chambers, Oliver Perry – Private. Enlisted age 17, July 20, 1862 Danville, Texas. First shown present September 1862. Captured Arkansas Post January 11, 1863. POW Camp Butler, Illinois January 31, 1863. Paroled and exchanged City Point, Virginia April 1863. Serving with Company B, 24th Texas Cavalry when it was reorganized as Company I, Granbury's Consolidated Brigade, Texas Cavalry (1st Consolidated Regiment), surrendered with General Joseph Johnston's army April 26, 1865, paroled at Greensboro, North Carolina.

Chambers, Thomas – Private. Enlisted age 20, March 29, 1862 Danville, Texas. First shown present April 28, 1862 Camp Carter, Hempstead, Texas. Captured Arkansas Post January 11, 1863. POW, Gratiot Street Prison, St. Louis, Missouri. Died of disease Gratiot Prison Hospital February 26, 1863, buried Jefferson Barracks Cemetery.

Childers, Jefferson P. – Corporal. Enlisted age 20, March 29, 1862 Danville, Texas. First shown present April 28, 1862 Camp Carter, Hempstead, Texas. Shown on roll of April 28-August 31, 1862 as sick in camp. Appears on list of refugees from Arkansas Post. Transferred to Trans-Mississippi Department.

Childers, Reuben – Private. Enlisted age 22, March 29, 1862 Danville, Texas. First shown present April 28, 1862 Camp Carter, Hempstead, Texas. Died of disease in Shreveport Confederate Hospital July 10, 1862.

Collard, Jonathan – Private. Enlisted age 24, March 29, 1862 Danville, Texas. First shown present April 28, 1862 Camp Carter, Hempstead, Texas. Appears on rolls of June-October 1862 as absent on sick furlough. Transferred to Trans-Mississippi Department.

Conn, John L. – Private. Enlisted age 46, March 29, 1862 Danville, Texas. Discharged July 28, 1862 El Dorado, Arkansas.

Copeland, Alex C. – Private. Enlisted age 17, April 8, 1862 Montgomery, Texas. First shown present April 28, 1862 Camp Carter, Hempstead, Texas. Died of disease in Smith County, Texas June 21, 1862.

Cude, Timothy Jackson – Private. Enlisted age 18, March 29, 1862 Danville, Texas. First shown present April 28, 1862 Camp Carter, Hempstead, Texas. Discharged on July 28, 1862.

Elam, M. L. – Private. Enlisted age 18, March 29, 1862 Danville, Texas. First shown present April 28, 1862 Camp Carter, Hempstead, Texas. Captured Arkansas Post January 11, 1863. POW Camp Butler, Illinois. Died Camp Butler, Illinois March 26, 1863. Buried in Camp Butler Cemetery.

Estill, Charles B. – Private. Enlisted age 26, March 29, 1862 Danville, Texas. First shown present April 28, 1862 Camp Carter, Hempstead, Texas. Captured Arkansas Post January 11, 1863. POW Camp Butler, Illinois. Died at Camp Butler, Illinois April 13, 1863. Buried in Camp Butler Cemetery.

Estill, Milton – Private. Enlisted age 18, March 29, 1862 Danville, Texas. First shown present April 28, 1862 Camp Carter, Hempstead, Texas. Killed in action at Battle of Arkansas Post. Burial site unknown.

Estill, George (Negro) – No age shown. Appears on roll of prisoners of war received at Camp Butler, Illinois January 31, 1863. Shown as liberated. No further records appear in file.

Forrest, William Whitfield – Private. Enlisted age 26, March 29, 1862 Danville, Texas. First shown present April 28, 1862 Camp Carter, Hempstead, Texas. Captured Arkansas Post January 11, 1863. POW Camp Butler, Illinois, January 31, 1863. Paroled and exchanged City Point, Virginia April 1863. Shown absent, sick in hospital January-April 1864. Serving with Company B, 24th Texas Cavalry when reorganized as Company I, Granbury's Consolidated Brigade, Texas Cavalry (1st Consolidated Regiment). Surrendered with General Joseph Johnston's army April 26, 1865 and paroled Greensboro, North Carolina.

Fowler, Charles A. – Private. Enlisted age 18, March 29, 1862 Danville, Texas. First shown present April 28, 1862 Camp Carter, Hempstead, Texas. Captured Arkansas Post January 11, 1863. POW Camp Butler, Illinois January 31, 1863. Paroled and exchanged City Point, Virginia April 1863. Killed in action Battle of Chickamauga September 20, 1863.

Golding, Thomas D. – Private. Enlisted age 19, March 29, 1862 Danville, Texas. First shown present April 28, 1862 Camp Carter, Hempstead, Texas.

Captured Arkansas Post January 11, 1863. POW Gratiot Street Prison, St. Louis, Missouri. Died of disease in Gratiot Prison Hospital February 13, 1863, buried Jefferson Barracks Cemetery.

Golding, Henry R. – Private. Enlisted age 18, March 29, 1862 Danville, Texas. First shown present April 28, 1862 Camp Carter, Hempstead, Texas. Captured Arkansas Post January 11, 1863. POW Gratiot Street Prison at St. Louis, Missouri. Paroled and exchanged City Point, Virginia April 1863. Shown sick in hospital through April 1864.

Green (Negro) – No age shown. Appears on roll of prisoners of war received at Camp Butler, Illinois January 31, 1863. Shown as liberated. No further records appear in file.

Green, Wiley – Private. Enlisted age 28, March 29, 1862 Danville, Texas. First shown present April 28, 1862 Camp Carter, Hempstead, Texas. Died of disease August 31, 1862 at Pine Bluff, Arkansas, believed to be buried in Camp White Sulphur Springs Cemetery.

Guynn, John A. – Private. Enlisted age 19, March 28, 1862 Danville, Texas. First shown present April 28, 1862 Camp Carter, Hempstead, Texas. Captured Arkansas Post January 11, 1863. POW Camp Butler, Illinois January 31, 1863. Paroled and exchanged City Point, Virginia April 1863. Last shown present on roll of March-April 1864. Signed Parole of Honor July 14, 1865 Columbus, Texas.

Guynn, William James (J. W.) – Private. Enlisted age 21, March 28, 1862 Danville, Texas. First shown present April 28, 1862 Camp Carter, Hempstead, Texas. Captured Arkansas Post January 11, 1863. POW Camp Butler, Illinois January 31, 1863. Paroled and exchanged City Point, Virginia April 1863. Roll of March-April 1864 shows as absent on furlough (possibly sick). Transferred to Trans-Mississippi Department.

Hayden, Samuel T. – Private. Enlisted age 29, March 29, 1862 Danville, Texas. First shown present April 28, 1862 Camp Carter, Hempstead, Texas. Received 60-day furlough November 8, 1862. Transferred to Trans-Mississippi Department.

Hewitt, Israel – Private. Enlisted age 53, December 11, 1862 Arkansas Post. Captured at Battle of Arkansas Post January 11, 1863. Died at City General Hospital St. Louis, Missouri February 3, 1863, buried Jefferson Barracks Cemetery.

Hoskins, John C. – Private. Enlisted age 24, March 29, 1862 Danville, Texas. First shown present April 28, 1862 Camp Carter, Hempstead, Texas. Captured Arkansas Post January 11, 1863, admitted to City General Hospital in St. Louis, Missouri with wounds received in battle. Transferred to Gratiot Street Military Prison May 7, 1863. Paroled and exchanged City Point, Virginia April 1863. Discharged October 12, 1863.

Hoskins, Thomas J. – Private. Enlisted age 25, March 29, 1862 Danville, Texas. First shown present April 28, 1862 Camp Carter, Hempstead, Texas. Died Arkansas Post October 29, 1862. Burial site unknown.

Hulon, James William – Private. Enlisted age 21, March 29, 1862 Danville, Texas. First shown present April 28, 1862 Camp Carter,

Hempstead, Texas. Captured Arkansas Post January 11, 1863. POW Camp Butler, Illinois January 31, 1863. Paroled and exchanged City Point, Virginia April 1863. Serving with Company B, 24th Texas Cavalry when it was reorganized as Company I, Granbury's Consolidated Brigade, Texas Cavalry (1st Consolidated Regiment) which surrendered with General Joseph Johnston's army April 26, 1865 and paroled at Greensboro, North Carolina.

Irvine, Peter Belles – Private. Enlisted age 38, March 29, 1862 Danville, Texas. First shown present April 28, 1862 Camp Carter, Hempstead, Texas. Killed in action Battle of Arkansas Post January 11, 1863.

King, Adam Meek – Private. Enlisted age 24, March 29, 1862 Danville, Texas. First shown present April 28, 1862 Camp Carter, Hempstead, Texas. Captured Arkansas Post January 11, 1863. POW Camp Butler, Illinois January 31, 1863. Paroled and exchanged City Point, Virginia April 1863. Serving with Company B, 24th Texas Cavalry when it was reorganized as Company I, Granbury's Consolidated Brigade, Texas Cavalry (1st Consolidated Regiment) which surrendered with General Joseph Johnston's army April 26, 1865 and paroled at Greensboro, North Carolina.

King, Henry Clay – Corporal. Enlisted age 28, March 24, 1862 Danville, Texas. First shown present April 28, 1862 Camp Carter, Hempstead, Texas. Captured Arkansas Post January 11, 1863. POW Camp Butler, Illinois January 31, 1863. Signed Oath of Allegiance at Camp Butler and was released. Returned to Texas.

King, Thomas Edward – Private. Enlisted age 22, March 29, 1862 Danville, Texas. First shown present April 28, 1862 Camp Carter, Hempstead, Texas. Captured Arkansas Post January 11, 1863. POW Camp Butler, Illinois January 31, 1863. Paroled and exchanged City Point, Virginia April 1863. Sent to hospital in Petersburg, Virginia July 1863. Transferred to Trans-Mississippi Dept.

Lewis, Eldon McKinley – Private. Enlisted age 27, March 29, 1862 Danville, Texas. First shown present April 28, 1862 Camp Carter, Hempstead, Texas. Captured Arkansas Post January 11, 1863. POW Camp Butler, Illinois January 31, 1863. Paroled and exchanged City Point, Virginia April 1863. Wounded at Ringgold Gap, November 1863. Wounded at Jonesboro, Georgia, August 31, 1864. Believed to have died in hospital at Cuthbert, Georgia.

Lindley, Elijah – Private. Enlisted age 27, March 29, 1862 Danville, Texas. First shown present April 28, 1862 Camp Carter, Hempstead, Texas. Absent, sick, furloughed for 60 days, June 25, 1862. Last shown on roll of March-April 1864 as sick on furlough.

Lindley, James – Private. Enlisted age 31, March 29, 1862 Danville, Texas. First shown present April 28, 1862 Camp Carter, Hempstead, Texas. Captured Arkansas Post January 11, 1863. POW Camp Butler, Illinois January 31, 1863. Roll of prisoners exchanged City Point, Virginia April 30, 1863 shows absent without leave having taken Oath of Allegiance to U.S.

Lindley, John – Private. Enlisted age 33, March 29, 1862 Danville, Texas. First shown present April 28, 1862 Camp Carter, Hempstead, Texas. Captured Arkansas Post January 11, 1863. POW Camp Butler, Illinois January 31, 1863. Shown present June-December 1863 and February-April 1864. Admitted to St. Mary's Hospital, La Grange, Georgia in summer 1864. Returned to duty August 17, 1864.

Little, Jonathan – Private. Enlisted age 33, March 29, 1862 Danville, Texas. First shown present April 28, 1862 Camp Carter, Hempstead, Texas. Detailed to return horses to Montgomery County in summer 1862. Shown sick on furlough October 1862. Believed to have died in Arkansas.

Malone, Henderson F. – Corporal. Enlisted age 24, March 29, 1862 Danville, Texas. First shown present April 28, 1862 Camp Carter, Hempstead, Texas. Discharged July 13, 1862. Joined 24th/25th Consolidated Texas Cavalry (Trans-Mississippi Dept.).

Malone, Thomas Monroe – Private. Enlisted age 26, March 29, 1862 Danville, Texas. First shown present April 28, 1862 Camp Carter, Hempstead, Texas. Transferred to 20th Texas Infantry.

Martin, Francis Marion – Private. Enlisted age 21, March 29, 1862 Danville, Texas. First shown present April 28, 1862 Camp Carter, Hempstead, Texas. Present, sick in hospital September-October 1862. Presumed to have died in Arkansas in winter 1862-1863.

McCan, James Marion – Private. Enlisted age 24, March 29, 1862 Danville, Texas. First shown present April 28, 1862 Camp Carter, Hempstead, Texas. Captured Arkansas Post January 11, 1863. POW Camp Butler, Illinois. Paroled and exchanged City Point, Virginia April 1863. Serving with Company B, 24th Texas Cavalry when it was reorganized as Company I, Granbury's Consolidated Brigade, Texas Cavalry (1st Consolidated Regiment) which surrendered with General Joseph Johnston's army April 26, 1865 and paroled at Greensboro, North Carolina.

McCarley, James – Private. Enlisted age 24, March 29, 1862 Danville, Texas. First shown present April 28, 1862 Camp Carter, Hempstead, Texas. Captured Arkansas Post January 11, 1863. POW Gratiot Street Prison, St. Louis, Missouri. Died February 8, 1863. Buried Jefferson Barracks National Cemetery, St. Louis County, Missouri.

McCrory, Marion A. – Sergeant. Enlisted age 28, March 29, 1862 Danville, Texas. First shown present April 28, 1862 Camp Carter, Hempstead, Texas. Captured Arkansas Post January 11, 1863. POW Camp Butler, Illinois. Signed Oath of Allegiance to U.S. and released. Returned to Texas.

McGary, Jonathan T. – Private. Enlisted age 22, March 29, 1862 Danville, Texas. First shown present April 28, 1862 Camp Carter, Hempstead, Texas. Captured Arkansas Post January 11, 1863. POW Gratiot Street Prison, St. Louis, Missouri. Died January 23, 1863. Buried Jefferson Barracks National Cemetery, St. Louis County, Missouri.

McGilvary, Alexander Murdock – Private. Enlisted age 18, March 29, 1862 Danville, Texas. First shown present April 28, 1862 Camp Carter, Hempstead,

Texas. Captured Arkansas Post January 11, 1863. POW Camp Butler, Illinois. Paroled and exchanged City Point, Virginia April 1863. KIA Battle of Franklin, Tennessee, November 30, 1864 (death unconfirmed).

McIntyre, James Robert – Private. Enlisted age 30, March 29, 1862 Danville, Texas. First shown present April 28, 1862 Camp Carter, Hempstead, Texas. Captured Arkansas Post January 11, 1863. POW Camp Butler, Illinois. Escaped from prison February 1863. Joined Trans-Mississippi Department.

McIntyre, Jesse Cothier – Private. Enlisted age 30, March 29, 1862 Danville, Texas. First shown present April 28, 1862 Camp Carter, Hempstead, Texas. Discharged (probably due to illness) May 26, 1862.

McKinney, Albert Wrinkles – Private. Enlisted age 19, March 29, 1862 Danville, Texas. First shown present April 28, 1862 Camp Carter, Hempstead, Texas. Captured Arkansas Post January 11, 1863. POW Camp Butler, Illinois. Paroled and exchanged City Point, Virginia April 1863. Serving with Company B, 24th Texas Cavalry when it was reorganized as Company I, Granbury's Consolidated Brigade, Texas Cavalry (1st Consolidated Regiment) which surrendered with General Joseph Johnston's army April 26, 1865 and paroled at Greensboro, North Carolina.

Milburn, M. J. – Private. Enlisted age 30, March 29, 1862 Danville, Texas. First shown present April 28, 1862 Camp Carter, Hempstead, Texas. Captured Arkansas Post January 11, 1863. POW Camp Butler, Illinois January 31, 1863. Died March 14, 1863. Buried Camp Butler National Cemetery, Springfield, Sangamon County, Illinois.

Moore, William C. – Private. Enlisted age 30, March 29, 1862 Danville, Texas. First shown present April 28, 1862 Camp Carter, Hempstead, Texas. Furloughed June 20, 1862. Transferred to Trans-Mississippi Dept.

Nelson (Negro) – No age shown. Appears on roll of prisoners of war received at Camp Butler, Illinois January 31, 1863. Shown as liberated. No further records appear in file.

Nichols, George J. – Private. Enlisted age 31, March 29, 1862 Danville, Texas. First shown present April 28, 1862 Camp Carter, Hempstead, Texas. Captured Arkansas Post January 11, 1863. POW Camp Butler, Illinois. Died March 18, 1863. Buried Camp Butler National Cemetery, Sangamon County, Illinois.

Nichols. Walter W. – Private. Enlisted age 27, March 29, 1862 Danville, Texas. First shown present April 28, 1862 Camp Carter, Hempstead, Texas. Discharged June 21, 1862. No further records found.

Nobles, John W. – Private. Enlisted age 28, March 29, 1862 Danville, Texas. First shown present April 28, 1862 Camp Carter, Hempstead, Texas. Discharged August 15, 1862. Believed to have died in Arkansas.

Norsworthy, James H. – Private. Enlisted age 22, April 19, 1862 Danville, Texas. First shown present April 28, 1862 Camp Carter, Hempstead, Texas. Died November 11, 1862 Arkansas.

O'Banion, John R. – Private. Enlisted age 32, March 28, 1862 Danville, Texas. First shown present April 28, 1862 Camp Carter, Hempstead, Texas.

Captured Arkansas Post January 11, 1863. POW Camp Butler, Illinois. Paroled and exchanged City Point, Virginia April 1863. May-June 1863 sick in hospital. Last shown present April 1864. Believed to have died during the Atlanta campaign.

Pace, John Pinckney – Private. Enlisted age 19, March 28, 1862 Danville, Texas. First shown present April 28, 1862 Camp Carter, Hempstead, Texas. Last shown present September-October 1862. No further records found.

Parker, David Henry – Private. Enlisted age 20, April 16, 1862 Danville, Texas. First shown present April 28, 1862 Camp Carter, Hempstead, Texas. Captured Arkansas Post January 11, 1863. POW Gratiot Street Prison, St. Louis, Missouri. Died February 18, 1863. Buried Jefferson Barracks National Cemetery, St. Louis County, Missouri.

Quick, George J. – Private. Enlisted age 31, March 28, 1862 Danville, Texas. First shown present April 28, 1862 Camp Carter, Hempstead, Texas. Captured Arkansas Post January 11, 1863. POW Camp Butler, Illinois. Died about March 1863. Buried Camp Butler National Cemetery, Sangamon County, Illinois.

Reding, John Baker – Corporal. Enlisted age 45, March 29, 1862 Danville, Texas. First shown present April 28, 1862 Camp Carter, Hempstead, Texas. Discharged July 28, 1862. Later enlisted in 17th Brigade TST.

Rogers, William D. – Private. Enlisted age 34, March 29, 1862 Danville, Texas. First shown present April 28, 1862 Camp Carter, Hempstead, Texas. Captured Arkansas Post January 11, 1863. POW Camp Butler, Illinois. Took Oath of Allegiance to U.S. and released. No further records found.

Roten (Rotten), Larkin J. – Private. Enlisted age 23, March 29, 1862 Danville, Texas. First shown present April 28, 1862 Camp Carter, Hempstead, Texas. Died in Smith County, Texas June 20, 1862.

Roten (Rotten), William W. – Private. Enlisted age 38, March 29, 1862 Danville, Texas. First shown present April 28, 1862 Camp Carter, Hempstead, Texas. Died after December 15, 1862.

Sandel (Sandell), John Oliver – Private. Enlisted age 31, March 29, 1862 Danville, Texas. First shown present April 28, 1862 Camp Carter, Hempstead, Texas. Captured Arkansas Post January 11, 1863. POW Camp Butler, Illinois. Paroled and exchanged City Point, Virginia April 1863. Killed in action at Battle of Franklin, Tennessee, November 30, 1864.

Sandel (Sandell), Peter Tabor – Private. Enlisted age 31, March 29, 1862 Danville, Texas. First shown present April 28, 1862 Camp Carter, Hempstead, Texas. Captured Arkansas Post January 11, 1863. POW Camp Butler, Illinois. Paroled and exchanged City Point, Virginia April 1863. Serving with Company B, 24th Texas Cavalry when it was reorganized as Company I, Granbury's Consolidated Brigade, Texas Cavalry (1st Consolidated Regiment) which surrendered with General Joseph Johnston's army April 26, 1865 and paroled at Greensboro, North Carolina.

Sell, Worthy (Negro) – No age shown. Appears on roll of prisoners of war received at Camp Butler, Illinois January 31, 1863. Shown as liberated. No further records appear in file.

Smith, John – Private. Enlisted age 21, March 29, 1862 Danville, Texas. First shown present April 28, 1862 Camp Carter, Hempstead, Texas. Died October 13, 1862 Arkansas.

Spear, Thomas Jackson – Private. Enlisted age 24, March 29, 1862 Danville, Texas. First shown present April 28, 1862 Camp Carter, Hempstead, Texas. Died August 2,1862.

Tarpley, Barbee – Private. Enlisted age 18, March 29, 1862 Danville, Texas. First shown present April 28, 1862 Camp Carter, Hempstead, Texas. Escaped from Battle of Arkansas Post January 11, 1863. Joined Trans-Mississippi Dept.

Terry, Samuel – Private. Enlisted age 31, March 29, 1862 Danville, Texas. First shown present April 28, 1862 Camp Carter, Hempstead, Texas. Escaped from Battle of Arkansas Post January 11, 1863. Joined Trans-Mississippi Dept.

Thomas, Charles Henry – Private. Enlisted age 26, March 29, 1862 Danville, Texas. First shown present April 28, 1862 Camp Carter, Hempstead, Texas. Died June 12, 1862.

Thomason, Frances Marion – Private. Enlisted age 18, March 29, 1862 Danville, Texas. First shown present April 28, 1862 Camp Carter, Hempstead, Texas. Captured Arkansas Post January 11, 1863. POW Camp Butler, Illinois. Paroled and exchanged City Point, Virginia April 1863. Muster rolls for June 1863-April 1864 show absent, sick at hospital. Transferred to Trans-Mississippi Dept.

Thomason, James Burke – Private. Enlisted age 30, April 16, 1862 Galveston, Texas. First shown present April 28, 1862 Camp Carter, Hempstead, Texas. Killed in action at Battle of Arkansas Post January 11, 1863.

Walker, Samuel T. (T. S.) – Private. Enlisted age 20, March 29, 1862 Danville, Texas. First shown present April 28, 1862 Camp Carter, Hempstead, Texas. Captured Arkansas Post January 11, 1863. POW Camp Butler, Illinois. Paroled and exchanged City Point, Virginia April 1863. Muster roll for March-April 1864 shows absent, sick in hospital. No further records found.

Walker, William – Corporal. Enlisted age 46, March 29, 1862 Danville, Texas. First shown present April 28, 1862 Camp Carter, Hempstead, Texas. Died November 11, 1862 Arkansas.

Westmoreland, John Thompson – Private. Enlisted age 33, April 25, 1862 Danville, Texas. First shown present April 28, 1862 Camp Carter, Hempstead, Texas. Captured Arkansas Post January 11, 1863. POW Camp Butler, Illinois. Paroled and exchanged City Point, Virginia April 1863. Captured at Battle of Chickamauga, Georgia September 19, 1863. POW Camp Douglas, Illinois. Forwarded to New Orleans for exchange on May 4, 1865.

White, Reuben Birch – Private. Enlisted age 35, April 25, 1862 Danville, Texas. First shown present April 28, 1862 Camp Carter, Hempstead, Texas. Killed at Battle of Arkansas Post January 11, 1863.

Whitten, John D. G. – Sergeant. Enlisted age 25, March 29, 1862 Danville, Texas. First shown present April 28, 1862 Camp Carter, Hempstead, Texas. Captured Arkansas Post January 11, 1863. POW Camp Butler, Illinois. Paroled and exchanged City Point, Virginia April 1863. Serving with Company B, 24th Texas Cavalry when it was reorganized as Company I, Granbury's Consolidated Brigade, Texas Cavalry (1st Consolidated Regiment) which surrendered with General Joseph Johnston's army April 26, 1865 and paroled at Greensboro, North Carolina.

Williams, L. (Negro) – No age shown. Appears on roll of prisoners of war received at Camp Butler, Illinois January 31, 1863. Shown as liberated. No further records appear in file.

Wilson, Thomas J. – Private. Enlisted age 22, March 29, 1862 Danville, Texas. First shown present April 28, 1862 Camp Carter, Hempstead, Texas. Died November 19, 1862 Arkansas.

Wood, Robert. L. – Sergeant. Enlisted age 28, April 25, 1862 Danville, Texas. First shown present April 28, 1862 Camp Carter, Hempstead, Texas. Captured Arkansas Post January 11, 1863. POW Camp Butler, Illinois. Paroled and exchanged City Point, Virginia April 1863. Taken prisoner in fall 1864 while scout for General Hood. Discharged at Chaneyville, Louisiana May 1865.

Worthy, Albert V. – Sergeant. Enlisted age 41, March 29, 1862, Danville, Texas. First shown present April 28, 1862 Camp Carter, Hempstead, Texas. Captured Arkansas Post January 11, 1863. POW Camp Butler, Illinois. Paroled and exchanged City Point, Virginia April 1863. Last shown present on roll of March-April 1864. No further records found.

---

*KAREN MCCANN HETT is the historian for Company B, 24th Regiment, Texas Cavalry, a company of 102 men who served under Montgomery County Captain Samuel D. Wooldridge. A number of these men first served with Captain Wooldridge in the Danville Mounted Riflemen (see pp. 95-97). For other works by Ms. Hett, see *The Herald* (Conroe, Tx: MCG&HS), Vols. 27-31 and her website at *http://freepages. genealogy.rootsweb.ancestry.com/~barrettbranches/Researchers/Karen%20Hett/ B24cavindex.html.*

Company D

Bobbitt, George Random, Sr. – Private. Enlisted age 22, March 20, 1862 Montgomery County, Texas. First shown present April 24, 1862 Camp Carter, Hempstead, Texas. Promoted to 5th sergeant summer 1862. Captured Arkansas Post January 11, 1863. POW Camp Butler, Illinois. Paroled and exchanged City Point, Virginia April 1863. Sick in hospital July 1863. Transferred to Trans-Mississippi Department

Springer, Greenberry B. – Private. Enlisted age 20, March 16, 1862 Hempstead, Texas. First shown present April 24, 1862 Camp Carter, Hempstead, Texas. Captured Arkansas Post January 11, 1863. POW Camp Butler, Illinois. Paroled and exchanged City Point, Virginia April 1863. Wounded at Battle of Chickamauga September 20, 1863. Discharged November 1863.

24ᵗʰ/25ᵗʰ Consolidated Regiment
&
Mann's Regiment, Texas Cavalry

Both the 24ᵗʰ Texas Cavalry (Dismounted) and the 25ᵗʰ Texas Cavalry (Dismounted) were engaged in the Battle of Arkansas Post on January 11, 1863. Although a small number of men managed to escape from Arkansas Post, those who were not killed in action were taken prisoner and sent to prisoner-of-war camps. A substantial number of men died in transit or during their incarceration. Those who survived were paroled and exchanged at City Point, Virginia in the spring of 1863. Many of the men were still suffering from debilitating illnesses or exposure to deplorable conditions in prison and were sent back to Texas. Others rejoined their regiments in Eastern Tennessee. After these regiments were reorganized as a part of the Confederate Army of Tennessee, some were found to be unfit to continue their service and were transferred to the Trans-Mississippi Department and furloughed back in Texas. Among those transferred to Texas was the former 25ᵗʰ Texas Cavalry commander, Colonel Clayton C. Gillespie.

Doctor Robert S. Poole of Montgomery County, the original commander of Company A, 24ᵗʰ Texas Cavalry (Dismounted), was not present at the Battle of Arkansas Post. He later became the commander of two other companies of Confederate troops. The story concerning his command of Company A, Mann's Regiment, Texas Cavalry and Company A, 24ᵗʰ/25ᵗʰ Consolidated Regiment is a very confused one. In January 1863, shortly after the fall of Fort Hindman at the Battle of Arkansas Post, Captain Poole, by means of Special Order No. 10 issued by Major General John G. Walker, was charged with organizing the men of the 24ᵗʰ Texas Cavalry not captured at Arkansas Post into a company of men to serve in the Trans-Mississippi Department. While this order was intended to be temporary, Captain Poole proceeded as if he were permanent commander of all remaining members of the 24ᵗʰ Texas Cavalry west of the Mississippi.

After receiving his orders from General Walker, Captain Poole returned to Texas and operating as commander of the 24ᵗʰ Texas Cavalry, Trans-Mississippi Department, began to round up deserters, conscripts, and men listed as absent without leave. On August 29, 1863, Major General John B. Magruder ordered all men who were members or former members of the 24ᵗʰ Texas Cavalry to report to Captain Robert S. Poole in Montgomery County, Texas. Soon an apparent struggle began to take shape between Captain Poole and Colonel Clayton C. Gillespie, the former commander of the 25ᵗʰ Texas Cavalry.

On December 1, 1863, General Magruder ordered Colonel Clayton Gillespie to take command of the 3ʳᵈ Brigade TST under General Slaughter. Displeased by having been placed in the militia, Colonel Gillespie bypassed the authority of General Magruder and on July 14, 1864 received authority from Lieutenant General E. Kirby Smith to organize all men from the 24ᵗʰ and 25ᵗʰ Texas Cavalries and the 17ᵗʰ Texas Consolidated Cavalry in the Trans-Mississippi into a regiment to be known as the 24ᵗʰ/25ᵗʰ Consolidated Texas Cavalry.

Obviously angered by Colonel Gillespie's action, General Magruder sent a letter to General Smith asking him to rescind his order, but to no avail. In response to Colonel Gillespie's actions, Captain Poole aligned his unit with Mann's Regiment, Texas Cavalry, becoming commander of Company A.

In August 1864, General Magruder was placed in temporary command of the Department of Arkansas and was replaced as commander of the Department of Texas, New Mexico, and Arizona by Major General John Walker. In November 1864, General Walker assigned Captain Poole's Company to the 24th/25th Consolidated Texas Cavalry under Colonel Gillespie's command. Captain Poole continued to operate as a detached company, did not report to the regiment, and refused to allow his company to be dismounted. General Magruder returned as commander of the Texas District in March 1865 but made no apparent effort to force Captain Poole to comply. For this reason, Confederate service records for Captain Poole's Company A in Mann's Regiment and his Company A in the 24th/25th Consolidated Regiment overlap. Fourteen of the sixteen men from Montgomery County who served in Mann's Regiment Texas Cavalry were in Captain Poole's Company A. Two sons of Peter James Willis, Private William Henry Willis and Private Peter James Willis, Jr., enlisted in Company B in Galveston. This company also was known as Captain W. M. Williamson's Company of Cadets.

The roster of Captain Poole's Company A in the 24th/25th Consolidated Regiment contains the names of ten men who are simultaneously listed in Company A of Mann's Regiment and the officers of the two companies are exactly the same. The names of other men from Montgomery County often appear in more than one company of the 24th/25th Consolidated. However, all but one appear on the rolls of Company E. These men were under the command of Colonel Gillespie and served in a wide variety of details but were most commonly detailed as guards in Austin and Washington Counties.

Montgomery County Men in Mann's Regiment, Texas Cavalry

Company A

Anders, James, Pvt	Sapp, John M., Sgt
Burden, George Larkum, Pvt	Sapp, Wyatt Allen, Pvt
Cartwright, J. C., Pvt	Simonton, Lucius H., Cpl
Cartwright, Pleasant L., 3rd Lt	Sones, Benson, Pvt
Chilton, Hugh Barclay, Pvt	Taylor, Charles L., Pvt
Finch, W. A., Cpl	Uzzell, Major M., 2nd Lt
Malone, Henderson F., Pvt	Woodson, Creed Taylor, 1st Lt
Poole, Robert S., Capt	

Company B

Willis, Peter James, Jr., Pvt	Willis, William Henry, Pvt

Montgomery County Men in the 24th/25th Consolidated Texas Cavalry

Company A

Anders, James, Pvt
Betts, Dexter, Pvt
Betts, Menter, Pvt
Cartwright, Joseph C., Pvt
Cartwright, Pleasant L., 3rd Lt
Chilton, Hugh Barclay, Pvt
Finch, W. A., Pvt
Golding, John Madison, Pvt
Golding, Nimrod Chiles, Pvt
Goodson, James W., Pvt
Griffith, Joshua Delos, Pvt

Harlan, George, Pvt
Malone, Henderson F., Pvt
Meeks, Zachariah T., Pvt
Morris, A. W., Pvt
Pool, Robert S., Capt
Sandel, Martin Luther, Pvt
Simonton, Lucius H., Pvt
Sones, Benson, Pvt
Uzell, Major May, 2nd Lt
Walker, James Madison, Pvt
Woodson, Creed Taylor, 1st Lt

Company E

Field, James M. B., Pvt
Guynn, William James, Pvt
Hayden, Samuel Turner, Pvt

Jones, M. D., 2nd Lt
King, Thomas Edward, Pvt
Womack, Daniel Harrison, Pvt

Company I

Thomason, Frances Marion, Pvt

26th Texas Cavalry

The regiment which became the 26th Texas Cavalry was originally organized from Davis's Mounted Battalion which also was known as the 7th Texas Cavalry Battalion. On October 10, 1861, Samuel Boyer Davis was appointed major in command of this battalion which consisted of seven companies of men from Caldwell, Fort Bend, Galveston, Harris, Leon, Liberty, Montgomery, and Washington Counties. In January 1862, three more companies were raised from Harris, Grimes, and Montgomery Counties. On April 15, 1862, Xavier Blanchard Debray was commissioned as a colonel in command of the regiment designated as the 26th Texas Cavalry.

The regiment was assigned to Brigadier General Hamilton Bee's brigade and took part in the Battle of Galveston on January 1, 1863. It is likely that some of the men from the regiment were used aboard the Confederate cottonclads during the assault on Union gunboats. During the remainder of 1863 and the winter of 1864, the 26th Texas Cavalry served in defense of the upper Texas coast. In the spring of 1864, the regiment marched to Louisiana and participated in the Red River Campaign. The 26th Texas Cavalry remained in Louisiana for several months after the Red River Campaign. After returning to Texas, the regiment remained intact until receiving news of the Confederate surrender.

The men were then discharged and allowed to return to their homes.

At least thirty-five men from Montgomery County served in the 26th Texas Cavalry. Ten of these men had previously been members of the Montgomery County Rifle Boys which was organized by Captain Lemuel G. Clepper who later organized and commanded Company K of the 20th Texas Infantry.

Five men from Montgomery County enlisted in Company E of the 26th Texas Cavalry under its original commander, Captain George W. Owens. Captain Owens was later promoted to major, and Captain William Harn replaced him as commander of the company.

Thirty men from Montgomery County enlisted in Company H of the 26th Texas Cavalry. This company was organized and originally commanded by Captain Franklin Goldstein Dupree from Montgomery County. His first cousin, John Lewis Dupree, and his brother-in-law, Zachariah Landrum Springer, served as lieutenants in the company. Three men from this company, 2nd Lieutenant Zachariah Landrum Springer, Private Leeberry H. Springer, and Private A. Ezekiel Springer, died of disease during their service in the 26th Texas Cavalry. Private A. E. Springer died in the Confederate Hospital in Houston and is buried beneath a parking lot adjacent to the old Jefferson Davis Hospital. The burial locations of Private L. H. Springer and Lieutenant Zachariah Springer are unknown at this time.

Montgomery County Men
in the 26th Texas Cavalry

Company E

Gatlin, John Davidson, Pvt
Pillow, Ransom Doc, Pvt
Pillow, Thomas J., Pvt
Roberts, Green, Pvt
Roberts, John W., Pvt

Company H

Boon, E. A., Pvt
Boon, J. A., Pvt
Brown, J. W., Cpl
Connell, M. A., Pvt
Cude, Timothy J., Pvt
Dupree, Franklin G., Capt
Dupree, Jesse G. T., Sgt
Dupree, John Lewis, 2nd Lt
Ford, James A., Pvt
Hicks, J. L., Pvt
Hicks, Lemuel M., Pvt
Johnson, John Wesley, Pvt
Matthews, T. R., Pvt
Norman, William H., Cpl
Nuner, William, Pvt
Roberts, James Eldridge, Pvt
Robertson, Jesse Wiley, Pvt
Shannon, Mathis Ward, Pvt
Smith, L. W., 2nd Lt
Springer, Zachariah Landrum, 2nd Lt
Springer, A. Ezekial, Pvt
Springer, Addis Emmet, Pvt
Springer, Leeberry H., Pvt
Springer, Franklin E., Pvt
Threadgill, William T., Pvt
Vance, Seaborn S., Pvt
Vance, Joshua J., Pvt
Vance, Davis W., Pvt
Wickson, Jesse, Pvt
Wickson, John, Pvt

Granbury's Consolidated Brigade, Texas Cavalry
(1st Consolidated Regiment)

The regiment which became Granbury's Consolidated Brigade, Texas Cavalry had one of the shortest histories of any regiment in the Confederate Army, but the path that these men took in becoming members of this regiment was almost inconceivable. Organized from the remnants of eight regiments that formed Granbury's Texas Brigade, a famed fighting unit of more than five-thousand battle-hardened soldiers, Granbury's Consolidated Regiment had been reduced to fewer than five hundred men.

Seven of the eight original regiments that would eventually carry the name of Brigadier General Hiram Bronson Granbury began their struggles after marching from Texas to Arkansas in the summer of 1862. All along the trail, the men of the 6th and 10th Texas Infantries and the 15th, 17th, 18th, 24th, and 25th Texas Cavalries experienced illness and death from disease and exposure. While preparing for war at camps in Arkansas, the problem only worsened. By the time of the first battle at Arkansas Post on January 11, 1863, many had died, and most of the remaining men were still ill and scarcely able to fight. The Confederates who survived the defeat at Arkansas Post were loaded onto transport ships in the dead of winter without coats or blankets and transported up the Mississippi River to prisoner-of-war camps. Some died during the trip up the river, and even more died from deplorable conditions in Union prisons. The remaining men of these regiments were paroled and exchanged at City Point, Virginia in the late spring of 1863. Many of the men were still suffering from disease and exposure to poor prison conditions and were sent directly to the hospital. Those who were no longer fit for service were transferred to the Trans-Mississippi Department. Captain Samuel Wooldridge was among those sent back to Texas. First Lieutenant Jabez S. Thomason took command of the company, but after a brief period of time, he too was transferred to the Trans-Mississippi Department. Those men who were still healthy or had recovered quickly enough to continue were assigned to the Confederate Army of Tennessee. At less than half their original numbers, the 6th and 7th Texas Infantries were consolidated with the 15th Texas Cavalry to form one regiment, and the 17th, 18th, 24th, and 25th Texas Cavalries were consolidated to form a second regiment.

The last of the original eight regiments, the 7th Texas Infantry, suffered a similar demise after marching from Shreveport, Louisiana to Hopkinsville, Kentucky where it arrived in November 1861. By February 1862, the regiment had lost more than one-hundred-thirty men to disease. At the Battle of Fort Donelson, in addition to heavy losses, more than three hundred of the men in the 7th Texas were captured and sent to Union prison camps where more than sixty died. Those men who managed to survive the prison ordeal were paroled and released at Vicksburg, Mississippi in September 1862. The 7th Texas Regiment was so depleted that for a short period, it was consolidated with two Tennessee regiments. By February 1863, the 7th Texas had received enough recruits to regain regimental status and was assigned to General John Gregg's brigade.

All eight regiments appeared on the same field together at the Battle of Chickamauga in September 1863. The two new consolidated regiments were assigned to Deshler's Brigade, and the 7th Texas remained with Gregg's Brigade. At the Battle of Missionary Ridge in the Chattanooga campaign, the men of the eight original regiments were combined under the command of newly-appointed Brigadier General Hiram B. Granbury. The new Texas Brigade was composed of the 6th, 10th, and 15th Texas Consolidated Regiment, the 7th Texas Infantry Regiment, and the 17th, 18th, 24th, and 25th Consolidated Texas Cavalry Regiment (Dismounted).

As part of General Patrick Cleburne's Division, Granbury's Texas Brigade was involved in more than seventeen major battles in the Atlanta campaign during the summer of 1864. In the fall of 1864, Cleburne's Division traveled with General John Bell Hood on his ill-fated invasion of Tennessee. On November 30, 1864, Granbury's Texas Brigade was in the lead down the Columbia Pike during the Confederate attack against Union forces at Franklin, Tennessee. The attack left six Confederate generals dead, including General Patrick Cleburne and General Hiram Granbury. At the Battle of Nashville in December 1865, the ragged Granbury's Brigade inflected heavy casualties on Union forces attempting an assault on a Confederate stronghold known as Granbury's Lunette, but the superior number of federal troops forced Hood's army to retreat into Mississippi.

After arriving in Mississippi, General Hood resigned. Hood's Army of the Tennessee and Granbury's Texas Brigade were assigned to the command of Lieutenant General Richard Taylor but were soon ordered to the east in support of General Joseph Johnston's forces in North Carolina. Granbury's Brigade arrived at Bentonville, North Carolina during the battle which took place March 19-March 21, 1865, but Granbury's Texas Brigade did not take an active role in the conflict.

During the following weeks, General Johnston reorganized his army, and the remaining men of the former Granbury's Texas Brigade became a single regiment known as Granbury's Consolidated Brigade, Texas Cavalry (1st Consolidated Regiment). This regiment was assigned to the brigade commanded by Brigadier General Daniel C. Govan. The former 24th Texas Cavalry became Company I of the new regiment. Company I was commanded by Captain Samuel Thompson Foster, a former first lieutenant in Company H of the 24th Cavalry. Foster had originally joined the Texas State Troops in Live Oak County, Texas in a unit commanded by Captain James Washington Winters, Jr. whose family was among the earliest to settle in an area near Waverly in Walker County, Texas.

By mid-April of 1865, General Johnston's Army had retreated to Durham Station, North Carolina. General Johnston met with Confederate President

Jefferson Davis who ordered him to disband his infantry and to escape with his mounted troops. Johnston disobeyed the president's order, and on April 18, 1865, he signed an armistice agreement with Union General William Tecumseh Sherman suspending hostilities until the formal surrender at Bennett Farm on April 26, 1865.

Out of the one-hundred-and-one men who had enlisted in Captain Samuel Wooldridge's Company of cavalry in Danville, Texas, only nine remained when Granbury's Consolidated Regiment was surrendered with General Joseph Johnson's Confederate Army on April 26, 1865. Aside from surviving deplorable conditions in a Union prison camp, these nine men participated in some of bloodiest battles of the War between the States, including Arkansas Post, Chickamauga, the Chattanooga campaign, the Atlanta campaign, Battle of Franklin, and the second Battle of Nashville.

Montgomery County Men
in Granbury's Consolidated Brigade
Company I

Private Oliver Perry Chambers

Oliver Perry Chambers was born in Texas about 1842. He was the son of Thomas and Isabella Barnhill Chambers. O. P. Chambers enlisted as a private in Captain Sam Wooldridge's company of Texas Lancers at Danville, Texas in the summer of 1862. After training at Camp Carter near Hempstead, Texas, he rode with this company to Arkansas where it became Company B, 24th Texas Cavalry (Dismounted). He was captured at the Battle of Arkansas Post on January 11, 1863 and sent to the Union prison at Camp Butler. Chambers was paroled and exchanged at City Point, Virginia in April 1863 and rejoined the ranks of the 24th Texas Cavalry which was then consolidated with the 17th, 18th, and 25th Texas Cavalries. Private Chambers participated in the Battle of Chickamauga, September 19-20, 1863 and the Battle of Missionary Ridge on November 25, 1863 where his regiment became part of Granbury's Texas Brigade. He participated in the Atlanta campaign, the Battle of Franklin, and the Battle of Nashville before the regiment was transferred to North Carolina and assigned to the command of General Joseph Johnston. Here the 24th Texas Cavalry became Company I, Granbury's Consolidated Brigade, Texas Cavalry and was a part of the Confederate surrender at Greensboro, North Carolina in April 1865.

Oliver was the only one of four Chambers brothers in Company B, 24th Texas Cavalry to survive the war. His brother, Thomas Chambers, Jr., died in Gatriot Street Prison Hospital, St. Louis, Missouri on February 26, 1863, and two other brothers, Daniel and John H. Chambers, were killed in action at the Battle of Chickamauga on September 20, 1863. After the war, Oliver returned to Montgomery County and became a preacher and a farmer. He married Elizabeth "Eliza" Vickers on December 20, 1865. After Eliza's death about

1897, Oliver married Sarah Jane Grimes Gilmore on October 16, 1899. Oliver Perry Chambers died September 6, 1922 and was buried in the Cleveland City Cemetery, Cleveland, Texas.

Private William W. Forrest

William W. Forrest was born in Montgomery County, North Carolina on January 15, 1834. He is believed to have been the son of John Gresham and Nancy Ingram Forrest. William arrived in Montgomery County, Texas on December 30, 1859. He married Tabitha J. Steed on December 28, 1860. Tabitha's father, Willis H. Steed, enlisted in the 17th Brigade of Texas State Troops at age 47. At age 26, William W. Forrest enlisted as a private in Captain Sam Wooldridge's company of Texas Lancers at Danville, Texas on March 29, 1862. After training at Camp Carter near Hempstead, Texas, William rode with this company to Arkansas where it became Company B, 24th Texas Cavalry (Dismounted). He was captured at the Battle of Arkansas Post on January 11, 1863 and sent to the Union prison at Camp Butler. William was paroled and exchanged at City Point, Virginia in April 1863 and rejoined the ranks of the 24th Texas Cavalry which was then consolidated with the 17th, 18th, and 25th Texas Cavalries. William was present at the Battle of Chickamauga, September 19-20, 1863 and the Battle of Missionary Ridge on November 25, 1863 where his regiment became part of Granbury's Texas Brigade. William was shown to be sick in the hospital through most of the winter and early spring of 1864. William participated in the Atlanta campaign, the Battle of Franklin, and the Battle of Nashville before the regiment was transferred to North Carolina and assigned to the command of General Joseph Johnston. Here the 24th Texas Cavalry became Company I, Granbury's Consolidated Brigade, Texas Cavalry and was a part of the Confederate surrender at Greensboro, North Carolina in April 1865.

After being paroled, William returned to Montgomery County, Texas. William's first wife, Tabitha, died sometime in the early 1870s, and William married Louisa Martin on July 12, 1874. William W. Forrest died July 16, 1914 and was buried at Bethel Cemetery near the town of Dacus in Montgomery County, Texas.

Private Gideon Johnson Gooch

Gideon Johnson Gooch was the only one of the nine men who started with Captain Wooldridge's company and served in Company I, Granbury's Consolidate Brigade who had never lived in Montgomery County, Texas. John, as he was known, was born April 3, 1844 in McLean County, Kentucky. He was the son of John Graham and Elizabeth Cravens Gooch. He enlisted in the 2nd Texas Lancers at Palestine, Texas on April 15, 1862. He trained with the rest of Captain Wooldridge's company at Camp Carter and rode with them to Arkansas where he was captured at the Battle of Arkansas Post on January 11, 1863. Private Gooch was transported to the Union prison at Camp Butler. He was paroled and exchanged at City Point, Virginia in April 1863 and rejoined the ranks of the 24th Texas Cavalry which was then consolidated with the 17th, 18th, and 25th Texas Cavalries. John was present at the Battle of Chickamauga,

September 19-20, 1863 and at the Battle of Missionary Ridge on November 25, 1863 where his regiment became part of Granbury's Texas Brigade. He participated in the Atlanta campaign, the Battle of Franklin, and the Battle of Nashville before the regiment was transferred to North Carolina and assigned to the command of General Joseph Johnston. Here the 24th Texas Cavalry became Company I, Granbury's Consolidated Brigade, Texas Cavalry and was a part of the Confederate surrender at Greensboro, North Carolina in April 1865.

After the surrender, John returned to Anderson County and became a lawyer. He married Sue Rebecca Kimborough on October 31, 1867. After Sue died in 1869, John married Frances (Fannie) Brooks on September 20, 1870. John served as mayor of Palestine, Texas from 1872 to 1873 and in 1886 was a member of the first board of directors of the Dallas and Greenville Railway Company which was chartered to build a railroad and telegraph line from Greenville to Dallas. Gideon Johnson Gooch died January 31, 1906 and was buried in the Palestine City Cemetery.

Private Adam Meek King

Adam Meek King was born in September 1836 in Jefferson County, Illinois. He was the son of Thomas and Margaret Meek King who moved their family from Illinois to Texas about 1839. Adam married Minerva Ellen Ezell in Montgomery County on March 29, 1860. Exactly two years later, Adam enlisted as a private in Captain Sam Wooldridge's company of Texas Lancers at Danville, Texas. His brother, Thomas Edward King, also served in Captain Wooldridge's company but after being paroled and exchanged from Camp Butler in Illinois, was transferred to the Trans-Mississippi Department. After training at Camp Carter near Hempstead, Texas, Private King rode with this company to Arkansas where it became Company B, 24th Texas Cavalry (Dismounted). He was captured at the Battle of Arkansas Post on January 11, 1863 and sent to the Union prison at Camp Butler. King was paroled and exchanged at City Point, Virginia in April 1863 and rejoined the ranks of the 24th Texas Cavalry which was then consolidated with the 17th, 18th, and 25th Texas Cavalries. Private A. M. King was wounded at the Battle of Chickamauga on September 20, 1863.

After recovering, he participated in the Atlanta campaign, the Battle of Franklin, and the Battle of Nashville before the regiment was transferred to North Carolina and assigned to the command of General Joseph Johnston. Here the 24th Texas Cavalry became Company I, Granbury's Consolidated Brigade, Texas Cavalry and was a part of the Confederate surrender at Greensboro, North Carolina in April 1865. After the surrender, Adam returned to Montgomery County and took up farming and preaching. He died November 20, 1900 and was buried in the Hickory Grove Cemetery in Montgomery County.

Private James William Hulon

James "Jim" William Hulon was born in Montgomery County, Republic of Texas in 1840. He was the son of William Henry and Phoebe Reese Spillers Hulon. He joined the Danville Mounted Riflemen, 17th Brigade of Texas State Troops in May 1861. He joined Captain Robert Oliver's Company I, 9th Texas Infantry in November 1861. This regiment was organized for a period of six months to defend Galveston Island. After mustering out of Nichols' regiment, Hulon enlisted in Captain Samuel Wooldridge's company at Galveston on April 16, 1862. Following his training at Camp Carter near Hempstead, Texas, he rode with this company to Arkansas where it became Company B, 24th Texas Cavalry (Dismounted). He was captured at the Battle of Arkansas Post on January 11, 1863 and sent to the Union prison at Camp Butler in Illinois. Jim was paroled and exchanged at City Point, Virginia in April 1863 and was sent directly to the Confederate hospital in Petersburg. A short time later, he rejoined the ranks of the 24th Texas Cavalry which was then consolidated with the 17th, 18th, and 25th Texas Cavalries. Private Hulon participated in the Battle of Chickamauga, September 19-20, 1863 and the Battle of Missionary Ridge on November 25, 1863 where his regiment became part of Granbury's Texas Brigade. He participated in the Atlanta campaign, the Battle of Franklin and the Battle of Nashville before the regiment was transferred to North Carolina and assigned to the command of General Joseph Johnston. Here the 24th Texas Cavalry became Company I, Granbury's Consolidated Brigade, Texas Cavalry and was a part of the Confederate surrender at Greensboro, North Carolina in April 1865.

After returning home to Montgomery County, William married Sarah Frances McCaleb Chambers on January 1, 1868. Sarah was one of three daughters of Zill McCaleb who were married to men in Company B, 24th Texas Cavalry. Sarah Frances Hulon died on September 5, 1889 and was buried in the Willis Cemetery. William was married a second time to a woman known only as Jennie. She filed an application for a Confederate widow's pension on June 1, 1915, but it was rejected. In the application, she states that she was fifty years old and that she was married to J. W. Hulon in Coryell County on March 10, 1892. She mistakenly claimed that J. W. Hulon had served in Hood's Brigade which could have contributed to the application being rejected. James William Hulon died April 16, 1907 and was buried in the Willis Cemetery, Montgomery County, Texas.

Private James Marion McCan

James Marion "Jim" McCan was born in Lawrence County, Alabama, on October 20, 1834. He was the son of James McCan and Sarah S. "Sally" Viser. His sister, Catherine Elizabeth McCan, married Dr. Samuel Dunbar Wooldridge who became the captain of the Danville Mounted Riflemen and Company B, 24th Cavalry (Dismounted). Jim first entered Confederate service on October 25, 1861 as a private in Captain James Gillaspie's Company E, 9th Texas Infantry (Nichols') for a period of six months, serving in defense of Galveston. After mustering out of Nichols' regiment, Jim McCan enlisted in Captain Samuel Wooldridge's Company at Galveston on April 16, 1862. After training at Camp Carter near Hempstead, Texas, Jim rode with this company to Arkansas where it became Company B, 24th Texas Cavalry (Dismounted). He was captured at the Battle of Arkansas Post on January 11, 1863 and

James Marion McCan
photo courtesy of Karen McCann Hett

sent to the Union prison at Camp Butler in Illinois. Jim was paroled and exchanged at City Point, Virginia in May 1863 and rejoined the ranks of the 24th Texas Cavalry which was then consolidated with the 17th, 18th, and 25th Texas Cavalries. Confederate service records indicate that Jim spent a considerable amount of time sick in the hospital from mid-summer until the end of 1863, so it is uncertain if he participated in the Battle of Chickamauga or the Chattanooga campaign. Jim returned to Company B in 1864 and participated in the Atlanta campaign, the Battle of Franklin and the Battle of Nashville before the regiment was transferred to North Carolina and assigned to the command of General Joseph Johnston. Here the 24th Texas Cavalry became Company I, Granbury's Consolidated Brigade, Texas Cavalry and was part of the Confederate surrender at Greensboro, North Carolina in April 1865.

After being paroled, Jim McCan returned to Texas and settled in Madison County. He married Amanda Catherine Barrett on January 20, 1869. Amanda was born in Montgomery County, Texas on May 2, 1849 and was the daughter of John Whitten and Hulda Reding Barrett. Amanda's cousin, John D. G. Whitten also had served in Company I of Granbury's Consolidated Regiment. Although most of Jim McCan's post-war years were spent in Madison County, he also spent time in Houston, Leon, and Montgomery Counties. In 1912, the Carrie Hannon Chapter #935 of the United Daughters of the Confederacy of Oakwood in Leon County awarded Jim McCan the Southern Cross of Honor for his distinguished service in the Confederate Army. James Marion McCan was killed in a carriage accident crossing Poole's Creek in Madison County on July 31, 1915 and was buried alongside his wife, Amanda, at nearby Barrett–Burroughs Cemetery.

Private Albert Wrinkles McKinney

Albert Wrinkles McKinney
photo courtesy of Billy McKinney

Albert Wrinkles McKinney was born on August 15, 1842 in Alexandria, Louisiana. He was the son of Mercer and Mary Sophronia Wrinkles McKinney. His father, Mercer, served as a 1st lieutenant in Captain Simms' Company, Texas Home Guards. According to Albert's biography, he first joined a militia unit known as the Galveston Rifles or Lone Star Rifles. This unit became Company L of the 1st Texas Infantry. The first Confederate service record for A. W. McKinney shows him on the rolls of Captain Robert M. Powell's Company D of the 5th Texas Infantry which consisted primarily of men from Grimes, Walker, and Montgomery Counties. This single muster roll indicates that A. W. McKinney deserted prior to the company leaving for Virginia. It is possible that Albert had gone home to visit family in nearby Lynchburg and simply did not make it back in time to catch the train before it departed. In January of 1862, Albert enlisted in Company I, 9th Texas Infantry (Nichols'). This company was commanded by Captain Robert F. Oliver and consisted of men from Montgomery County, Texas. Another member of this company was 5th Sergeant Gilbert Harris McKinney who appears to have been related to Albert. After mustering out of Nichols' regiment, Albert McKinney made his way to Montgomery County and was enrolled in Captain Samuel Wooldridge's Company of the 2nd Texas Lancers by Charles L. S. Jones on June 1, 1862. After training at Camp Carter near Hempstead, Texas, Albert rode with this company to Arkansas where it became Company B, 24th Texas Cavalry (Dismounted). He was captured at the Battle of Arkansas Post on January 11, 1863 and sent to the Union prison at Camp Butler in Illinois. Albert was paroled and exchanged at City Point, Virginia in the spring of 1863 and rejoined the ranks of the 24th Texas Cavalry which was then consolidated with the 17th, 18th, and 25th Texas Cavalries. Private McKinney participated in the Battle of Chickamauga, September 19-20, 1863 and the Battle of Missionary Ridge on November 25, 1863 where his regiment became part of Granbury's Texas Brigade. He participated in the Atlanta campaign, the Battle of Franklin and the Battle of Nashville. Albert was one of the men who went back onto the battlefield, under enemy fire, to retrieve the body of General Hiram Granbury after the Battle of Franklin on November 30, 1864. Albert was with the regiment when it was transferred to North Carolina and assigned to the command of General Joseph Johnston. Here the 24th Texas Cavalry became Company I, Granbury's Consolidated Brigade, Texas Cavalry and was a part of the Confederate surrender at Greensboro, North Carolina in April 1865.

After being paroled, Albert returned to Harris County and worked on his father's farm. On December 20, 1866, he married Miss Sarah Jane Singleton. In addition to being a farmer, Albert became a Harris County deputy sheriff and later became a precinct constable. He was elected Harris County Tax Assessor in November of 1884 and held the position through 1895. Albert Wrinkles McKinney died August 2, 1908 and was buried in White's Chapel Cemetery near Highlands, Texas.

Private Peter Tabor Sandel

Peter Tabor Sandel was born on September 15, 1842 in Pike County, Mississippi. His father, Reverend Peter Warren Sandel, was a Methodist minister. His mother, Winifred Tabor Sandel, died the day after giving birth to Peter. She was the daughter of Reverend Isaac Tabor who was an early settler in Montgomery County, Texas. Another of Isaac's daughters, Minerva Tabor, was married to Peter Belles Irvine who served in Company B, 24th Texas Cavalry and was killed in action at the Battle of Arkansas Post. Peter's brother, John Oliver Sandel, was killed in action at the Battle of Franklin. On October 10, 1861, Peter Sandel enlisted in Captain Robert F. Oliver's Company I, 9th Texas Infantry (Nichols'). After mustering out of the 9th Infantry and while still in Galveston,

Peter Tabor Sandel
photo courtesy of Rayford Sandel

Peter enlisted in Captain Sam Wooldridge's Company of Texas Lancers on April 16, 1862. After training at Camp Carter near Hempstead, Texas, Peter rode with this company to Arkansas where it became Company B, 24th Texas Cavalry (Dismounted). He was captured at the Battle of Arkansas Post on January 11, 1863. While most of the men captured at Arkansas Post were sent to Camp Butler in Illinois, Peter was sent to the City General Hospital in St. Louis, Missouri on January 22, 1863 to be treated for a gunshot wound. On February 27, 1863, Private Sandel had the great misfortune of being transferred to the infamous Gratiot Street Prison in St. Louis. He was paroled in April 1863 and sent to City Point, Virginia where he was exchanged.

After being exchanged, Peter was sent to the hospital where he remained until August. Peter was present at the Battle of Chickamauga, September 19-20, 1863 and the Battle of Missionary Ridge on November 25, 1863 where his regiment became part of Granbury's Texas Brigade. He participated in the Atlanta campaign, the Battle of Franklin, and the Battle of Nashville before the regiment was transferred to North Carolina and assigned to the command of General Joseph Johnston. Here the 24th Texas Cavalry became Company I, Granbury's Consolidated Brigade, Texas Cavalry and was a part of the Confederate surrender at Greensboro, North Carolina in April 1865.

Private John D. G. Whitten

John D. G. Whitten was born on October 27, 1836 in Fayette County, Tennessee. He was the son of Alfred and Bridget Graham Whitten. His sister Ellen was married to Marion A. McCrory who served in Company B, 24th Texas Cavalry (Dismounted). John D. Whitten and his family arrived in Montgomery County prior to 1850. On March 7, 1861, John married Antoinette Folks. On May 4, 1861, John joined the Danville Mounted Rifles, 17th Brigade, Texas State Troops. On March 29, 1862, John enlisted as a 4th sergeant in Captain Sam Wooldridge's Company of Texas Lancers. After training at Camp Carter near Hempstead, Texas, John rode with this company to Arkansas where it became Company B, 24th Texas Cavalry (Dismounted). He was captured at the Battle of Arkansas Post on January 11, 1863 and sent to the Union prison at Camp Butler in Illinois. He was paroled in the spring of 1863 and sent to City Point, Virginia where he was exchanged. After the exchange, he rejoined the ranks of the 24th Texas Cavalry which was then consolidated with the 17th, 18th, and 25th Texas Cavalries. Confederate service records indicate that John Whitten was on furlough from September through December of 1863. He returned to his company in January 1863 and went on to participate the Atlanta campaign, the Battle of Franklin, and the Battle of Nashville before the regiment was transferred to North Carolina and assigned to the command of General Joseph Johnston. Here the 24th Texas Cavalry became Company I, Granbury's Consolidated Brigade, Texas Cavalry and was a part of the Confederate surrender at Greensboro, North Carolina in April 1865.

After the war, John returned to Montgomery County, but by 1870, he had settled in Brazos County near Bryan. John Whitten and his family moved to the Elwood Community in Madison County about 1883. John D. G. Whitten died there on October 20, 1894 and was buried in Elwood Cemetery.

Terry's Regiment, Texas Cavalry

At some date prior to February 1864, Samuel Houston Brooks was instructed by David Smith Terry to begin organizing a regiment of Texas men to serve in the Confederate Army. Permission to raise this regiment was originally given to David Terry by authority of Special Order No. 32, paragraph three, issued by the Confederate Secretary of War on August 24, 1862. Final approval to begin organizing this regiment was received from the Houston headquarters of the District of Texas, New Mexico, and Arizona on February 1, 1864.

Prior to the war, both David Terry and Samuel Brooks were prominent politicians in California and were very closely acquainted. David Terry, who had been serving as a justice of the California Supreme Court, was the brother of the famed Benjamin Franklin Terry who organized and commanded the 8th Texas Cavalry, better known as Terry's Texas Rangers. For this reason, Terry's Regiment of Texas Cavalry is often confused with Terry's Texas Rangers. Samuel H. Brooks had been serving as California State Treasurer/ Controller but resigned in order to accept a commission as major on the staff of Confederate General Benjamin F. Cheatham. Samuel Brooks was the son of Samuel Clifford Brooks who was an early settler near Danville in Montgomery County, Texas.

Samuel Brooks began organizing the new regiment at Danville in Montgomery County. Headquarters had dictated that the new regiment could be either infantry or cavalry and must be comprised of non-conscripts. The substantial number of men in Terry's Regiment who were drawn from the 17th Brigade of Texas State Troops effectively dissolved the militia in Montgomery County. It is unlikely that there were enough men left in the 17th Brigade to form even a small company.

Although there are very few Confederate service records for Terry's Cavalry, it is known that its total strength in numbers was less than five-hundred men. One of the earliest records shows that on March 28, 1864, Forsyth H. Sapp of Montgomery County was elected captain of Company K, and Captain Joseph M. Evans of Montgomery County was promoted to major. One record in the individual files of Major Evans states that he signed the roster as commander of the regiment. This record was not dated. Thomas Wesley Smith of Montgomery County was elected captain of Company C on April 14, 1864. Although a letter signed by Colonel D. S. Terry shows him to be at camp near

Plantersville on April 19, 1864, official records show that Terry's Regiment was mustered into Confederate service on July 6, 1864 at which time David S. Terry was appointed as colonel and later confirmed by election. A letter from Colonel Terry dated September 26, 1864 relates that many of his companies had not arrived in camp. The letter also states that some of the men were still at Danville in Montgomery County while others were near Navasota in Grimes County. Other officer elections are shown to have been held on November 11, 1864. A muster roll dated March 1865 shows Terry's Regiment to be at camp in Austin County, and a return dated April 1865 shows the regiment to be a part of the Second Brigade, Maxey's Division. The regiment was disbanded prior to Confederate General E. Kirby Smith's surrender in June 1865.

Montgomery County Men
Terry's Regiment, Texas Cavalry

Officers

Brooks, Samuel Houston, Lt Col

Evans, Joseph M., Maj

Company A

Dyer, Shepherd Franklin, Pvt

Morris, Benjamin Franklin, Pvt

McLeod, William, Pvt

Liles, Thomas Jefferson, Pvt

Company B

Chilton, Matthias Dayton, Pvt

Shannon, Owen, Pvt

Shannon, William T., Pvt

Company C

Baker, Benjamin Franklin, Pvt

Boone, E. A., Pvt

Deadrick, John, Pvt

Elliott, Sanford E., Pvt

Griffin, Joseph E., Pvt

Lynch, D. B., Pvt

McKinzie, Joseph, 1st Lt

Smith, Thomas Wesley, Capt

Williamson, John H., 2nd Lt

Company K

Glass, William, Pvt

Goodrich, J. M., Pvt

Goodson, William Walter, Pvt

McKinney, Gilbert Harris, 1st Lt

Pace, John Pinckney, Pvt

Sanders, John F., Pvt

Sapp, Forsyth H., Capt

Scott, John Franklin, Pvt

Thomas, William, Pvt

Waul's Texas Legion

Waul's Texas Legion was organized in and around Washington County in the spring of 1862 by Colonel Thomas Neville Waul. Large numbers of men were recruited from the ranks of the 9th Texas Infantry (Nichol's) after it was disbanded at Galveston. The legion was unique in contrast to other Texas units in that it was a mixture of infantry, cavalry, and artillery components. Initially there were two infantry battalions commanded by Lieutenant Colonel Barnard Timmons and Lieutenant Colonel James Wrigley; one cavalry battalion commanded by Major Leonidas M. Willis; and an artillery battery commanded by Captain William Edgar.

Because of the difficulty in managing mixed components, Waul's Texas Legion was later stripped of most of its artillery and cavalry units at which time Captain William Edgar's company was assigned to the Trans-Mississippi Department as the 1st Field Battery, Texas Light Artillery (Edgar's Company), and Leonidas Willis was promoted to lieutenant colonel in command of Willis' Battalion Texas Cavalry assigned to the Confederate Department of Mississippi and East Louisiana. In the late summer of 1862, the two infantry units were attached to General John C. Pemberton's army in Vicksburg, Mississippi.

Most of the men in Waul's Texas Legion were captured at the fall of Vicksburg on July 4, 1863. These men were paroled by mid-July, and the legion was later reorganized in Houston. After Colonel Waul was promoted to brigadier general in September 1863, Bernard Timmons was promoted to colonel in command of Waul's Texas Legion. The legion was sent to Velasco in December 1863 to defend against a Union invasion along the Texas coast. On March, 23 1864, the legion was reorganized and designated Timmons' Regiment, Texas Infantry. The unit was officially discharged on May 5, 1865.

There were thirteen men from Montgomery County who are known to have served in Waul's Texas Legion. Eleven of these men served in Company C of the 2nd Infantry Battalion and enlisted at Galveston after being discharged from the 9th Texas Infantry (Nichols') in March 1862. Company C was originally commanded by Captain Allen Cameron who was later promoted to major and was killed in action during the Siege of Vicksburg. For most of these men, the story was the same. They all were engaged at the Battle of Vicksburg, captured, paroled, and returned to Texas. The lone exception was Private Clause Groth who died at Camp Pemberton.

John Barber Nuner, who was married to Maria Cartwright in Montgomery County on December 30, 1858, served in Company B of Captain B. J. Hogue's Light Artillery. Two Montgomery County men, Jesse Wiley Robertson and his son, Louis Thomas Robertson, appear on the census rolls in Montgomery County in 1850 and 1860 but moved to Navarro County prior to enlisting in the Confederate Army. Louis Thomas Robertson served in Company B, 2nd Infantry Battalion of Waul's Texas Legion, and his father Jesse transferred from Bradford's Regiment to Timmons' Regiment in 1864.

Montgomery County Men
In Waul's Texas Legion

Company B, Light Artillery

Nuner, John Barber – Enlisted at Houston, May 8, 1862. Sent to hospital at Grenada, Mississippi December 28, 1862. Captured at Vicksburg, Mississippi July 4, 1863. Paroled July 9, 1863. Transferred to Company A, 1st Infantry Battalion.

Company B, 2nd Infantry Battalion

Robertson, Lewis Thomas – Enlisted at age 17 as a private, Fairfield, Texas February 10, 1862. Captured at Vicksburg, Mississippi July 4, 1863. Paroled July 17, 1863.

Company C, 2nd Infantry Battalion

Downing, Timothy – Enlisted at age 38 as a private, Galveston, Texas October 18, 1861. Captured at Vicksburg, Mississippi July 4, 1863. Paroled July 17, 1863. Absent sick in hospital with pneumonia December 18, 1863. Sick in hospital at Hempstead, Texas January 1864. Transferred to Company F, Timmons Regiment, Texas Infantry.

Groth, Clause – Enlisted at age 29 as a 2nd sergeant, Galveston, Texas October 18, 1861. Died at Camp Pemberton, Mississippi February 25, 1863.

Mack, Edward – Enlisted at age 50 as a private, Galveston, Texas October 18, 1861. Sick in hospital November 5, 1862. Sent to hospital in Vicksburg February 25, 1863. Detached to Company G, 7th Texas Infantry July 1863. Transferred to Company F, Timmons Regiment, Texas Infantry. Discharged March 23, 1864.

Mack, George W. – Enlisted at age 18 as a private, Galveston, Texas October 18, 1861. Sick in hospital November 5, 1862. Captured at Vicksburg, Mississippi July 4, 1863. Paroled July 9, 1863. Transferred to Company F, Timmons Regiment.

Mack, Jesse – Enlisted at age 18 as a private, Galveston, Texas October 18, 1861. Captured at Vicksburg, Mississippi July 4, 1863. Paroled July 9, 1863. Admitted to hospital December 15, 1863. Transferred to Company F, Timmons Regiment.

Mack, John – Enlisted at age 19 as a private, Houston, Texas December 1, 1863. Transferred to Company F, Timmons Regiment.

Martin, Benjamin F. – Enlisted at age 18 as a private, Galveston, Texas October 18, 1861. Sick in hospital at Grenada, Mississippi December 29, 1862. Detached to Company G, 7th Texas Infantry July 1863. Transferred to Company F, Timmons Regiment.

McLeod, Christopher Charles – Enlisted at age 20 as a private, Galveston, Texas October 18, 1861. Sick in hospital September 1862. Captured at Vicksburg, Mississippi July 4, 1863. Paroled July 9, 1863. Sick July 13, 1863. Transferred to Company F, Timmons Regiment,

McLeod, George – Enlisted at age 17 as a private, Galveston, Texas October 18, 1861. Captured at Vicksburg, Mississippi July 4, 1863. Paroled July 9, 1863. Transferred to Company F, Timmons Regiment.

Metts, Frances Marion – Enlisted at age 18 as a private, Galveston, Texas October 18, 1861. Captured at Vicksburg, Mississippi July 4, 1863. Paroled July 9, 1863. Transferred to Company F, Timmons Regiment. Transferred to Company K, 20th Texas Infantry.

Metts, Joseph Robert – Enlisted at age 18 as a private, Galveston, Texas October 18, 1861. Sent to hospital in Vicksburg February 15, 1863. No further records found.

Chapter 4
Post War
&
Reconstruction

photo courtesy of the author

Home from the War

Unlike most Confederate states, the State of Texas saw very few battles on its own soil. After Union troops were driven from the Texas coast near Velasco in the spring of 1864, there was no longer a threat of Union invasion. Boredom and disease had become the biggest enemy of Confederate troops in Texas. Overcrowded camps with poor facilities led to chronic illnesses, and outbreaks of diseases such as measles sent many soldiers to hospitals that were equally overcrowded.

By the summer of 1864, the war in Louisiana was essentially over, and most of the Texas regiments were preparing for their return home. Men from Montgomery County who had enlisted late in the war found themselves chasing deserters or guarding Union prisoners of war. Others who enlisted in newly-formed regiments such as Terry's Cavalry discovered that they had no place to go, and the units were soon disbanded. By 1865, the morale among Confederate troops in Texas was in serious decline. Many of the men simply packed up and went home without orders.

General Robert E. Lee's surrender at Appomattox Court House on April 9, 1865 allowed the Montgomery County men in the 4th and 5th Texas Infantries to be paroled and returned to Texas. These men were furnished transportation as far as Louisiana. From that point, they were on their own to find their way back to Montgomery County.

For many of the Montgomery County men in the 24th Texas Cavalry, the war ended with the Atlanta campaign in the summer of 1864 or the Tennessee campaign in the fall of 1864. How and when most of these men made their way home is uncertain. The nine remaining men in the 24th Texas Cavalry were paroled in North Carolina. Several Montgomery County men remained in Northern prison camps well into the summer of 1865.

More than ninety soldiers from Montgomery County are known to have died during the war along with substantial numbers of men missing and unaccounted for. In addition to the men who did not return home from the war, even greater numbers sustained wounds or ailments from which they would never fully recover. According to U.S. census records, the number of white males in Montgomery County who were born in the years 1812 through 1847 declined from 778 in 1860 to only 584 in 1870, reflecting a twenty-five-percent decrease in a short ten-year period.

Amnesty

Conditional amnesty was included in the terms and conditions when General Robert E. Lee surrendered to General Ulysses S. Grant at Appomattox Court House, Virginia on April 9th 1865. The enlisted men and the officers of the Confederate Army of Northern Virginia were allowed to return to their homes and terms stated that they were not to be disturbed by United States authorities so long as they observed their paroles and the laws in force where they resided. This eliminated the threat of these soldiers being tried for treason. Similar terms were provided in General Joseph Johnston's surrender to General William T. Sherman in North Carolina, but not all subsequent Confederate surrenders contained these conditions.

On May 29, 1865, President Andrew Johnson provided conditional amnesty to Confederate soldiers who would take an oath of allegiance. This amnesty did not apply to Confederate government officials, to Confederate Army officers with the rank of colonel and above, or to Confederate navy officers with the rank of lieutenant and above. While thousands of Confederate Army and navy officers did ask for and receive amnesty, many of them refused to take the oath of allegiance and fled to other countries. When President Johnson granted an unconditional pardon to everyone except the very highest-ranking military and civil officials on Christmas Day of 1868, many of the officers returned to the United States.

The 14th Amendment to the Constitution barred all Confederate soldiers and sailors from holding U. S. public office until the passage of the Congressional Amnesty in May 1872. Robert E. Lee signed his Amnesty Oath on October 2, 1865, but he did not receive a pardon, and his citizenship was not restored prior to his death. A worker at the National Archives discovered Lee's Amnesty Oath among State Department records in 1970. Robert E. Lee's citizenship was posthumously restored by a joint resolution of the U.S. Congress in 1975. It was signed by President Gerald R. Ford on August 5, 1975. President Jimmy Carter's signing of S. J. Resolution Number 16 on October 17, 1978 posthumously restored the U.S. citizenship of former Confederate Jefferson Davis.

Reconstruction

The period of time in American history which is commonly referred to as the Reconstruction era could likely be better defined as the "re-destruction" era. For more than a decade after the War between the States, political, social, and economic turmoil plagued the former Confederate states. Texas was no exception.

After the war, the Confederate soldiers from Montgomery County returned home to face a new set of problems. Many were charged with caring for family members who had been widowed or orphaned by the war. Their currency was worthless, and their prospects for future earnings were grim. Now under military rule, the men who had been political leaders prior to the war had to struggle for even the slightest leadership roles and were required to sign an oath of allegiance to the United States in order to reinstate their voting rights. The local tax base was ravaged by the end of slavery, and plummeting property values left the door open for Northerners to move in and take advantage of an economically depressed population. Those Northerners who came to Texas for financial gain and political prominence became known as "carpetbaggers."

On June 17, 1865, President Andrew Johnson appointed Andrew Jackson Hamilton as provisional Governor of Texas. Hamilton was a former Texas State Representative and a former U.S. Representative from Texas. In 1861, Hamilton won a special election to the Texas State Senate but was forced to resign for refusing to take the oath to the Confederacy. After threats to his life for his pro-Union statements, Hamilton fled to Mexico in 1862. Hamilton later returned to the United States, giving pro-Union speeches in the North. President Lincoln appointed him brigadier general for the Texas troops fighting for the Union, an empty position which he held until the end of the war. When Hamilton was appointed provisional governor, he was generally viewed as a traitor by the citizens of Texas. Southerners like Hamilton who supported the Union during the war were commonly referred to as "scalawags."

On June 18, 1865, Union General Gordon Granger arrived on Galveston Island with 2,000 federal troops, taking possession of the State of Texas and declaring that all acts of the Texas Confederate government were illegal. On June 19, 1865, General Gordon stood on the balcony of Galveston's Ashton Villa and announced that, in accordance with the emancipation proclamation, all slaves were free. Although the federal government had created the Bureau of Refugees, Freedmen, and Abandoned Lands (Freedmen's Bureau) to support the former slaves, Reconstruction was also a devastating period for blacks. While most blacks celebrated their newly- found freedom, they soon found themselves to be no more than poverty-stricken share-croppers who never realized the promises that were made to them by the federal government. In Montgomery County, as in the rest of the South, it was common in the late 19th century for blacks to be found living on the same property as their former owners, having never left.

In the late summer of 1865, General George A. Custer and five regiments of U.S. Cavalry passed through Montgomery County on his way to Liendo Plantation near Hempstead. Custer made Liendo his first headquarters during the military occupation of Texas. He later moved his headquarters to Austin, Texas. The U.S. Cavalry's presence so soon after the war generated bitterness among Texas residents.

By the fall of 1865, the number of freed blacks that were homeless and wandering around Montgomery County had reached alarming proportions. As winter approached, rumors of a black insurrection began to circulate. Citizens became so uneasy that they petitioned the governor to send state troops for protection, but no black uprising occurred.

For the next five years, radical Republicans controlled Texas politics with little interruption. President Andrew Johnson accepted a provisional Texas Constitution and in 1866 allowed Texas to hold elections for the first time since the end of the war. Democrat James W. Throckmorton won the governorship's election over Republican opponent Elisha M. Pease by a margin of four-to-one but was removed from office in 1867 by General Phillip Sheridan, commander of the military district. Throckmorton was replaced by Elisha

Pease. In 1870, Texas was readmitted to the Union. Montgomery County was still deep in debt at that time, and carpetbaggers continued to seize property in the county for more than a decade. The towns of Danville and Montgomery were still struggling to survive. The Houston and Great Northern Railroad began surveying Montgomery County for a new rail line. Peter James Willis, treasurer for the railroad, and his brother, Richard Short Willis, donated land for a townsite along the proposed route. The town was later named Willis in their honor. Some historians believe that the railroad was responsible for the demise of Danville, but it is likely that the railroad was only the last nail in the coffin of a dying community. Despite at an attempt to move the county courthouse to Willis, the City of Montgomery remained the county seat until 1889, managing to survive despite the devastation of war.

Confederate Pensions

Pension benefits for Confederate veterans were paid by the individual states, and applications were submitted to the state wherein the veteran was living at the time that the application was filed. In 1899, the State of Texas began awarding pensions for Confederate service to veterans or their widows who had resided in Texas since 1880 and who were disabled or indigent. Veterans who had significant income or owned substantial amounts of property were not eligible for benefits. Nearly 55,000 applications were submitted to the State of Texas between 1899 and 1975. The last Confederate benefits paid by the State of Texas was the $50.00 balance of a $200 mortuary warrant on November 19, 1979 to the estate of Lucy Victoria Spires Stark, the widow of Confederate veteran William Kilgore.

The last application for Confederate pension benefits filed in Montgomery County was that of Mary Florence Clarke Shepperd. She claimed her benefits as the widow of Private William M. Shepperd who served in Company A of the 21st Texas Cavalry. Mrs. Sheppard was also the daughter of Private Pickens R. Clarke, a Confederate soldier from the State of Georgia. It is likely that the last pension benefits paid to a Confederate veteran from Montgomery County were to Private Charles Robert Scott who served in Company A, 7th Texas Cavalry. Charles Scott filed his application on January 29, 1914. He died twenty-six years later on July 5, 1940.

In 1958, Confederate veterans won a final victory when U.S. Public Law 85-425, approved by the second session of the eighty-fifth U.S. Congress, provided pension benefits for veterans who had served honorably in the Confederate military. Unfortunately, there were no surviving Confederate veterans to receive these benefits.

The Texas Confederate Home

In 1884, the John B. Hood Camp of the United Confederate Veterans obtained a charter from the State of Texas for the purpose of establishing a home for disabled and indigent Confederate veterans. With the help of fundraising by the Albert Sidney Johnston Chapter of the United Daughters of the Confederacy, the Hood Camp purchased sixteen and two-thirds acres of land at 1600 West 6th Street in Austin, Texas and built the home which opened on November 1, 1886. A board of managers was established consisting of five Confederate veterans appointed by the governor. A superintendent who was also a Confederate veteran was selected by the board. In 1920, the Texas State Board of Control took responsibility for managing the facility. An annual report filed by the Board of Control for the fiscal year ending August 31, 1920 stated that the grounds of the home embraced twenty-six and two-thirds acres overlooking the Colorado River and included twenty small-to-fair-size brick-and-frame buildings capable of housing about four-hundred-and-twenty men. Officers of the home included a superintendent, eye and ear doctor, surgeon, druggist, and a storekeeper. In 1949, management of the home was transferred to the Board for Texas State Hospitals and Special Schools which continued to maintain the home until it closed in 1954.

From 1886 to 1954, more than 2,000 Confederate veterans were admitted to the Texas Confederate Home. During the first two years of operation, 113 veterans were admitted to the home. The Board of Control report in August of 1920 indicated 441 residents. Residents in the home dwindled to 312 in 1929, 80 in 1936, and 38 in 1938.

Although his Confederate service has not been conclusively verified, Thomas Evans Riddle was the last resident of the Texas Confederate Home. He died on April 2, 1954 and was buried in Burkburnett Cemetery, Wichita County, Texas. Unlike Thomas Riddle, most of the men who died in the Confederate Home were buried in the Texas State Cemetery. This is the case with the four veterans from Montgomery County who were known to have been residents of the home. These four men were: Matthias Dayton Chilton, John W. Fowler, Jabez N. Mitchell, and William Franklin Sanders.

Texas Confederate Women's Home

In 1905, the United Daughters of Confederacy purchased a small piece of property north of Austin for the purpose of establishing a home to care for the wives and widows of Confederate veterans. A two-story building with fifteen bedrooms was completed in 1907. The organization opened the doors of the Texas Confederate Women's Home on June 3, 1908, admitting three women. The United Daughters of the Confederacy operated the home with private funds and donations until 1911 when the property was deeded to the State of Texas. In 1913 the State of Texas constructed an additional two-story brick building, twenty-four new bedrooms, and added a brick hospital building in 1916. Management of the facility was transferred to the Texas Board of Control in 1920. The Board of Control reported 102 residents at that time. The population of the home had dwindled to only 55 residents by 1945. The facility closed in 1963 and its three remaining residents were transferred to private nursing facilities at the State's expense. The State of Texas sold the property in 1986. In approximately fifty-five years of operation, the home cared for more than 3,400 hundred women. It is unknown if any women from Montgomery County were ever residents of the home.

Graves of Confederate Veterans

A trip to a national cemetery at any of the battlefields of the War between the States can be an awe-inspiring experience. Gazing across a field dotted with thousands of white markers can cause your mind to question what possible cause could have motivated so many men to risk their lives in such a brutal conflict. While viewing one of these great cemeteries, many visitors are unaware that there are few if any Confederate soldiers buried beneath these markers.

The sad and unfortunate truth is that the final resting place for most of the Confederate soldiers who were killed in action was on the battlefield or near the spot where they fell. Those who were buried by their comrades were most often hurriedly placed in shallow graves that allowed the bodies to become prey for animals or grave robbers. In time, some fallen soldiers' remains were taken to nearby communities where local citizens assisted in properly burying the soldiers in a city or private cemetery. Those who were mortally wounded but managed to live long enough to reach a hospital were normally buried in proper graves that were commonly marked and recorded. Those who were buried by the enemy were usually piled in mass graves, leaving no records of their identities nor locations.

Confederate graves that are found in national cemeteries today are most frequently for those men who died while confined to prisoner-of-war camps. The Confederate graves in these cemeteries number in the thousands. Because of the high mortality rate, U.S. Congress established a national cemetery system in 1862. Although many Confederate soldiers who died as prisoners of war were buried in these cemeteries, they were not provided with military markers until 1906 when an act by Congress authorized the furnishing of headstones for the graves of Confederate soldiers who died primarily in Union prison camps and were buried in federal cemeteries.

Another sad and unfortunate truth is that many thousands of Confederate veterans' graves are lost and may never be found. The soldiers who suffered their way through the war and managed to make it home to their friends and family returned to a homeland of poverty. Many were still suffering from wounds or debilitating illnesses. Death came soon after the war for countless thousands. These men were usually buried in family plots with handmade wooden markers for tombstones that soon decayed and left no traces.

Confederate military markers found in cemeteries today were likely placed long after the veterans' deaths. Most have been placed by organizations such as the Sons of Confederate Veterans or the United Daughters of the Confederacy. It was not until 1929 that the United States government began to furnish military markers for Confederate veterans not buried in national cemeteries, but many Confederate graves had long since been lost by then.

During the siege of Vicksburg, Mississippi in 1863, the Confederate government contracted a local undertaker to bury those who had died from illness or were killed in action. These soldiers were buried in a special section of the old city cemetery now known as Cedar Hill. This section of the cemetery is called Soldier's Rest and is maintained by the United Daughters of the Confederacy. Although the undertaker took great care in documenting the burials, these records disappeared after the surrender of the Confederate Army at Vicksburg. A portion of these records were discovered in the 1960s and used in the 1980s to mark approximately 1,600 of the more the 5,000 graves.

The two largest Confederate cemeteries are located in Richmond, Virginia. Hollywood Cemetery is the final resting place for more than 18,000 Confederate soldiers including General George Pickett and General J. E. B. Stuart. Confederate President Jefferson Davis is also buried at Hollywood. Three Montgomery County men are known to be buried in Hollywood Cemetery. These men are Privates Henry Reid Irvine and James Tomlinson of Company D, 5th Texas Infantry along with Captain Procter P. Porter, Company H, 4th Texas Infantry. The second largest Confederate cemetery in Richmond is Oakwood Cemetery which contains almost 17,000 Confederate graves.

This book contains a list of Confederate soldiers and veterans buried in Montgomery County, Texas as well as soldiers from across Texas and soldiers from ten other Confederate states. At the time of publication, there were 234 Confederate soldiers and veterans found in forty-eight cemeteries within the county.

Bibliography

Books

Barnickel, Linda A. *Milliken's Bend: A Civil War Battle in History and Memory.* Baton Rouge, Louisiana: LSU Press, 2013.

Cottrell, Steve. *Civil War in Texas and New Mexico Territory.* Gretna, Louisiana: Pelican Publishing, 1998.

Dupree, Stephen. *Dupree: A Family History, Memoir, and Journal of My Times.* Lincoln, Nebraska: iUniverse Publishers, 2007.

History of Montgomery County, Texas. Conroe, Texas: Montgomery County Genealogical & Historical Society, Inc., 1981.

Hughes, Nathaniel Cheairs, Jr. *Bentonville: The Final Battle of Sherman and Johnston.* Raleigh, North Carolina: UNC Press Books, 1996.

Lubbock, Francis Richard. *Six Decades in Texas: Or, Memoirs of Francis Richard. Lubbock, Confederate Governor of Texas in War Time, 1861-63, a Personal Experience in Business, War, and Politics.* Austin, Texas: B. C. Jones & Co., 1900.

McCaffrey, James M. *This Band of Heroes: Granbury's Texas Brigade, C.S.A.* College Station, Texas: Texas A&M University Press, 1996.

Moneyhon, Carl H. *Republicanism in Reconstruction Texas.* College Station, Texas: Texas A&M University Press, 2002.

Murray, Lois Smith. *Baylor at Independence.* Waco, Texas: Baylor University Press, 1972.

Reichardt, Robert E. *Forever the Cause: the Life and Legacy of Confederate Colonel Robert M. Powell, 5th Texas Infantry.* St. Louis, Missouri: privately published, 2007.

Taylor, John. *Bloody Valverde: a Civil War Battle on the Rio Grande, February 21, 1862.* Albuquerque, New Mexico: UNM Press, 1999.

Thompson, Jerry, Ph.D. *Civil War in the Southwest: Recollections of the Sibley Brigade.* College Station, Texas: Texas A&M University Press, 2001.

Thompson, Kevin P. *Leaf, Stem, Branch, and Root: Muskegon County, Michigan. Thompson Ancestry, Walker County, Texas & Baldwin Ancestry.* Colorado Springs, Colorado: privately published, 2010.

Periodicals and Other Publications

Gandy, William Harley. "A History of Montgomery County, Texas." Master's thesis, University of Houston, 1952.

Hett, Karen McCann, *The Herald* 27-30. Conroe, Texas: Montgomery County Genealogical & Historical Society, Inc., 2004-2007.

Hett, Karen McCann, Karen Lucas-Lawless, Elsa Vorwerk, David Frame. "Old Danville." *The Herald* 31. Conroe, Texas: Montgomery County Genealogical & Historical Society, Inc., 2008.

Archives and Databases

Civil War Compiled Service Records. National Archives and Records. Washington, D.C.: National Archives and Records Administration, 2011. *https://www.tsl.state.tx.us/arc/.*

Confederate Service Records 1861-1865. *Ancestry.com*. Provo, Utah: *Ancestry.com* Operations, Inc., 2007. *www.ancestry.com.*

"Danville Mounted Riflemen." compiler, Karen McCann Hett. http://freepages. genealogy.rootsweb.ancestry.com/~barrettbranches/Researchers/Karen%20Hett/ B24cavindex.html.

Soldiers and Sailors Database. National Park Service, U.S. Department of the Interior. Washington, D.C.: National Park Service, 2012. *www.nps.gov/ civilwar/search-soldiers.htm.*

Texas Adjutant General Service Records 1836-1935. Texas State Library and Archives. Austin, Texas: Texas State Library and Archives Commission, 2011. *https://www.tsl.state.tx.us/apps/arc/service/.*

Texas Compiled Censuses and Census Substitutes Index 1820-1890. Texas State Library and Archives. Austin, Texas: Texas State Library and Archives Commission, 2011. https://www.tsl.state.tx.us/apps/arc/censuses/.

Texas Confederate Pension Applications Index. Texas State Library and Archives. Austin, Texas: Texas State Library and Archives Commission, 2011. https://www.tsl.state.tx.us/apps/arc/pensions/.

Texas Muster Roll Index Cards, 1838-1900. *Ancestry.com*. Provo, Utah: *Ancestry.com* Operations, 2011. *www.ancestry.com.*

Texas Voters Registration of 1867. Texas State Library and Archives. Austin, Texas: Texas State Library and Archives Commission, 2007. *https://www.tsl. state.tx.us/apps/arc/votersreg.html.*

Appendices
Appendix A
Alphabetical Listing of Soldiers

Abbott, George – Pvt. Co. D, 4th Texas Infantry, TST. Born about 1820, died about 1892. Father: Lewis Abbott. Spouse: Sarah Jane Adams.

Abbott, Johnson – Pvt. Co. G, 20th Texas Infantry. Born about 1825, died unknown. Spouse: Mary Abbott.

Abney, Hezekiah H. – 1st Lt. Company B, 17th Brigade TST. Born about 1827, died about 1870. Spouse: Nancy Ellen Milburn

Adams, Edwin Wesley – Pvt. Co. I, 9th Texas Infantry (Nichols')/Pvt. Co. K, 20th Texas Infantry. Born about 1841, died 03/11/1903. Father: T. C. E. Adams. Spouse: Caroline Matilda Oglesby.

Adams, Thomas R. – Pvt. Co. I, 9th Texas Infantry (Nichols')/Pvt. Co. G, 20th Texas Infantry. Born about 1845, died unknown.

Adams, William G. – Sgt. Co. B, 24th Texas Cavalry. Born about 1822, died before 1879. Spouse: Sarah E. Chambliss.

Alexander, Negro – Co. B, 24th Texas Cavalry. Vitals unknown. Last record shows Camp Butler, Illinois POW.

Alford, John Peachman – Pvt. Co. A, 10th Texas Infantry. Born 09/12/1841, died 4/27/1913. Buried: Mostyn–Tillis Prairie Cemetery, Montgomery County, Texas. Father: William B. Alford. Spouse: Margaret Jane Mostyn.

Anders, Burrel (Burrill) – Pvt. Co. H, 4th Texas Infantry. Born 04/14/1829, died 07/30/1896. Buried: Saint Elmo Cemetery, Freestone County, Texas. Spouse: Elizabeth Martin.

Anders, Jacob – Pvt. Co. A, 17th Brigade TST. Born 02/14/1827, died 06/27/1909. Buried: Mount Pleasant Cemetery, Montgomery County, Texas. Father: James Anders. Spouse: Cynthia E. Rankin.

Anders, James – Pvt. Co. G, 20th Texas Infantry/Pvt. Co. A, 24th/25th Consolidated Regiment, Texas Cavalry/Pvt. Co. A. Mann's Regiment, Texas Cavalry (Bradford's). Born 04/29/1833, died 01/03/1900. Buried: Mount Pleasant Cemetery, Montgomery County, Texas. Father: James Anders. Spouse: Nancy Gilleland.

Anderson, Edward Americus – Pvt. 17th Brigade TST. Born 02/01/1820, died 12/11/1896. Buried: Willis Cemetery, Montgomery County, Texas. Father: James Alexander Anderson. Spouse: Mary Jane Whitten/Lucy A. Hulon.

Arnold, Eliphalet Lester Jr. – Pvt. Co. G, 20th Texas Infantry. Born 06/12/1838, died 05/29/1924. Buried: Arnold/Dean Cemetery, Montgomery County, Texas. Father: Eliphalet Lester Arnold, Sr. Spouse: Mary S. Boyd.

Arnold, Owen William – Sgt. Co. G, 20th Texas Infantry. Born 06/22/1836, died 07/14/1913. Buried: Arnold/Dean Cemetery, Montgomery County, Texas. Father: Eliphalet Lester Arnold, Sr. Spouse: Minnie Dean Alban/Lucereta Arnold.

Atchison, James W. – Pvt. Co. I, 9th Texas Infantry (Nichols')/Pvt. Co. K, 20th Texas Infantry. Born about 1842 in Kentucky, died 12/23/1927.

Baggerly, Isaac J. – Pvt. Co. K, 20th Texas Infantry. Born 1839, died 02/14/1922. Buried: North Elm Cemetery, Milam County, Texas. Father: John W. Baggerly. Spouse: Carine Matilda Coward.

Bailey, James A. – Pvt. Montgomery County Rifle Boys, 17th Brigade TST. Born 05/07/1829, died 6/3/1911. Burial: Bradshaw Cemetery, Taylor County, Texas. Father: Wyatt Bailey. Spouse: Perniece Caroline Gatlin.

Bailey, Pitser (Pittser) M. – Pvt. Co. K, 20th Texas Infantry. Born 09/22/1823, died 10/26/1889. Buried: Live Oak Cemetery, Erath County, Texas. Spouse: Mary Lewin Waterhouse.

Bailey, William Henry – Pvt. Co. A, 17th Brigade TST/Pvt. Co. D, 4th Infantry TST. Born 04/12/1821, died 01/11/1895. Buried: New Montgomery Cemetery, Montgomery County, Texas. Spouse: Clarissa Millie Orr.

Baker, Benjamin Franklin – Pvt. Co. C, Terry's Regiment Texas Cavalry. Born 02/04/1847, died 05/06/1934. Buried: Willow Creek Cemetery, Harris County, Texas. Father: Basil Caleb Baker. Spouse: Ida Lee Wren.

Baker, William Henry – Pvt. Montgomery County Rifle Boys, 17th Brigade TST. Born about 1844, died unknown. Buried: Baker Cemetery (unmarked grave), Montgomery County Texas. Father: Basil Caleb Baker. Spouse: Nancy Elizabeth Williamson.

Barker, G. F. – Sgt. Company G, 20th Texas Infantry. Born about 1834, died 09/27/1864 of yellow fever in Galveston.

Barrett, David Albert – Pvt. Co. G, 7th Texas Cavalry. Born 05/02/1849, died 12/28/1928. Buried: Barrett–Burroughs Cemetery, Madison County, Texas. Father: John Whitten Barrett. Spouse: Martha J. Tolbert.

Barrett, Stephen Reding – Pvt. Co. G, 7th Texas Cavalry. Born 09/08/1840, died 12/08/1863 in Louisiana. Father: John Whitten Barrett. Spouse: Sarah Larrison.

Barrett, William Robert – Cpl. Co. G, 7th Texas Cavalry. Born 12/30/1842, died 01/01/1903. Buried: Madisonville City Cemetery, Madison County, Texas. Father: John Whitten Barrett. Spouse: Elizabeth Waters.

Bass, B. E. – Pvt. Company I, 9th Texas Infantry (Nichols'). Born about 1833, died unknown.

Bass, Thomas W. – Pvt. Company I, 9th Texas Infantry (Nichols'), Pvt. Company K, 20th Texas Infantry. Born about 1837 in Tennessee.

Baugass (Bauguss), J. R. – Cpl. Co. B, 24th Texas Cavalry. Born about 1835 in Tennessee, died 03/26/1863. Buried: Camp Butler National Cemetery, Sangamon County, Illinois.

Bay, Andrew Foster – Pvt. 17th Brigade TST. Born 04/01/1817, died 04/25/1878. Buried: Bay's Chapel Cemetery, Montgomery County, Texas. Father: Robert Thomas Bay. Spouse: Elizabeth B. Jones.

Bay, James Henry, Sr. – Pvt. Co. B, 17th Texas Militia/Pvt. Co. D, 4th Infantry, TST. Born 03/22/1821, died 07/19/1901. Buried: Bay's Chapel Cemetery, Montgomery County, Texas. Father: Robert Thomas Bay.

Bay, James Henry, Jr. – Pvt. Co. I, 20th Texas Infantry. Born 10/11/1842, died 05/17/1905. Buried: Bay's Chapel Cemetery, Montgomery County, Texas. Father: James Henry Bay. Spouse: Nancy E. Bay.

Bay, Thomas Bowen – Pvt. Co. I, 20th Texas Infantry. Born 03/22/1831, died 7/19/1901. Buried: Bay's Chapel Cemetery, Montgomery County, Texas. Father: Robert Thomas Bay. Spouse: Julia M. Harman.

Bay, William Harrison . Pvt. Co. C, 17th Texas Militia. Born 11/10/1815, died 08/10/1897. Buried: Bay's Chapel Cemetery, Montgomery County, Texas. Father: Robert Thomas Bay, Spouse: Cynthia Pryor Jones.

Bell, Henry Ellsworth – Pvt. Co. B, 24th Texas Cavalry. Born about 1844, died 10/20/1930. Father: J. H. Bell. Spouse: Adner Childers.

Bell, James Henry – Pvt. Co. B, 1st Texas Heavy Artillery. Born about 1821 in Alabama, died about 1897 in Walker County, Texas. Father: James Henry Bell. Spouse: Sarah Ann Elizabeth McGill.

Bell, James Jefferson – Pvt. Montgomery County Rifle Boys, 17th Brigade TST/Pvt. Co. C, 21st Texas Cavalry. Born about 1829, died 04/17/1915. Buried: Sabanno Cemetery, Eastland County, Texas. Father: John Bell. Spouse: May Jane Sanders.

Bender, John F. – Pvt. 17th Brigade TST/Pvt. Co. K, 20th Texas Infantry. Born 10/22/1829, died 10/19/1904. Buried: Goodson–Pinehurst Cemetery, Montgomery County, Texas. Father: Johann G. Bender. Spouse: Elizabeth "Lizzie" Goodson.

Berkley, William Henry – Pvt. Co. I, 9th Texas Infantry (Nichols'). Born 05/11/1844, died 03/31/1905. Buried: New Montgomery Cemetery, Montgomery County, Texas. Father: N. H. Berkley. Spouse: Mary Alice Mattingly.

Betts, Dexter – Pvt. Co. A, 24th/25th Consolidated Texas Cavalry. Born about 1843, died unknown. Father: Thomas J. Betts.

Betts, Menter – Pvt. Co. G, 7th Texas Cavalry/Pvt. Co. A, 24th/25th Consolidated Texas Cavalry. Born about 1841, died unknown. Father: Thomas J. Betts.

Blount, James Koen – Pvt. Co. A, 36th Texas Cavalry (Woods). Born 10/04/1832, died 04/28/1918. Buried: Live Oak Cemetery, McCulloch County, Texas. Father: John Thomas Blount. Spouse: Lydia Ann Moore.

Blount, Joseph Shaw – Pvt. Co. C, 17th Texas Infantry Infantry/Pvt. Co. G, 13th Texas Cavalry. Born about 1835 in Washington County, Alabama, died before 1883 in Texas. Father: John Thomas Blount. Spouse: Mary Jane Yates.

Blount, Francis Marion – Pvt. Co. C, 17th Texas Infantry/Pvt. Co. G, 13th Texas Cavalry. Born about 1839 in Mississippi, died before 1880 in Texas. Father: John Thomas Blount. Spouse: Isabella Saxton.

Bobbitt, George Random, Sr. – Sgt. Co. D, E, 24th Texas Cavalry. Born about 1839, died 04/11/1905. Buried: New Montgomery Cemetery, Montgomery County, Texas. Father: Robert Roderick Bobbitt. Spouse: Elizabeth C. "Ella" Carson.

Bolton, John T. – Pvt. Co. B, 24th Texas Cavalry. Born about 1830, died unknown.

Boone, E. A. – Pvt. Montgomery County Rifle Boys, 17th Brigade TST/ Pvt. Company H, 26th Texas Cavalry/Pvt. Co. C, Terry's Regiment, Texas Cavalry. Born 06/22/1822, died 8/26/1902. Buried: Trent Garden, Taylor County, Texas.

Boone, J. A. – Pvt. Montgomery County Rifle Boys, 17th Brigade TST/Pvt. Company H, 26th Texas Cavalry. Born about 1845, died unknown. Father: E. A. Boone.

Boyd, Alexander R. – Pvt. Co, 9th Texas Infantry (Nichols')/Pvt. Co. G, K, 20th Texas Infantry. Born about 1842, died unknown. Father: David Boyd.

Boyd, Theodore David – Pvt. Co. K, 20th Texas Infantry. Born about 1844, died about 1926. Buried: Knickerbocker Cemetery, Tom Green County, Texas. Father: David Boyd. Spouse: Cherry M. Etheridge.

Bradley, R. R. – 2nd Lt. Co. K, 20th Texas Infantry. Born about 1820 in Alabama, died after 1880.

Brake, William B. – Pvt. Co. B, 24th Texas Cavalry. Born about 1843, died 03/04/1863. Buried: Camp Butler National Cemetery, Sangamon County, Illinois.

Brantley, Edward – Pvt. Co. K, 20th Texas Infantry. Born about 1846, died unknown.

Brantley, Robert Augustus – Cpl. Co. D, 5th Texas Infantry. Born about 1838 in Georgia, died 08/03/1911. Buried: Oaklawn Cemetery, Burleson County, Texas. Spouse: Anna Wilson.

Brantner, George H. – Pvt. 17th Brigade TST/Pvt. Co. D, 4th Infantry TST. Born about 1827, died about 1871. Buried: Heards Prairie–Petteway Cemetery, Robertson County, Texas. Father: George Brantner. Spouse: Eliza Shaffner/Susana Lambkin.

Brautigam, Frederick – Pvt. Co. K, 20th Texas Infantry. Born 02/23/1839, died 03/20/1904. Buried: Salem Luthern Cemetery, Harris County, Texas. Father: Christoph Brautigam. Spouse: Mary Elizabeth Heaton.

Brautigam, George C. – Pvt. Co. K, 20th Texas Infantry. Born 08/06/1837, died 01/17/1916. Buried: Salem Luthern Cemetery, Harris County, Texas. Father: Christoph Brautigam.

Bridgers, C. A. – Pvt. Co. A, 24th Texas Cavalry. Born about 1839, died 04/15/1863. Buried: Camp Butler National Cemetery, Sangamon County, Illinois. Father: Willis Bridgers.

Bridgers, Leonidas Moore – Pvt. Co. I, 9th Texas Infantry (Nichols')/Pvt. Co. A, 24th Texas Cavalry. Born 05/14/1842, died 4/19/1918. Buried: Oak Hill Cemetery, Lampasas County, Texas. Father: Willis Bridgers. Spouse: Mary Margaret "Maggie" Smith.

Brooks, Andrew Jackson – Pvt. Co. B, 24th Texas Cavalry. Born 11/08/1844, died 01/12/1863. Buried: unmarked grave, Arkansas Post (Ft. Hindman), Arkansas. Father: Samuel Clifford Brooks.

Brooks, Calvin Herlock – Chaplain, 20th Texas Infantry. Born 02/20/1827, died 08/03/1916. Buried: Elgin City Cemetery, Bastrop County, Texas. Father: Richard Simms Brooks. Spouse: Letitia (Lettia) Worsham.

Brooks, John Caperton – Pvt. Co. B, 6th Texas Cavalry (Gould's). Born 06/13/1825, died 05/30/1870. Buried: Cedar Hill–Price Cemetery, Madison County, Texas. Father: Samuel Clifford Brooks. Spouse: Emily Yarbrough Montague.

Brooks, Montgomery Somerville – Pvt. Co. B, 17th Brigade TST. Born about 1844, died 02/05/1908. Buried: Midway Cemetery, Madison County, Texas. Father: Samuel Clifford Brooks. Spouse: Lauretta Brooks.

Brooks, Reding LaFayette – Cpl. Co. B, 6th Texas Cavalry (Gould's). Born 03/14/1832, died 08/10/1908. Buried: Oakwood Cemetery, Walker County, Texas. Father: Samuel Clifford Brooks. Spouse: Mary Emily Whitley.

Brooks, Samuel Houston – Major, A.D.C., Cheatham's Division, CSA/Lt. Col. Terry's Regiment, Texas Cavalry. Born: 01/01/1829, died 9/16/1910. Buried: California. Father: Samuel Clifford Brooks. Spouse: Lucy C. Thornton Judge.

Brooks, William Haley – Sgt. Co. G, 20th Texas Infantry. Born 06/09/1833, died 04/23/1916. Buried: Greenwood Cemetery, Freestone County, Texas. Father: Samuel Clifford Brooks. Spouse: Julia Helen Besser.

Broomfield, John W. – Pvt. 17th Brigade TST. Born about 1811 in Virginia, died about 1881 in Texas. Spouse: Julia Ann Stubbs.

Brown, J. W. – Cpl. Co. H, 26th Texas Cavalry. Born about 1835 in Virginia, died unknown.

Brown, Robert J. – Pvt. Co. I, 9th Texas Infantry (Nichols')/Pvt. Co. G, 20th Texas Infantry. Born about 1837, died unknown. Spouse: C. M. Brown.

Bryant, Jacob – Pvt. Co. I, 9th Texas Infantry (Nichols')/Pvt. Co. K, 20th Texas Infantry. Born about 1832, died unknown. Spouse: Amanda Cheatham Roten.

Burden, George Larkum – Pvt. Co. G, 7th Texas Cavalry/Pvt. Co. A, Mann's Regiment, Texas Cavalry (Bradford's). Born 05/23/1842, died 03/07/1918. Buried: Concord Cemetery, Grimes County, Texas. Father: John Gillard Burden. Spouse: Rebecca Miller.

Burden, John Gillard – Pvt. Co. D, 5th Texas Infantry. Born 01/08/1812, died 07/28/1875. Father: Henry Roe Burden. Spouse: Mathilda Stotts Harris.

Burden, Joseph Castine – Pvt. Co. D, 5th Texas Infantry. Born 02/28/1840, died 08/31/1862 from wounds at Manassas. Father: John Gillard Burden.

Burgess, I. J. – Pvt. Co. B, 24th Texas Cavalry. Born about 1844, died 04/25/1863. Buried: Camp Butler National Cemetery, Sangamon County, Illinois.

Burke, Charles – Pvt. Co. G, 20th Texas Infantry. Born about 1845, died after 1902. Father: N. Burke.

Burke, Ephraim – Pvt. Co. D, 5th Texas Infantry. Born about 1835 in Kentucky, died after 1880. Father: N. Burke. Spouse: Araminta Burke.

Burke, Lee – Pvt. Co. G, 7th Texas Cavalry. Born about 1836, died unknown. Father: N. Burke. Spouse: Tabitha Gibson.

Burke, Levi Zim – Pvt. Co. G, 7th Texas Cavalry. Born about 1839, died unknown. Father: N. Burke.

Burke, Nathan – Pvt. Co. G, 7th Texas Cavalry. Born about 1840, died after 1880. Father: N. Burke. Spouse: Mary Posey.

Burrows, Thomas J. – Pvt. Co. K, 8th Texas Cavalry. Born about 1833, died unknown.

Burton, George – Pvt. Co. K, 20th Texas Infantry. Born about 1843 in Louisiana, died unknown.

Caldwell, S. H. – Pvt. Co. D, 4th Infantry TST. Born about 1846, died unknown. Buried: Bay's Chapel Cemetery, Montgomery County, Texas.

Caldwell, William – Pvt. 17th Brigade TST. Born 03/10/1844, died 08/15/1897. Buried: Bay's Chapel Cemetery, Montgomery County, Texas.

Campbell, Archibald Roland – 5th Sgt. Company B, 35th Texas Cavalry (Brown's). Born 05/08/1841, died 05/01/1920. Buried: Trinity Episcopal Cemetery, Galveston County, Texas. Father: John Wesley Campbell. Spouse: Alice Lee Matthews.

Campbell, Clark Calhoun – Pvt. Co. B, 17th Brigade TST/Surgeon, Co. D, 4th Texas Infantry TST. Born about 1824, died 07/27/1907. Buried: Old City Cemetery, Galveston County, Texas. Father: John Wesley Campbell, Sr. Spouse: Lucille Caroline Goree.

Campbell, Douglas McQueen – Pvt. Co. D, 5th Texas Infantry. Born 01/24/1844, died 10/20/1925. Buried: Orange Grove Cemetery, Calcasieu Parish, Louisiana. Father: John Wesley Campbell, Sr. Spouse: Ella Abercrombie Wood.

Campbell, John Wesley, Jr. – Sgt. Co. D, 5th Texas Infantry/1st Lt. Co. D, 4th Infantry TST. Born 05/12/1829, died 12/08/1915. Father: John Wesley Campbell, Sr. Spouse: Sarah Louise Davis.

Campbell, William L. Barnes "Bose" – Sgt. Co. D, 5th Texas Infantry. Born about 1834, died unknown. Father: William Archibald Campbell.

Carrington, Edward William – Pvt. Co. I, 20th Texas Infantry. Born about 1838 in Virginia, died 04/15/1863 in hospital at Galveston, Texas. Father: William Edward Carrington.

Carrington, Thomas Preston – Pvt. Co. I, 20th Texas Infantry. Born about 1841 in Virginia, died about 1890. Father: William Edward Carrington.

Carroll, David Allison – Cpl. Co. K, 20th Texas Infantry. Born about 1827 in South Carolina, died 01/15/1900. Spouse: Louisa M. Wheeler/Ada Carroll.

Carson, Elihis Lemuel – Cpl. Co. G, 20th Texas Infantry. Born 05/26/1829, died 01/23/1900. Buried: Willis Cemetery, Montgomery County, Texas. Spouse: Elizabeth Caroline Uzzell.

Carson, R. L. – Pvt. Co. K, 20th Texas Infantry. Born about 1842 in North Carolina, died after 1880. Spouse: Narcissa Uzzell.

Carter, Hampton Wesley – Pvt. Co. H, 21st Texas Cavalry. Born 12/15/1835, died 06/18/1896. Buried: Martin's Prairie Cemetery, Grimes County, Texas. Father: Ebenezer A. "Nace" Carter. Spouse: Amanda C. Walker.

Carter, Jessie P. – Pvt. Co. C, 17th Brigade TST. Born 10/28/1825, died 05/11/1905. Buried: Splendora Cemetery, Montgomery County, Texas. Spouse: Melvina Beeks/Catherine Carr.

Cartwright, E. G. – Pvt. Co. H, 4th Texas Infantry. Born about 1836, died 09/11/1861 train accident, Holly Springs, Mississippi. Father: Williford B. Cartwright.

Cartwright, James G. W. – Sgt. Co. H, 4th Texas Infantry. Born about 1842, died 06/05/1864 from wounds in Wilderness campaign. Buried: Old Lynchburg City Cemetery, Lynchburg City, Virginia. Father: Williford B. Cartwright.

Cartwright, Joseph C. – Pvt. Co. A, 24th/25th Consolidated Texas Cavalry/ Pvt. Co. D, 4th Infantry TST/Pvt. Co. A. Mann's Regiment, Texas Cavalry (Bradford's). Born 05/31/1821, died 1/24/1904. Buried: Cartwright–Rabun Chapel Cemetery, Montgomery County, Texas. Father: T. P. Cartwright, Jr.

Cartwright, Lemuel C. – Pvt. Co. H, 4th Texas Infantry. Born 12/15/1836, died about 1891. Buried: Cartwright–Rabun Chapel Cemetery, Montgomery County, Texas. Father: Williford B. Cartwright.

Cartwright, Pleasant L. – Pvt. Co. K, 8th Texas Cavalry/Pvt. Co. A, 24th Texas Cavalry/2nd Lt. Co. A, 24th/25th Consolidated Texas Cavalry/2nd Lt. Co. A. Mann's Regiment, Texas Cavalry (Bradford's). Born: 09/06/1840, died 01/06/1899. Buried: Cartwright–Rabun Chapel Cemetery, Montgomery County, Texas. Father: Matthew Winston Cartwright.

Carvell, William M. – Pvt. Co. C, 21st Texas Cavalry. Born 05/24/1819, died 02/14/1891. Buried: Mt. Pleasant Cemetery, Montgomery County, Texas. Spouse: Elizabeth Anders.

Cates, Benjamin Franklin – Pvt. Danville Mounted Riflemen/Pvt. Co. G, 7th Texas Cavalry. Born about 1839, died 12/19/1861.

Catharino, David – Pvt. Co. K, 20th Texas Infantry. Born about 1813 in New York, died unknown.

Cathey, Bennett H. – Pvt. Co. H, 4th Texas Infantry. Born about 1839, died 04/30/1863 in Virginia.

Cathey, John C. – Pvt. Montgomery County Rifle Boys, 17th Brigade TST. Born about 1817 in Tennessee, died after 1870. Spouse: Elender Rhoden.

Chambers, Daniel L. – Pvt. Co. B, 24th Texas Cavalry. Born about 1841, killed in action 09/20/1863 at Chickamauga. Place of burial unknown. Father: Thomas Chambers.

Chambers, Edward C. – Pvt. Co. G, 20th Texas Infantry. Born 03/1831, died about 1912. Buried: Thornton Cemetery, Limestone County, Texas. Spouse: Annie Jean.

Chambers, John F. – Pvt. Co. B, 24th Texas Cavalry. Born about 1828 in South Carolina, died 01/17/1863 from wounds at Arkansas Post. Place of burial unknown.

Chambers, John H. – Sgt. Co. B, 24th Texas Cavalry. Born about 1838, killed in action 09/20/1863 at Chickamauga. Place of burial unknown. Father: Thomas Chambers.

Chambers, Oliver Perry – Pvt. Co. B, 24th Texas Cavalry. Born 05/17/1844 died 09/06/1922. Buried: Cleveland City Cemetery, Liberty County, Texas. Father: Thomas Chambers. Spouse: Sarah Jane Grimes.

Chambers, Thomas, Jr. – Pvt. Co. B, 24th Texas Cavalry. Born about 1842, died 02/26/1863 from disease at prison hospital in St. Louis. Buried: Jefferson Barracks National Cemetery, St. Louis County, Missouri. Father: Thomas Chambers.

Chatham, Andrew Singleton – Pvt. Co. G, 20th Texas Infantry. Born 01/21/1830, died 08/07/1911. Buried: Copeland Chapel Cemetery, Montgomery County, Texas. Father: Thomas Chatham. Spouse: Martha Jane Bauguss.

Chatham, Thomas Jefferson – Pvt. Co. K, 8th Texas Cavalry. Born 03/24/1841, died 11/18/1891. Father: Thomas Chatham. Spouse: Emma J. Gafford.

Chatham, Noah W. – Pvt. Co. K, 8th Texas Cavalry. Born 11/17/1836, died unknown. Father: Thomas Chatham.

Cheatham, William A. – Cpl. Co. C, 21st Texas Cavalry. Born 12/27/1837, died 01/04/1900. Buried: Cude Cemetery, Montgomery County, Texas. Father: Robert Cheatham. Spouse: Sarah Elizabeth Walker.

Chesher, James F. – Pvt. Co. G, 7th Texas Cavalry. Born about 1843 in Tennessee, died unknown.

Childers, Douglas – Pvt. Co. A, 17th Brigade TST. Born 10/19/1819, died 08/09/1911. Father: Abraham Childers. Spouse: Amanda Cheshire.

Childers, Jefferson Pearse – Sgt. Co. I, 9th Texas Infantry (Nichols')/Cpl. Co. B, 24th Texas Cavalry. Born 11/23/1841, died 12/10/1913. Father: Douglas Childers. Spouse: Elizabeth L. Bell.

Childers, Reuben – Pvt. Co. B, 24th Texas Cavalry. Born about 1840 in Georgia, died 07/10/1862 in hospital Shreveport, Caddo Parish, Louisiana. Father: Douglas Childers.

Chilton, Franklin Bowden – Pvt. Co. H, 4th Texas Infantry. Born 02/27/1845, died 5/19/1926. Buried: Willis Cemetery, Montgomery County, Texas. Father: Thomas Chilton. Spouse: Annie R. Briscoe/Lelia Thornton/Emma Belle Preston/Mable Bowers.

Chilton, Hugh Barclay – Pvt. Co. A, Mann's Regiment, Texas Cavalry/ Pvt. Co. A, 24th/25th Consolidated Texas Cavalry. Born 05/22/1848, died 01/12/1872. Father: Thomas Chilton.

Chilton, Matthias Dayton – Pvt. Co. B, Madison's Regiment, Texas Cavalry/Pvt. Co. C, Terry's Regiment, Texas Cavalry. Born 11/06/1846, died 03/19/1918. Buried: Texas State Cemetery, Travis County, Texas. Father: Thomas Chilton.

Chilton, William Henry – Pvt. Co. B, 8th Texas Infantry (Hobby's). Born 10/06/1843, died 11/02/1897. Father: Thomas Chilton.

Clark, E. A. – Cpl. Co. G, 7th Texas Cavalry. Born about 1824, died unknown.

Clark, J. Edward – Pvt. Co. K, 20th Texas Infantry. Born about 1844 in Texas, died unknown. Father: E. A. Clark.

Clark, John – Pvt. Co. K, 20th Texas Infantry. Born about 1835 in Ireland, died unknown.

Clepper, Charles Duncan – Pvt. Co. I, 9th Texas Infantry (Nichols')/Sgt. Co. K, 20th Texas Infantry. Born 11/06/1840, died about 1923. Buried: Fields Store Cemetery, Waller County, Texas. Father: John Clepper. Spouse: Mary Jane McAlpine.

Clepper, James – Pvt. Co. I, 9th Texas Infantry (Nichols')/Pvt. Co. K, 20th Texas Infantry. Born about 1844 in Tennessee, died unknown. Father: John Clepper.

Clepper, Joseph Collier – Pvt. Co. K, 8th Texas Cavalry. Born 06/30/1831, died 5/14/1910. Father: James Clepper. Spouse: Penelope Hatfield Burney.

Clepper, Lemuel Gilliam – Capt. Montgomery County Rifle Boys, 17th Brigade TST/Capt. Co. K, 20th Texas Infantry. Born 10/28/1813, died 06/19/1893. Buried: Magnolia Cemetery, Montgomery County, Texas. Father: James Clepper. Spouse: Mary Ann Faulkner.

Clepper, Lorenzo Dow – Pvt. Co. H, 4th Texas Infantry/Pvt. Co. K, 20th Texas Infantry. Born 01/30/1839, died 7/1/1904. Buried: Shiloh Cemetery, Waller County, Texas. Father: John Clepper. Spouse: Sarah Ann Travis.

Close, J. E. – Pvt. Montgomery County Rifle Boys, 17th Brigade TST/Pvt. Co. D, 4th Infantry TST. Born about 1825 in Missouri, died unknown. Spouse: Lucinda Decker.

Cobb, J. G. – 2nd Lt. Co. I, 9th Texas Infantry (Nichols')/Sgt. Co. G, 20th Texas Infantry. Born about 1830, died 09/17/1894. Spouse: Sarah Cobb.

Collard, Felix R. – Pvt. Co. G, 7th Texas Cavalry. Born 03/16/1844, died 12/13/1922. Buried: Wheelock Cemetery, Robertson County, Texas.

Collard, Jonathan Stark – Pvt. Co. B, 24th Texas Cavalry, Pvt. Co. E, F, 24th/25 Consolidated Texas Cavalry/Pvt. Co., E, 25th Texas Cavalry (Trans-Mississippi). Born 06/16/1837, died 11/22/1900. Buried: Oakwood Cemetery, Walker County, Texas. Father: Lemuel M. Collard. Spouse: Lydia Vick.

Collier, Arthur H. – Pvt. Co. H, 4th Texas Infantry. Born about 1834 in Alabama, died unknown. Father: Erasmus Collier. Spouse: Mary McDaniel.

Collier, Austin B. – Pvt. in Captain S. M. Drake's Company, Rough & Ready Guards TST. Born about 1825, died about 1908. Buried: Collier Cemetery, Montgomery County, Texas. Father: Erasmus Collier. Spouse: Elizabeth Ann Talley.

Collins, Isom S. – Pvt. Co. C, 9th Texas Infantry (Nichols')/Cpl. Co. K, 16th Texas Infantry. Born about 1844 in Mississippi, died unknown. Father: Meshak Collins.

Collins, John J. – Pvt. Co. C, 9th Texas Infantry (Nichols')/Pvt. Co. K, 16th Texas Infantry. Born about 1839 in Mississippi, died unknown.

Collins, Johnson – Pvt. Co. C, 9th Texas Infantry (Nichols')/Pvt. Co. K, 16th Texas Infantry. Born 04/21/1837 in Mississippi, died 03/11/1899. Buried: Old Collins Cemetery, Williamson County, Texas. Father: Meshak Collins. Spouse: Mary McEy/Sarah Jane Parthenia Coursey Evans.

Collins, Meshak – Pvt. Co. C, 9th Texas Infantry (Nichols'). Born about 1812 in South Carolina, died about 1880 in Williamson County, Texas. Father: Shadrack Collins, Sr. Spouse: Elizabeth "Eliza Jane" Pounds.

Collins, R. D. – Pvt. 17th Brigade TST. Born about 1841 in Mississippi, died about 1865. Father: Meshak Collins. Spouse: Jemima Thompson.

Compton, Barton William – Cpl. Co. G, 20th Texas Infantry. Born 06/11/1830, died 08/13/1902. Buried: East End Cemetery, Erath County, Texas. Father: Richard J. Compton. Spouse: Francis Ann Brooks.

Cone, Monroe Martin – Pvt. Co. A, 17th Brigade TST. Born 06/22/1846, died 09/12/1921. Buried: Odd Fellows Cemetery, Grimes County, Texas. Father: C. S. Cone. Spouse: Arabella Stevens.

Cone, Thomas Jefferson – Pvt. Co. I, 9th Texas Infantry (Nichols'), Cpl. Co. K, 20th Texas Infantry. Born 03/19/1843, died 03/18/1917. Buried: Glenwood Cemetery, Harris County, Texas. Father: C. S. Cone.

Conn, John L. – Pvt. Co. B, 24th Texas Cavalry. Born about 1816, died after 1880. Spouse: Nancy B. Reding Malone.

Connell, J. William – Pvt. Co. G, 20th Texas Cavalry. Born about 1842, died unknown.

Connell, M. A. – Pvt. Co. G. 20th Texas Infantry/Pvt. Co. H. 26th Texas Cavalry. Born about 1835 in Alabama, died after 1880. Spouse: Josephine Shannon.

Conrow, C. M. – Cpl. Co. H, 4th Texas Infantry. Born unknown, died 06/27/1862. Buried: unknown grave in Virginia.

Cooper, Francis – Pvt. Co. F, Ragsdale's Battalion, Texas Cavalry. Born about 1832 in Mississippi, died unknown. Spouse: Elizabeth Goodson.

Copeland, Alex C. – Pvt. Co. B, 24th Texas Cavalry. Born about 1843, died 06/21/1862. Father: William Campbell Copeland (Coopland).

Copeland, Reuben Campbell – Pvt. Co. C, Ragsdale's Battalion, Texas Cavalry. Born 11/22/1849, died 10/15/1925. Buried: Salem Cemetery, Cherokee County, Texas. Father: William Campbell Copeland (Coopland). Spouse: Elizabeth (Betty) Wilcox/Huberta James/Lucinda E. Carruth/Mary (Mollie) Elizabeth Outlaw.

Corgey, Henry – Pvt. Co. K, 20th Texas Infantry. Born 07/01/1836, died 09/29/1885. Buried: New Church Cemetery, Brazos County, Texas. Father: Ludwig Kage. Spouse: Elizabeth Goodson Cooper.

Corgey, Louis – Pvt. Co. K, 20th Texas Infantry. Born 08/09/1833, died 01/02/1901. Buried: Corgey Cemetery, Montgomery County, Texas. Father: Ludwig Kage. Spouse: Sarah Jane Griffin.

Coward, Myrick Milburn – Pvt. Co. K, 16th Texas Infantry. Born about 1835 in South Carolina, died after 1900 in Walker County, Texas. Father: James R. Coward. Spouse: Mary A. Clark.

Cude, Alfred Jackson – Cpl. Co. K, 2nd Texas Cavalry. Born about 1840, died about 1867. Father: William A. Cude, Jr. Spouse: Ann Elizabeth Battle.

Cude, George Travis – Pvt. Co. G, 7th Texas Cavalry. Born 11/09/1845, died 01/06/1933. Buried: Cleveland City Cemetery, Liberty County, Texas. Father: Timothy Wright Cude. Spouse: Sarah Ferguson.

Cude, James Hyrum– Pvt. Co. G, 7th Texas Cavalry. Born 03/15/1839, died 06/02/1907. Buried: Boring Cemetery, Robertson County, Texas. Father: Timothy Wright Cude. Spouse: Nancy Ann Patrick Thomas/Ann Dryman.

Cude, James Washington – Pvt. in Captain Malvern Harrell's Company, Hopkinsville Mounted Cavalry, 25th Brigade TST. Born 04/27/1822, died 05/15/1908. Father: William Arthur Cude, Jr. Spouse: Rachel Walker/Ann Elizabeth Battle.

Cude, John M. – Pvt. Co. C, 16th Texas Infantry. Born 11/19/1833, died 03/07/1895. Buried: Longview Cemetery, Frio County, Texas. Father: William A. Cude, Jr. Spouse: Nancy Naomi Winters.

Cude, Nathanial Wiley – Pvt. Co. K, 2nd Texas Cavalry. Born 02/16/1836, died 12/11/1916. Buried: Longview Cemetery, Frio County, Texas. Father: William A. Cude, Jr. Spouse: Cassandra Steward/Sarah Stewart/Kaziah Ellis.

Cude, Richard Dowling – Sgt. Co. K, 2nd Texas Cavalry/McCord's Frontier Regiment, Texas Cavalry. Born 03/26/1842, died 06/1895. Buried: Wrightsboro Cemetery, Gonzales County, Texas. Father: William A. Cude, Jr. Spouse: Adelia "Delia" Williams.

Cude, Solomon Marion – Pvt. Co. C, 16th Texas Infantry. Born 10/03/1831, died 03/23/1877. Buried: Delhi Cemetery, Caldwell County, Texas. Father: William A. Cude, Jr. Spouse: Mary Ann Jones.

Cude, Timothy J. – Pvt. Co. K, 2nd Texas Cavalry. Born 03/29/1846, died 09/17/1929. Buried: Oakville Cemetery, Live Oak County, Texas. Father: William A. Cude, Jr. Spouse: Mary Tullis.

Cude, Timothy Jackson – Pvt. Co. B, 24th Texas Cavalry/Co. H, 26th Texas Cavalry. Born 06/30/1843, died 10/27/1877. Father: Timothy Wright Cude. Spouse: Martha Irene "Mattie" Foshee (Forshee).

Cude, Tobias A. – Pvt. Co. K, 2nd Texas Cavalry. Born about 1825, died 07/13/1863. Father: William A. Cude, Jr.

Cude, William Johnson – Pvt. Co. H, 4th Texas Infantry. Born 09/25/1834, died 11/10/1908. Buried: Plantersville Cemetery, Grimes County, Texas. Father: Timothy Wright Cude. Spouse: Helen Ann Davis/Gatsy Ann Mixon.

Cude, Willis Franklin – Pvt. Co. K, 2nd Texas Cavalry. Born 04/04/1844, died 11/07/1932. Buried: Pearsall Cemetery, Frio County, Texas. Father: William A. Cude, Jr. Spouse: Mary Elizabeth Harrell.

Culbertson, James M. – Pvt. Co. D, 4th Infantry TST. Born about 1826 in Missouri, died about 1889. Father: James Duncan Culbertson. Spouse: Mildred Hulder Schropshire.

Curling, William Thomas – Sgt. Co. G, 7th Texas Cavalry. Born about 1833, died 04/12/1912. Spouse: Tirzah Anne Gratin Wade.

Curry, Frances M. – Cpl. Co. C, 9th Texas Infantry (Nichols')/Cpl. Co. G, 20th Texas Infantry. Born 12/02/1837, died 9/1/1919. Father: Thomas C. Curry. Spouse: Lavinia Washington Herrington.

Curry, James L. – Pvt. 17th Brigade TST. Born about 1824 in Georgia, died unknown. Father: Thomas C. Curry. Spouse: Celia A. Horton.

Curry, Tobias Franklin – Sgt. Co. C, 9th Texas Infantry (Nichols')/Pvt. Co. K, 20th Texas Infantry. Born 12/20/1840, died 10/17/1877. Buried: Norris Cemetery, Limestone County, Texas. Father: Thomas C. Curry. Spouse: Margaret G. Gainey.

Curtis, F. S. – Pvt. Co. C, 21st Texas Cavalry. Born about 1834 in New York, died unknown. No further records found.

Dabney, Joel G. – Pvt. Co. B, 17th Brigade TST. Born about 1825 in Alabama, died unknown. Buried: Evergreen Cemetery, San Jacinto County, Texas. Spouse: Sarah Catherine Ellisor.

Daffan, Lawrence Aylette – Pvt. Co. G, 4th Texas Infantry. Born 04/30/1845, died 01/28/1907. Buried: Myrtle Cemetery, Ellis County, Texas. Father: John Warren Daffin. Spouse: Mary Anna Day.

Daffan, Stanfield Churchill – Pvt. C, 3rd Battalion, Texas Cavalry (Yager's). Born about 1843 in Alabama, died unknown. Father: John Warren Daffin.

Dafford, Alfred – Pvt. Co. A, 24th Texas Cavalry. Born about 1824, died 02/17/1863. Buried: Camp Butler National Cemetery, Sangamon County, Illinois.

Dale, G. W. – Sgt. Co. H, 4th Texas Infantry. Born about 1829 in Kentucky, died 07/1866. Spouse: Clarinda Dale.

Darden, William T. – Pvt. Co. D, 4th Infantry TST. Born about 1823 in Georgia, died before 1870. Spouse: Sarah A. Murphy.

Davis, A. J. – Pvt. 17th Brigade TST/Sgt. Co. K, 8th Texas Cavalry. Born about 1835 in Georgia, died unknown. No further records found.

Davis, Franklin C. – Pvt. Co. K, 20th Texas Infantry. Born 01/1843, died 05/16/1910. Buried: Hickory Grove Cemetery, Montgomery County, Texas. Father: Daniel Davis. Spouse: Martha E. Sapp/Mary M. Sweet.

Davis, Gary – Pvt. Co. A, 17th Brigade TST/Pvt. Co. D. 4th Texas Infantry TST. No further records found.

Davis, James R. – Pvt. Co. C, 21st Texas Cavalry. Born 08/27/1827, died 8/26/1900. Buried: New Montgomery Cemetery, Montgomery County, Texas. Father: Nathaniel Bowe Davis.

Davis, John C. – Pvt. Co. K, 20th Texas Infantry. Born about 1834, died unknown. Father: Daniel Davis.

Davis, Nathaniel Hart – Pvt. 17th Brigade TST. Born 11/06/1815, died 10/08/1893. Buried New Montgomery Cemetery, Montgomery County, Texas. Father: Nathaniel Bowe Davis. Spouse: Sarah Elizabeth White.

Davis, William Humphrey – Pvt. Montgomery County Rifle Boys, 17th Brigade TST. Born about 1826, died about 1899. Father: Daniel Davis. Spouse: Mary Jane Cagle.

Day, E. S. – Pvt. Montgomery County Rifle Boys, 17th Brigade TST. No further records found.

Deadrick, John – Pvt. Co. A, 17th Brigade TST/Pvt. Co. D, 4th Infantry TST/Pvt. Co. C, Terry's Regiment, Texas Cavalry. Born about 1818, died unknown. No further records found.

Dean, Henry Ingraham – Pvt. Co. I, 9th Texas Infantry (Nichols'), Pvt. Co. A, 24th Texas Cavalry. Born about 1843 in Alabama, died 12/1903. Buried: G. I. Dean Cemetery, Montgomery County, Texas. Father: George Dean. Spouse: Sarah Elizabeth Tucker.

Dean, John – Pvt. Co. A, 17th Brigade TST/Pvt. Co. D, 4th Texas Infantry TST. Born 01/08/1822, died 1879. Buried: Arnold–Dean Cemetery, Montgomery County, Texas. Father: Aylett Dean. Spouse: Lucinda Boyd.

Dean, Robert T. – Pvt. Co. I, 9th Texas Infantry (Nichols'), Pvt. Co. A, 24th Texas Cavalry. Born about 1841 in Alabama, died 09/06/1882. Father: George Dean.

Dean, Reuben B. – Pvt. Co. G, 20th Texas Infantry. Born about 1829 in Alabama, died unknown. Father: George Dean.

Dean, Rufus R. – Pvt. Co. A, 24th Texas Cavalry. Born about 1846, died 06/01/1864. Buried: Rose Hill Cemetery, Bibb County, Georgia. Father: George Dean.

Dean, William Aylett – Pvt. Co. A, 17th Brigade TST. Born 03/22/1827, died 01/19/1899. Buried: Arnold–Dean Cemetery, Montgomery County, Texas. Father: Aylett Dean. Spouse: Margaret Shannon/Maria Clarissa Arnold.

Decker, Christler – Pvt. Montgomery County Rifle Boys, 17th Brigade TST/Pvt. Co. G, 20th Texas Infantry. Born 02/23/1832, died about 1873. Father: Isaac Decker. Spouse: Mary Ann E. Lewis.

Decker, Isaac Cryle – Pvt. 17th Brigade TST. Born 02/18/1829, died between 1874-1876 Grimes County, Texas. Father: Isaac Decker. Spouse: Rachel Elizabeth Sanders.

Denman, Chapleigh Hampton – Pvt. 17th Brigade TST. Born 5/16/1819, died 06/07/1894. Buried: Willowhole Cemetery, Madison County, Texas. Father: Moses Denman. Spouse: Sarah Shannon.

Denman, William Absolum – Pvt. Co. B, 17th Brigade TST/Pvt. Co. E, 4th Infantry TST. Born 03/25/1846, died 09/01/1919. Buried: Willowhole Cemetery, North Zulch, Madison County, Texas. Father: Chapleigh Hampton Denman. Spouse: Eliza Ann E. Green.

Dennis, George W. – Pvt. Co. G, 20th Texas Infantry. Born about 1814 in Georgia, died after 1880. Spouse: Caroline Wright.

Dickinson, W. W. – Pvt. Montgomery County Rifle Boys, 17th Brigade TST. Born About 1838 in Tennessee, died unknown.

Dikeman, William Kellogg – Pvt. Co. D, 5th Texas Infantry/Sgt. Co. K, 20th Texas Infantry. Born 05/19/1834, died 07/4/1913. Buried: New Montgomery Cemetery, Montgomery County, Texas. Father: Cyrus Dikeman. Spouse: Nancy Cynthelia Gay.

Dildia (Dilday), George W. – Pvt. Co. I, 9th Texas Infantry (Nichols'). Born about 1837 in North Carolina, died unknown.

Dooley, Jesse – Pvt. Co. I, 20th Texas Infantry. Born about 1833 in Alabama, died 04/04/1897 in Robertson County, Texas. Father: Elijah Dooley. Spouse: Sarah J. Chandler.

Dorwin, W. H. C. – Pvt. Co. A, 24th Texas Cavalry. Born 05/03/1835, died 02/21/1894. Buried: New Montgomery Cemetery, Montgomery County, Texas. Father: Samuel Dorwin. Spouse. Sarah E. Dorwin.

Doughtie, Jacob – Pvt. Co. I, 9th Texas Infantry (Nichols')/Pvt. Co. K, 20th Texas Infantry. Born July 13, 1843, died December 4, 1895. Buried: Farris Cemetery, Walker County, Texas. Father: Daniel Doughtie. Spouse: Mary Sophia Collins.

Downing, Timothy – Pvt. Co. I, 9th Texas Infantry (Nichols')/Pvt. Co. C, Waul's Texas Legion. Born about 1824 in Ireland, died unknown. No further records found.

Duckworth, George H. – Pvt. Co. A, 10th Texas Infantry. Born about 1845 in Tennessee. Killed in action 11/25/1863 at Battle of Missionary Ridge, Tennessee.

Dunlap, James Marion, 2nd Lt. 17th Brigade TST. Born 07/04/1826, died 10/03/1908. Buried New Montgomery Cemetery, Montgomery County, Texas. Father: William Dunlap. Spouse: Rachel Ann Oliver.

Dupree, Franklin Goldstein – Capt. Co. H, 26th Texas Cavalry. Born 04/14/1826, died 04/22/1914. Buried: Magnolia Cemetery, Montgomery County, Texas. Father: Lewis Dupree. Spouse: Canzada Tynes Springer/ Samantha M. Heflin.

Dupree, Jesse G. – Sgt. Co. H, 26th Texas Cavalry. Born 12/10/1834, died 05/11/1922. Father: Lewis Dupree. Spouse: Lydia Ann Springer.

Dupree, Joel Reed – Pvt. Co. G, 20th Texas Infantry. Born 11/28/1827, died 08/05/1912. Buried: Glenwood Cemetery, Harris County, Texas. Father: Lewis Dupree. Spouse: Roana Collier/Amanda Perkins/Susan Jane Ellis.

Dupree, John Lewis – Pvt. Co. C, 5th Texas Cavalry/2nd Lt. Co H, 26th Texas Cavalry. Born about 1841 in Georgia, died 1925. Buried: Washington Cemetery, Harris County, Texas. Father: Louis G. Dupree. Spouse: Carrie A. Dupree.

Dupree, Samuel Francis – Pvt. Co. C, 5th Texas Cavalry. Born about 1841, died 04/1862, Santa Fe, New Mexico from wounds Battle of Glorieta Pass. Father: Lewis Dupree.

Dyer, Shepherd Franklin – Pvt. Co. A, Terry's Regiment, Texas Cavalry.

Born 08/15/1841, died 01/14/1923. Buried: Bedias Baptist Cemetery, Grimes County, Texas. Father: William Dyer. Spouse: Virginia Adeline Blount.

Edwards, James Lemic – Pvt. Co. G, 20th Texas Infantry. Born 03/14/1832, died 11/15/1915. Buried: Willis Cemetery, Montgomery County, Texas. Spouse: Martha Ellendor Ellisor/Margaret Mahala King.

Edwards, T. J. – Pvt. Co. D, 5th Texas Infantry. Born about 1829 in Alabama, killed in action 09/17/1862 at Sharpsburg, Maryland.

Elam, Frances Marion – Cpl. Co. K, 8th Texas Cavalry. Born about 1836 in Georgia, died in 1900. Buried: Willis Cemetery, Montgomery County, Texas. Father: Hodijah Elam. Spouse: Anna Lucy Weisinger.

Elam, Martin L. – Pvt. Co. B, 24th Texas Cavalry. Born about 1844, died 03/16/1863. Buried: Camp Butler National Cemetery, Sangamon County, Illinois.

Elliott, Mason Henderson – Lt. Co. I, 9th Texas Infantry (Nichols')/Lt. Co. K, 20th Texas Infantry. Born about 1836 in South Carolina, died in 1911. Buried: Oakland Cemetery, Grimes County, Texas. Spouse: Martha Ann "Mattie" Presley.

Elliott, Sanford E. – Pvt. Co. C, Terry's Regiment, Texas Cavalry. Born about 1824 in South Carolina, died after 1910. Spouse: Sarah A. Campbell.

Elliott, William D. – Pvt. Co. K, 20th Texas Infantry. Born 10/30/1846, died 09/15/1920. Buried: West Hill Cemetery, Grayson County, Texas. Father: Sanford E. Elliott. Spouse: Elizabeth Melroy.

Ellis, John – Pvt. Co. I, 9th Texas Infantry (Nichols')/Pvt. Co. G, 20th Texas Infantry. Born about 1835 in Alabama, died 02/04/1912. Buried: Oakwood Cemetery, Montgomery County, Texas.

Ellisor, Drayton David – Pvt. Co. D, 1st Texas Cavalry (Hardeman's). Born about 1834 in South Carolina, died about 1910. Buried: Montgomery County, Texas. Father: John George Ellisor. Spouse: Mary Dubard Noble/Annie Boykin Hightower.

Ellisor, G. Willis – Pvt. Co. G, 7th Texas Cavalry. Born about 1846 in Alabama, died 01/01/1863 at the Battle of Galveston. Father: John George Ellisor.

Ellisor, Nathan Thomas – Pvt. Co. G, 7th Texas Cavalry. Born 10/13/1832, died 01/15/1918. Buried: Oakwood Cemetery, McLennan County, Texas. Father: John George Ellisor. Spouse: Martha Eugenia Stewart.

English, Joshua – Pvt. Co. A,17th Brigade TST. Born about 1816 in South Carolina, died in 1886. Buried: Bryan City Cemetery, Brazos County, Texas. Spouse: Charlotte House.

Epperson, Samuel – Pvt. Co. K, 8th Texas Cavalry. Born about 1821, died as POW at Camp Douglas, Illinois. Buried: Oak Wood Cemetery, Cook County, Illinois. Spouse: Rachael Epperson.

Estill, Benjamin P. – Pvt. Co. D, 5th Texas Infantry. Born about 1839 in Tennessee, died 10/05/1862 from wounds Battle of Manassas. Buried: Warrenton Cemetery, Fauquier County, Virginia. Father: Milton Estill.

Estill, Charles B. – Pvt. Co. B, 24th Texas Cavalry. Born about 1836 in Tennessee, died 04/13/1863. Buried: Camp Butler National Cemetery, Sangamon County, Illinois. Father: Milton Estill.

Estill, James Black – Pvt. Co. D, 5th Texas Infantry. Born about 1841 in Texas, died 05/21/1862. Buried: Oakwood Cemetery, Richmond, Virginia. Father: Milton Estill.

Estill, Milton – Pvt. Co. B, 24th Texas Cavalry. Born about 1844, killed in action 01/11/1863 at Battle of Arkansas Post. Burial: unknown. Father: Milton Estill.

Estill, George (Negro) – Co. B, 24th Texas Cavalry. Vitals unknown. Last record shows Camp Butler, Illinois POW.

Etheridge, B. R. – Pvt. Co. K, 20th Texas Infantry. Born 02/03/1828, died 04/22/1906. Buried: Mt. Calm Cemetery, Limestone County, Texas. Spouse: Lucretia Boyd.

Etheridge, Horatio D. – Pvt. Co. I, 9th Texas Infantry (Nichols')/2nd Lt. Co. K, 20th Texas Infantry. Born about 1835, died unknown.

Evans, Henry – Pvt. Co. I, 9th Texas Infantry (Nichols')/Pvt. Co. K, 20th Texas Infantry. Born about 1841, died after 1910. Spouse: Sallie Evans.

Evans, Joseph M. – Capt. Co. A, 7th Brigade TST/Captain, Co. D, 4th Infantry TST/Maj. Terry's Regiment, Texas Cavalry. Born about 1820, died in 1876. Spouse: Harriet E. Devereux.

Farmer, David – Pvt. Co. I, 9th Texas Infantry (Nichols')/Pvt. Co. G, 20th Texas Infantry. Born about 1840, died 09/20/1896. Buried: Martin Hill Cemetery, Montgomery County, Texas.

Farrow, D. D. – Pvt. Co. H, 4th Texas Infantry. Born about 1842, died 12/12/1861. Father: Samuel Farrow.

Farrow, Samuel William – Sgt. Co. H, 4th Texas Infantry. Born 08/22/1821, died 01/04/1903. Buried: Barclay Cemetery, Falls County, Texas. Father: Samuel Farrow. Spouse: Elizabeth W. Jones.

Faulkner, Albert – Pvt. Co. H, 4th Texas Infantry. Born about 1835 in England, killed in action 09/17/1862 at Battle of Antietam.

Field, James M. B. – Pvt. Co. E, 24th/25th Consolidated Texas Cavalry. Born about 1847 in Texas, died 12/26/1923. Buried: Mount Pleasant Cemetery, Montgomery County, Texas. Father: M. W. Field. Spouse: Josephine Emily Taylor.

Ferguson, George – Pvt. Co. G, 20th Texas Infantry. Born 12/30/1841, died 04/19/1867. Buried: Old Methodist Church Cemetery, Montgomery County, Texas. Father: George Ferguson.

Ferguson, J. H. – Pvt. Co. G, 20th Texas Infantry. Born unknown, died 03/01/1863 of disease in field hospital at Dickinson Bayou.

Ferguson, John L. – Pvt. Co. I, 9th Texas Infantry (Nichols')/Pvt. Co. G, 20th Texas Infantry. Born about 1839, died 01/15/1886. Buried: Calvary Rd. Cemetery, Montgomery County, Texas. Spouse: Mattie Oliver.

Finch, W. A. – Pvt. Co. B, 17th Brigade TST/Pvt. Co. A, Mann's Regiment, Texas Cavalry. Born about 1830, died unknown.

Fisher, William S. – Pvt. Co. H, 4th Texas Infantry. Born 10/24/1844, died 02/29/1876. Buried: Honey Creek Cemetery, Hamilton County, Texas. Spouse: Martha Elizabeth Compton.

Ford, James A. – Pvt. Co. A, 17th Brigade TST/Pvt. Co. E, H, 26th Texas Cavalry. Born about 1839 in Texas, died 12/28/1899. Buried: New Montgomery Cemetery, Montgomery County, Texas. Father: James B. Ford.

Ford, Thomas M. – Pvt. Co. C, 21st Texas Cavalry. Born about 1840, died unknown.

Forrest, William Whitfield – Pvt. Co. B, 24th Texas Cavalry. Born 01/15/1834, died 07/16/1914. Buried: Bethel Cemetery, Montgomery County, Texas. Spouse: Tabitha Steel/Louisa Martin.

Forshee, George Washington – Pvt. 17th Brigade TST. Born about 1820, died 10/15/1881. Father: Charles B. Forshee. Spouse: Sarah Louvinda Cheatham.

Foster, John A. – Pvt. Co. K, 8th Texas Cavalry. Born about 1834, died about 1868. Father: James Foster. Spouse: Frances C. Clepper.

Fowler, Charles A. – Pvt. Co. B, 24th Texas Cavalry. Born about 1843 in South Carolina, killed in action 09/20/1863 at Battle of Chickamauga. Father: David Ramsey Fowler.

Fowler, John W. – Pvt. 17th Brigade TST. Born about 1816, died 05/28/1899. Buried: Texas State Cemetery, Travis County, Texas.

Fox, Richard – Pvt. Co. H, 4th Texas Infantry. Born about 1838, killed in action 09/17/1862 at Battle of Antietam.

Fox, Samuel – Sgt. Danville Mounted Riflemen, 17th Brigade TST. Born about 1825 in Germany, died unknown.

Frierson, William Screven – Staff Surgeon, CSA. Born 06/25/1834, died 12/14/1898. Father: George Phillip Frierson. Spouse: Flora McIver.

Gafford, James O. – Pvt. Co. A, 17th Brigade TST/Pvt. Co. D, 4th Infantry TST. Born about 1824, died 12/1879. Father: Daniel Gafford. Spouse: Susan Gafford.

Gafford, R. D. – Pvt. Co. H, 4th Texas Infantry. Born about 1841 in Alabama, died 05/25/1862 of disease in hospital at Richmond, Virginia. Father: Abner W. Gafford.

Gafford, Seaborn W. – Pvt. Co. I, 9th Texas Infantry (Nichols')/Pvt. Co. K, 20th Texas Infantry. Born about 1844 in Alabama, died after 1880. Father: Abner W. Gafford. Spouse: Ida Gafford.

Gary, James M. – Pvt. Co. C, 5th Texas Cavalry. Born 06/01/1835, died 04/24/1897. Buried: New Cemetery, Montgomery County, Texas. Spouse: Susan E. Nobles.

Gatlin, John Davidson – Pvt. Co. C, 17th Brigade TST/Pvt. Co. E, 26th Texas Cavalry. Born 03/22/1841, died 02/08/1916. Father: Jesse Gatlin.

Gatlin, William Riley – Pvt. Co. C, 17th Brigade TST. Born 05/13/1833, died 06/29/1908. Father: Jesse Gatlin.

George, John Edmond – Pvt. 17th Brigade TST. Born 07/22/1821, died 09/24/1875. Buried: Willis City Cemetery, Montgomery County, Texas. Spouse: Martha Sandel.

Gerloff, C. H. L. – Pvt. Co. K, 20th Texas Infantry. Born about 1815 in Germany, died unknown. Spouse: Anna M. Gerloff.

Gerloff, Carl – Pvt. Co. G, 20th Texas Infantry. Born 10/14/1842, died 01/11/1927. Buried: Galveston Memorial Park, Galveston County, Texas. Father: C. H. L. Gerloff. Spouse: Susan Landers.

Gibson, Anthony Palmer – Pvt. 17th Brigade TST. Born 11/17/1818, died 02/24/1895. Buried: Allphin Cemetery, Madison County, Texas. Father: Samuel Gibson. Spouse: Katherine Green/Martha Lindley Crowson/Mary Elizabeth Reynolds Corley.

Gilliam, James Wiley – Sgt. Co. K, 20th Texas Infantry. Born about 1836, died 10/26/1920. Father: Lemuel Gilliam. Spouse: Elizabeth J. Clepper.

Gilmore, Simeon E. – Pvt. Co. A, 21st Texas Cavalry. Born about 1838, died 06/27/1862. Father: James Gilmore.

Glass, William – Pvt. Co. D, 4th Infantry TST/Pvt. Co. K, Terry's Regiment, Texas Cavalry. Born about 1829, died 11/15/1894. Spouse: Elizabeth Mitchell.

Glenn, Joseph C. – Pvt. Co. K, 20th Texas Infantry. Born about 1815, died unknown. Father: Joseph C. Glenn. Spouse: Lucretia D. Whitaker.

Glover, John Allen – Pvt. Co. K, 8th Texas Cavalry. Born 06/22/1827, died 08/27/1892. Buried: New Montgomery Cemetery, Montgomery County, Texas. Spouse: Belle Glover.

Goalder, Theodore O. – Pvt. Co. K, 8th Texas Cavalry. Born about 1844, died 11/28/1922. Buried: Fort Stanton Cemetery, Lincoln County, New Mexico.

Goble, Thaddeus Lynn – Pvt. Co. K, 20th Texas Infantry. Born 05/19/1847, died 08/31/1920. Buried: Live Oak Cemetery, Paulding County, Ohio. Father: John Goble. Spouse: Harriet Elizabeth Manges.

Golding, Anthony Foster – Pvt. Co. D, 5th Texas Infantry. Born 03/27/1841, died 09/07/1886. Buried: Willis City Cemetery, Montgomery County, Texas. Father: Reuben Griffin Golding. Spouse: Sally A. Sample.

Golding, Henry R. – Pvt. Co. B, 24th Texas Cavalry. Born 10/31/1844, died 11/20/1883. Father: John Madison Golding. Spouse: Sidney Elizabeth Sapp Alston.

Golding, John Madison – Pvt. Co. A, 24th/25th Consolidated Texas Cavalry. Born 08/06/1846, died 05/18/1920. Buried: Cude Cemetery, Montgomery County, Texas. Father: John Madison Golding, Sr. Spouse: Emily Elizabeth Ferguson/Nancy Delia Sunday.

Golding, Nimrod Chiles – Pvt. Co. A, 24th/25th Consolidated Texas Cavalry. Born 03/09/1845, died 02/16/1912. Buried: Willis City Cemetery, Montgomery County, Texas. Father: Reuben Griffin Golding.

Golding, Reuben Griffin – Pvt. Co. B, 17th Brigade TST. Born about 1815, died unknown. Father: Reuben Griffin Golding, Sr. Spouse: Helena Cheatham.

Golding, Thomas D. – Pvt. Co. B, 24th Texas Cavalry. Born 12/06/1843, died 02/13/1863. Buried: Jefferson Barracks National Cemetery, St. Louis County, Missouri. Father. Reuben Griffin Golding.

Goodrich, J. M. – Pvt. Co. A, 17th Brigade TST/Pvt. Co. D, 4th Infantry TST/ Pvt. Co. K, Terry's Regiment, Texas Cavalry. Born about 1819, died unknown.

Goodson, Arthur – Pvt. Montgomery County Rifle Boys, 17th Brigade TST. Born about 1799, died 02/18/1863. Spouse: Rhoda Ward.

Goodson, Edmond – Pvt. Co. K, 20th Texas Infantry. Born about 1832, died unknown. Father: Arthur Goodson. Spouse: Mary Martin.

Goodson, James W. – Pvt. Co. A, 24th/25th Consolidated Texas Cavalry. Born 10/27/1820, died 01/25/1891. Father: Arthur Goodson.

Goodson, William Walter – Pvt. 17th Brigade TST/Pvt. Co. D, 4th Infantry TST/Pvt. Co. K, Terry's Regiment, Texas Cavalry. Born about 1824, died 03/30/1899. Buried: Oklahoma Cemetery, Montgomery County, Texas. Father: Arthur Goodson. Prudence Peavehause/Malinda Lynn Pyles.

Goree, Thomas Jewett – Maj./ADC, Longstreet's Corps, Army of Northern Virginia. Born 11/14/1835, died 03/04/1905. Buried: Oakwood Cemetery, Walker County, Texas. Father: Langston James Goree. Spouse: Eliza Thomas Nolley.

Gott, Thomas R. – Pvt. Co. C, 21st Texas Cavalry. Born 03/29/1811, died 12/04/1872. Spouse: Susan Virginia Thorne.

Gott, Samuel Sutton – Pvt. 17th Brigade TST. Born 01/16/1836, died 03/20/1914. Buried: Powers Chapel Cemetery, Falls County, Texas. Father: Robert L. Gott. Spouse: Vincia Gott.

Graham, James C. – Pvt. Co. K, 20th Texas Infantry. Born about 1832 in Mississippi, died unknown. Father: Anthony Graham. Spouse: Nancy A. Chambers.

Graham, Moses – 1st Lt. Company B, 24th Texas Cavalry. Born 03/04/1825, died 1/13/1904. Buried: Wesson Cemetery, Brazos County, Texas. Spouse: Mary J. Pincham Folks.

Graves, James W. – Pvt. Co. K, 20th Texas Infantry. Born about 1839 in Ohio, died unknown. Father: John William Graves.

Graves, Jesse Cox – Pvt. Montgomery County Rifle Boys, 17th Brigade TST/ Pvt. Co. I, 9th Texas Infantry (Nichols')/Pvt. Co. K, 20th Texas Infantry. Born 09/21/1841, died 1/6/1923. Buried: Resthaven Cemetery, Bell County, Texas. Father: John William Graves. Spouse: Josephine Amanda Coward.

Green, Levi – Pvt. Co. K, 20th Texas Infantry. Born about 1831 in Alabama, died 08/04/1867. Father: Wiley Green. Spouse: Elizabeth C. Walker.

Green, (Negro) – Co. B, 24th Texas Cavalry. Vitals unknown. Last record shows Camp Butler, Illinois POW.

Green, Wiley – Pvt. Co. B, 24th Texas Cavalry. Born 10/16/1833, died 08/31/1862 in camp near Pine Bluff, Arkansas. Father Wylie Green. Spouse: Margaret Frances Spear.

Griffin, Benjamin Devane – 1st Lt.-Adjutant, 24th Texas Cavalry. Born 08/12/1833, died 04/21/1898. Buried: Oakwood Cemetery, Montgomery County, Texas. Spouse: Mary Hester Spiller.

Griffin, Joseph Ezekial – Pvt. Co. D, 4th Infantry TST/Pvt. Co. C, Terry's Regiment, Texas Cavalry. Born about 1823, died 12/19/1888. Spouse: Martha A. Walker.

Griffin, S. D. – Pvt. Montgomery County Rifle Boys 17th Brigade TST/Pvt. Co. K, 20th Texas Infantry. Born about 1842, died 08/07/1862 at Camp Groce, Harris County, Texas. Father: Gilbert Griffin.

Griffin, W. R. – Pvt. Co. D, 4th Infantry TST/Pvt. Co. K, 20th Texas Infantry. Born about 1844, died 12/19/1932 Titus County, Texas. Father: Gilbert Griffin.

Griffith, Joshua Delos – Pvt. Co. A, 24th/25th Consolidate Texas Cavalry. Born about 1825, died about 06/14/1887. Buried: Griffith Family Cemetery, Montgomery County, Texas. Father: Noah Griffith. Spouse: Amelia Ellen Conley.

Griffith, Leroy Alonzo – Pvt. Co. A, 24th Texas Cavalry/Sgt. Co. D, 17th (Consolidated) Texas Dismounted Cavalry. Born 12/17/1821, died 02/29/1883. Buried: Salado Cemetery, Bell County, Texas. Father: Noah Griffith. Spouse: Nancy Rebecca Hogan.

Groth, Claus – Sgt. Co. C, Waul's Texas Legion. Born in Germany about 1833, died 02/25/1863 at Camp Pemberton, Mississippi.

Guynn, John A. – Pvt. Co. I, 9th Texas Infantry (Nichols')/Pvt. Co. B, 24th Texas Cavalry. Born 05/22/1843, died 06/08/1894. Buried: Odd Fellows Rest Cemetery, Colorado County, Texas. Father: Isom Guynn. Spouse: Ella A. Harris.

Guynn, William James (J. W.) – Pvt. Co. B, 24th Texas Cavalry/Pvt. Co. D, 5th Texas Infantry/Pvt. Co. E, 24th/25th Consolidated Texas Cavalry. Born 09/17/1840, died 07/02/1882. Buried: Odd Fellows Rest Cemetery, Colorado County, Texas. Father: Isom Guynn. Spouse: Mary Anne (Kittie) Bridge.

Hall, C. C. – Pvt. Co. A, 24th Texas Cavalry. Born about 1841 in Tennessee, died in 1864.

Hall, Hiram H. – Pvt. Co. I, 9th Texas Infantry (Nichols')/Pvt. Co. K, 20th Texas Infantry. Born about 1844, died unknown.

Hall, James H. "Kit" – Pvt. Co. H, 4th Texas Infantry. Born about 1841, died unknown.

Hall, James Henry – Pvt. Co. G, 20th Texas Infantry. Born 07/17/1824, died 03/15/1905. Buried: Danville–Shepard Hill Cemetery, Montgomery County, Texas. Father: John Hall. Spouse: Sarah Ann George/Mary Jane Wester.

Hamby, Isaac – Pvt. Co. K, 20th Texas Infantry. Born about 1820 in Alabama, died unknown.

Hardy, John – Pvt. Danville Mounted Riflemen, 17th Brigade TST. Born about 1808, died 09/01/1884. Spouse: Sarah.

Harlan, George – Pvt. Co. K, 20th Texas Cavalry/Pvt. Co. A, 24th/25th

Consolidated Texas Cavalry. Born 02/02/1835, died 12/30/1919. Buried: Blue Ridge Baptist Church Cemetery, Falls County, Texas. Father: Isaiah Harlan. Spouse: Palina Jane McCaleb/Margaret Ann Denson.

Harrington, Robert Calvin – Pvt. Co. I, 9th Texas Infantry (Nichols'). Born 12/24/1845, died 05/23/1918. Buried: New Hope Cemetery, Limestone County, Texas. Father: William Calvin Harrington. Spouse: Louisa Johnson/ Minerva Caroline Cude.

Harrington, William Calvin – Pvt. Co. 17th Brigade TST. Born about 1822, died 07/05/1882. Buried: Hughey Cemetery, Grimes County, Texas. Spouse: Holland Martin Liles/Sarah Suthard.

Harris, James K. P. – Pvt. Co. D, 5th Texas Infantry. Born about 1830, died 09/20/1862. Spouse: Margaret Cude.

Harrison, William – Pvt. Danville Mounted Riflemen, 17th Brigade TST. Born about 1821, died after 1870. Spouse: Frances O'Banion.

Hayden, Samuel Turner – Pvt. Co. B, 24th Texas Cavalry/Pvt. Co. E, 24th/25th Consolidated Texas Cavalry. Born about 1832, died about 1876. Father: James Hayden. Spouse: Emily Metts.

Hays, Lewis – Pvt. Co. D, 4th Infantry TST. Born about 1840, died unknown.

Henry, John K. – Pvt. Co. I, 9th Texas Infantry (Nichols')/Pvt. Co. K, 20th Texas Infantry. Born about 1839 in Alabama, died unknown.

Herring, Asa Franklin – Pvt. Co. G, 20th Texas Infantry. Born 10/28/1831, died 04/11/1909. Buried Apolonia Cemetery, Grimes County, Texas. Father: Joseph Herring. Spouse: Amanda M. Herring/Nellie Herring.

Hewitt, Israel – Pvt. Co. B, 24th Texas Cavalry. Born about 1809, died 02/02/1863. Buried: Jefferson Barracks National Cemetery, St. Louis County, Missouri. Spouse: Mary Rhine/Selena Forshee.

Hewitt, Robert – Pvt. Co. D, 5th Texas Infantry. Born about 1820 in Alabama, died unknown.

Hicks, J. L. – Pvt. Co. H, 26th Texas Cavalry. Born about 1846, died unknown. Father: James Monroe Hicks.

Hicks, James Monroe – Pvt. Co. D, 4th Infantry TST. Born about 1818 in Georgia, died unknown. Spouse: Margaret Elvira Franklin.

Hicks, Lemuel M. – Pvt. Co. H, 26th Texas Cavalry. Born about 1844, died about 1880. Buried: Bald Prairie Cemetery, Robertson County, Texas. Father: James Monroe Hicks. Spouse: Mary Elizabeth Williams.

Holland, W. P. – Pvt. Co. B, 17th Brigade TST. Born about 1821 in Georgia, died unknown.

Holt, Albert C. – Pvt. Co. H, 4th Texas Infantry. Born about 1843 in Georgia, died unknown.

Horton, Thomas – Pvt. Co. H, 4th Infantry TST. Born about 1822 in Georgia, died unknown.

Hoskins, John C. – Pvt. Co. B, 24th Texas Cavalry. Born about 1837, died about 1868. Buried: Thomson Cemetery, Burleson County, Texas. Father:

Hugh Clayborn Hoskins. Spouse: Virginia A. Hoskins.

Hoskins, Thomas J. – Pvt. Co. B, 24th Texas Cavalry. Born about 1836, died 10/29/1862 at Battle of Arkansas Post. Father: Hugh Clayborn Hoskins.

Hostetter, John – Cpl. Danville Mounted Riflemen, 17th Brigade TST. Born 03/01/1799, died 04/06/1871. Buried: Hostetter Cemetery, Pike County, Missouri. Father: Isaac Hostetter. Spouse: Hannah.

Hottlel (Hottle), A. W. – 1st Sgt. Co. K, 8th Texas Cavalry. Promoted to Major & Quartermaster. Born about 1828, died 1864 in Harris County, Texas.

Hughes, Henry S. – Pvt. 17th Brigade TST. Born about 1815 in Connecticut, died unknown. Spouse: Theodora L. Baker.

Hulon, James William – Pvt. Co. I, 9th Texas Infantry (Nichols')/Pvt. Co. B, 24th Texas Cavalry/Pvt. Co. I, Granbury's Consolidated Brigade, Texas Cavalry (1st Consolidated Regiment). Born about 1840, died 4/16/1907. Buried: Willis City Cemetery, Montgomery County, Texas. Father: William Henry Hulon. Sarah F. McCaleb Chambers/Jennie Hulon.

Hulon, John Spiller – Pvt. Danville Mounted Riflemen, 17th Brigade TST. Born 10/30/1845, died 09/09/1915. Buried: Willis City Cemetery, Montgomery County, Texas. Father: William Henry Hulon. Spouse: Sallie M. Williamson.

Hulon, William Henry – Pvt. Danville Mounted Riflemen, 17th Brigade TST. Born about 1803 in Virginia, died unknown.

Irion, John L. – Asst. Surgeon, 20th Texas Infantry. Born 08/28/1828, died 12/31/1904. Buried: New Montgomery Cemetery, Montgomery County, Texas. Father: McKinney F. Irion. Spouse: Martha Ann Elizabeth Griggs.

Irvine, Benjamin Franklin – Pvt. Danville Mounted Riflemen, 17th Brigade TST. Born 08/19/1821, died 01/06/1902. Eureka Cemetery, Navarro County, Texas. Father: Benjamin Fielding Irvine. Spouse: Catherine L. (Kitty) Tabor.

Irvine, Henry Reid – Pvt. Co. D, 5th Texas Infantry. Born about 1842, died 07/01/1862. Buried: Hollywood Cemetery, Richmond, Virginia. Father: Benjamin Fielding Irvine.

Irvine, Peter Belles – Pvt. Co. B, 24th Texas Cavalry. Born 1823, killed in action 01/11/1863 at the Battle of Arkansas Post. Father: Benjamin Fielding Irvine. Spouse: Minerva Angelina Tabor.

Jefferies, William Cantrel – Pvt. 17th Brigade TST. Born about 1826 in South Carolina, died 05/17/1888. Buried: Laredo City Cemetery, Webb County, Texas. Spouse: Tabatha Ann Womack.

Jeffers, Manlins S. – Pvt. Co. H, 4th Texas Infantry.

Jenkins, J. F. – Pvt. Co. K, 16th Texas Infantry. Born about 1834 in Alabama, died unknown.

Jenkins, James C. – Pvt. Montgomery County Rifle Boys, 17th Brigade TST/ Pvt. Co. E, 14th Texas Infantry. Born about 1830, died after 1920. Buried: Cedar Creek Cemetery, Anderson County, Texas. Father: Jesse B. Jenkins. Spouse: Eliza A. Jenkins.

Jett, J. R. P. – Pvt. Co. H, 4th Texas Infantry. Born about 1835, died unknown.

Johnson, G. W. – Pvt. Co. D, 4th Infantry TST. Born about 1833, died unknown.

Johnson, Jesse – Pvt. Montgomery County Rifle Boys, 17th Brigade TST/ Pvt. Co. G, 20th Texas Infantry. Born about 1818, died 04/18/1914. Father: William Johnson. Spouse: Melinda Parker.

Johnson, John Wesley – Pvt. Montgomery County Rifle Boys, 17th Brigade TST/Pvt. Co. H, 26th Texas Cavalry. Born 03/22/1843, died 05/18/1925. Buried: Splendora, Cemetery, Montgomery County, Texas. Father: Jesse Johnson. Spouse: Nancy Mary Cowart.

Johnson, John T. – Sgt.-Adjutant, Co. E, 11th Battalion, Texas Volunteers/1st Lt.-Adjutant 21st Texas Infantry. Born about 1827, died about 1868. Father: Bede D. Johnson. Spouse: Elizabeth C. Reding.

Johnson, William Wilburn – Pvt. Co. K, 20th Texas Infantry. Born 01/19/1829, died 06/06/1910. Buried: Petteway Cemetery, Robertson County, Texas. Father: William Johnson. Spouse: Luranie Parker.

Jones, Charles Edward – 2nd Lt. Co. H, 4th Texas Infantry. Born about 1831, died 08/30/1862. Father: Charles L. S. Jones.

Jones, Matthew Davis – Pvt. Co. A, 24th Texas Cavalry. Born about 1835, died 05/02/1912. Buried: Woodland Cemetery, Falls County, Texas. Father: Charles L. S. Jones. Spouse: Sallie W. Morrison.

Jones, William T. – 3rd Lt. Montgomery County Rifle Boys, 17th Brigade TST. Born about 1839 in Ohio, died unknown.

Judson, John – Pvt. 17th Brigade TST/Pvt. Co. D, 4th Infantry TST. Born about 1817, died unknown.

Katchler, John A. – Pvt. Co. K, 8th Texas Cavalry. Born about 1833, died 09/26/1905. Buried: Jonesboro Cemetery, Hamilton County, Texas. Spouse: Emily J. Clepper.

Kellet, John Garland – Pvt. Danville Mounted Riflemen, 17th Brigade TST. Born about 1826 in South Carolina, died 07/29/1865. Spouse: Susan Elizabeth Ezell.

Kellet, James Madison – Pvt. Danville Mounted Riflemen, 17th Brigade TST. Born about 1811 in South Carolina, died before 1870. Spouse: Sarah A. Dunlap.

Kelsey, Samuel L. – Pvt. Danville Mounted Riflemen, 17th Brigade TST. Born about 1816 in South Carolina, died 02/10/1878. Buried: Waverly Cemetery, Walker County, Texas. Spouse: Mary Mariah Richardson.

Kerr, William – Pvt. Co. K, 20th Texas Infantry. Born about 1833 in Ireland, died unknown.

King, Adam Meek – Pvt. Co. B, 24th Texas Cavalry. Born 07/21/1838, died 11/20/1900. Buried: Hickory Grove Cemetery, Montgomery County, Texas. Father: Thomas King. Spouse: Minerva Ellen Ezell.

King, Henry C. – Pvt. Co. B, 24th Texas Cavalry. Born 01/16/1834, died 03/20/1911. Buried: Evergreen Cemetery, Crawford County, Wisconsin. Father: Lyman King. Spouse: Susannah (Susan) Mellor/Mary Seaman.

King, Thomas Edward – Pvt. Co. B, 24th Texas Cavalry/24th/25th Consolidated Texas Cavalry. Born 03/21/1840, died 02/08/1919. Buried: Park Cemetery, Madison County, Texas. Father: Thomas King. Spouse: Henrietta R. Park.

Kirby, James A. – Pvt. Co. H, 4th Texas Infantry. Born about 1839 in Georgia, killed in action 09/19/1863 at the Battle of Chickamauga. Father: Lewis Kirby.

Kirby, Jeff – Pvt. Co. A, 17th Brigade TST. Born about 1821 in South Carolina, died unknown.

Lacey, Cicero Daniel – Pvt. Montgomery County Rifle Boys, 17th Brigade TST. Born 06/22/1839, died 01/12/1927. Buried: Weaver Cemetery, Montgomery County, Texas. Father: Daniel L. Lacey. Spouse: Catherine Celia Williamson/Mary Jane Goodrum.

Lacey, Milan Carile – Pvt. Montgomery County Rifle Boys, 17th Brigade TST. Born about 1844, died about 1873. Father: Daniel L. Lacey.

Laishonce, Louis – Cpl. Co. I, 9th Texas Infantry. Born about 1817 in Missouri, died unknown. Buried: Cartwright–Rabon Chapel Cemetery, Montgomery County, Texas. Spouse: Martha Ann Cartwright.

Landrum, Willis J. – Pvt. Co. H, 4th Texas Infantry. Born 08/10/1845, died 03/19/1927. Buried: New Montgomery Cemetery, Montgomery County, Texas. Father: William Landrum. Spouse: Elizabeth Harris.

Landrum, Zachariah – Cpl. Co. H, 4th Texas Infantry. Born about 1839, died about 1868. Buried: Old Methodist Church Cemetery, Montgomery, Montgomery County, Texas. Father: William Landrum.

Lauderdale, Thomas Josiah – Pvt. Co. I, 9th Texas Infantry (Nichols'). Born about 1833, died about 1885. Buried: LaSalle Cemetery, Limestone County, Texas. Father: Jeremiah Lauderdale. Spouse: Frances Margaret Coe.

Leach, William G. – Pvt. Co. H, 4th Texas Infantry. Born about 1836 in Georgia, died 06/20/1862 in Virginia.

Lee, Andrew E. – Pvt. Co. G, 20th Texas Cavalry. Born 08/26/1841, died 12/15/1887. Buried: Laurel Hill Cemetery, San Jacinto County, Texas. Father: John J. Lee. Spouse: Mollie Lee.

Lee, Alexander – Pvt. Co. K, 20th Texas Infantry. Born 02/20/1820, died 02/19/1879. Buried: Martin Hill Cemetery, Montgomery County, Texas. Spouse: Martha Lee.

Leigh, Walter – Pvt. Co. K, 20th Texas Infantry/Pvt. Co. B, 4th Engineers, CSA. Born 02/03/1830, died 08/05/1896. Buried: Zion Cemetery, Grimes County, Texas. Father: John Leigh. Spouse: Rebecca Shannon.

Lewin, Charles W. – Pvt. Co. G, K, 20th Texas Infantry. Born about 1839 in Alabama, died unknown. Father: Charles W. Lewin, Sr.

Lewis, Clint A. – Pvt. Co. H, 4th Texas Infantry. Born about 1836 in Alabama, died 07/28/1862 at Fincastle, Virginia. Father: John McClanahan Lewis, Sr.

Lewis, Eldon McKinley – Pvt. Co. B, 24th Texas Cavalry. Born 10/29/1833 in Alabama, died 1864 in Georgia. Father: John McClanahan Lewis, Sr. Spouse: Frances A. (Fannie) Arnold.

Lewis, John McClanahan, Jr. – Pvt. Co. I, 9th Texas Infantry (Nichols')/Lt.

Co. B, 24th Texas Cavalry. Born 11/29/1837, died 04/08/1908. Buried: Willis Cemetery, Montgomery County, Texas. Father: John McClanahan Lewis, Sr. Spouse. Martha (Mattie) C. Woodson.

Lewis, William Marion – Pvt. Co. H, 4th Texas Infantry. Born about 1833 in North Carolina, died 08/26/1915. Buried: Florence Cemetery, Williamson County, Texas. Father: Henry Lewis. Spouse: Drusilla Hobson.

Liles, Thomas Jefferson – Pvt. Co. A, 17th Brigade TST/Pvt. Co. D, 4th Infantry TST/Pvt. Co. A, Terry's Regiment, Texas Cavalry/Pvt. Co. F, 20th Texas Infantry. Born 07/14/1840, died 06/26/1881. Buried: Sardis Cemetery, Leon County, Texas. Spouse: Elizabeth Helena (Beth) Golding.

Lindley, Elijah – Pvt. Co. B, 24th Texas Cavalry. Born 03/20/1835, died 07/28/1880. Buried: Ferguson Cemetery, Limestone County, Texas. Father: Samuel Washington Lindley. Spouse: Eliza Tolbert Kelton/Margaret E. McGill.

Lindley, James – Pvt. Co. B, 24th Texas Cavalry. Born 03/13/1831, died 10/18/1895. Buried: Danville–Shepard Hill Cemetery, Montgomery County, Texas. Father: Samuel Washington Lindley. Spouse: Mary Lee R. Irvine.

Lindley, John – Pvt. Co. B, 24th Texas Cavalry. Born 06/08/1829, died 02/20/1911. Buried: Madisonville City Cemetery, Madison County, Texas. Father: Samuel Washington Lindley. Spouse: Eliza Ann Martin.

Lindley, John Wood – Pvt. Co. G, 7th Texas Cavalry. Born 04/25/1842, died 09/30/1928. Buried: Oakland Cemetery, Grimes County, Texas. Father: William Nathan Lindley. Spouse: Cynthia Edna Goodnight.

Lindsey, G. W. – Pvt. 17th Brigade TST. Born about 1828, died unknown.

Linton, William – Pvt. 17th Brigade TST. Born about 1831, died 05/21/1898. Father: Samuel L. Linton. Spouse: Eliza Murray Backstrom.

Lipscomb, Albert S. – Pvt. 17th Brigade TST. Born 07/26/1826, died 04/01/1873. Buried: New Montgomery Cemetery, Montgomery County, Texas.

Lipscomb, Nathan Lee – Pvt. Co. I, 9th Texas Infantry (Nichols')/Pvt. Co. G, 20th Texas Infantry. Born about 1836, died 1913. Buried: Magnolia Cemetery, Jefferson County, Texas. Father: Lee Lipscomb. Spouse: Caledonia (Callie) Porter.

Little, Hiram – Pvt. Danville Mounted Riflemen, 17th Brigade TST. Born 04/09/1809, died 09/13/1891. Buried: Willis Cemetery, Montgomery County, Texas. Spouse: Mary (Polly) Lindley.

Little, Jonathan – Pvt. Co. B, 24th Texas Cavalry. Born 05/26/1836, died in Arkansas, date unknown. Father: Hiram Little. Spouse: Elizabeth Smith.

Little, Samuel – Pvt. Co. A, 24th Texas Cavalry. Born 11/04/1842, died about 1874. Father: Hiram Little. Spouse: Mary Mahalia Ellisor.

Little, William M. (Doc) – Pvt. Co. G, 7th Texas Cavalry. Born 11/18/1840, died 02/01/1913. Buried: Willis Cemetery, Montgomery County, Texas. Father: Hiram Little. Spouse: Sarah Catherine Paulsel.

E. A. Long – Pvt. Danville Mounted Riflemen, 17th Brigade TST.

Love, A. J. – Pvt. Capt. Powell's Co. 17th Brigade TST.

Love, R. O. – Pvt. Co. D, 4th Infantry TST/Transferred to Engineers. Born about 1818, died unknown.

Lowery, Allen – Cpl. Co. A, 17th Brigade TST. Born about 1818 in Virginia, died after 1900. Spouse: Sarah A. L. Wheeler.

Lowry, Simpson – Pvt. Co. I, 9th Texas Infantry (Nichols'). Born about 1839, died unknown.

Lucky, John F. – Pvt. 17th Brigade TST/Pvt. Co. D, 4th Infantry TST. Born about 1820 in North Carolina. Spouse: Susannah Baker.

Lynch, D. B. – Pvt. 17th Brigade TST/Pvt. Co. D, 4th Infantry TST/Pvt. Co. C, Terry's Regiment, Texas Cavalry. Born 02/14/1823, died 06/20/1878. Buried: Cartwright–Rabon Chapel Cemetery, Montgomery County, Texas.

Mack, Edward – Pvt. Co. I, 9th Texas Infantry (Nichols')/Pvt. Co. C, Waul's Texas Legion/Pvt. Co. F, Timmons Regiment, Texas Infantry. Born 10/29/1810, died about 1880. Spouse: Mary Jenkins.

Mack, George W. – Pvt. Co. C, Waul's Texas Legion/Pvt. Co. F, Timmons Regiment, Texas Infantry. Born 11/08/1842, died   02/19/1907. Buried: Cedar Creek Cemetery, Anderson County, Texas. Father: Edward Mack.

Mack, Jesse – Pvt. Co. I, 9th Texas Infantry (Nichols')/Pvt. Co. C, Waul's Texas Legion/Pvt. Co. K, 20th Texas Infantry. Born 11/15/1840, died 06/23/1910. Buried: Lone Grove Cemetery, Carter County, OK. Father: Edward Mack. Spouse: Arzilla Harrington.

Mack, John – Pvt. Co. C, Waul's Texas Legion/Pvt. Co. F, Timmons Regiment, Texas Infantry. Born 12/31/1844, died about 12/02/1902. Buried: Salem Cemetery, Lee County, Texas. Father: Edward Mack. Spouse: Georgia Ann Tomme.

Malone, Henderson F. – Pvt. Co. D, 5th Texas Infantry/Cpl. Co. B, 24th Texas Cavalry/Pvt. Co. A, 24th/25th Consolidated Texas Cavalry/Pvt. Co. A, Mann's Regiment, Texas Cavalry. Born about 1838 in Tennessee, died unknown. Father: Andrew J. Malone.

Malone, Thomas Monroe – Pvt. Co. B, 24th Texas Cavalry/Pvt. Co. H, 20th Texas Infantry. Born 11/18/1835, died about 1866. Father: Andrew J. Malone. Spouse: Cynthia Ann Johnson.

Malone, William Farrington – Sgt. Co. I, 9th Texas Infantry (Nichols')/Pvt. Co. H, 20th Texas Infantry. Born about 1835, died 10/08/1907. Buried: Willis Cemetery, Montgomery County, Texas. Father: Andrew J. Malone. Spouse: Willie A. Caperton.

Martin, Benjamin F. – Pvt. Co. D, 1st Texas Heavy Artillery/Pvt. Co. C, 9th Texas Infantry (Nichols')/Pvt. Co. C, Waul's Texas Legion/Pvt. Co. F, Timmons Regiment, Texas Infantry. Born about 1844 in Alabama, died unknown. Father: Lewis Martin.

Martin, Claiborne A. – Pvt. Co. K, 20th Texas Infantry/Pvt. Co. D, 4th Infantry TST. Born about 1844, died after 1880. Buried: Martin–Sugar Hill Cemetery, Montgomery County, Texas. Father: Anthony Martin.

Martin, Francis Marion – Pvt. Co. B, 24th Texas Cavalry. Born about 1841, died about 1863 in Arkansas. Father: Lewis Martin.

Martin, Gould D. – Sgt. Co. F, 31st Texas Cavalry. Born 03/20/1833, died 5/17/1907. Buried: Greenwood Cemetery, Travis County, Texas. Spouse: Elizabeth "Lizzie" Maddox.

Martin, James P. – Co. I, 9th Texas Infantry (Nichols')/Pvt. Co. K, 20th Texas Infantry. Born 02/22/1832, died 01/08/1904. Buried: Cow Creek Cemetery, Erath County, Texas. Father: Lewis Martin. Spouse: Louisa Metts/Indiana Cagle.

Martin, John William – Pvt. Co. K, 20th Texas Infantry. Born 05/14/1836, died 10/4/1904. Buried: Martin Hill Cemetery, Montgomery County, Texas. Father: Anthony Martin. Spouse: Josephine Gaines Moore.

Martin, Robert Ball – Sgt. Co. G, 20th Texas Infantry. Born 11/09/1810, died 01/13/1868. Buried: Old Methodist Church Cemetery, Montgomery County, Texas. Father: William Harvey Martin. Spouse: Mary Rebecca Warner.

Martin, William Edward – Pvt. Co. F, 31st Texas Cavalry. Born 01/03/1828, died 12/21/1886. Buried: Bagdad Cemetery, Williamson County, Texas. Spouse: Nancy Cathrine Wilson.

Matthews, George A. – Pvt. Co. K, 20th Texas Infantry. Born about 1832 in Virginia, died unknown. Spouse: Margaret C. Matthews.

Matthews, Harmon – Pvt. Co. I, 9th Texas Infantry (Nichols')/Pvt. Co. D, 4th Infantry TST. Born about 1845, died unknown.

Matthews, Jacob – Pvt. Co. I, 9th Texas Infantry (Nichols')/Pvt. Co. K, 20th Texas Infantry. Born about 1843, died 08/01/1862 at Camp Groce.

Matthews, Lamar Littleberry – Cpl. Co. G, K, 20th Texas Infantry. Born about 1839, died 11/30/1920. Father: Littleberry William Matthews. Spouse: Laura Sapp.

Matthews, Neuman (Newman) Isaac – Pvt. Co. I, 9th Texas Infantry (Nichols')/Pvt. Co. K, 20th Texas Infantry. Born about 1844, died 10/30/1890. Spouse: Tennessee Jane Adams.

Matthews, T. R. – Pvt. Co. H, 4th Texas Infantry/Pvt. Co. K, 20th Texas Infantry/Pvt. Co. H, 26th Texas Cavalry.

Mayfield, Samuel Brooks – Pvt. Danville Mounted Riflemen, Co. B, 17th Brigade TST. Born about 1825, died in 02/1899. Buried: Glenwood Cemetery, Houston, Harris County, Texas. Father: Ambrose Mayfield. Spouse: Mary Louisa Seymour.

McAlpine, William Kennedy – Pvt. Co. I, 9th Texas Infantry (Nichols')/ Pvt. Co. K, 20th Texas Infantry. Born 12/12/1843, died 06/09/1918. Buried: Fairview Cemetery, Grimes County, Texas. Father: Alexander Smith McAlpine. Spouse: Lucy Ophelia Long.

McCaleb, George Washington – Cpl. Co. F, 20th Texas Infantry. Born 09/30/1825, died 11/11/1890. Buried: Powers Family Cemetery, Falls County, Texas. Father: Zill McCaleb. Spouse: Mary Cude/Mary J. McCaleb.

McCaleb, Jesse H. – Pvt. Co. C, 12th Texas Infantry. Born 06/26/1827, died 06/06/1888. Buried: Cude Cemetery, Montgomery County, Texas. Father: Zill McCaleb. Spouse: Emma Chambers/Dorcus Cude.

McCan, James Marion – Pvt. Co. F, 9th Texas Infantry (Nichols')/Pvt. Co. B, 24th Texas Cavalry/Pvt. Co. I, Granbury's Consolidated Regiment. Born 10/20/1834, died 07/31/1915. Buried: Burroughs Cemetery, Madison County, Texas. Father: James McCan. Spouse: Amanda Catherine Barrett.

McCarley, James – Pvt. Co. I, 9th Texas Infantry (Nichols')/Pvt. Co. B, 24th Texas Cavalry. Born about 1840, died 02/08/1863. Buried: Jefferson Barracks National Cemetery, St. Louis County, Missouri. Father: Dean McCarley.

McCaskill, Daniel A. – Pvt. Co. D, 1st Texas Heavy Artillery/Pvt. Co. G, K, 20th Texas Infantry. Born about 1837 in Florida, died 12/21/1902. Buried: Confederate Cemetery, Bexar County, Texas. Father: Alexander McCaskill. Spouse: Lizzie M. McCaskill.

McCaskill, Henry Clay – Pvt. Co. K, 20th Texas Infantry. Born about 1844 in Florida, died 01/01/1919. Father: Alexander McCaskill.

McCaskill, James Marion – Pvt. Co. C, 21st Texas Cavalry. Born 1842 in Florida, died 07/19/1900. Father: Alexander McCaskill.

McClure, A. J. – Pvt. Co. A, 17th Brigade TST. Born about 1817, died after 1880. Spouse: Martha McClure.

McCormick, James P. – Pvt. Co. G, 20th Texas Infantry. Born about 1843, died unknown. Father: Calvin McCormick.

McCrory, Marion A. – Sgt. Co. B, 24th Texas Cavalry. Born about 1834, died 12/30/1895. Buried: Cotopaxi Cemetery, Fremont County, Colorado. Spouse: Sarah Eleanor "Ellen" Whitten.

McFadin, John Franklin – Pvt. Co. K, Morgan's Texas Cavalry. Born 02/09/1827, died 09/10/1868. Buried: Enloe Cemetery, Montgomery County, Texas. Spouse: Sarah A. Stanley.

McGary, Jonathan T. – Pvt. Co. B, 24th Texas Cavalry. Born about 1839, died 01/23/1863. Buried: Jefferson Barracks National Cemetery, St. Louis County, Missouri.

McGaughey, John Clarence – Sgt. Co. G, 20th Texas Infantry. Born 07/28/1830, died 04/19/1915. Buried: New Montgomery Cemetery, Montgomery County, Texas. Father: William M. McGaughey. Spouse: Mary Jane McCord.

McGilvary, Alexander Murdock – Pvt. Co. B, 24th Texas Cavalry. Born about 1844, died 11/30/1864 in Tennessee. Father: John Martin McGilvary.

McGilvary, John Martin – Pvt. Co. B, 17th Brigade TST. Born 12/20/1812, died 05/18/1878. Buried: Birdston Cemetery, Navarro County, Texas. Spouse: Eleanor McIver.

McGilvary, William Thomas – Pvt. Co. D, 5th Texas Infantry. Born 07/13/1839, died 12/28/1888. Buried: Robinson Cemetery, Freestone County, Texas. Father: John Martin McGilvary.

McGrew, William J. – Pvt. Co. I, 9th Texas Infantry (Nichols')/1st Lieutenant, Co. K, 20th Texas Infantry. Born about 1844, died 12/28/1868. Buried: New Montgomery Cemetery, Montgomery County, Texas. Father: William McGrew. Spouse: Rebecca "Lucy" Martin.

McGuffin, John Ford – Pvt. Co. A, 17th Brigade TST. Born about 1813 in South Carolina, died 09/10/1887. Buried: Riverside Cemetery, Gonzales County, Texas. Father: Hugh Moses McGuffin. Spouse: Sarah Montgomery.

McIntyre, James Robert – Pvt. Co. B, 24th Texas Cavalry. Born about 1832 in North Carolina, died after 1911. Buried: Oakland Cemetery, Grimes County, Texas. Father: Malachi Stokes McIntyre. Spouse: Elizabeth Ann Spear/Augusta C. Hall.

McIntyre, Jesse Cothier – Pvt. Co. B, 24th Texas Cavalry. Born 03/03/1835 in North Carolina, died 6/13/1903. Buried: Oakland Cemetery, Grimes County, Texas. Father: Malachi Stokes McIntyre. Spouse: Hannah Caroline Lindley.

McKinney, Albert Wrinkles – Pvt. Co. I, 9th Texas Infantry (Nichols')/Pvt. Co. B, 24th Texas Cavalry/Pvt. Co. I, Granbury's Consolidated Regiment. Born 08/15/1842 in Louisiana, died 08/02/1908. Buried: White's Chapel Cemetery, Harris County, Texas. Father: Mercer McKinney. Spouse: Sarah Jane Singleton.

McKinney, Gilbert Harris – 5th Sgt. Co. I, 9th Texas Infantry (Nichols')/1st Lt. Co. K, Terry's Regiment, Texas Cavalry. Born about 1823, died 03/29/1905. Buried: New Montgomery Cemetery, Montgomery County, Texas. Spouse: Mary Harris Pace McKinney/Melissa Davis/Melinda Peterson.

McKinzie, Joseph – 1st Sgt. Co. I, 9th Texas Infantry (Nichols')/1st Lt. Co. C, Terry's Regiment, Texas Cavalry. Born about 1831 in North Carolina, died unknown.

McLain, Joseph – Pvt. Co. I, 9th Texas Infantry (Nichols')/Pvt. Co. K, 20th Texas Infantry. Born about 1845, died 02/10/1934. Buried: Enron Cemetery, Grimes County, Texas. Spouse: Letha "Lettie" R. Cartwright.

McLain, Moses – Pvt. Co. I, 9th Texas Infantry (Nichols')/Pvt. Co. K, 20th Texas Infantry. Born about 1842, died 12/20/1922. Buried: Enron Cemetery, Grimes County, Texas. Spouse: Narcissa Cartwright.

McLeod, Christopher Charles – Pvt. Co. I, 9th Texas Infantry (Nichols')/Pvt. Co. C, Waul's Texas Legion. Born about 1841 in Georgia, died unknown. Father: Malcom McLeod. Spouse: Frances Martin.

McLeod, George – Pvt. Co. I, 9th Texas Infantry (Nichols')/Pvt. Co. C, Waul's Texas Legion. Born about 1843 in Georgia, died 02/04/1875. Father: Malcom McLeod. Spouse: Martha Jane McGuffin.

McLeod, William – Pvt. Co. A, Terry's Regiment, Texas Cavalry. Born about 1844 in Georgia, died about 1917. Buried: Bether Cemetery, Montgomery County, Texas. Father: Malcom McLeod. Spouse: Piananer Ratliff.

McNeese, Ivy – Pvt. 17th Brigade TST. Born about 1811 in North Carolina, died unknown.

McRae, Cyrus D. – Pvt. Co. G, 20th Texas Infantry. Born about 1844, died 10/02/1864 in Galveston, Texas. Father: Colin McRae.

McRae, Richard W. – Pvt. Co. K, 20th Texas Infantry. Born about 1845 in Texas, died unknown. Father: Colin McRae.

Meeks, Archibald – 2nd Lt. Co. F, 17th Brigade TST/Pvt. Co. D, 4th Infantry Regiment, TST. Born about 1818 in Georgia, died after 1870. Spouse: Margaret Metts.

Meeks, Zachariah T. – Pvt. Co. A, 24th/25th Consolidated Texas Cavalry. Born 05/10/1846, died after 1920. Father: Archibald Meeks. Spouse: Josephine Meeks.

Meredith, Jacob A. – Pvt. Co. I, 9th Texas Infantry (Nichols')/Cpl. Co. K, 20th Texas Infantry. Born about 1832 in Pennsylvania, died unknown. Spouse: Matilda Meredith.

Metts, Francis Marion – Pvt. Co. C, 9th Texas Infantry (Nichols')/Pvt. Co. D, 1st Texas Heavy Artillery/Pvt. Co. C, Waul's Texas Legion/Pvt. Co. F, Timmons Regiment, Texas Infantry/Pvt. Co. K, 20th Texas Infantry. Born about 1844 in Georgia. Father: Zachariah Metts.

Metts, George Washington – Sgt. Co. C, G. 9th Texas Infantry (Nichols')/2nd Lt. Co. K, 20th Texas Infantry. Born about 1831 in Georgia, died unknown. Father: Zachariah Metts.

Metts, Joseph Robert – Cpl. Co. C, 9th Texas Infantry (Nichols')/Pvt. Co. D, 1st Texas Heavy Artillery/Cpl. Co. C, Waul's Texas Legion. Born about 1842 in Georgia. Father: Zachariah Metts.

Milburn, Joseph E. – Pvt. Co. K, 3rd Texas Cavalry. Born 10/04/1829, died 07/16/1915. Buried: Fairmount Cemetery, Harmon County, Oklahoma. Father: Williamson Milburn. Spouses: Mary Norsworthy/Mary E. Brantley.

Milburn, M. J. – Pvt. Co. B, 24th Texas Cavalry. Born about 1832, died 03/14/1863. Buried: Camp Butler National Cemetery, Sangamon County, Illinois. Father: Williamson Milburn.

Mitchell, Daniel – Pvt. Co. K, 8th Texas Cavalry. Born about 1841, died 10/30/1863. Buried: Green Lawn Cemetery, Marion County, Indiana.

Mitchell, Jabez N. – Pvt. Co. K, 8th Texas Cavalry. Born about 1844, died 2/28/1919. Buried: Texas State Cemetery, Travis County, Texas.

Mitchell, John M. – Pvt. Co. I, 9th Texas Infantry (Nichols'). Born about 1817 in South Carolina, died unknown.

Mitchell, Thomas – Pvt. Co. H, 4th Texas Infantry. Born about 1835, died unknown.

Mochman, Wilhelm Robert E. – Pvt. Co. A, 17th Brigade TST/Pvt. Co. D, 4th Infantry Regiment, TST. Born 04/28/1828, died 01/01/1880. Spouse: Sarah Sallie Somers.

Moore, William C. – Pvt. Co. B, 24th Texas Cavalry. Born in 1838, died in 1922. Buried: Willis Cemetery, Montgomery County, Texas. Father: Isham Moore. Spouse: Sarephta Amanda Horton/Lucy A. Fortner.

Moorefield, Henry – Pvt. Co. B, 17th Brigade TST. Born about 1824 in North Carolina, died after 1900. Spouse: Malinda Johnson.

Morehead, Sanford V. – 1st Lt. Co. A, 17th Brigade TST/Sgt. Co. D, 4th Infantry Regiment, TST. Born about 1816 in Georgia, died unknown. Spouse: Elizabeth S. Holland.

Morris, A. C. – Pvt. Co. H, 4th Texas Infantry. Born about 1841 in Texas, died 02/02/1862 in Virginia.

Morris, Alfred William, Sr. – 1st Lt. Co. K, 8th Texas Cavalry. Born 06/11/1821, died 09/29/1866. Buried: Old Methodist Church Cemetery, Montgomery County, Texas. Father: John P. Morris. Spouse: Matilda Parmer.

Morris, Alfred William, Jr. – Pvt. Co. K, 8th Texas Cavalry/Pvt. Co. A, 24th/25th Consolidated Texas Cavalry. Born 01/10/1846, died 06/25/1925. Buried: Palestine City Cemetery, Anderson County, Texas. Father: Alfred William Morris, Sr. Spouse: Mary Permilia Bobbitt/Irene Lois Kimbrough/Anna C. Parsons/Mayme Bradshaw.

Morris, Benjamin F. – Pvt. Co. A, 17th Brigade TST/Pvt. Co. D, 4th Infantry Regiment, TST/Pvt. Co. A, Terry's Regiment, Texas Cavalry. Born about 1822 in South Carolina, died before 1880. Spouse: Mary J. Morris.

Morris, Samuel – Pvt. Montgomery County Rifle Boys, 17th Brigade TST. Born about 1825 in Ohio, died unknown.

Morse, M. H. – Pvt. Co. C, 21st Texas Cavalry. Born about 1834 in Ohio, died unknown. Spouse: J. Morse.

Mostyn, Henry – Pvt. Montgomery County Rifle Boys, 17th Brigade TST. Born about 1841, died before 1866.

Muckle, David C. – Pvt. Co. K, 8th Texas Cavalry. Born about 1840, killed in action near Savannah, Georgia 11/28/1864. Father: William Muckle.

Muckle, Jeptha – Pvt. 17th Brigade TST. Born 03/17/1828, died 07/20/1899. Buried: Shannon–Evergreen Cemetery, Montgomery County, Texas. Father: William Muckle. Spouse: Martha E. Muckle.

Myers, Thomas J. – Pvt. Co. H, 4th Texas Infantry. Born about 1839 in South Carolina, died in Virginia 08/25/1862. Father: James F. Myers.

Neal, Lewis – Pvt. Co. 9th Texas Infantry (Nichols'). Born about 1810 in Virginia, died unknown. Spouse: Sarah Runfield.

Needham, Kyle Grundy – Pvt. Co. K, 16th Texas Infantry. Born 02/18/1829, died in 1884. Buried: Enloe Cemetery, Montgomery County, Texas. Father: Enoch Needham. Spouse: Samantha Marelda Cheairs.

Nelson, (Negro) – Co. B, 24th Texas Cavalry. Vitals unknown. Last record shows Camp Butler, Illinois POW.

Nichols, George J. – Pvt. Co. B, 24th Texas Cavalry. Born about 1831, died 03/18/1863. Buried: Camp Butler National Cemetery, Sangamon County, Illinois. Spouse: Sarah Nichols.

Nichols. Walter W. – Pvt. Co. B, 24th Texas Cavalry. Born 11/22/1834, died 08/28/1890. Buried: Odd Fellows Cemetery, Williamson County, Texas. Spouse: Sarah G. Chessher.

Noble, P. H. – Pvt. Co. I, 9th Texas Infantry (Nichols'). Born about 1825 in Virginia, died unknown.

Nobles, John W. – Pvt. Co. B, 24th Texas Cavalry. Born about 1833 in Alabama, died unknown. Spouse: Mary Dubard.

Nobles, Warren Tillet – Cpl. Co. G, 20th Texas Infantry. Born 12/23/1839, died 3/22/1910. Buried: New Montgomery Cemetery, Montgomery County,

Texas. Father: Warren Nobles. Spouse: Sally Cook.

Norman, J. – Pvt. Co. A, 17th Brigade TST/Pvt. Co. D, 4th Infantry Regiment, TST. Born about 1816, died unknown.

Norman, William H. – Cpl. Co. H, 26th Texas Cavalry. Born about 1814 in Mississippi, died about 1885. Father: William Norman. Spouse: Nancy Ann Parker.

Norsworthy, James H. – Pvt. Co. I, 9th Texas Infantry (Nichols')/Pvt. Co. B, 24th Texas Cavalry. Born about 1840, died 11/11/1862 in Arkansas. Father: Wiley B. Norsworthy.

Norsworthy, Thomas Wiley – Pvt. Co. K, 20th Texas Infantry. Born 06/06/1845, died 06/09/1906. Buried: Oakwood Cemetery, Walker County, Texas. Father: Wiley B. Norsworthy. Spouse: Lucy C. Wardlaw.

Nuner, John Barber – Pvt. Co. B, Waul's Texas Legion. Born about 1829 in Tennessee, died unknown. Father: William McMinn Nuner. Spouse: Maria Cartwright.

Nuner, William P. – Pvt. Co. K, 20th Texas Infantry/Cpl. Co. H, 26th Texas Cavalry. Born about 1828 in Tennessee, died unknown.

Oats, Stephen – Pvt. Co. K, 20th Texas Infantry. Born about 1825, died 02/24/1864. Father: Stephen Oats. Spouse: Martha Compton.

O'Banion, John R. – Pvt. Co. B, 24th Texas Cavalry. Born about 1831, died after 04/1864. Father: Green H. O'Banion.

O'Banion, William Hamilton – Pvt. Danville Mounted Riflemen, 17th Brigade TST. Born 04/22/1827, died 05/09/1913. Buried: Willis City Cemetery, Montgomery County, Texas. Father: Green H. O'Banion. Spouse: Rachel Morris Lindley Kelton.

Oglesby, Calvin – Pvt. Co. G, 1st Texas Heavy Artillery. Born about 1834 in Mississippi, died unknown. Father: Sabert Oglesby.

Oglesby, Daniel – Pvt. Co. G, 1st Texas Heavy Artillery. Born about 1817 in Mississippi, died 02/1865 in camp at Galveston. Father: Sabert Oglesby.

Oglesby, Henry – Pvt. Co. G, 1st Texas Heavy Artillery. Born about 1830 in Mississippi. Father: Sabert Oglesby

Oglesby, Sabert – Pvt. Co. G, 1st Texas Heavy Artillery. Born about 1825 in Mississippi, died unknown. Father: Sabert Oglesby

Oliver, Robert F. – Capt. Co. I, 9th Texas Infantry (Nichols')/Pvt. Co. D, 4th Infantry Regiment, TST. Born about 1817 in Tennessee, died after 1890. Spouse: Martha "Mattie" Anders/Elizabeth J. Oliver.

Outlaw, Alexander – Pvt. Co. K, 16th Texas Infantry/Pvt. Co. K, 20th Texas Infantry. Born about 1836 in Tennessee, died about 1880. Father: Lewis Outlaw.

Outlaw, Francis Marion – Pvt. Co. K, 16th Texas Infantry/Pvt. Co. K, 20th Texas Infantry. Born 12/23/1839, died 3/22/1910. Buried: Vick Cemetery, Montgomery County, Texas. Father: Lewis Outlaw. Spouse: Sibannia "Sibbie" Vick.

Outlaw, Richard – Pvt. Co. D, 1st Texas Heavy Artillery/Pvt. Co C, 9th Texas Infantry (Nichols'). Born about 1840 in Tennessee, died 02/28/1862 in Galveston. Father: Lewis Outlaw.

Pace, John Pinckney – Pvt. Co. B, 24th Texas Cavalry/Pvt. Co. K, Terry's Regiment, Texas Cavalry. Born about 1843, died about 1889. Father: Richard E. Pace. Spouse: Mary Ellen McKinney.

Palmer, Reuben Jonathan – Pvt. 17th Brigade TST. Delegate to 1861 Texas Secession Convention.

Parker, A. M. (N.) – Pvt. Co. G, 20th Texas Infantry. Born about 1846 in Georgia, died unknown. Father: H. C. Parker.

Parker, David Henry – Pvt. Co. I, 9th Texas Infantry (Nichols')/Pvt. Co. B, 24th Texas Cavalry. Born about 1842, died 02/18/1863. Buried: Jefferson Barracks National Cemetery, St. Louis County, Missouri. Father: John R. Parker.

Parker, Joseph C. – Pvt. Co. K, 20th Texas Infantry. Born about 1834, died 04/13/1863. Buried: Confederate Hospital Cemetery, Harris County, Texas. Father: Isaiah Parker. Spouse: C. Parker.

Peel, John R. – Sgt. Co. E, 9th Texas Infantry (Nichols')/Capt. Co. K, 16th Texas Infantry/Capt. Co. G, Bradford's Regiment, Texas Cavalry. Born about 1832 in Arkansas, died after 1880. Father: Thomas Ray Peel. Spouse: Sarah "Sallie" E. Creath.

Peel, Thomas Jefferson – 2nd Lt. Co. I, 9th Texas Infantry (Nichols')/Capt. Co. K, 16th Texas Infantry. Born 02/02/1837, died 10/31/1901. Buried: Old Methodist Church Cemetery, Montgomery County, Texas. Father: Thomas Ray Peel. Spouse: Anamelia "Annie" Arnold.

Peel, Thomas Ray – Pvt. Co. K, 16th Texas Infantry. Born about 1807 in Kentucky, died 05/25/1888. Buried: New Montgomery Cemetery, Montgomery County, Texas. Father: Richard Peel. Spouse: Ann E. Wood.

Perry, C. William – Pvt. Co. G, 7th Texas Cavalry. Born about 1838 in Alabama, died unknown. Spouse: Louisa Jane Spear.

Perry, William F. – Pvt. Danville Mounted Riflemen, 17th Brigade TST. Born about 1835 in Maryland, died unknown.

Phillips, Abram B. – Capt. Company F, 17th Brigade TST. Born about 1820, died about 1877. Father: Charles Phillips. Spouse: Ann Bell Walker.

Phillips, George Nix – 2nd Lt. Co. F, 17th Brigade TST. Born 10/09/1825, died 03/11/1877. Father: Charles Phillips. Spouse: Lucinda Walker.

Pillow, Andrew Montgomery – Pvt. Co. K, 20th Texas Infantry. Born 10/03/1838, died 08/18/1913. Buried: Huffines Cemetery, Cass County, Texas. Father: William Barton Pillow. Spouse: Lou Self/Mahalia J. Flippen/W. J. Biley.

Pillow, Ransom "Doc" – Pvt. Co. E, 26th Texas Cavalry. Born 05/01/1842, died 10/14/1914. Buried: Huffines Cemetery, Cass County, Texas. Father: William Barton Pillow. Spouse: Martha Josephine Coe/Sarah Mary Cryer/Mary Boudreaux/Josephine Teresa Lee.

Pillow, Thomas Jefferson – Pvt. Co. E, 26th Texas Cavalry. Born 02/23/1844, died 05/06/1889. Father: William Barton Pillow. Spouse: Mary Jane Gates/Theodsia "Docia" Hoover.

Pincham, Peter – 1st Sgt. Danville Mounted Riflemen, 17th Brigade TST. Born about 1797 in Virginia, died 10/15/1867. Spouse: Ann Dorris Wilson.

Pinchback, James Howard – Pvt. Co. K, 8th Texas Cavalry. Born 08/24/1843, died 06/01/1919. Buried: Marlow Cemetery, Stephens County, Oklahoma. Father: George P. Pinchback. Spouse: Missouri Juliette "Julie" Mattingly.

Pinchback, George F. – Pvt. Co. K, 20th Texas Infantry. Born 08/13/1835, died 09/01/1871. Buried: Old Homer Cemetery, Claiborne Parish, Louisiana. Father: George P. Pinchback.

Pinkston, Nathaniel – Pvt. 17th Brigade TST. Born about 1834 in Alabama, died 02/28/1905. Buried: Oakwood Cemetery, Navarro County, Texas. Father: Lucian Pinkston. Spouse: M. L. Pinkston/Medora Eva Pinkston.

Pitts, James Harrison – Capt. Co. A, 17th Brigade TST/2n. Lt. Co. D, 4th Infantry Regiment, TST. Born 10/02/1818, died 04/20/1884. Buried: New Montgomery Cemetery, Montgomery County, Texas. Father: John Pitts. Spouse: Elizabeth Muckle.

Pitts, William L. – Pvt. Co. K, 8th Texas Cavalry. Born about 1844 in Alabama, died 12/01/1861. Buried: Mt. Olivet Cemetery, Davidson County, Tennessee. Father: James Harrison Pitts.

Pool, Henry Joseph – Pvt. Co. G, 20th Texas Infantry. Born 06/30/1825, died 1897. Buried: Poole Cemetery, Montgomery County, Texas. Father: Jacob Pool. Spouse: Cebell Birdsong.

Pool, John William – Pvt. Co. G, 20th Texas Infantry. Born 06/23/1823, died 02/18/1901. Buried: Poole Cemetery, Montgomery County, Texas. Father: Jacob Pool. Spouse: Johanna Welch.

Poole, Robert S. – Capt. Co. A, 24th Texas Cavalry/Capt. Co. A, Mann's Regiment, Texas Cavalry/Capt. Co. A, 24th/25th Consolidated Texas Cavalry. Born about 1826 in Virginia, died before 1880. Spouse: Harriet Amelia Jones/ Sarah Bustin/Eliza A. Poole.

Porter, Procter Prentice – Capt. Co. H, 4th Texas Infantry. Born about 1826 in Tennessee, died 07/20/1862 in Richmond, Virginia.

Powell, J. G. – Pvt. Co. I, 9th Texas Infantry. Born about 1831, died unknown.

Powell, Robert Micajah – Capt. Waverly Confederates, 17th Brigade TST/ Capt. Co. D, 5th Texas Infantry/Col. 5th Texas Infantry/Col. commanding Hood's Texas Brigade. Born 09/23/1826, died 01/15/1916. Buried: Calvary Cemetery, St. Louis County, Missouri. Father: George Francis Powell. Spouse: Elizabeth Green Wood/Elizabeth Grace.

Quick, George J. – Pvt. Co. B, 24th Texas Cavalry. Born about 1830, died about 1863. Buried: Camp Butler National Cemetery, Sangamon County, Illinois.

Quigley, Reverious – Pvt. Co. H, 4th Texas Infantry. Born about 1828, killed in action 06/27/1862 at the Battle of Gaines' Mill in Virginia.

Ramsdell, Charles H. – Pvt. Co. C, 21st Texas Cavalry. Born 02/21/1842, died 07/13/1903. Father: Charles Ramsdell. Spouse: Augusta Fredonia Halley.

Rankin, Robert – Pvt. Co. H, 4th Texas Infantry. Born about 1831 in Texas, died 02/17/1910. Spouse: Ellen J. Rankin.

Rankin, Thomas Berry – Pvt. 17th Brigade TST. Born 03/30/1815, died 09/30/1885. Buried: New Montgomery Cemetery, Montgomery County, Texas. Father: William Marshall Rankin. Spouse: Lucy V. Ellington/Helen M. Rankin.

Rankin, William – Pvt. Co. G, 20th Texas Infantry. Born about 1837 in Texas, died after 1900. Spouse: Matilda Ann Hall.

Ratliff (Ratcliff), James R. – Pvt. Co. I, 9th Texas Infantry (Nichols')/Pvt. Co. K, 20th Texas Infantry. Born about 1832 in Mississippi, died 03/10/1899. Spouse: Ruth E. Wood.

Reding, George Washington – 1st Corp. Danville Mounted Riflemen, 17th Brigade TST/1st Sgt. Co. A, 17th Brigade TST/Pvt. Co. D, 4th Infantry Regiment, TST. Born 02/12/1825, died 10/18/1888. Buried: Zion Cemetery, Grimes County, Texas. Father: Iredell Reding. Spouse: Betty Ann Neeley.

Reding, James Adniel – Pvt. 17th Brigade TST. Born about 1825 in Tennessee, died about 1864. Father: Iredell Reding. Spouse: Martha Eliza Spear.

Reding, John Baker – Pvt. Co. B, 24th Texas Cavalry/3rd Cpl. Co, A, 17th Brigade TST. Pvt. Co. D, 4th Infantry Regiment, TST. Born 03/05/1817, died 10/27/1877. Buried: Danville–Shepard Hill Cemetery, Montgomery County, Texas. Father: Robert Reding. Spouse: Martha (Patsy) Hallum/Eliza J. Cheshire.

Reynolds (Rennolds), W. B. – Cpl. Co. C, 21st Texas Cavalry. Born about 1827, died in Texas 09/1862. Spouse: Sarah (R. M. D.) Shannon.

Richards, Augustus – Maj. 17th Brigade TST. Born 10/02/1816, died 11/18/1913. Buried: Danville–Shepard Hill Cemetery, Montgomery County, Texas. Spouse: Mary Scanlan.

Ridg(e)way, F. M. – Pvt. Co. D, 5th Texas Infantry. Born about 1838 in Alabama, killed in action 09/17/1862 at the Battle of Antietam.

Rigby, A. H. . Cpl. Co. K, 20th Texas Infantry. Born about 1834 in Texas, died after 1870. Father: Benjamin F. Rigby. Spouse: Caroline Rigby.

Rigby, Eli – Pvt. Co. I, 9th Texas Infantry/Pvt. Co. K, 20th Texas Infantry. Born about 1839 in Texas, died after 1880. Father: Benjamin F. Rigby. Spouse: Nannie Rigby.

Rigby, William M. – 1st Lt. Co. K, 20th Texas Infantry. Born about 1829 in Louisiana, died 09/13/1864. Father: Benjamin F. Rigby. Spouse: Julia Betts.

Robb, J. A. – Jr. 2nd Lt. Co. A, 17th Brigade TST. Born about 1817, died unknown.

Roberts, Green, Sr. – Pvt. Montgomery County Rifle Boys, 17th Brigade TST. Born about 1811 in Georgia, died about 1870 in Falls County, Texas. Father: John Roberts. Spouse: Harriet Riley/Mary A. Brooks/Elizabeth Jane Thames.

Roberts, Green, Jr. – Pvt. Co. E, 26th Texas Cavalry. Born about 1841 in Alabama, died after 1880 in Montgomery County, Texas. Father: Green Roberts. Spouse: Sarah Miller/Missouri Presswood.

Roberts, James Eldridge – Pvt. Co. H, 26th Texas Cavalry. Born about 1834, died about 1897. Buried: Morgan's Point Cemetery, Harris County, Texas. Father: Green Roberts. Spouse: Nancy Jenny Lynn Rose.

Roberts, James Monroe – Pvt. Co. C, 21st Texas Cavalry. Born about 1833 in Alabama, died 01/07/1913. Buried: Devine Cemetery, Medina County, Texas. Father: Tyrie Roberts. Spouse: Lucinda Henrietta Thames.

Roberts, John W. – Pvt. Co. E, 26th Texas Cavalry. Born about 1840 in Alabama, died 07/06/1927. Buried: Speaks Cemetery, Lavaca County, Texas. Father: Green Roberts. Spouse: Mary Farrow/Martha Jane Wells/ Willie Speaks.

Robertson, Jesse Wiley – Pvt. Co. A, Timmons Regiment, Texas Infantry. Born about 1823 in Tennessee, died after 1900 in Waller County, Texas. Father: Lewis Robertson. Spouse: Mary Elizabeth Dorris.

Robertson, Louis Thomas – Pvt. Co. B, Waul's Texas Legion. Born about 1844 in Tennessee, died unknown. Father: Jesse Wiley Robertson.

Rodgerson, William – Pvt. Montgomery County Rifle Boys, 17th Brigade TST/Pvt. 4th Infantry Regiment, TST. Born 11/30/1816, died 12/13/1900. Buried: Magnolia Cemetery, Montgomery County, Texas. Father: Thomas Rodgers. Spouse: Jane Elizabeth Thames.

Rogers, Charles Lewis – Pvt. Co. G, 20th Texas Infantry. Born 06/30/1839, died 08/12/1862. Buried: Yell Cemetery, Montgomery County, Texas. Father: Raleigh Rogers.

Rogers, James M. – Pvt. 17th Brigade TST. Born 09/06/1824, died 01/28/1871. Buried: Odd Fellows Cemetery, Grimes County, Texas. Spouse: Smytha Uzell.

Rogers, William D. – Pvt. Co. B, 24th Texas Cavalry. Born about 1827 in Tennessee, died after 1900. Father: Cullen Rogers. Spouse: Margaret Adeline Moore.

Rose, Elisha Alexander – Pvt. Co. G, 7th Texas Cavalry. Born about 1842, died 04/28/1892. Father: Samuel Rose. Spouse: Almedia McDonald.

Rose, Joseph D. – Pvt. Co. D, 5th Texas Infantry. Born about 1841, died 06/03/1862 in Virginia. Father: Samuel Rose.

Rose, Sterling A. – Pvt. Co. G, 7th Texas Infantry. Born about 1844, died unknown. Father: Samuel Rose.

Roten (Rotten), David Edward – Pvt. Co. I, 9th Texas Infantry (Nichols')/Cpl. Co. K, 20th Texas Infantry. Born 05/01/1834, died 9/10/1917. Buried: Cedar Hill Cemetery, Cherokee County, Texas. Father: Thomas Roten. Spouse: Alice Anderson Whitten.

Roten (Rotten), Larkin J. – Pvt. Co. B, 24th Texas Cavalry. Born about 1838 in South Carolina, died 06/20/1862 in Smith County, Texas. Father: Thomas Roten.

Roten (Rotten), William W. – Pvt. Co. B, 24th Texas Cavalry. Born about 1823 in South Carolina, died after 12/15/1862. Father: Thomas Roten. Spouse: Amanda E. Cheatham.

Ryals, William Alexander – 2nd Lt. Co. C, 21st Texas Cavalry. Born 12/10/1838, died 01/04/1933. Buried: Cartwright–Rabon Chapel Cemetery, Montgomery County, Texas. Father: Handy Ryals. Spouse: Martha Francis Carson/Rebecca Elizabeth Ogg.

Sandel (Sandell), Erastus Emory – Pvt. Co. I, 9th Texas Infantry (Nichols')/ Pvt. Co. H, 20th Texas Infantry. Born 06/27/1836, died about 1901. Father: Henry Sandel. Spouse: Rachel S. Lindley.

Sandel (Sandell), James Monroe – Cpl. Co. I, 9th Texas Infantry (Nichols')/ Cpl. Co. K, 20th Texas Infantry. Born 07/08/1835, died 12/03/1881. Buried: Willis Cemetery, Montgomery County, Texas. Father: Darius Sandel. Spouse: Minervia Ann Smart.

Sandel (Sandell), John Oliver – Pvt. Co. B, 24th Texas Cavalry. Born 01/07/1831, killed in action 11/30/1864 at Franklin, Tennessee. Father: Peter Warren Sandel.

Sandel (Sandell), Martin Luther – Pvt. Co. A, 24th/25th Consolidated Texas Cavalry. Born 12/20/1826, died 04/21/1882. Buried: Buck Foster Cemetery, Walker County, Texas. Father: Henry Sandel. Spouse: Sarah Jackson Bay.

Sandel (Sandell), Peter Tabor – Pvt. Co. I, 9th Texas Infantry (Nichols')/Pvt. Co. B, 24th Texas Cavalry/Pvt. Co. I, Granbury's Consolidated Regiment. Born 09/15/1842, died 04/02/1932. Father: Peter Warren Sandel. Spouse: Priscilla A. Samuels/Mollie E. Gibson.

Sanderlin, J. M. – Pvt. Co. H, 4th Texas Infantry. Born about 1837 in Tennessee, died unknown. Father: J. H. Sanderlin.

Sanders, Claiborne B. – Pvt. Co. H, 4th Texas Infantry. Born about 1813, died after 1880. Father: Samuel Sanders. Spouse: Nancy Holder.

Sanders, James Madison – Pvt. Co. I, 9th Texas Infantry (Nichols')/Pvt. Co. K, 20th Texas Infantry. Born 07/10/1842, died 01/26/1897. Buried in White Cemetery, Harris County, Texas. Father: Claiborne B. Sanders. Spouse: Ann.

Sanders, John – Pvt. Co. I, 9th Texas Infantry (Nichols')/Sgt. Co. K, 20th Texas Infantry. Born about 1838, died 06/18/1864. Father: Claiborne B. Sanders.

Sanders, John F. – Pvt. Co. D, 4th Infantry Regiment, TST/Pvt. Co. K, Terry's Regiment, Texas Cavalry. Born about 1823 in North Carolina, died unknown. Spouse: Nancy Sanders.

Sanders, William Franklin – Pvt. Co. K, 20th Texas Infantry. Born 02/27/1831, died 3/25/1917. Buried: Texas State Cemetery, Travis County, Texas. Father: Thomas Saunders. Spouse: Mary Elizabeth Worsham.

Sapp, Forsyth H. – Pvt. Co. G, 31st Georgia Infantry/Capt. Co. H, 4th Infantry TST/Capt. Co. K, Terry's Regiment, Texas Cavalry. Born 02/14/1834, died 04/07/1908. Buried: Moody Cemetery, McLennon County, Texas. Father: Madison Sapp. Spouse: Cinderella Nancy Ella Redding.

Sapp, Hartwell T. – Cpl. Co. H, 4th Texas Infantry. Born 09/09/1839, died 05/26/1919. Buried: Hollywood Cemetery, Harris County, Texas. Father: Madison Sapp. Spouse: Elizabeth Rabie.

Sapp, John M. . Sgt. Co. G, 20th Texas Infantry/Sgt. Co. A, Mann's Regiment, Texas Cavalry. Born about 1828 in Georgia, died unknown. Spouse: Sarah R. Sapp.

Sapp, Wyatt Allen – Pvt. Co. A, Mann's Regiment, Texas Cavalry. Born about 1846 in Georgia, died about 1895 in Texas. Father: Forsyth B. Sapp. Spouse: Sarah A. Felker/Emilene Eliza Maywald.

Schilling, Christopher – Pvt. Co. C, 21st Texas Cavalry. Born 12/03/1833, died 05/30/1874. Father: Christof Friedrich Schilling. Spouse: Aramintia Wickson.

Scott, Charles Robert – Pvt. Co. A, 7th Texas Cavalry. Born 11/13/1843, died 07/05/1940. Buried: New Montgomery Cemetery, Montgomery County, Texas. Father: George W. Scott.

Scott, John Franklin – Pvt. Co. D, 5th Texas Infantry/Pvt. Co. D, 4th Infantry TST/Pvt. Co. K, Terry's Regiment, Texas Cavalry. Born 06/05/1838, died 9/16/1916. Buried: Evergreen Cemetery, Harris County, Texas. Father: Joseph Scott. Spouse: Nannie H. Scott.

Scott, John Newton – Capt. Beat 4, 17th Brigade TST. Born 08/15/1825, died 01/01/1913. Buried: Rhodes Cemetery (Bay's Chapel), Montgomery County, Texas. Susan Elizabeth Womack.

Seale, William J. – Pvt. Co. G, 7th Texas Cavalry. Born about 1844 in Mississippi, died unknown. Place of burial unknown. Father: John A. Seale.

Sell, Worthy (Negro) – Co. B, 24th Texas Cavalry. Vitals unknown. Last record shows Camp Butler, Illinois POW.

Sessums, Blount D. – 2nd Lt. Co. G, 7th Texas Cavalry. Born about 1835, died 08/26/1868. Father: Richard H. C. Sessums. Spouse: Harriet Pecter.

Sessums, George W. – Pvt. Co. G, 7th Texas Cavalry. Born about 1838, died unknown. Father: Richard H. C. Sessums. Spouse: Susan H. Curry.

Sessums, Peter Thomas – Pvt. Co. G, 7th Texas Cavalry. Born 12/27/1836, died 11/07/1906. Buried: Rayburn Cemetery, Madison County, Texas. Father: Richard H. C. Sessums. Spouse: Josephine E. Curry.

Shannon, Aaron, Jr. – 1st Lt. Co. C, 21st Texas Cavalry. Born about 1838, died 02/12/1864. Buried: Shannon–Evergreen Cemetery, Montgomery County, Texas. Father: Aaron Shannon.

Shannon, Benjamin Franklin – Pvt. Co. G, 20th Texas Infantry. Born 02/21/1843, died 03/05/1922. Buried: Shannon–Evergreen Cemetery, Montgomery County, Texas. Father: Jacob Montgomery Shannon. Spouse: Mary E. Scott/Anna Davidson Harbin.

Shannon, Jacob Montgomery, Jr. – Pvt. Co. K, 8th Texas Cavalry. Born 09/29/1828, died 12/04/1877. Buried: Shannon–Evergreen Cemetery, Montgomery County, Texas. Father: Jacob Montgomery Shannon.

Shannon, Mathis Ward – Pvt. Co. H, 26th Texas Cavalry. Born 04/24/1824, died 04/13/1909. Buried: Shannon–Evergreen Cemetery, Montgomery County, Texas. Father: Jacob Montgomery Shannon. Spouse: Mary Steele.

Shannon, Owen – Pvt. Co. C, 17th Brigade TST/Pvt. Co. B, Terry's Regiment, Texas Cavalry. Born about 1821, died 02/05/1880. Buried: Cleburne Memorial Cemetery, Johnson County, Texas. Father: John Shannon. Spouse: Miranda Raney.

Shannon, Thomas Brandon – Capt. Co. C, 21st Texas Cavalry. Born 01/01/1831, died 06/01/1921. Buried: Old Independence Cemetery, Washington County, Texas. Father: Aaron Shannon. Spouse: Mary Jane Hayes.

Shannon, William Alexander – 1st Lt. Co. C, 5th Texas Cavalry. Born about 1828 in Alabama, died after 03/1862. Father: Aaron Shannon. Spouse: Celesta Ann Farquhar.

Shannon, William Thomas – Pvt. Co. B, Terry's Regiment, Texas Cavalry. Born 03/31/1848, died 05/15/1936. Buried: Cleburne Memorial Cemetery, Johnson County, Texas. Father: Owen Shannon.

Sharp, James H. – Pvt. Co. H, 4th Texas Infantry. Born about 1841 in Texas, killed in action 06/22/1864 at Petersburg, Virginia. Father: M. P. Sharp.

Shaw, John – Pvt. Co. A, 24th Texas Cavalry. Born about 1843 in Germany, died unknown.

Sheets, A. – Pvt. Co. A, 17th Brigade TST/Pvt. Co. D, 4th Infantry Regiment, TST. Born about 1834 in Germany, died unknown.

Simonton, Lucius H. – Cpl. Co. A, Mann's Regiment. Born 09/10/1846, died 09/09/1865. Buried: Old Methodist Cemetery, Montgomery County, Texas. Father: William Sylvester Simonton.

Simonton, Reuben Davis – Sgt. Co. K, 8th Texas Cavalry. Born about 1842 in Texas, died in 1900. Buried: New Montgomery Cemetery, Montgomery County, Texas. Father: William Sylvester Simonton. Spouse: Louisa "Ludy" Arnold.

Simonton, Robert S. – Pvt. 17th Brigade TST. Born about 1816, died about 1863. Father: Henry Smith Simonton. Spouse: Susanna D. Simonton.

Singletary, J. M. – Pvt. 17th Brigade TST. Born about 1838 in Georgia, died unknown.

Slaughter, Henry Travis – Pvt. Co. H, 20th Texas Infantry. Born about 1845 in Colorado County, Texas, died unknown. Father: Pleasant Slaughter. Spouse: Sarah Dennis.

Smith, Lewis Andrew – Pvt. Co. K, 20th Texas Infantry. Born 12/01/1842, died 01/06/1917. Buried: Magnolia Cemetery, Jefferson County, Texas. Spouse: Eva Smith.

Smith, L. W. – 1st Lt. Montgomery County Rifle Boys, 17th Brigade TST/2nd Lt. Co. H, 26th Texas Cavalry. Born before 1828, died unknown.

Smith, John – Pvt. Co. B, 24th Texas Cavalry. Born about 1841, died 10/13/1862 in Arkansas.

Smith, John I. – Cpl. Co. H, 4th Texas Infantry. Born 03/27/1839, died 12/28/1924. Buried: Cedar Bayou Masonic Cemetery, Harris County, Texas. Spouse: Laura Cobb.

Smith, Robert T. – Pvt. Co. G, 20th Texas Infantry. Born 07/16/1840, died 9/10/1927. Buried: Magnolia Cemetery, Montgomery County, Texas. Spouse: Mary Louise Clepper.

Smith, Thomas Wesley – 1st Lt. Co. I, 9th Texas Infantry (Nichols')/Capt. Co. C, Terry's Regiment, Texas Cavalry. Born 07/13/1829, died 3/20/1902. Buried: Willis Cemetery, Montgomery County, Texas. Father: Joseph Smith. Spouse: Margaret Hope Arnold.

Smith, William Oliver – Cpl. Co. D, 5th Texas Infantry. Born 04/03/1838, died 7/16/1906. Buried: Bedias Methodist Cemetery, Grimes County, Texas. Father: Saul Smith. Spouse: Penelope Ann Wilson.

Sones, Benson – Pvt. Co. G, 20th Texas Infantry. Born about 1834 in Mississippi, died 03/20/1880. Buried: Mostyn–Tillis Prairie Cemetery, Montgomery County, Texas. Spouse: Catherine Martin.

Spear, Thomas Jackson – Pvt. Co. B, 24th Texas Cavalry. Born 09/27/1837, died 08/02/1862. Father: Malachai Moore Spear. Spouse: Mary J. Childers.

Spiller, Preston Hampden – Pvt. 17th Brigade TST. Born about 1824 in Virginia, died unknown. Father: George W. Spiller. Spouse: Mary Elizabeth Gary.

Springer, A. Ezekiel – Pvt. Co. H, 26th Texas Cavalry. Born unknown, died 08/04/1862 in Confederate Hospital, Houston, Texas. Buried: Jefferson Davis Hospital Cemetery, Houston, Harris County, Texas.

Springer, Addis Emmett – Pvt. Co. E, H, 26th Texas Cavalry. Born about 1842 in Texas, died 09/15/1882. Father: Alford Uriah Springer. Spouse: Delia Springer.

Springer, Franklin E. – Pvt. Co. H, 26th Texas Cavalry. Born 10/23/1848, died 01/29/1911. Buried: Plantersville Cemetery, Grimes County, Texas. Father: John May Springer. Spouse: Emma Dean.

Springer, Greenberry B. – Pvt. Co. D, 24th Texas Cavalry. Born about 1841, died 05/14/1909. Father: Alfred Ezekiel Springer. Spouse: Sallie Springer.

Springer, J. P. – Pvt. Co. H, 26th Texas Cavalry. Born about 1839 in Texas, died after 1899. Father: Alford Uriah Springer.

Springer, L. H. – Pvt. Co. H, 26th Texas Cavalry. Born unknown, died of disease, 07/31/1862 at Camp C. L. Owen.

Springer, Uriah – Pvt. Co. E, 17th Brigade TST. Born about 1834 in Texas, died unknown. Father: John May Springer.

Springer, Zachariah Landrum – 2nd Lt. Co. H, 26th Texas Cavalry. Born about 1828 in Alabama, died 1862. Father: John May Springer.

Stanley, Stephen S. – Pvt. Co. K, 16th Texas Infantry. Born about 1834, died about 1878 in Montgomery County, Texas. Father: Willaford Stanley. Spouse: Mary Ann Talitha Cheairs/Mary Ann Bowles Smith/Elizabeth J. Bowles.

Stanton, Robert – Pvt. Co. D, 5th Texas Infantry. Born about 1829 in England, died unknown.

Steed, Willis H. – Pvt. Co. C, 17th Brigade TST. Born about 1818 in Alabama, died after 1880. Spouse: Elizabeth Welch.

Steussy (Steussey), Jacob – Pvt. Co. H, 4th Texas Infantry. Born about 1827 in Switzerland, died 05/18/1880. Buried: Oakwood Cemetery, Travis County, Texas. Spouse: Maria Albertina Klein.

Steussy (Steussey), Matthew – Pvt. Co. H, 4th Texas Infantry. Born about 1842 in Texas, died unknown. Father: Fredrich Steussy.

Stewart, Charles W. – Cpl. Co. A, Hart's South Carolina Artillery (Hampton's Legion). Born 02/10/1837, died 03/07/1907. Buried: Oakland Cemetery, Grimes County, Texas. Father: Charles Bellinger Stewart. Spouse: Anna Peebles.

Stewart, James Samuel – Pvt. Co. B, 17th Brigade TST. Born 09/11/1823, died 02/07/1908. Buried: Moore's Grove Cemetery, Walker County, Texas. Spouse: Nancy Ann Roten/Mary Eliza O'Banion.

Stowe, John W. – Pvt. Co. D, 4th Infantry TST. Born about 1817, died about 1871. Father: Ferdinand W. Stowe. Spouse: Elizabeth Freeman/Sarah Mercer.

Surghnor, Lloyd Walter – 2nd Lt. Co. C, 17th Brigade TST/Sgt. Co. I, 9th Texas Infantry (Nichols')/Pvt. Co. A, 16th Texas Infantry. Born 09/12/1833, died 03/05/1883. Buried: Old City Cemetery, Ouachita Parish, Louisiana. Spouse: Martha Frances Joiner.

Surles, Robert – Pvt. Co. K, 20th Texas Infantry. Born about 1838 in North Carolina, died 02/10/1864. Spouse: S. Surles.

Talley, James C. – Pvt. Co. H, 4th Texas Infantry. Born about 1828 in Alabama, died about 1864 in Virginia. Father: Reuben Talley. Spouse: Charlotte Talley.

Talley, Reuben – Pvt. Co. H, 4th Texas Infantry. Born 08/22/1830, died 07/01/1905. Buried: New Montgomery Cemetery, Montgomery County, Texas. Father: Reuben Talley. Spouse: Mary Ellen Jones.

Talley, Thomas J. – Pvt. 17th Brigade TST. Born about 1834 in Alabama, died about 1905 in Montgomery County, Texas. Father: Reuben Talley. Spouse: Sarah Wade Jones.

Tarpley, Barbee – Pvt. Co. B, 24th Texas Cavalry. Born 01/29/1842, died 4/8/1909. Buried: Allphin Cemetery, Madison County, Texas. Father: Saxon Tarpley. Spouse: Lizzie Jane Hawkins.

Taylor, Alexander C. – Pvt. Co. H, 4th Texas Infantry. Born about 1842 in Texas, died about 1878. Father: William Stanhope Taylor. Spouse: Josephine C. Broomfield.

Taylor, Charles L. – Pvt. Co. H, 4th Texas Infantry/Pvt. Co. A, Mann's Regiment, Texas Cavalry. Born about 1840 in Texas, died unknown. Father: William Stanhope Taylor. Spouse: Mary Dealy.

Taylor, William Washington – Pvt. Co. A, 11th Brigade TST. Born 12/12/1848, died 02/01/1914. Buried: Bear Creek Cemetery, Burnet County, Texas. Father: William Stanhope Taylor. Spouse: Mary Elizabeth Field.

Terry, Samuel – Pvt. Co. B, 24th Texas Cavalry. Born about 1831 in Alabama, died after 04/1865. Father: Joseph W. Terry. Spouse: Sarah Ann "Sallie" Norsworthy.

Thomas, Charles Henry – Pvt. Co. B, 24th Texas Cavalry. Born about 1836 in Alabama, died 1862. Father: Ila Thomas. Spouse: Amanda Eliza McCaleb.

Thomas, D. J. L. – Pvt. Co. I, 9th Texas Infantry (Nichols'). Born about 1838, died unknown.

Thomas, Simeon – Pvt. Co. I, 20th Texas Infantry. Born 12/27/1827, died 02/01/1897. Buried: Bay's Chapel Cemetery, Montgomery County, Texas. Father: John Thomas. Spouse: Mary Sarah Gilmore.

Thomas, William – Pvt. Co. D, 4th Infantry Regiment, TST/Pvt. Co. K, Terry's Regiment, Texas Cavalry. Born about 1823 in Alabama, died about 1870 in Montgomery County, Texas. Father: John Thomas. Spouse: Lydia Uman.

Thomason, Frances Marion – Pvt. Co. B, 24th Texas Cavalry. Born 01/26/1843, died 12/16/1876. Father: George Thomason. Spouse: Elizabeth M. Fowler.

Thomason, Jabez Smyth, Sr. – 1st Lt. Co. B, 24th Texas Cavalry. Born 11/27/1827, died 6/13/1908. Buried: Madisonville City Cemetery, Madison County, Texas. Father: George Thomason. Spouse: Margaret Jane Cheshire/ Sophia H. McCaleb.

Thomason, James Burke – Cpl. Co. I, 9th Texas Infantry (Nichols')/Pvt. Co. B, 24th Texas Cavalry. Born about 1832 in Alabama, killed in action 01/11/1863 at the Battle of Arkansas Post. Father: George Thomason.

Threadgill, William T. . Pvt. Co. H, 26th Texas Cavalry. Born about 1846 in Alabama, died unknown. Father: John Threadgill.

Tolson, Thomas T. – Staff Surgeon, CSA. Born about 1829 in Alabama, died about 1885. Spouse: Mary Ann Tribble.

Tomlinson, James – Pvt. Co. D. 5th Texas Infantry. Born about 1838 in North Carolina, died of disease in Virginia 05/26/1862. Buried: Hollywood Cemetery, Richmond, Virginia.

Tomlinson, John – Pvt. Co. D. 5th Texas Infantry. Born about 1841 in North Carolina, killed in action 09/19/1863 at Battle of Chickamauga.

Travis, Amos – Pvt. Co. B, 20th Texas Cavalry. Born 02/02/1841, died 01/23/1924. Buried: Spring Hill Cemetery, Sabine County, Texas. Father: John Travis. Spouse: Mary Josephine Davidson Hines.

Travis, Henry – Cpl. Co. H, 4th Texas Infantry. Born about 1843 in Mississippi, killed in action 05/06/1864 at the Battle of the Wilderness. Buried: Confederate Cemetery, Fredericksburg City, Spotsylvania County, Virginia. Father: John Travis.

Travis, Joseph – Pvt. Co. K, 20th Texas Infantry. Born about 1837 in Mississippi, died after 1907. Father: John Travis. Spouse: Emily Ratliff.

Traylor, Alexander Hamilton – Pvt. Co. D, 5th Texas Infantry. Born 02/18/1841, died 10/21/1903. Buried: Old Waverly Cemetery, Walker County, Texas. Father: Samuel Traylor.

Traylor, Joseph Derry – Pvt. Co. G, 20th Texas Infantry. Born about 1844 in Alabama, died unknown. Father: William Parker Traylor. Spouse: Elizabeth "Elsie" Wilson Hardy.

Traylor, William A. – Pvt. Co. D, 5th Texas Infantry. Born 02/10/1843, died 12/13/1909. Buried: Old Waverly Cemetery, Walker County, Texas. Father: William Parker Traylor. Spouse: Mary Susanna Hardy.

Truitt, Roland K. – Pvt. Danville Mounted Riflemen, 17th Brigade TST/Pvt. Co. K, 12th Texas Cavalry. Born 08/23/1841, died 5/18/1930. Oak Mound Cemetery, Sonoma County, California. Father: James Hayden Truitt. Spouse: Sina Gentry Brooks.

Tubb, James M. – Pvt. Co. K, 20th Texas Infantry. Born about 1820 in Tennessee, died unknown. Father: James F. Tubb. Spouse: Emily Jane Boyd.

Uzzell, Calvin Dunn – Pvt. Co. G, 20th Texas Infantry. Born 12/22/1838, died 03/24/1921. Buried: Apolonia Cemetery, Grimes County, Texas. Father: Major Ben Uzzell. Spouse: Susan Elizabeth Kennard.

Uzzell, Elisha Bryant – Pvt. Co. D, 4th Infantry Regiment, TST/Pvt. Co. G, 20th Texas Infantry. Born 12/26/1843, died 5/25/1928. Buried: Clareville Cemetery, Bee County, Texas. Father: Major B. Uzell. Spouse: Julia Ann Reed/Sallie B. Uzzell.

Uzzell, Major May – Pvt. Co. A, 24th Texas Cavalry/2nd Lt. Co. A, 24th/25th Consolidated Texas Cavalry/2nd Lt. Co. A, Mann's Regiment, Texas Cavalry. Born: 08/16/1835, died 10/09/1878. Buried: M. M. Uzzell Cemetery, Montgomery County, Texas. Father: Elisha Uzzell. Spouse: Margaret Uzzell.

Vance, D. W. – Pvt. Co. H, 26th Texas Cavalry. Born about 1829 in Alabama, died after 1880. Father: Lorenzo D. Vance. Spouse: Sarah Vance.

Joshua J. Vance – Pvt. Co. H, 26th Texas Cavalry. Born about 1841 in Alabama, died unknown. Father: Lorenzo D. Vance.

Vance, Seaborn S. – Pvt. Co. H, 26th Texas Cavalry. Born about 1836 in Alabama, died unknown. Father: Lorenzo D. Vance.

Vaught, Columbus Wright – Pvt. Co. K, 8th Texas Cavalry. Born 03/23/1843, died 9/23/1923. Buried: Mart Cemetery, McLennan County, Texas. Father: William Vaught. Spouse: Jennie Ellen Ector.

Vick, Jesse – Pvt. Co. K, 20th Texas Infantry. Born about 1841 in Louisiana, died in 1888. Buried: Vick Cemetery, Montgomery County, Texas. Father: Hamon C. Vick. Spouse: Fredonia Presswood.

Vick, Vincent C. – Pvt. Co. K, 20th Texas Infantry. Born about 1843 in Louisiana, died 01/07/1878. Buried: Vick Cemetery, Montgomery County, Texas. Father: Hamon C. Vick. Spouse: Elizabeth E. McIntosh.

Viser, William Wallace – Pvt. Danville Mounted Riflemen, 17th Brigade TST/Capt. Co. B, Gould's Battalion, Texas Cavalry/Major, Gould's Battalion, Texas Cavalry. Born 06/19/1830, died 9/25/1901. Buried: Madisonville City Cemetery, Madison County, Texas. Father: William Viser. Spouse: Amanda M. Johnson/Cynthia Ann Johnson Malone/Elizabeth Ann Wycough Hawkins.

Wade, John Marshall – Cpl. Co. K, 20th Texas Infantry. Born about 1815 in New York, died 10/09/1879. Buried: Oakwood Cemetery, Travis County, Texas. Spouse: Ruth M. Boston/Louisa Virginia Tinsley.

Wade, Frank H. – Cpl. Co. H, 4th Texas Infantry. Born about 1843 in Texas, died unknown. Father: John Marshal Wade.

Walker, James Madison – Pvt. Co. A, 24th/25th Consolidated Texas Cavalry. Born 02/07/1845, died 10/29/1906. Father: William Walker. Spouse: Serena "Sarah" A. McCaleb.

Walker, Samuel T. (T. S.) – Pvt. Co. I, 9th Texas Infantry (Nichols')/Pvt. Co. B, 24th Texas Cavalry. Born about 1840 in Alabama, died unknown. Father: William Walker.

Walker, William – Cpl. Co. B, 24th Texas Cavalry. Born about 1816 in South Carolina, died 11/11/1862 in Arkansas. Father: John Newstep Walker. Spouse: Mary E. Howerton.

Wallace, Hugh Theodore – Pvt. Co. G, 20th Texas Infantry. Born 1844, died about 1928. Father: John Wallace.

Wallace, Thomas R. – Pvt. Co. D, 5th Texas Infantry. Born about 1843, 06/12/1862 in Richmond, Virginia. Father: John Wallace.

Wallace, William Goodwin – Pvt. Co. G, 20th Texas Infantry. Born about 1838, died 05/20/1874. Buried: Byrne Cemetery, Grimes County, Texas. Father: John Wallace.

Walters, August – Pvt. Co. K, 20th Texas Infantry. Born unknown, died 04/14/1865 at Confederate Hospital in Houston.

Walters, William W. – Pvt. Danville Mounted Riflemen, 17th Brigade TST/Cpl. Co. A, 17th Brigade TST. Born 02/07/1825, died 5/6/1907. Buried: Barrett–Burrows Cemetery, Madison County, Texas. Spouse: Eliza McDow.

Warren, William H. – 1st Sgt. Co. I, 9th Texas Infantry (Nichols'). Born about 1838, died 12/30/1861 in Galveston, Texas.

Waters, N. M. – Pvt. Co. I, 9th Texas Infantry (Nichols'). Born about 1840, died unknown.

Weatherford, Jones E. – Pvt. 17th Brigade TST. Born 05/15/1828, died 06/01/1883. Buried: Mount Pleasant Cemetery, Montgomery County, Texas. Father: Major Weatherford. Spouse: Mary Ann Anders.

Weatherly, Thomas Jefferson – Pvt. Co. G, 7th Texas Cavalry. Born 09/30/1838, died 01/22/1888. Buried: Danville–Shepard Hill Cemetery, Montgomery County, Texas. Father: Francis A. Weatherly. Spouse: Sarah Ann Frances "Fannie" Weisinger.

Webb, George Washington – Pvt. Danville Mounted Riflemen, 17th Brigade TST. Born 08/02/1820, died 05/02/1898. Buried: San Domingo Cemetery, Bee County, Texas. Spouse: Henrietta Jane Owen.

Weisinger, Samuel D. – Pvt. Danville Mounted Riflemen, 17th Brigade TST/ Pvt. Co. D, 4th Infantry Regiment, TST. Born 06/27/1818, died 01/16/1897. Buried: New Montgomery Cemetery, Montgomery County, Texas. Father: John Weisinger. Spouse: Nancy A. Weatherly.

Welch, John – Pvt. Co. A, 16th Texas Infantry. Born about 1830 in Alabama, died about 1908. Father: John Welch. Spouse: Nancy Welch.

Welch, Thomas – Pvt. Co. A, 16th Texas Infantry. Born 05/18/1835, died 02/09/1908. Buried: Bethel Cemetery, Montgomery County, Texas. Father: John Welch.

West, James M. – Cpl. Co. G, 20th Texas Infantry. Born 1829, died after 1880. Spouse: Masena M. Rankin.

Westbrook, James A. – Pvt. Co. G, 20th Texas Infantry. Born about 1834 in North Carolina, died before 1868. Father: Frederick F. Westbrook. Spouse: Mary Bathers Cox.

Westmoreland, John Thompson – Pvt. Co. B, 24th Texas Cavalry. Born about 1838 in Alabama, died 10/29/1911. Buried: Lakeside Cemetery, Colorado County, Texas. Father: Wilburn Dennison Westmoreland. Spouse: Nancy Guynn.

Westmoreland, Joseph Mark – 2nd Lt. Danville Mounted Riflemen, 17th Brigade TST. Born about 1827 in Alabama, died about 1904. Buried: Danville–Shepard Hill Cemetery, Montgomery County, Texas. Father: Wilburn Dennison Westmoreland. Spouse: Mary Sarah McGill.

Whitaker, Thomas J. – Pvt. Montgomery County Rifle Boys, 17th Brigade TST. Born about 1841 in Texas, died unknown. Father: Alexander Whitaker.

White, Reuben Birch – Pvt. Co. B, 24th Texas Cavalry. Born about 1830 in Mississippi, killed in action 01/11/1863 at the Battle of Arkansas Post. Father: Reuben White. Spouse: Charlotte Horton.

Whitten, John D. G. – Sgt. Co. B, 24th Texas Cavalry. Born 10/27/1836, died 10/20/1894. Buried: Elwood Cemetery, Madison County, Texas. Father: Alfred Whitten. Spouse: Antoinette Folks.

Wickson, Cyrus – Pvt. Co. K, 20th Texas Infantry. Born about 1845, died after 1880. Father: Cyrus Wickson. Spouse: Hannah Lou Burns.

Wickson, James – Pvt. Montgomery County Rifle Boys, 17th Brigade TST. Born about 1836 in Texas, died unknown. Father: Asa Wickson.

Wickson, Jesse – Pvt. Co. H, 26th Texas Cavalry. Born about 1845, died unknown.

Wickson, John – Pvt. Co. H, 26th Texas Cavalry. Born about 1845, died unknown.

Wickson, Peter – Pvt. Montgomery County Rifle Boys, 17th Brigade TST. Born about 1841 in Texas, died unknown. Father: Asa Wickson.

Wilkes, Britton B. – Pvt. Co. H, 4th Texas Infantry/Midshipman, Confederate States Navy. Born about 1844, died unknown. Father: Britton B. Wilkes.

Wilkes, T. O. – Pvt. Co. H, 4th Texas Infantry. Born unknown, killed in action 06/27/1862 at Battle of Gaines' Mill. Father: Britton B. Wilkes.

Willcox, Theodore W. – Pvt. Co. H. 4th Texas Infantry. Born about 1841 in Louisiana, died 05/12/1862 in Fredericksburg, Virginia.

Williams, Francis James – Pvt. Co. K, 20th Texas Infantry. Born 08/13/1842, died

06/02/1888. Buried: New Montgomery Cemetery, Montgomery County, Texas. Father: Williamston Williams. Spouse: Mary Margaret Dean/Emily F. Williams.

Williams, L. (Negro) – Co. B, 24th Texas Cavalry. Vitals unknown. Last record shows Camp Butler, Illinois POW.

Williams, Williamston – Pvt. 17th Brigade TST. Born 05/15/1817, died 10/18/1897. Buried: New Montgomery Cemetery, Montgomery County, Texas. Spouse: Martha Ann Davenport.

Williamson, John H. – 2nd Lt. Co. B, 17th Brigade TST/Pvt. Co. D, 4th Infantry Regiment, TST/2nd Lt. Co. C, Terry's Regiment, Texas Cavalry. Born 11/03/1823, died 5/16/1905. Buried: New Montgomery Cemetery, Montgomery County, Texas.

Willis, Peter James, Jr. – Pvt. Co. B, Mann's Regiment, Texas Cavalry. Born 11/09/1847, died 10/31/1912. Buried: Trinity Episcopal Cemetery, Galveston, Texas. Father: Peter James Willis. Spouse: Martha Sterling Stella Dolly Price.

Willis, Peter James, Sr. – Adjutant, 3rd Regiment, 17th Brigade TST/Pvt. Co. G, 20th Texas Infantry. Born 03/26/1815, died 11/28/1873. Buried: Trinity Episcopal Cemetery, Galveston, Texas. Father: Short Adam Willis. Spouse: Caroline Womack.

Willis, Richard Short – Pvt. Co. K, 20th Texas Infantry. Born 10/17/1821, died 01/27/1892. Buried: Old City Cemetery, Galveston, Texas. Father: Short Adam Willis. Spouse: Narcissa Worsham.

Willis, William Henry – Pvt. Co. B, Mann's Regiment, Texas Cavalry. Born 12/07/1845, died 05/16/1886. Buried: Trinity Episcopal Cemetery, Galveston, Texas. Father: Peter James Willis. Spouse: Emma Price.

Wilson, Thomas J. – Pvt. Co. B, 24th Texas Cavalry. Born about 1838 in Tennessee, died 11/19/1862 in Arkansas. Father: Drury Wilson.

Winslow, William – Pvt. Co. D, 4th Infantry Regiment, TST. Born 06/10/1824, died 06/18/1896. Buried: Tillis Prairie Cemetery, Montgomery County, Texas. Father: William Winslow. Spouse: Elizabeth Jane Winslow.

Womack, Daniel Harrison – Pvt. Co. D, 24th Texas Cavalry/Pvt. Co. E, 25th Texas Cavalry (Trans-Mississippi Dept.)/Pvt. Co. F, 24th/25th Consolidated Texas Cavalry. Born 08/25/1840, died 12/14/1881. Buried: New Montgomery Cemetery, Montgomery County, Texas. Father: John Womack. Spouse: Virginia Springer.

Womack, Francis Hancock – Pvt. Co. D, 4th Infantry Regiment, TST. Born 05/26/1815, died about 1875 in Montgomery County, Texas. Father: John Womack. Spouse: Nancy Grimes.

Womack, John Calvin – Pvt. Co. D, 24th Texas Cavalry. Born 05/05/1838, died about 1882. Father: John Womack. Spouse: Lucy J. Sturges.

Womack, John Francis – Cpl. Co. G, 20th Texas Infantry. Born about 1842 in Alabama, died about 1893. Buried: Willis Cemetery, Montgomery County, Texas. Father: Francis Hancock Womack.

Womack, William Grimes – Pvt. Co. G, 20th Texas Infantry. Born 05/01/1845, died 9/28/1928. Buried: Womack–Springer Cemetery, Montgomery County, Texas. Father: Francis Hancock Womack. Spouse: Annie.

Wood, Campbell – 2nd Lt. Co. D, 5th Texas Infantry. Born 12/05/1842, died 10/28/1914. Buried: Sunset Memorial Park, Bexar County, Texas. Father: Green Wood. Spouse: Ann Hall Mitchell.

Wood, Green Mark – Pvt. Co. B, 17th Brigade TST. Born 09/07/1814, died 03/05/1898. Buried: Oakland Cemetery, Grimes County, Texas. Father: Green Wood. Spouse: Mary Jane LeGrand.

Wood, Robert. L. – Pvt. Co. D, 5th Texas Infantry/Sgt. Co. B, 24th Texas Cavalry. Born 10/09/1833, died 08/19/1917. Father: John Wood. Spouse: Josephine Cousins.

Wood, Rush Brevard – Pvt. Co. G, 7th Texas Cavalry. Born 01/31/1847, died 12/01/1932. Buried: Fairview Cemetery, Grimes County, Texas. Father: Green Mark Wood. Spouse: Katie Bertha Reed/Mahalah J. Hamilton.

Wood, William H. Pvt. – Co. B, 17th Brigade TST. Born 05/17/1814, died 02/20/1884. Burried: Willis Cemetery, Montgomery County, Texas. Spouse: Elizabeth Ann Irvine.

Woodson, Creed Taylor – Cpl. Co. D, 5th Texas Infantry/1st Lt. Co. A, Mann's Regiment, Texas Cavalry/1st Lt. Co. A, 24th/25th Consolidated Texas Cavalry. Born about 1839 in Georgia, died 02/16/1900. Father: Creed Taylor Woodson. Spouse: Ophelia Frances Worsham.

Woodson, John C. – 3rd Cpl. Danville Mounted Riflemen, 17th Brigade TST. Born about 1844 in Georgia, died after 1880. Father: Creed Taylor Woodson.

Woodson, Miller Alexander – Pvt. Co. D, 24th Texas Cavalry. Born 08/25/1836, died after 1868. Father: Creed Taylor Woodson. Spouse: Lanthe Alabama Lewis.

Woodson, Phillip T. – Pvt. 17th Brigade TST. Born about 1832 in Georgia, died after 1870. Father: Creed Taylor Woodson. Spouse: Lou C. Woodson.

Woodson, William Henry – 2nd Lt. Co. B, 24th Texas Cavalry. Born 04/13/1834, died 01/13/1894. Father: Creed Taylor Woodson. Spouse: Emily Caroline Glenn/Carrie Woodson/Emily Woodson.

Wooldridge, Samuel Dunbar – Capt. Co. B, 24th Texas Cavalry. Born 09/21/1823, died 05/18/1890. Born 09/21/1823, died 05/18/1890. Buried: Willis Cemetery, Montgomery County, Texas. Father: Samuel C. Wooldridge. Spouse: Catherine Elizabeth McCan.

Worsham, Israel – Lt. Colonel, 17th Brigade TST. Born about 1820 in Alabama, died about 1882 in Montgomery County, Texas. Father: Jeremiah Worsham. Spouse: Emily Frances Womack.

Worthy, Albert V. – Sgt. Co. B, 24th Texas Cavalry. Born about 1820 in Georgia, died after 1880. Spouse: Mary Gwinn (Guynn).

Wren, L. W. – Pvt. 17th Brigade TST. Born about 1810 in Virginia, died unknown. Spouse; Mary E. Wren.

Wyche, George W. – Pvt. Co. B, 17th Brigade TST. Born about 1823 in Mississippi, died 03/04/1871. Father: George Wyche. Spouse: Flora Kent Kane.

Appendix B
Confederate Soldiers
Buried in Montgomery County, Texas

Soldier's Name	Unit	State	Function	Cemetery
Addison, William S.	3rd	Louisiana	Cavalry	Montgomery (New)
Alford, John P.	10th	Texas	Infantry	Mostyn
Anders, James	20th	Texas	Infantry	Mt. Pleasant
Anderson, Edward A.	17th	Texas	Militia	Willis
Anderson, J.K. P.	13th	Texas	Cavalry	Pilgreen
Arnold, E. L.	20th	Texas	Infantry	Arnold/Dean
Arnold, Owen W.	20th	Texas	Infantry	Arnold/Dean
Athey, E. J.	60th	Alabama	Infantry	Pilgreen
Bailey, Haymon L.	4th	Mississippi	Infantry	Goodson
Bailey, William H.	4th	Texas	TST	Montgomery (New)
Baker, James D.	15th	CSA	Cavalry	Bays Chapel
Baker, William H.	17th	Texas	Militia	Baker
Barfield, Macon	23rd	Alabama	Infantry	Shannon-Evergreen
Bay, James H. Jr.	20th	Texas	Infantry	Bays Chapel
Bay, James H. Sr.	17th	Texas	Militia	Bays Chapel
Bay, Thomas B.	20th	Texas	Infantry	Bays Chapel
Bay, William H.	17th	Texas	Militia	Bays Chapel
Beason, Edward G.	37th	Texas	Cavalry	Stowe
Bender, John F.	20th	Texas	Infantry	Goodson
Berkely, William H.	9th	Texas	Infantry	Montgomery (New)
Black, Thomas A.	43rd	Georgia	Infantry	Oakwood (Conroe)
Blackman, James M.	3rd	Texas	Cavalry	Mt. Zion
Bobbitt, George R. Sr.	24th	Texas	Cavalry	Montgomery (New)
Brice, Jer. James	Byrd's	CSA	Courier	Willis
Butler, John Beech	1st	Texas	Infantry	Rabon Chapel
Bybee, Clinton	4th	Kentucky	Mtd Inf	Willis
Caldwell, S. H.	4th	Texas	TST	Bays Chapel
Caldwell, W.	17th	Texas	Militia	Bays Chapel
Carnochan, Nicholas	45th	Alabama	Infantry	Oakwood (Conroe)
Carson, E. L.	20th	Texas	Infantry	Willis
Carter, Jessie P.	17th	Texas	Militia	Splendora
Cartwright, Joseph C.	24th/25th	Texas	Cavalry	Rabon Chapel
Cartwright, Lemuel C.	4th	Texas	Infantry	Rabon Chapel
Cartwright, P. L.	24th	Texas	Cavalry	Rabon Chapel
Carvell, William M.	21st	Texas	Cavalry	Mt. Pleasant
Chatham, Andrew S.	20th	Texas	Infantry	Copeland Chapel
Cheatham, William A.	21st	Texas	Cavalry	Cude
Cheshire, J. B.	21st	Tennessee	Cavalry	Mt. Pleasant
Chilton, Franklin B.	4th	Texas	Infantry	Willis

Name	Unit	State	Branch	Cemetery
Clark, William Chester	28th	Alabama	Infantry	East River
Clarke, Pickens R	-	Georgia	Infantry	Morgan
Clepper, Lemuel G.	20th	Texas	Infantry	Magnolia
Clopton, Reuben M.	1st	Mississippi	Cavalry	Shannon-Evergreen
Cochran, R. F.	12th	Texas	Cavalry	Willis
Coley, John C	2nd	Louisiana	Infantry	Morgan
Collier, A. B.	Drake's	Texas	Militia	Collier
Corgey, Louis	20th	Texas	Infantry	Corgey
Curry, Felix	38th	Mississippi	Infantry	Oakwood (Conroe)
Dacus, J. B.	Scoggins	Georgia	L Artillery	Montgomery (New)
Dampier, Hamilton	26th	Georgia	Infantry	Oakwood (Conroe)
Davis, Franklin C	20th	Texas	Infantry	Hickory Grove
Davis, James R.	21st	Texas	Cavalry	Montgomery (New)
Dean, Henry Ingraham	24th	Texas	Cavalry	G. I. Dean
Dean, John	4th	Texas	TST	Arnold/Dean
Dean, William Aylett	17th	Texas	Militia	Arnold/Dean
Dikeman, William K.	20th	Texas	Infantry	Montgomery (New)
Dixon, Jasper Newton	6th	Florida	Infantry	Enloe
Dorwin, W. H. C.	24th	Texas	Cavalry	Montgomery (New)
Dupree, Franklin G.	26th	Texas	Cavalry	Magnolia
Edwards, James L.	20th	Texas	Infantry	Willis
Elam, Frances M	8th	Texas	Cavalry	Willis
Ellis, John	9th	Texas	Infantry	Oakwood (Conroe)
Epperson, William H.	2nd	Texas	Infantry	White Oak
Ethridge, George Guy		Arkansas		Oakwood (Conroe)
Evans, George Brown	5th	Georgia	Reserves	Montgomery (New)
Fairchild, Samuel A.	13th	Texas	Cavalry	Oakwood (Conroe)
Farmer, David	20th	Texas	Infantry	Martin Hill
Ferguson, George	20th	Texas	Infantry	Montgomery (Old)
Ferguson, John Lewis	20th	Texas	Infantry	Calvary Road
Field, J. M.	24th/25th	Texas	Cavalry	Mt. Pleasant
Ford, James	26th	Texas	Cavalry	Montgomery (New)
Forrest, William W.	24th	Texas	Cavalry	Bethel
Fox, Dr. Samuel Irvin	1st	Kentucky	Infantry	Willis
Fultz, T. B. (Theobold)	16th	Mississippi	Infantry	Willis
Fussell, Calvin R.	Madison	Texas	Cavalry	Wilburton
Gary, James M.	5th	Texas	Cavalry	Montgomery (New)
Gentry, T. N.	23rd	Texas	Militia	Montgomery (New)
George, John Edmund	17th	Texas	Militia	Willis
Glover, John Allen	8th	Texas	Cavalry	Montgomery (New)
Golding, Anthony Foster	5th	Texas	Infantry	Willis
Golding, John Madison	24th/25th	Texas	Cavalry	Cude
Golding, Nimrod Chiles	24th/25th	Texas	Cavalry	Willis
Goodrum, Seaborn	10th	Texas	Infantry	Morgan

Goodson, William Walter	17th	Texas	Militia	Oklahoma
Gregg, Hyram John	22nd	Alabama	Infantry	Pilgreen
Griffin, Benjamin D	24th	Texas	Cavalry	Oakwood (Conroe)
Griffith, Joshua D.	24th/25th	Texas	Cavalry	Griffith Cemetery
Gunter, Francis Marion	18th	Alabama	Infantry	Willis
Hall, James H.	20th	Texas	Infantry	Danville-Shepard Hill
Harbin, Morgan Priestly	3rd	Mississippi	Infantry	Shannon-Evergreen
Harman, Jonathan D.	5th	S. Carolina	Cavalry	Bays Chapel
Harper, James Randolph	6th	Missouri	Infantry	Montgomery (New)
Harris, Andrew J.	8th	Texas	Cavalry	Oakwood (Conroe)
Hart, Jacob Gibson	15th	Arkansas	Infantry	Pilgreen
Harvell, David Crockett	2nd	N. Carolina	Cavalry	Montgomery (New)
Hastey, Richard L.	17th	Louisiana	Infantry	Montgomery (New)
Hoke, Thomas W.	20th	Texas	Infantry	Bays Chapel
Holmes, Oscar F.	Madison	Texas	Cavalry	Willis
Horton, Joseph L.	21st	Tennessee	Cavalry	Montgomery (New)
Hulon, James William	24th	Texas	Infantry	Willis
Hulon, John Spiller	17th	Texas	Militia	Willis
Irion, J. L.	20th	Texas	Infantry	Montgomery (New)
Jackson, Henry F.	3rd	Alabama	Reserves	Montgomery (New)
Johnson, John Wesley	26th	Texas	Cavalry	Splendora
Johnson, Napoleon B.	27th	Louisiana	Infantry	Copeland Chapel
Jones, D. C.	20th	Texas	Infantry	Freeman
Jones, James M.	33rd	Alabama	Infantry	Bethel
Jordan, George W.	17th	Alabama	Infantry	Security
Kelley, Columbus N.	18th	N. Carolina	Infantry	Oakwood (Conroe)
Kidd, John Quincy	14th	Mississsippi	Infantry	Kidd (Conroe)
King, Adam Meek	24th	Texas	Cavalry	Hickory Grove
Lacey, Cicero Daniel	17th	Texas	Militia	Weaver
Laishonce, Louis	9th	Texas	Infantry	Rabon Chapel
Landrum, W. J.	4th	Texas	Infantry	Montgomery (New)
Landrum, Zachariah	4th	Texas	Infantry	Montgomery (Old)
Lee, Alexander	20th	Texas	Infantry	Martin Hill
Lewis, John M.	24th	Texas	Cavalry	Willis
Lindley, James	24th	Texas	Cavalry	Danville-Shepard Hill
Little, Hiram	17th	Texas	Militia	Willis
Little, William M.	7th	Texas	Cavalry	Willis
Long, Jeptha Dupree	Howell's	Florida	Infantry	Mt. Pleasant
Lynch, D. B.	17th	Texas	Militia	Rabon Chapel
Malone, William Farrington	9th	Texas	Infantry	Willis
Martin, Ben	57th	Alabama	Infantry	China Grove
Martin, Claiborne A.	17th	Texas	Militia	Martin-Sugar Hill
Martin, John William	20th	Texas	Infantry	Martin Hill
Martin, Robert Ball	20th	Texas	Infantry	Montgomery (Old)

Massey, Warren	1st	S. Carolina	Rifles	Dry Creek
McCaleb, Jesse H.	12th	Texas	Infantry	Cude
McCurdy, George	12th	Georgia	Cavalry	Willis
McFadin, John Franklin	Morgan's	Texas	Cavalry	Enloe
McFarland, Haywood A.	19th	Louisiana	Infantry	Willis
McGaughey, J. C.	20th	Texas	Infantry	Montgomery (New)
McGinnis, Robert L.	20th	Texas	Infantry	Oakwood (Conroe)
McGrew, William J.	20th	Texas	Infantry	Montgomery (New)
McKibbin, Robert E.	17th	Texas	Militia	Willis
McKinney, Gilbert H.	Terry's	Texas	Cavalry	Montgomery (New)
McLeod, William	Terry's	Texas	Cavalry	Bethel
Mickler, William C.	33rd	Alabama	Infantry	Montgomery (New)
Mills, James A.	1st	Texas	H Artillery	Mt. Zion
Moore, William C.	24th	Texas	Cavalry	Willis
Morgan, James S.	55th	Alabama	Infantry	White Oak
Morris, Alfred W., Sr	8th	Texas	Cavalary	Montgomery (Old)
Morris, James W.	62nd	Alabama	Infantry	Montgomery (New)
Myers, Henry	6th	Mississippi	Infantry	Calvary Road
Needham, Kyle G.	16th	Texas	Infantry	Enloe
Nobles, Warren T.	20th	Texas	Infantry	Montgomery (New)
O'Banion, William H.	17th	Texas	Militia	Willis
Outlaw, F. M.	16th	Texas	Infantry	Vick
Parsons, E. C. B	28th	Texas	Cavalry	Montgomery (New)
Pate, William N.	5th Bat	Florida	Cavalry	Pate
Peel, Thomas J.	16th	Texas	Infantry	Montgomery (Old)
Phears, A. H.	35th	Texas	Cavalry	Mt. Pleasant
Pitts, James H.	17th	Texas	Militia	Montgomery (New)
Pool, Henry Joseph	20th	Texas	Infantry	Pool
Pool, John William	20th	Texas	Infantry	Pool
Powell, A. A.	1st	Mississippi	Artillery	Montgomery (New)
Price, Morgan L.	5th	Texas	Cavalry	Montgomery (New)
Rabun, Richard	38th	Alabama	Infantry	Rabon Chapel
Rankin, Thomas B.	17th	Texas	Militia	Montgomery (New)
Reding, John B	17th	Texas	Militia	Danville-Shepard Hill
Redmon, Samuel R.	8th Bat	Georgia	Infantry	Hickory Grove
Rembert, W. E	2nd	Louisiana	Infantry	Bays Chapel
Richards, Augustus	17th	Texas	Militia	Danville-Shepard Hill
Rodgerson, William	4th	Texas	TST	Magnolia
Rogers, Charles L.	20th	Texas	Infantry	Yell
Ryals, W. A.	21st	Texas	Cavalry	Rabon Chapel
Sandell, J. M.	9th	Texas	Infantry	Willis
Sanders, Julius J.	53rd	Alabama	Cavalry	Sanders
Sanderson, A. M.	23rd	Alabama	Infantry	Oakwood (Conroe)
Scott, Charles R.	7th	Texas	Cavalry	Montgomery (New)

Scott, James J	6th	Georgia	Infantry	Montgomery (New)
Scott, John Newton	17th	Texas	Militia	Rhodes
Shannon, Aaron	21st	Texas	Cavalry	Shannon-Evergreen
Shannon, F	20th	Texas	Infantry	Shannon-Evergreen
Shannon, Jacob M.	8th	Texas	Cavalry	Shannon-Evergreen
Shannon, Matt W.	26th	Texas	Cavalry	Shannon-Evergreen
Shepperd, W. M.	21st	Texas	Cavalry	Morgan
Simonton, Lucius H.	Mann's	Texas	Cavalry	Montgomery (Old)
Simonton, Reubin D.	8th	Texas	Cavalry	Montgomery (New)
Sims, Charles W.	4th	Florida	Infantry	Oakwood (Conroe)
Skelton, William R.	16th	Georgia	Infantry	Willis
Smith, Albert	2nd	Texas	Infantry	Splendora
Smith, R. T.	20th	Texas	Infantry	Magnolia
Smith, Thomas W.	Terry's	Texas	Cavalry	Willis
Smith, Williford Stanley	8th	Texas	Infantry	Stowe
Smyth, Reginald	8th	Texas	Cavalry	Shannon-Evergreen
Sones, Benson	20th	Texas	Infantry	Mostyn
Strozier, Augustus B.		Georgia	Militia	Willis
Sunday, George W.	15th	CSA	Cavalry	Rabon Chapel
Sunday, Thomas J.	1st	Florida	Reserves	Collier
Sweet, Benjamin S.	5th Bat	Florida	Cavalry	Hickory Grove
Talley, Reuben	4th	Texas	Infantry	Montgomery (New)
Taylor, W. (William) E.	4th	Alabama	Infantry	Willis
Terrell, William Jones	12th	Texas	Infantry	Oakwood (Conroe)
Thomas, Daniel J.	5th	S. Carolina	Cavalry	Hickory Grove
Trice, Benjamin A.	3rd Bat	Georgia	Infantry	Willis
Turner, John L.	43rd	Mississippi	Infantry	Turner-Thomas
Turner, Leonidas W.	63rd	Alabama	Infantry	Willis
Urquhart, William N.	Kolb's	Alabama	Artillery	Oakwood (Conroe)
Uzzell, M. M.	24th	Texas	Cavalry	Uzzell
Vick, Jesse	20th	Texas	Infantry	Vick
Vick, Vincent C.	20th	Texas	Infantry	Vick
Walker, James M.	24th/25th	Texas	Cavalry	Cude
Waller, Henry E.	1st	Alabama	Infantry	Bethel
Walters, Richard W.	7th	Mississippi	Infantry	Mt. Zion
Ward, B. F.	20th	Alabama	Infantry	Mt. Pleasant
Weatherly, Thomas J.	7th	Texas	Cavalry	Danville-Shepard Hill
Welch, Thomas	16th	Texas	Infantry	Bethel
Wells, F. M.	24th/25th	Texas	Cavalry	Vick
Westmoreland, J. M.	17th	Texas	Militia	Danville-Shepard Hill
Wilcox, R. E.	15th	Texas	Militia	Mt. Zion
Williams, Frank J	17th	Texas	Militia	Montgomery (New)
Williams, Henry E.	45th	Alabama	Infantry	Pool
Williams, Williamston	17th	Texas	Militia	Montgomery (New)

Williamson, John H.	Terry's	Texas	Cavalry	Montgomery (New)
Winslow, William	4th	Texas	TST	Mostyn
Womack, Daniel H.	24th	Texas	Cavalry	Montgomery (New)
Womack, John F.	20th	Texas	Infantry	Willis
Womack, William G.	20th	Texas	Infantry	Womack-Springer
Wood, William Franklin	20th	Texas	Infantry	Calvary Road
Woodson, Miller	24th	Texas	Cavalry	Willis
Wooldridge, Samuel D.	24th	Texas	Cavalry	Willis

www.ingramcontent.com/pod-product-compliance
Lightning Source LLC
Chambersburg PA
CBHW032048080426
42733CB00006B/203